Eating History

Arts and Traditions of the Table

Arts and Traditions of the Table: Perspectives on Culinary History

ALBERT SONNENFELD, SERIES EDITOR

Eating History

30 Turning Points *in the*
Making of American Cuisine

Andrew F. Smith

Columbia University Press New York

Columbia University Press
Publishers Since 1893
New York   Chichester, West Sussex
Copyright © 2009 Andrew F. Smith
Paperback edition, 2011

Library of Congress Cataloging-in-Publication Data
Smith, Andrew F., 1946–
Eating history : thirty turning points in the making of American cuisine /
Andrew F. Smith.
p. cm.
Includes bibliographical references and index.
ISBN 978-0-231-14092-8 (cloth : alk. paper)—ISBN 978-0-231-14093-5 (pbk. : alk.
paper)—ISBN 978-0-231-51175-9 (e-book)
1. Cookery, American. 2. Cookery, American —History. 3. Food habits—
United States—History.   I. Title.

TX715.S651315   2009
641.30973—dc22

∞

Columbia University Press books are printed on permanent and durable
acid-free paper.

Designed by Lisa Hamm

References to Internet Web sites (URLs) were accurate at the time of writing. Neither the author nor Columbia University Press is responsible for URLs that may have expired or changed since the manuscript was prepared.

Contents

Contents

Preface

FOR THE PAST few years, I've asked audiences across America several questions related to food: Do you prefer organic food to food grown with petrochemical fertilizers and synthetic pesticides? Inevitably, the majority indicate, with a show of hands, that they prefer organic foods. When asked, How about a choice between processed food laced with additives, preservatives, and stabilizers and fresh food straight from the farm or garden? On this question, fresh food wins—hands up. To the question, Do those of you who eat meat prefer that the animals be free-range, organic, and slaughtered humanely, or doused with hormones and steroids and raised in highly concentrated animal-feeding operations? By far, most respondents want the former. Would you prefer buying food from family farms, or from corporate farms? Not surprisingly, family farms win every time. Do you prefer eating home-baked bread, or supermarket bread? No one argues against homemade bread, provided that the respondents don't actually have to bake it themselves. Would you prefer eating food made from fresh ingredients, or processed food from boxes, cans, and bottles? Again, the results are inevitable: processed foods never have a chance, everyone prefers fresh ingredients. Do you prefer homemade meals prepared from scratch, or convenient fast food? No surprise here either: homemade food wins. Would you prefer buying food produced locally, or the same foods shipped in from hundreds or thousands of miles away? Respondents want food grown or raised locally rather than imports. In the choice between fast food and slow food, slow is always the big winner. And finally, when asked about foods with transgenic ingredients, few have admitted to preferring or wanting them.

I always find these responses heartwarming—not because I oppose processed, industrial, imported, or even transgenic food but because I'm a culinary historian, and the system that most responders say they favor is pretty much what existed in America two centuries ago. At that time, there were no biotech foods. Chemical additives and preservatives were virtually unknown (vinegar, salt, and sweeteners being the millennia-old exceptions), and farmers used no commercial fertilizers and few insecticides. There were no commercially canned, packaged, or frozen foods, either. Most bread was baked in the home, and most food was grown or raised locally. Most American farms were family owned or family operated. Families ate at home, as there were few restaurants or other public eating establishments.

Moving from preferences to behavior, let me provide a few facts. The total market share of organic food in the United States is only a little more than 3 percent—a share that is mainly due to the production of big organic farms, which sell their produce to big box retail chains.[1] At the present time, large factory farms control about 77 percent of total food production.[2] Most Americans, then, are still buying and eating industrially processed foods. Home-baked bread is largely a thing of the past, although artisan bread has recently made a comeback in cities across America. Somewhere between 25 and 40 percent of Americans eat at fast-food outlets every day, and more than half the meals Americans eat are now prepared outside the home.[3] As for buying food produced locally, observers estimate that the components of the American meal have likely traveled thousands of miles from the farm to the consumer's plate.[4] Regarding buying only domestic food, the Economic Research Service of the U.S. Department of Agriculture estimates that 17 percent of all food consumed in the United States is imported. Food imports swelled from $24 billion in 1996 to almost $82 billion in 2007. Some observers worry that the United States may become a net food importer within a decade.[5] And one final fact about our food supply: the vast majority of processed food sold in the United States contain some transgenic corn or soy ingredients.[6]

The point of my supplying these facts is neither to condemn hypocrisy—saying we prefer one food system while eating in another—nor to downplay the nostalgic yearning for the simpler, less commercial way of life our ancestors may have enjoyed. Over the past two centuries, Americans have made choices regarding their food resulting in a food system that is largely industrialized, mechanized, and controlled by large multinational corporations. To be sure, most such changes were integrated into the food system piecemeal, and the full effects were often not apparent until decades after these changes were first introduced. Nevertheless, to the extent that Americans were aware of these changes, they broadly supported them—and continue to demonstrate their support by buying ever larger quantities of foods produced in that way.

For the past several years, I've grappled with two related questions: Why did Americans shift so easily and quickly from a local food system based largely on family farms with simple standards of living to one that is highly complex, industrial, commercial, and globally dependent? And how can these shifts and changes be presented so that they are readily understandable to the general public? The American food system is immense, complex, and integrated—it would be impossible to condense it all into a single book. I have selected threads of culinary history introduced by turning points—some obscure, others well known—that connect choices made in the past with what we eat today. These historical threads were selected because they are representative of underlying currents affecting America's system of food production, processing, and distribution, and our cooking styles and eating habits, that are embedded in broader societal trends, such as those related to industrialization and mechanization, transportation systems, internal migrations and external immigration, political and economic reform efforts, nutrition and health, scientific discoveries and new technologies, governmental involvement and regulation, advertising and new communication systems, as well as corporate centralization and globalization. The relationships between the American food system and these broader trends are significant, but they are only tangentially touched upon here.

This book introduces American culinary history, its significant topics, inventors, celebrities, and shapers. My approach is mainly explanatory and descriptive rather than normative. While this is primarily a book about America's culinary past, it is also about how we think about food today. For those who believe that the modern American approach to food is on the right track, this book offers a partial history of how we arrived at a system that has emphasized convenience, superabundance, low cost, and consumer choice. For those interested in changing the current system, it offers insight into how we ended up where we are today, and perhaps this will suggest alternative approaches for the future.

Acknowledgments

I'D LIKE TO thank Barry Popik for his research into culinary linguistics, especially his work on hamburgers. I thank Rynn Berry for his comments on the Graham and Kellogg chapters; Forest Wanberg and George Brown for their assistance with the Cracker Jack chapter; the late Jerry Thomas for his firsthand account of the creation and launching of Swanson's TV dinner; Anne Mendelson for her help with the chapters on Gourmet and Gail Borden; Glenn Mack for his assistance on the chapter about culinary schools. For the chapter on Julia Child, I'd like to thank Judith Jones, Molly O'Neill, Mark DeVoto, Geoffrey Drummond, Fern Berman, and especially Laura Shapiro, Joan Reardon, and Dana Polan for their reviews of the Child chapter and their participation in my class, Julia Child: Culinary Revolutionary, at the New School. For the section on Chinese immigration and food, I'd like to thank Andy Coe for his sources and suggestions. For the chapters on Wilbur O. Atwater and the Flavr Savr, I thank Marion Nestle. I'd also like to thank David Strauss and Michael Batterberry for their comments about the early years of Gourmet and other food magazines; and Tanya Steel, for her help with the history of Epicurious.com.

Much to my surprise, little had been written on some turning points selected for this book. This was especially true for the chapter on the founding of the Food Network. Writing about TVFN required extensive interviews, and I'd like to thank the following: Trygve Myhren, Reese Schonfeld, Jack Clifford, David

Rosengarten, Tina Sharpe, Georgia Downard, Allen Reid, Dorie Greenspan for their interviews; thanks to Trygve Myhren, Joe Langhan, Dana Polan, and Kathleen Collins for their comments on that chapter; and special thanks to Stephen Cunningham for his permission to examine his files on the planning stage for TVFN.

I'd also like to warmly thank Charles Roebuck, Bonnie Slotnick, and Tatiana Kling, who read, edited, and commented on the manuscript, and my agent, Giles Anderson, for his comments on the book proposal and constant encouragement.

Finally, I'd like to thank my students at the New School, who have listened, considered, and argued with me about these past turning points and current implications. I've enjoyed every moment of our formal and informal dialogues and I thank you all for your thoughtful disagreements and kind encouragements over the years.

While all comments and responses have been appreciated, not all have been accepted or incorporated. I accept all responsibility for any errors that may appear in this work, and I look forward to continuing the discussions with leaders in the food industry, academics, foodies, culinary professionals, and interested readers.

Eating History

Prologue

FROM THE BEGINNING of European colonization of eastern North America, the population embraced myriad groups that differed culturally, linguistically, religiously, and racially. In addition to hundreds of different Native American nations, there were British, Dutch, Swedish, German, Spanish and French Huguenot settlers, and enslaved peoples were shipped in chains from Africa and the Caribbean. While each of these groups contributed to Colonial life, English settlers put down the deepest roots. Not only were English settlers most numerous, but also many considered themselves forever English and maintained strong connections with Great Britain.[1]

Eastern North America's diverse climates, soil conditions, and settlement patterns created broad culinary regions—New England, the South, the Middle Colonies, and the Western frontier—where particular foods and culinary styles predominated.[2] New England's landscape was rocky and mountainous, its soil was poor, and the winters were cold and the summer growing season was short. Most settlers lived on small, family farms, growing much of their own food.[3] Diet was based largely on what could be easily grown, raised, and produced, such as corn, apples, hard cider, dairy, and poultry, and what could be hunted in forests or caught in local waters and inland rivers and streams. Wheat was not easily grown, and New Englanders imported considerable flour.[4] In the South, the land was richer, winters were milder, and summers were longer and hotter. On large plantations powered by slaves, large-scale export crops, such as tobacco, rice, indigo, and later cotton, were common. A highly sophisticated cuisine emerged in the plantation South based on pork, poultry, rice, and fruits and vegetables largely raised and prepared by slaves—as well as on imported goods from Europe and the other English colonies.[5] The ethnically and religiously diverse Middle Colonies had a fairly long growing season and rich soil, so agriculture flourished there. Large farms grew wheat for export, and this region was known as the Bread Colonies. In the Western frontier—which, in Colonial times, began within a few hundred miles inland from the Atlantic—frontiersmen carved primitive farms out of the wilderness and depended largely on hunting, fishing, corn, and a few other crops.[6] Tenant farming was common in rich agricultural areas, and subsistence farming was common in all regions.

Those who lived in towns supplied their tables from their own gardens, local farmers' markets, and small general stores that sold mainly generic foods stored in barrels, casks, or other large containers. There were few brands or trademarks for common food products. The small proportion of colonists who lived in such cities as Philadelphia, Boston, Charleston, and New York had access to a fairly sophisticated bounty of foods, both from the hinterlands and from abroad, but even in such cities, residents often grew their own fruit and vegetables and raised their own poultry, pigs, and milk cows.

In every region, food was generally plentiful, as was noted by the many observers who contrasted the culinary abundance in America with the scarcity of food, especially meat, in Britain and Europe.[7] Except for luxury items, such as coffee, tea, sugar, molasses, rum, wine, and spices, as well as some staples, such as wheat, rice, and salt, that may not have been available locally, most food consumed in America was grown locally during the Colonial period. Most food at that time was organic because there were few chemical herbicides, pesticides, or fungicides, with some exceptions, such nicotine from tobacco plants. To the small extent that fertilizer was used, it was usually generated from animal manure, ashes, or agricultural waste, although Revolutionary War leader Ben Franklin, America's foremost scientist, advocated using plaster composed of lime or gypsum to fertilize the soil. He demonstrated his views by sowing plaster on a field so that it spelled out, in full capitals, "This field has been plastered."[8]

As for eating outside the home, taverns, inns, hotel restaurants, and a few independent restaurants existed, mostly to serve travelers and visitors. Americans ate most meals at home and food was cooked from scratch. Prior to the American War for Independence, few cookbooks were published in the Colonies and all were written by British authors. There were no food magazines, and newspapers generally did not publish recipes or discuss culinary matters.

Instead, cookery techniques and knowledge were handed down from mother to daughter, occasionally through the medium of family cookery manuscripts. On the whole, women did the food assembling, preparing, cooking, and cleaning up afterward; they also maintained kitchen gardens, handled the dairy, raised poultry, fed pigs, and, when necessary, assisted with planting and harvesting.[9]

The food served in Colonial homes varied according to region and season, the religion and social status of the diners, and whether the family lived in a town, in the country, or on the frontier. Breakfasts frequently consisted of hasty pudding, porridge, mush, corn dodgers, oatmeal, johnnycake, fritters, molasses, bread and butter; heavier breakfasts might have included eggs, smoked or pickled beef, ham, fish, or cheese, and available fruit. Coffee, tea, milk, cider, and occasionally chocolate were served at breakfast. Dinner, usually a large meal served at midday, often consisted of a buffet with meats, fish, poultry, side dishes, seasonal fruit and vegetables, bread, and perhaps butter and jam. The meal might end with fruit and nuts or cheese. Sweet dishes ordinarily were not served at dinner but rather were offered at afternoon tea or on special, festive, evening occasions. Alcoholic beverages, notably ale and hard cider, were served with meals depending on the wealth of the host. The third meal of the day was supper, usually a light repast served in the evening, often quite late. It typically consisted of porridge or soup and a dessert—perhaps cheese, fruit, nuts, or pastries. For all meals, the well-to-do had more complicated menus, while the poor ate whatever was cheap and at hand.[10]

Americans were conservative in their food choices and dietary patterns, and farmers maintained similar agricultural practices throughout most of the Colonial era. During the late eighteenth century, the methods of growing, raising, and processing food began to change: some farmers began adopting enhanced European agricultural practices, such as the use of organic fertilizers, crop rotation, and livestock breeding systems.[11] The resulting boost in productivity encouraged farmers to be more open to further agricultural innovation. Thomas Jefferson, for instance, experimented with moldboards (curved metal plow blades that lift and turn over soil), and others pioneered with the manufacture of cast-iron plows.[12] Concomitant with the changes in agricultural production were shifts in food processing. Oliver Evans, for example, experimented with an automated gristmill that would shape what Americans would eat for the next two centuries.

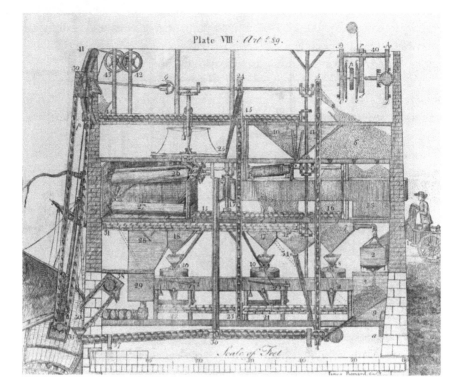

Oliver Evans's automated mill (Library of Congress Rare Book and Special Collections Division)

1.

Oliver Evans's Automated Mill

THE SAME YEAR that the American War for Independence ended, a new revolution was brewing, although it started slowly enough. At the time, the American landscape was dotted with labor-intensive gristmills. Millers carried sacks of grain to the mill's top floor and dumped the grain into a rolling screen that removed the dirt and chaff. The clean grain was ground between millstones on the first floor and then shoveled into buckets. These were then hoisted by hand to the mill's third floor, where the meal was spread out on the floor to cool and dry. Finally it was pushed to the center of the floor and down a chute to a bolting cylinder, which separated the finer flour from the lower-grade middlings, which generally consisted of bran, germ, and coarse flour remnants. Middlings flour was sold at a lower price or used for animal feed. The finer flour was then shoveled into barrels, which were sealed for shipment. The flour produced by these mills varied in quality and was often dirty.[1] As this milled flour contained oil found in the wheat germ, it spoiled quickly, and therefore customers brought only small amounts of grain to the mill for milling at any one time.

Oliver Evans, a tinkerer by nature, inspected several mills and concluded that he could optimize their efficiency by connecting each component of the mill with elevators and buckets so that the whole process required no human assistance from the time the grain was lifted from the cart to the time that flour was poured into a bag. Even though he'd never built such a thing before, and there were plenty of highly skilled millwrights who could have done the job, Evans began construction of his mill and, in 1784, completed it. He invited local millers to come see his new automatic design: they were unimpressed, declaring "the whole contrivance" to be "a set of 'rattle traps,' not worthy of the attention of men of common sense."[2] It was not an auspicious beginning for Evans's mill, and virtually no one (not even Evans himself) imagined that his innovations would forever change the milling industry and food processing.

Milling History

European colonists introduced wheat from Europe, but the initial varieties did not fare well. Within a few decades, however, European wheat varieties acclimatized to eastern North America, and large wheat farms emerged, especially in the Middle Colonies.[3] Gristmills were constructed in communities that had streams, and animal-powered mills and windmills were built in communities lacking streams; in areas where there were no mills, Colonial families ground their own grain in hand mills.[4] Large mills were constructed on rivers in cities, such as Baltimore, Philadelphia, and New York, and these mills produced large quantities of flour that was exported to the other English colonies, the West Indies, and Great Britain.

Both hard and soft wheat varieties were grown in Colonial America. Soft wheat was used for making all sorts of baked goods, such as pies, cakes, cookies, pastries, and pancakes. Soft wheat was not generally used for making bread, however, as important a staple in Colonial America as in Europe. Hard wheat was best for bread making because its starchy endosperm contains more protein than that of soft wheat. The problem was that traditional mills did a poor job of grinding hard wheat, so the resulting flour was coarse, and brownish, and it was discolored by specks of bran and small, flinty pieces of grain. As this flour was often not bolted, or sifted, bread made with it had a thick crust and was riddled with cracks. This may have been advantageous: according to historian Jayme A. Sokolow, this created a sturdy shell that "formed a natural protection against spoilage and dehydration."[5]

Evans's Mill

Oliver Evans, the man who changed the centuries-old process of milling, was born near Newark, Delaware. Little is known of his early life, or of his formal education (if indeed he had any). At age sixteen he was apprenticed to a wheelwright, giving him a trade skills he put to good use throughout his life. When he completed his apprenticeship four years later, he began manufacturing wire, and then proceeded to invent a machine that made carding combs for wool and cotton.[6] The Revolutionary War brought uncertainty to America, and Evans chose to make himself available for service, although it is unlikely that he served during the war. After the British surrender at Yorktown, in 1781, active military engagements declined while peace negotiations were under way. Evans opened a store selling simple commodities in Tuckahoe, Maryland. The local wheat farmers traded with Evans, as did the millers who ground that wheat into flour; through his customers, Evans familiarized himself with the labor-intensive milling practices, which had not changed much since the Middle Ages.[7]

Evans's previous experience as an apprentice wheelwright, wire manufacturer, and industrial inventor clearly gave him opportunities to hone his mechanical skills. He believed that he could improve the standard mills of the time by moving the grain and flour through the process more quickly and efficiently and with less human muscle power. He figured out how to connect the different machines through the use of bucket elevators, conveying devices, and a "hopper boy," a mechanical device that cooled and dried the meal before feeding it into the bolting cylinder. With these enhancements, wheat could be taken directly from a wagon or boat, cleaned, ground, dried, cooled, sifted, and packed without the need for a human operator, except to make adjustments to the machinery and cart away the flour. Evans acquired property along Red Clay Creek, near Newark, Delaware, and built a model of his automatic mill the following year. The model worked, so he began construction on the mill itself, which he finished in 1784.[8] The main advantage of Evans's design was that the mill could be run with far less manpower than that required by traditional mills—and it consistently produced a cleaner, finer flour.

Most millers ignored Evans's design changes. They were not interested in upgrading their traditional mills, which they felt worked just fine. Their mills served local communities and usually had little competition. Most millers did not have a large enough volume of business to justify the expense of installing Evans's inventions; it was easier to mill flour as they had always done.

Undaunted, Evans pushed ahead. He believed that his devices were important enough to patent, and he requested and received patents from state legislatures in Delaware, Maryland, New Hampshire, and Pennsylvania.[9] When Congress set up the Patent Office, in 1790, Evans was the third inventor to receive a patent from the United States. He also sent a model of his mill to England and applied for a patent there. Once the legal details were in place, Evans launched a business designing new mills that incorporated his inventions.

Evans did convince some large millers to try his devices. Joseph Tatnall, of Brandywine Village in Delaware, was one and he was delighted with the results: he estimated that his Evans mill wasted less grain and reduced labor costs, generating $37,000 in annual savings—a small fortune at the time.[10] When President George Washington visited Tatnall, in 1790, to thank him for the flour Tatnall had supplied to the Continental army during the Revolution, Washington viewed Tatnall's mills, which were fitted out with Evans's improvements, and was so impressed that he ordered one for himself.[11]

Millers using this new technology were able to substantially lower the price of their flour. Those not employing Evans's inventions began to lose business. Millers saw the writing on their balance sheets. Evans's machinery began to be installed in older mills, but where it really made a difference was in new mill construction. Mid-Atlantic merchant millers built larger, state-of-the-art mills based on Evans's design, at a cost of $8,000. These mills dwarfed previous works, often standing five stories tall, with an annual grinding capacity of 150,000 bushels of wheat.[12]

An even greater application of Evans's milling technology was made in upstate New York. Two years before Evans's death, in 1819, New York State commenced construction of the Erie Canal. While the canal was being dug, wheat farmers began acquiring large tracts of land adjacent to the canal path. Larger flour mills could handle enormous amounts of grain compared with traditional gristmills, and these big mills were constructed strategically along the canal's route. By the 1840s, there were an estimated 24,000 gristmills in the United States, and most contained one or more of Evans's devices.[13] Their improved efficiency had the added advantage of producing more superfine flour: when used for bread making, it resulted in a thin-crusted bread that was softer, lighter, and whiter—characteristics that were highly desirable at the time. Commercial bakers also preferred the superfine flour because it took less time to bake, thus reducing their operating costs and their prices charged to customers. It became less costly to buy bread from bakers than to make it at home, and city dwellers increasingly became consumers rather than producers of bread.[14]

New Inventions

To promote sales of his automatic mills, Evans wrote a book, *The Young Mill-Wright and Miller's Guide*, which was published in 1795. It was well received in the United States, where it went through at least fourteen editions before going out of print almost six decades later. Evans's book made an even bigger splash in Europe, where his inventions were referred to as scientific milling machines.[15] European millers quickly adopted many of Evans's innovations. European nations were engaged in almost continuous war from 1793 to 1815, and when there's war, there's a burgeoning demand for food to feed the military and war-disrupted civilian populations. Mills with Evans's devices in the United States and Europe helped satisfy this need.[16]

European millers not only adopted Evans's labor-saving equipment, but they also modified and enhanced his mill design. In Switzerland and Hungary, for instance, millstones were replaced with iron and later steel rollers. During the 1830s, steam power was introduced, and mills no longer needed to be located on streams or rivers. These innovations improved the efficiency and productivity of European flour mills, and their inventions in turn influenced American mill construction.[17] After the Civil War, entrepreneurs in the Midwest, particularly around Minneapolis, began constructing mills featuring steam and steel rollers. These new mills reduced the cost of flour, permitting these mill owners to undersell their competition.[18]

Unlike the old gristmills, flour mills employing steel rollers could grind hard wheat, which grew easily in the upper Midwest. These mills incorporated new technology that was more efficient in removing the bran, germ, and oil from the flour. Millers then bleached the flour, creating a bright white product, which appealed to consumers, and the refined flour's extended shelf life pleased grocers. Although it was not known at the time, the appealing-looking white flour, and the bread made from it, lacked the vitamins, minerals, and fiber found in whole-wheat flour and bread.

Roller mills were costly to build, and most millers did not have the capital to invest in them. However, the flour produced by roller mills was much cheaper than flour ground by millstones. Larger mills ground out more flour, but the new flour also represented a loss in flavor and texture. To compensate, commercial bakers began adding more sugar to their doughs, resulting in sweeter and puffier bread. As most manufacturers used more or less the same technology and ingredients, the breads they produced had a similar appearance and taste. To distinguish their products in the minds of consumers, food processors came to rely on advertising.

Milled Effects

Writing at the end of the nineteenth century, two English mill historians credited Evans as the "first to materially affect the milling processes." Evans's innovations, they concluded, effected a "vast improvement" in the conditions under which millers labored.[19] But it wasn't just the mill workers who got a break. Mill owners learned from the experience: Those who maximized efficiency through technology decreased their costs and could lower the price of their flour. Lower prices meant more sales and greater profits than they had through the old system. Then there was the corollary. Millers who did not adopt new technology were unable to compete: they either shifted their focus to producing other products, moved to a new location, or went out of business. To generate even more efficiency and profits, millers needed to install newer technology and build larger facilities. Large, efficient operations drove small millers out of business, and the result was the concentration of the milling industry into fewer and fewer hands. The milling industry thus became increasingly centralized. In the mid-1800s, there were an estimated 25,000 mills in America; by 1900 there were only 13,000, and a century later there were only 100 flour-milling companies in the nation.

Evans's influence was not limited to the milling industry: all forms of food production and processing were soon viewed through the efficiency lens. Evans's automated production on an assembly line from raw material to finished good was later called continuous processing. Evans is credited with inventing it in the United States.[20] As it turned out, the principles behind Evans's innovations— efficiency, automation, and continuous processing—eventually became the standard operating principles in the American food industry.

Postscript

Oliver Evans went on to develop many other inventions, such as high-pressure steam engines, boilers, and dredging machines. He also published a second book, *The Young Steam Engineers' Guide*, in 1805, and it went through several additional printings. Later in life, he spent considerable time and money in court trying to protect his patents. None of his inventions generated much revenue, but when he died, in 1819, he was financially solvent.

George Washington built his mill near his home in Mount Vernon. It has recently been reconstructed, and it is the only operating Evans mill in America.

Celebration poster for the opening of the Erie Canal (New York State Library, Manuscripts and Special Collections)

2.

The Erie Canal

AT 10:00 A.M. on October 25, 1825, the canal boat *Seneca Chief* entered the Erie Canal's western terminus, near Buffalo, New York, and headed for Albany. As the canal boat got under way, a thirty-two-pound cannon roared. Within a few seconds, another cannon's boom could be heard off to the east. A series of cannons (many used by Admiral Oliver Hazard Perry on Lake Erie during the War of 1812) had been placed at intervals along the canal's length, and from Albany, down the Hudson River and through New York Harbor; the last cannon was placed at Sandy Hook, New Jersey, on the Atlantic shore. As one cannon's boom echoed forth, the next one fired, until the chain of reports reached the Atlantic; the cannonade was then returned, and the roar rolled back up the Hudson and westward to Buffalo, where it had started three hours and twenty minutes earlier.[1] So began the celebration of the opening of a channel that revolutionized agriculture and commerce in New York, New England, and the midwestern states, and in the process helped shape what Americans eat today.[2]

Canal History

The Erie Canal was not the first canal built in the United States. In South Carolina, a canal connecting the Santee River with Charleston Harbor began operating in 1800; in Massachusetts, the Middlesex Canal, uniting the Merrimack River with Boston Harbor, opened in 1803.[3] But these projects were dwarfed by the Erie Canal—a four-foot-deep, forty-two-foot-wide hand-dug ditch that extended 363 miles from Albany, on the upper Hudson River, to Buffalo, on Lake Erie.

Compared with the areas adjacent to the Hudson, the central and western regions of New York were largely unoccupied except for American Indians, especially the Six Nations of the Iroquois. Since the arrival of the Europeans, these Indians had been under constant pressure from the French moving south from Canada and the Dutch and English colonists pushing westward from Albany and East Coast settlements. During the American Revolution, the Iroquois split their allegiance: two nations supported the Americans, four allied with the British. With British instigation, Iroquois raided Colonial settlements and pro-American Indian villages in New York and New England. These raids led to American retaliation, beginning in the summer of 1779, when General John Sullivan along with Indian allies methodically destroyed hostile villages, orchards, and cornfields in upstate New York. Disease and starvation did the rest.[4] Regardless of which side the Indians had chosen at the war's outset, the result was the final destruction of their lands and societal infrastructures.

With the Indians out of the way, the New York legislature began annual discussions of a possible canal to the west. Surveys had been made and canal projects begun, but none were completed. The War of 1812 was a decisive factor in the final decision to construct the canal. During the war, American forces attempted to invade Canada, and fighting occurred on both sides of Lake Ontario. One of the few American military successes in the war was Commodore Oliver Perry's defeat of a small English fleet on Lake Ontario in 1813. One problem uncovered during the war was that there was no easy way to ship men and supplies across New York to support these military efforts. After the war, the pressure to build a canal mounted, and construction finally commenced on July 4, 1817.[5] Those who proposed and approved the Erie Canal's construction, and those who bought bonds to finance it, hoped that the canal would encourage settlement around the new waterway, and that farms along the route would ensure an adequate food supply for New York's rapidly growing population.[6]

Even before the canal's completion, its construction began to have the economic impact predicted by those who had fought for the project. As the canal stretched westward toward Buffalo, land prices in the Mohawk Valley, especially along the projected canal's route, escalated. But acreage there was plentiful, and settlers flocked to the central part of the state, establishing farms on large tracts of land. They planted their crops on land previously cultivated by Indians, and where necessary, they cut or burned down forests. The soil and climatic conditions were particularly conducive to growing grain, specifically wheat. Wheat had been grown in upstate New York prior to the canal's construction, but shipping it to the East Coast over the inadequate turnpikes was expensive and time-consuming. As sections were completed, agricultural commodities, particularly wheat, began to flow through the canal.[7] This was only the beginning of a flood of grain that would traverse the canal by barge and head for New York City, where it would be milled into flour and then loaded onto oceangoing vessels for shipment to coastal cities in the eastern and southern United States, the Caribbean, and Europe. Likewise, most goods that were shipped westward via the canal came through New York City. Within fifteen years of the canal's opening, more tonnage was moving through the Port of New York than the combined tonnage of the nation's three other largest ports—Boston, Baltimore, and New Orleans.[8]

When wheat production proliferated in upstate New York, many farmers realized that it would be more economical to grind their wheat locally rather than shipping the heavy, bulky grain downstate for processing. If the wheat could be milled locally, shipping costs would drop, as the flour was lighter and more compact than the whole grain. This meant more money in the pockets of farmers and millers in upstate New York, and cities such as Rochester, Oswego, and Troy became milling centers. By 1840, Rochester was grinding more flour than any other city in the world.[9]

The farmlands adjacent to the newly completed sections of the Erie Canal were ideal for the type of mill Oliver Evans had designed. There were few existing mills, and when a new mill was constructed, it was outfitted with Evans's equipment. Mill builders used Evans's devices and added their own technological advancements, such as new high-grinding techniques that reduced the grain by successive grindings, resulting in an even finer flour.[10] The combination of large farms, high yields, efficient mills, and whiter flour meant that even with the cost of transportation factored in, wheat grown in central and western New York was less costly and more appealing to customers than grain grown locally in the traditional wheat-growing areas along the eastern seaboard.

The Erie Canal was a financial success well before its completion. The eastern portion was completed by 1823, a time when Rochester mills were shipping 10,000 barrels of flour to Albany. The grain trade expanded every year thereafter. The price of shipping grain dropped from about $100 per ton by wagon overland, before the canal was completed, to $10 a ton by canal boat. In 1836 alone Albany received almost 1 million barrels of wheat through the canal.[11] The canal was so heavily trafficked that bottlenecks were a common occurrence; nine years after its completion, an enlargement was ordered, increasing its width to seventy feet and its depth to seven feet.[12]

Canal Effects

The Erie Canal was the technological wonder of its day, and the engineering feat alone was revered by Americans in the same way that subsequent generations would view the completion of the transcontinental railroad, in 1869, the digging of the Panama Canal, in 1912, and the Apollo moon landing, in 1969.

The Erie Canal's financial success set off a frenzy of canal building, but there were relatively few places where cost-effective canals could be constructed. Canal systems blossomed in Maryland and Pennsylvania, but the best geographical locations for canals were in the flat, sparsely populated Midwest. In the decade beginning in 1830, canal mileage in the United States swelled from 1,270 miles to 3,320 miles—and most of this new construction was in the Midwest.[13] By the 1840s, it was possible to go from New York City to New Orleans through the country's interior traveling solely on river and canal boats.

Although the Erie Canal's economic importance waned eighty years after its completion, the canal's transforming effects on the American food supply and foodways remain with us today. The canal created an aquatic superhighway through which passed produce from western New York and the Midwest. Historically, wheat had been grown mainly in the middle states, from downstate New York to northern Virginia. By 1839, Ohio, Indiana, Illinois, Wisconsin, and Iowa were producing a quarter of the nation's wheat and corn. Just before the Civil War began, the production of these states had soared to half the national total, while wheat production along the Atlantic coast tumbled from 69 percent in 1840 to 39 percent by 1860.[14]

East Coast farmers, especially those in New England, could not compete with the inexpensive wheat and flour pouring through the canal. New Englanders had undertaken to raise wheat since the first colonists arrived in the 1620s, but, with the exception of the Connecticut valley, they never produced enough wheat to feed New England's growing population. When grain from the Mohawk valley began underselling their wheat, even after the transportation costs had been factored in, many New Englanders abandoned their farms and headed west.[15] Not only did the Erie Canal open up central and western New York to settlement, it also made the Midwest accessible to population growth and agricultural production. When the land along the Erie Canal became less productive, farmers just moved to the Great Lakes and Midwest regions, where they could more easily grow wheat that was then shipped by canal to population centers along the eastern seaboard.[16]

Canals spurred the construction of railroads, which could connect places that were unreachable by canals or navigable rivers. Railroads could also ship commodities to many more locations much faster, and their efficiency doomed canals as an important food-transportation system. The efficacy of the transportation grid cast aside the idea that foods had to be purchased from nearby farms or farmers' markets; it replaced the habit of buying locally with the mandate for buying cheaply. Once the preference for the least-expensive product was established, there was no reason why the concept should not spread to a wide range of other food products, such as vegetables and fruit from California or Chile, beef from Australia or Argentina, avocados and sugar from the Caribbean, or bananas and coffee from Latin America. Estimates vary, but the components of today's American meal have likely traveled 1,300 to 2,500 miles from their point of origin to the table.[17]

Postscript

In the summer of 1834, John Preston Kellogg and his family left his failed farm in Connecticut. Like tens of thousands of others, they traveled west via the Erie Canal, finally settling in Tyrone, Michigan Territory, where future health gurus and cereal magnates John Harvey Kellogg and Will Keith Kellogg would be born.

One unexpected effect of the Erie Canal was the sale of bonds to pay for its construction. At the time, the canal was the largest public works project ever attempted in the United States, and its cost was likewise unprecedentedly high. Eventually the canal paid for its operation through tolls, but, for its initial construction, bonds had to be sold. As they were sold mainly in New York, the city was strengthened as America's financial center.

Beginning in the latter part of the nineteenth century, commercial traffic on the canal gradually declined. During the early twentieth century, parts of the original canal were abandoned, while other sections were enlarged and deepened to form the New York State Barge Canal. In time, commercial traffic ceased on the canal, due largely to competition from railroads, trucking, and the Saint Lawrence Seaway. Today, the Erie Canal is used mainly by recreational craft and tourist boats.

Delmonico's second restaurant at Beaver and South William Streets, 1891 (Lately Thomas, *Delmonico's: A Century of Splendor* [Boston: Houghton Mifflin, 1967])

3.
Delmonico's

AMONG THOSE ENJOYING the 1825 festivities in New York City surrounding the Erie Canal's opening was a Swiss-born sea captain named Giovanni Del-Monico. He had sold his ship, and with the proceeds opened a wine shop in the city in 1824. At the time, most Americans did not drink wine, so his customers were mostly Frenchmen and other European immigrants or foreign visitors. To maximize profits, Del-Monico imported casks of wine and did the bottling himself, but he wasn't satisfied with the business and decided to try his hand at something new. Del-Monico sold his wine shop in 1826 and traveled to Switzerland to visit his family. There, he convinced his brother Pietro, a pastry chef, to return with him to New York and open a café and pastry shop. In December 1827, under their Americanized names, John and Peter Delmonico, the brothers opened their little café. This first enterprise, on William Street, near the harbor, had just six tables; its patrons could enjoy European-style pastries, ices, bonbons, cakes, and coffee.[1] In March 1830, the café was expanded into a fine-dining establishment, listed in the city directory as Delmonico & Brother, Restaurant Français. Delmonico's veneration of French haute cuisine set the stage for the nation's restaurant industry.

French Cuisine in America

For much of Colonial history, the French were the major enemy of the American colonists, who had fought frequently with the English against the French. Thanks to the French and Indian War, the English gained control of Canada and the French territories east of the Mississippi River. During the War for American Independence, the French became allies of the American colonists, and French naval and military officers visited and operated in America. As most Americans had had little previous contact with the French, they harbored many prejudices, several relating to what the French ate. When the French naval squadron arrived in Boston in 1778, a wealthy Cambridge resident, Nathaniel Tracy, tendered a dinner for Admiral d'Estaing and his officers. As a special treat for his guests, Tracy directed his servants to catch frogs, which he believed were the French national dish. The French officers broke into laughter when they found whole frogs floating in their soup bowls.[2]

Though no lover of the French, John Adams, the Revolutionary War leader and future president, charged that the English had duped Americans into disliking Parisian cookery. He loved French wine and, while minister to Great Britain, ordered 500 cases of it.[3] Thomas Jefferson fell in love with French cookery and French wine while serving as the American minister to France. While in Paris, he had one of his slaves, James Hemming, trained as a French chef, and Jefferson shipped French wine to George Washington and John Adams. While in the White House, Jefferson hired a French chef and regularly served French dishes. Jefferson's enjoyment of French food did raise eyebrows. Patrick Henry, for example, the Revolutionary War leader famous for his "Give me liberty, or give me death" speech in 1775, denounced Jefferson for having "abjured his native victuals."[4]

American exposure to French cookery expanded after the French Revolution of 1789, when many noblemen and their chefs fled France. Some refugees moved to England; others to the United States, where they shared their legacy of French cuisine. One of those who came to American shores was the gastronome and culinary philosopher Jean Anthelme Brillat-Savarin, who lived in New York for three years during the 1790s. He particularly liked to visit a fellow Frenchman, Captain Joseph Collet, who had opened an ice cream parlor. Brillat-Savarin wrote admiringly of Collet, who "earned a great deal of money in New York in 1794 and 1795, by making ices and sherbets for the inhabitants of that commercial town. It was the ladies above all, who could not get enough of a pleasure so new to them as frozen food; nothing was more amusing than to watch the little grimaces they made while savoring it."[5] Brillat-Savarin returned to France, where he wrote his famous *La physiologie du goût* (*The Physiology of Taste*), but Collet remained in New York, where he opened the Commercial Hotel, a fancy name for a boardinghouse with a coffee shop on the lower floor.[6] In 1835, Collet sold the boardinghouse to the Delmonico brothers, whose restaurant had burned down in a fire that swept through lower Manhattan.

An enlarged Delmonico's opened in 1837. It offered salads and other novel French dishes,[7] and the restaurant became popular. Its eleven-page menu listed a full selection of French dishes (with English translations opposite), such as *potage aux huitres, salade de chicorée, blanquette de veau à la perigueux, meringues à la crème*, and an impressive French wine list, with a Bordeaux vintage 1825.[8]

The success of Delmonico's encouraged the establishment of other French restaurants in the city. By the mid-1830s, many New York hotels were serving French food in their restaurants. The palatial Astor, which began construction in 1834, employed French chefs to run its dining rooms, and a number of these men became famous. New York's first stand-alone restaurants appeared during the second and third decades of the nineteenth century, and the French influence was clearly visible in the menus of these restaurants. Frederick Marryat, an English naval officer, traveler, and novelist, visited Delmonico's and other French restaurants in the 1830s, and reported that they served "excellent" French food.[9]

French restaurants continued to open in New York and other large cities. Their clientele consisted of businessmen and an increasingly affluent American upper class. English visitor and travel writer George Sala dined at Delmonico's in the 1880s. "How many tens of thousands of dollars a week Mr. Delmonico is clearing I do not know," wrote Sala, "but his palatial establishment, as well as scores of these restaurants and cafés, continually overflow with guests." Delmonico's consisted of a first floor with "an immense café, and a public restaurant of equal dimensions, while on the second floor," Sala continued, "there are first a magnificent saloon which can be used as a ball room or as a dining hall, and next a series of private rooms for select dinner parties; on the upper floors are a limited number of furnished apartments for gentlemen." Sala dined at several other restaurants, all of which, he wrote, served French food as good as that offered at Delmonico's.[10]

Delmonico's remained one of the city's premier restaurants throughout the nineteenth century, moving to new premises every so often as the city grew northward. In 1848, Alessandro Filippini was hired as a cook; over the years he rose to the post of *chef de cuisine*, and finally became manager of one of the Delmonico's restaurants. Filippini, who, like his employers, was Swiss, was one of the driving forces promoting the restaurant's culinary renown. When he retired in 1888, he began writing cookbooks. The first, *The Table*, presented simplified recipes based on those prepared at the restaurant.

The French-born Charles Ranhofer, who had been hired at Delmonico's in 1862 and became Filippini's successor as *chef de cuisine*, flattered the egos of his wealthy patrons by occasionally naming dishes after them. He named his lobster a la Wenberg after a ship's captain who was a frequent customer. When Ben Wenberg fell out with the management of Delmonico's, they changed the dish's name to lobster Newberg, or so the story goes. Ranhofer was among the first American chefs to achieve international acclaim. George Sala recorded for his British readers this description of Ranhofer's latest novelty, baked Alaska: "The nucleus or core of the *entremet* is an ice cream. This is surrounded by an envelope of carefully whipped cream, which, just before the dainty dish is served, is popped into the oven, or is brought under the scorching influence of a red hot salamander; so that its surface is covered with a light brown crust. So you go on discussing the warm cream *soufflé* till you come, with somewhat painful suddenness, on the row of ice."[11]

In 1894, Ranhofer produced his masterwork, *The Epicurean*, the most comprehensive French cookbook published in the United States up to that time.[12] Unlike Filippini's simplified version of the cookery of Delmonico's, Ranhofer's imposing tome was extremely detailed and featured menus for every imaginable event and occasion. Leopold Rimmer, who was in charge of one of the restaurant's dining rooms, reported that there was "hardly one hotel in New-York to-day whose chef did not learn his cooking at Delmonico's, every one of them." When *The Epicurean* was published, Rimmer bitterly complained that Ranhofer had given "away all the secrets of the house." Rimmer believed that, after the publication of *The Epicurean*, anyone could prepare French food.[13]

Cookbooks written by Americans in the late 1800s were filled with French-sounding recipes for *soufflés, potages, omelettes, croûtons, filets, fricassées, ragoûts, purées, croquettes, consommés,* and *patés.* Waiters affected French accents, while restaurant menus were replete with French words, albeit often misused or misspelled. A visitor from France recorded such bloopers as "Hors d'noeurves" and "Poummie de Terre Dauphin."[14] Other words changed in meaning when used in America—the word *entrée*, for instance, came to mean a main course, while in France it refers to a small dish served between main courses. French or French-trained chefs in America's most prestigious restaurants published still more cookbooks. Felix Déliée, chef at the New York Club and the Union and Manhattan Club, published *The Franco-American Cookery Book* in 1884; Oscar Tschirky, maître d'hôtel at the Waldorf, wrote *The Cook Book of Oscar of the Waldorf* in 1943.

French cookery in America reached a peak during the twentieth century, when hotel restaurants run by French or French-trained chefs—at the Waldorf-

Astoria, Essex House, and the Ritz-Carlton, among others—were among the nation's premier eating places. The hiring of French chefs by wealthy Americans to preside over their household kitchens also contributed to its rise.

When Prohibition went into effect in 1920, upscale restaurants were hit hard. French restaurants featured fine wines as part of the dining experience, and the sale of alcoholic beverages played an important role in a restaurant's profits. There was a loss of clientele as America's wealthy decamped for France during the summer. One casualty was the venerable Delmonico's, which closed in 1923, after nearly a hundred years of feeding the cream of New York society. When the Depression hit in 1929, frugality and simplicity became the keys to survival for American restaurants. French names were removed from menus and many French chefs lost their jobs.[15]

French Revival

On April 30, 1939, President Franklin Roosevelt opened the New York World's Fair, whose optimistic theme was "The World of Tomorrow." One exhibit that did indeed presage the future was the restaurant at the French pavilion, which the *New York Times* called "an epicure's delight."[16] Of course, America's aristocracy had long enjoyed classic French food. For almost 200 years, restaurants such as Delmonico's serving classic French dishes dominated the American culinary landscape. And wealthy Americans traveled to France, where they dined at the world's finest restaurants. The French restaurant at the World's Fair, however, attracted a much wider audience.[17] Many Americans who had never before sampled French food did so at the fair, and they liked what they tasted.

The French government had selected Charles Drouant, owner of the Café de Paris and several other restaurants in France, to run the restaurant at the fair. Henri Soulé, who had been an assistant maître d'hôtel at Café de Paris, was responsible for the dining room. The restaurant was staffed by workers from Parisian restaurants. By the time the fair closed on October 27, 1940, war had begun in Europe; a defeated France was divided, part under German occupation and the rest controlled by the collaborationist Vichy government. Most of those who had come from France to cook and serve at the French pavilion's restaurant decided not to return to their home country at that time.

After the fair closed, Charles Drouant thought he would open a French restaurant in New York City. He sought investors, one of whom was reputed to have been Joseph P. Kennedy, the father of the future American president, John F. Kennedy. When Drouant decided to return to France, Henri Soulé took over the project. Soulé found a space for the restaurant on New York's fashionable Upper East Side, and, hoping to trade on the restaurant's popularity at the fair, he named the establishment Le Pavillon. Soulé was joined by many of his former colleagues, such as Pierre Franey, who, at the fair, had been the *poisson commis* (assistant fish cook).[18]

For the restaurant's opening, on October 15, 1941, Soulé invited the rich and famous to dine.[19] Le Pavillon was a solid success from the beginning, even as, less than two months later, the United States entered the war. Franey enlisted in the U.S. Army and helped liberate France. When he returned, he rejoined the staff of Le Pavillon and moved up the ranks, becoming executive chef in the early 1950s.[20]

The social and economic elites—Astors, Cabots, Kennedys, Rockefellers, and Vanderbilts—were regulars at Le Pavillon.[21] Soulé made a virtue of snobbery. Presumably to protect the sensibilities of his refined customers, he refused entrance to those who did not meet his standards. Soulé is also said to have coined the term Siberia, referring to the tables closest to the kitchen (considered the worst in any restaurant).[22] Le Pavillon thrived, and, in October 1958, Soulé opened La Côte Basque—a less-formal alternative to Le Pavillon.[23]

The year 1960 was an unfortunate one for Le Pavillon. The nation's economy took a dip, affecting the restaurant's bottom line. Soulé ordered a staff reduction, but Chef Franey refused to discharge anyone from his *brigade de cuisine*. Newcomer Jacques Pépin, a rising star who had been at Le Pavillon for just eight months, joined Franey in his protest, and the two walked out, forcing Le Pavillon to close temporarily.[24] Both Franey and Pépin went to work for the Howard Johnson's restaurant chain—the money was better and the working hours were limited. Chef Roger Fessaguet also left Le Pavillon, to become executive chef at La Caravelle, owned by Fred Decré and Robert Meyzen.[25]

When John F. Kennedy was elected president, René Verdon, the executive chef at Essex House, in New York, was selected as the White House chef.[26] The presence of a French chef in the "Camelot" White House (his salary was paid personally by the Kennedys) brought new attention to haute cuisine. Suddenly Americans wanted to know more about French food.[27]

Delmonico's Effects

Americans paid a price for trying to imitate French haute cuisine. At the time Delmonico's opened, indigenous local and regional cuisines had been developing in New England and the American South. Delmonico's came to serve as a model for successful restaurants, and its fame helped popularize French food. The elite taste for French food filtered down to America's growing moneyed middle class during the late nineteenth century. So prestigious was French cooking in the nineteenth century that many American chefs claimed to have been born in France, although most were not even trained in French cookery. A wholesale invasion of French dishes and French terminology swept America.[28] French culinary terms commonly appeared on restaurant menus, and French food words were further popularized in the United States when some wealthy American families employed French chefs.[29] Veneration of a reified haute cuisine among many of America's elite undercut regional and local food almost as much as eating out later undermined home cooking. When French restaurants and haute cuisine declined in importance during the early twentieth century, American food had taken a different direction—toward fast and inexpensive industrialized food, which occasionally employed French-sounding words, such as "au gratin" or "à la," to attract customers.

Even so, for almost 200 years, French restaurants, French chefs, and French-inspired recipes dominated the elite American culinary foodscape. Wealthy Americans believed that French food was refined and delicious and expected their cooks to be able to prepare elaborate dishes of that cuisine. Well-to-do Americans traveled to France, where they dined at the world's finest restaurants. Writers followed in their footsteps and praised haute cuisine in the pages of *Gourmet* and other culinary publications, and, despite predictions to the contrary, haute cuisine thrives today.

But the influence of Delmonico's is not limited to haute cuisine. Before Delmonico's arrived on the scene, few Americans ate at restaurants and fewer ate French food. Restaurants like Delmonico's helped popularize the notion that Americans could eat in restaurants. The pseudonymous author Lately Thomas, who wrote *Delmonico's: A Century of Splendor*, concluded that the restaurant broadened the American palate and established "the pattern of purveying food in America that would be adopted universally." "Restaurants, on the Delmonico principle," he continued, "quickly appeared in imitation, spread to other cities, and long before Delmonico's career closed they had become fixtures in American life. Delmonico's modest beginnings laid the foundation of the restaurant industry of today: every eating house in the United States, be it good, bad, or indifferent, derives from the coffee shop on William Street, and the later establishment at Beaver and South William."[30] Today, Americans eat an average of five meals away from home every week, expending more money on food prepared outside the home than on that made in their own kitchens.

Postscript

Giovanni Del-Monico died in 1842, and his son Lorenzo took over the restaurant's management. Peter Delmonico retired in 1848 and sold his interest to Lorenzo. It was Lorenzo who, in 1862, hired Charles Ranhofer. Lorenzo died in 1881, and Delmonico's began a long, slow decline.

When Henri Soulé died in 1966, Craig Claiborne eulogized him as the "Michelangelo, the Mozart and Leonardo of the French restaurant in America."[31] Soulé's greatest achievement, according to Claiborne, was his nurturing of restaurateurs and other influential individuals on America's food scene.[32] Pierre Belin and Paul Arepejou, who started at Le Pavillon, opened La Poinière in 1954.[33] Roger Fessaguet, who had moved from Le Pavillon to La Caravelle, made La Caravelle the "incubator for some of New York's better-known chefs." Michael Romano worked with Fessaguet until Danny Meyer tapped him to become the chef at Union Square Café. David Ruggerio went from La Caravelle to Le Chantilly, and Cyril Renaud became the chef and owner of Fleur de Sel.[34]

In 1998, the Bice Group opened a restaurant in the former location of one of the Delmonico's incarnations. The restaurant on South William Street continues today under the name Delmonico's Restaurant, and is now owned by the Ocinomled Group.[35]

"Sylvester Graham," 1832 (Library of Congress Prints and Photographs Division)

4.

Sylvester Graham's Reforms

NOT EVERYONE IN America was happy with the dietary changes brought about by Oliver Evans's mills, the introduction of refined white flour, or the fancy food served in restaurants. One person particularly perturbed by the direction the American diet was taking was a Presbyterian minister and would-be food reformer named Sylvester Graham, who was a temperance advocate and a vegetarian. In 1830 he began delivering lectures from Philadelphia to Boston presenting his culinary views on such topics as gluttony, vegetarianism, and the use of bran bread. An impassioned speaker, Graham attracted large audiences, and the crusading minister became an overnight sensation.

Cholera, a new disease, emerged from Asia in the late 1820s and ravaged Europe in the early 1830s. Its arrival in the United States appeared imminent. Graham was determined to lecture on cholera before it hit New York. In March 1832 he announced that he would lecture on diseases, focusing on the prevention of cholera. Two thousand people turned up to hear him speak. He argued that eating fresh fruits and vegetables and drinking pure water could prevent cholera.[1] Many medical professionals disagreed: Dr. Martyn Paine, of the New York University Medical School, argued the opposite—eat no fruits or vegetables, just lean meat and bread.[2] When the disease hit New York in June 1832, Graham's followers appeared to thrive, and he alleged that no one who had followed his regimen had died of cholera. Sylvester Graham's views achieved instant national visibility, and he received fan mail from people who claimed that they had survived because they had followed his advice. Proud of his work and not one to avoid a good promotional activity, Graham immediately published dozens of these testimonials. And so America's first major food reform movement was born, and many of the culinary beliefs espoused by Graham continue to influence us today.

Graham History

That Graham was able to inspire such a monumental effort is surprising in the light of his early life. He was the seventeenth child of his seventy-two-year-old father, John Graham, an ordained Presbyterian minister, who died two years after Sylvester Graham was born, in 1794. His mother was unable to cope with his father's death and raising her large family, so for much of Sylvester Graham's early years, she was in and out of hospitals. Graham "was much neglected" and was a sickly child. For much of his early life, he lived with different sets of relatives. Even as a young adult he had a hard time establishing himself. He worked at a paper mill and as a horse trader, a clerk in a country store, and a merchant in New York—to name but a few of his early employments. He also acted in plays, wrote for newspapers, composed poetry, and taught in several schools. At the late age of twenty-nine, Graham entered Amherst Academy, a preparatory school for Amherst College, but his arrogance irritated the other students. They falsely accused him of assaulting a woman, and he was expelled. He suffered a nervous breakdown. While recovering, he met his future wife, who nursed him back to health. Later, to support his family, Graham studied privately to become a minister, and in 1828 he embarked on a career as an itinerant preacher in New Jersey.[3] Graham was a popular and energetic speaker, but his ministerial career was brief. When, in June 1830, he was offered a position as general agent for the Pennsylvania Temperance Society, he jumped at it.

Beginning in the early nineteenth century, Quakers and Methodists had begun to speak out against overindulgence in alcohol. Along with other denominations, they formed temperance organizations, which, by the late 1820s, were well established. Philadelphia had its own temperance advocates, but, unlike other groups, which were largely dominated by religious leaders, Philadelphia's was led mainly by the city's medical professionals, who were concerned by the effects of alcoholism on health. It was this medical aspect, not his religious beliefs, that motivated Graham to support temperance.[4]

Graham was successful in his lectures but quit the temperance job after six months.[5] He had become interested in medicine and immersed himself in the foremost medical works of the day, especially François J. V. Broussais's *Treatise on Physiology*, published in Philadelphia in 1826. Broussais maintained that gastronomical problems were responsible for most human illnesses. Based on Broussais and other readings, Graham pieced together his own physiological approach to health. He concluded that intemperance in food was an even greater evil than alcoholic intemperance, and that overindulgence in food frequently led to alcoholism, particularly among men. Graham believed that gluttony, and not alcoholism, was "the greatest of all causes of evil." Graham wasn't the only person who believed this. In 1832 a medical professor at the Transylvania University in Kentucky, Charles Caldwell, declared a similar conviction: "For every reeling drunkard that disgraces our country, it contains a hundred gluttons—I mean, who eat to excess and suffer by the practice."[6]

Graham's concern with temperance may have led him to vegetarianism. He was not the first prominent vegetarian in America, however: William Metcalfe, a clergyman from England who established a church in Philadelphia in 1817, created America's first vegetarian church. For Metcalfe, vegetarianism was supported by Scripture; the eating of flesh had brought about humanity's fall from grace. Another prominent convert to vegetarianism was William A. Alcott, a prominent physician (and the uncle of author Louisa May Alcott). Dr. Alcott wrote extensively in support of the vegetarian diet. In 1835, he commenced publishing the *Moral Reformer*, a monthly journal dedicated to healthful living, and three years later he wrote America's first vegetarian cookbook, *Vegetable Diet*.[7] Graham likely met both Metcalfe and Alcott, but his support for vegetarianism stemmed from his own studies of physiology. He believed that to be healthy, Americans needed to give up meat.[8]

Another source of Graham's culinary views was the literature on adulteration of food, particularly bread. The English chemist Henry Jackson had published, in 1758, *An Essay on Bread*, the first book-length attack on British bread making. He followed up this criticism with frequent articles in journals and newspapers.[9] By the late eighteenth century, English cookbooks routinely described methods for determining whether flour or bread was contaminated, which it often was. The German-born chemist Frederick Accum reported, in his *Treatise on Adulterations of Food, and Culinary Poisons*, 1820, that bread made by bakers was frequently adulterated with alum, subcarbonate of ammonia, and carbonate of magnesia, in addition to ground beans, peas, and potatoes. Although Accum was writing about London's bakers, Graham later leveled similar charges against commercial bread making in America. According to Accum, the reason for this adulteration was that it was difficult for bread bakers to turn a profit, so they cut costs by using cheap but extremely poor-quality wheat. The adulterants they added to their flour were intended to remove unpleasant odors and unappetizing discoloration. Accum's book generated excitement throughout Europe and America, and it was often cited in literature dealing with the adulteration of foods. The following year, Accum published another work, *Treatise on the Art of Making Good and Wholesome Bread*, which gave clear directions for how to make good bread. It's very likely that Graham read both of Accum's books, as he repeated these indictments of baker's bread in his own *Treatise on Bread and Bread-Making*.

Graham's views about medicine and food would probably never have garnered much attention had he not been invited by New York temperance leaders to lecture on the relationship between diet and disease. In his lectures, beginning in 1831, Graham argued in part that people were unable to survive the ravages of diseases because they did not eat the proper diet.[10] But it wasn't until the following year that Graham presented his culinary views, in his *Lecture to Young Men on Chastity*.[11] Graham believed that food in its natural state, uncooked, was best, and he condemned the use of all "stimulating foods"—liquor, meat, tea, coffee, condiments, spices, salt, and pepper. Unlike many contemporary medical professionals, who were leery of fresh fruits and vegetables because they purportedly caused a variety of summer diseases, Graham advocated eating fresh produce.[12]

The construction of the Erie Canal allowed cheap wheat and flour to flow into New England. Graham was deeply concerned about the bread made with this cheap wheat. He objected to the way wheat was grown, milled, and baked into bread. He believed that farmers tried to extort "the greatest amount of produce, with the least expense of tillage, and with little or no regard to the quality of that produce."[13] He particularly objected to the use of fertilizers, claiming that one could smell the difference between breads made with fertilizer and those baked with unfertilized wheat.[14] In regard to milling, Graham's objections concerned the way wheat was cleaned before it was ground, insisting that millers did not take enough time to remove impurities. He was also concerned with the bolting process, which eliminated much of the bran from the flour. Graham considered the bran to be healthful and condemned the flour produced in the Evans-type mills as unhealthful. On the subject of commercial bakers, Graham wrote that they served "the public more for the sake of securing their own emolument than for the public good."[15] Like Accum, Graham exposed adulteration in commercial baking, such as the addition of alum and sulfate of zinc. Graham also revealed that bakers added chalk, pipe clay, and plaster of Paris to boost the weight and whiteness of their breads.[16]

According to Graham, even if commercial bakers used wholesome grain, abjured adulterations, and prepared the dough properly, the bread they produced would still be nutritionally deficient and unpalatable. Why? Commercial bakers used brewer's yeast, which was employed in manufacturing alcoholic beverages, and "superfine flour," bolted and ground to the point where the granular texture had been "tortured into an unnatural state of concentration." Graham's solution was that every family should grind its own wheat with a hand mill and bake bread in its own oven. According to Graham, this was the only way a family could ensure that its bread was properly made and safe to eat.[17]

Graham advised everyone to eat bread made of coarse, stone-ground, unbolted flour, and he believed that bread should be baked at home. According to Graham, "the most perfect loaf of raised bread, is that which, being made of the best material, is light, and sweet, and well baked, and still most nearly retains all the natural proportions and properties of the original material."[18] By 1834, bread made this way—as it had been made for centuries—came to be called Graham bread.[19]

Graham expounded on these views in his *Treatise on Bread and Bread-Making*, the first book published in America, in 1837, focused solely on bread. Shortly after its publication, large crowds gathered in New York and New England to hear Graham speak. His harangues on the subjects of commercial bread and vegetarianism provoked the ire of bakers, who disagreed with his views on commercial bread, and butchers, who opposed his vegetarian advocacy. In the fall of 1837, Graham had planned a lecture at Boston's Amory Hall, but the threat of violence pressured the proprietors to cancel it. Not one to be intimidated by threats, Graham moved his lecture to the dining room of the almost completed Marlborough Hotel, planned as the first "temperance house" in America. While Graham was lecturing, bakers outside the hotel rioted. Graham's supporters, waiting on the roof, shoveled lime down onto the rioters, whereupon, as *Harper's Magazine* later reported it, "the 'eyes' had it, and the rabble incontinently adjourned."[20]

In addition to his concerns about bread, Graham found fault in flavor-enhancing condiments. In his magnum opus and final work, *Lectures on the Science of Human Life*, he advocated banning condiments—mustard, ketchup, pepper, cinnamon, and salt—because they were stimulating and "all highly exciting and exhausting." Graham concluded, "The stern truth is, that no purely stimulating substances of any kind can be habitually used by man, without injury to the whole nature."[21]

Graham's Effects

Graham's ideas struck a responsive chord in many Americans, thousands of whom listened to his lectures, read his essays, and changed their diets and habits based on his ideas.[22] In 1833 Asenath Nicholson, a temperance boardinghouse owner in New York, teamed up with Graham to institutionalize his dietary principles in her boardinghouse, and she later published the first "Graham" recipes devised in accordance with his precepts.[23] Graham boardinghouses soon opened in Boston and other cities. Many survived until late in the nineteenth century. Noted guests at such boardinghouses included newspapermen Horace Greeley and William Lloyd Garrison. Meanwhile, students at Oberlin, Wesleyan, and Williams colleges conformed to Graham's dietetic strictures—at least for a time. Oberlin discontinued the regimen in 1841 when students protested against the all vegetable and fruit diet and rumors of mass starvation began to circulate.[24]

The furor surrounding Sylvester Graham and his ideas had begun to wane by 1840, and fewer people attended his lectures. Believing himself to be a professional failure, Graham retired from public life. He was, however, anything but a failure. Medical periodicals, such as the *Graham Journal of Health and Longevity*, with which Graham was unconnected, promoted his views, and several medical and other groups, such as the American Vegetarian Society, created in 1850, popularized vegetarianism among a wide audience.

Graham's objection to condiments and spicy foods was a common theme throughout the nineteenth century. In 1835, Dr. William Alcott campaigned against condiments, which he defined as substances used "to season or give relish to dishes which would be otherwise less agreeable to the taste." In addition to those condiments cited by Graham, Alcott also opposed such spices as ginger, fennel, cardamom, mace, nutmeg, and coriander; he also rejected molasses, garlic, cucumbers, pickles, gravies, sauces, lettuce, and horseradish, which he considered disgusting and indecent "drugs."[25] Alcott and Graham both opposed the consumption of coffee and tea.[26] Others echoed their concerns, among them Dio Lewis, a Harvard-trained physician who campaigned around the country against the use of condiments. In his *Chastity, or Our Secret Sins*, he announced, "Everything which inflames one's appetite is likely to arouse the other also. Pepper, mustard, ketchup and Worcestershire [*sic*] sauce—shun them all. And even salt, in any but the smallest quantity, is objectionable; it is such a goad toward carnalism."[27]

In the mid-nineteenth century, Graham's successors became interested in hydropathy, an idea imported from Germany in 1840. Hydropathists believed in a water cure, a therapeutic system for improving health that emphasized frequent bathing and consumption of water. Joel Shew, a hydropath, began publishing the *Water Cure Journal* in 1845; Russell T. Trall, a hydropath and vegetarian, became its editor in 1849.[28] In 1857, Trall chartered the Hygeio-Therapeutic College, which was the first-known commercial firm to sell Graham flour. Another hydropath, James Caleb Jackson, had started his professional life as a farmer and then became a newspaperman, but throughout his early life he had been plagued with ill health. In 1847 he visited a spa specializing in the water cure and avowed that his ailments had been cleared up. That same year he opened a hydropathic institute in Cortland County, New York; when it burned down eleven years later, he moved his operation to Dansville, New York. The patients at Jackson's spa, Our Home Hygienic Institute or Our Home on the Hill Side, as Jackson variously called it, were offered a health-enhancing food regimen while they took the water cure. Patients received only two meals a day—breakfast and dinner, the latter served at 2:30 p.m. While the menu was not strictly vegetarian, it did emphasize raw fruits and vegetables and Graham (whole-wheat) bread. Like Graham, Jackson ruled out the use of such stimulants as tea, coffee, and alcohol in his spa. It attracted thousands of patients during its almost forty years of operation.[29]

One visitor to Jackson's spa was Ellen G. White, the prophetess of the Seventh-Day Adventist Church, which was then centered at Battle Creek, Michigan. Like Graham, she believed that "intemperance in eating and drinking" caused the greatest human degeneracy. She argued similarly against the consumption of coffee, tea, and meat. In 1865, the church's publication arm reprinted extracts of Graham's publications.[30] Graham's and Jackson's ideas, though revised, remain a part of Seventh-Day Adventist Church teaching today.

Sylvester Graham advocated many things—vegetarianism, temperance, homemade whole-grain bread as a dietary staple, and abstinence from spicy food—but the most lasting monument to his work, according to historian Stephen Nissenbaum, was the "rise of the modern American breakfast cereal industry."[31]

Postscript

Soon after Graham retired, he became ill; he felt compelled to explain in a local newspaper that his illness resulted from medical problems he had had prior to promulgating his views on diet. In fact, he postulated, had he not followed the Graham diet, he would have died.[32] Despite his strong views, at his wife's insistence he began eating meat and drinking alcoholic beverages before he died, at the age of fifty-seven, in 1851.

One of William Alcott's brothers, Bronson Alcott, and Bronson's wife, Abba, were also followers of Sylvester Graham. In 1843, Bronson Alcott cofounded the utopian community Fruitlands based on Graham's views. His daughter, Louisa May Alcott, had strong memories of the vegetarian fare with Graham bread.[33]

Today's commercial "graham" crackers are made with sugar, preservatives, and other ingredients that Sylvester Graham would have strongly opposed.

"Cyrus McCormick's Reaper" (Library of Congress Prints and Photographs Division)

5.

Cyrus McCormick's Reaper

CYRUS MCCORMICK BEGAN work on developing a horse- or ox-drawn mechanical reaper in 1831. Within a few years he had a working device, but it wasn't until 1847 that McCormick felt he had a reliable machine that farmers would accept. His enhanced reaper, he guaranteed, could harvest ten acres a day—five times more than a large crew could harvest by hand—using far fewer workers. Mechanical reaper sales expanded, and in 1848 McCormick sold 1,500 of them. McCormick moved his operation to Chicago, where he began mass-producing reapers to capitalize on the expansion of grain farming in the Midwest. The McCormick reaper soon became the gold standard in farming equipment, and mechanization took command of American agriculture.

Reaping History

Families living on farms and plantations ate much of what they grew and raised; excess produce was sold to or bartered with people they knew at local markets. Late eighteenth century American farms had much in common with European farms of the Middle Ages. By nature, farmers were conservative, and little had changed on American farms since early Colonial times. Farms were labor-intensive: fields were cultivated, plowed, and harrowed with horse-drawn equipment, the crops seeded, weeded, harvested, threshed, and winnowed largely by hand.

At the same time that Oliver Evans's mill engendered a spirit of innovation in food processing and the Erie Canal began a revolution in food transportation, a revolution was also under way in food production, with hand harvesting remaining as one obstinate bottleneck. This was particularly true for small grains—corn, oats, and wheat—which were America's most important staple crops. There was some flexibility in a farmer's deciding when to plow, sow, weed, winnow, and thresh his grain, but harvesting was a high-stakes task that had to be completed within ten to fourteen days—sometimes less if the weather didn't cooperate. If the harvest was not completed during this brief period, the grain would fall from the seed heads and be lost. Harvesting wheat by hand was an arduous and exhausting task: using handheld sickles, scythes, reaping hooks, and grain cradles, laborers mowed down the standing grain while others followed, tying the stalks into bales or assembling the sheaves into shocks. On a good day, fifteen laborers working from dawn to dusk might harvest about two acres of wheat.[1]

Once the grain was ready, the harvest couldn't wait, so farmers in an area needed to harvest their crops at virtually the same time. This required the efforts of everyone on the farm as well as any able-bodied workers from the local villages, regardless of age or gender. Yet even when things ran smoothly, large amounts of grain were still lost, due usually to shattering, when the grain split off from the stalk and ended up on the ground. Weather presented other difficulties—if it was hot, grain matured faster and had to be harvested faster; if a downpour occurred during harvesting, the seeds might begin to sprout. As a result of such constraints, farmers had to limit how much they planted in accordance with what they could reasonably expect to harvest in the fall.

Since the late eighteenth century, inventors in England and the United States had unsuccessfully tried to create a workable mechanical reaper. In fact, the designs needed for a mechanical reaper had already been patented by that time, but no one had pulled these inventions together.[2] That was about to change, however. Beginning in 1815, a Virginia farmer, Robert Hall McCormick, tried to design a horse-drawn reaper. During the following years, he continued to refine and patent various designs, but he never got the reaper to work properly. In 1831, after sixteen years of on-again off-again experimentation, Robert McCormick gave up and turned the project over to his son, Cyrus, who had already invented several agricultural devices and had a keen mechanical sense. After two months of tinkering, Cyrus purported to have developed a workable prototype. The device had a field trial in the fall of 1831, but it wasn't until 1834 that Cyrus McCormick patented his mechanical reaper. Despite this early apparent success, he spent another ten years refining his invention.

Even with the obvious potential of McCormick's mechanical reaper, farmers were leery of change, and sales were slow. In 1842, McCormick advertised that purchasers of his reaper ran no risk since, if the reapers could "not cut fifteen acres a day and save one bushel of wheat per acre, ordinarily lost by shelling when the cradle was used, they could be returned."[3] In fact, many of his early reapers *were* returned. Rather than give up and pursue some other line, Cyrus McCormick continued to tinker with his invention; he designed and patented additional equipment for the reaper, and sales started to pick up, particularly in the Midwest, where the opening of the prairie led to larger farms on level land. With small grains as the main crops, mechanical reapers made midwestern farming particularly profitable. Recognizing this geographical advantage, McCormick moved his operation from Virginia to Chicago and, in 1847, created the McCormick Harvesting Machine Company. At the time, with only 25,000 residents, Chicago was hardly a metropolis, but it was situated at an important canal and river junction. The city was rapidly expanding due largely to its strategic location, and railroads would soon connect it with the East. Chicago lay at the center of the Midwest, where grain was fast becoming the main crop on farms far bigger than those back East. In Chicago, sales of the mechanical reaper picked up.

In addition to being an inspired inventor, Cyrus McCormick was a smart businessman. He guaranteed farmers that his reaper would cut between one and two acres of small grains per hour. He also gave his customers credit to pay for the machine. Farmers thus had little to lose by buying a McCormick reaper. McCormick was also a good promoter: He displayed and competitively demonstrated his reaper at agricultural exhibitions and fairs throughout America, and it won many prizes. In 1851, McCormick displayed his reaper at London's Great Exhibition at the Crystal Palace, where it won a gold medal, leading to international visibility and substantial sales.[4] In 1852, McCormick sold 5,000 reapers, and during the next seven years he sold 100,000 more. At the time of the American Civil War, an astounding 250,000 reapers were operating on American farms.[5]

Reaping Success

Grain production in the United States soared throughout the 1850s and 1860s. Many factors contributed to this expansion, and McCormick's reaper was not the only agricultural invention that contributed to the rise in grain production. Many novel farm implements, "unthinkable previously, became the norm by the mid-1830s."[6] A self-polishing steel plow, for example, patented by John Deere in 1837, made it easier to break up the thick sod in the Midwest. In the same year, a practical threshing machine was patented. Mowing machines were being used on farms by 1844. Widespread adoption of such equipment signaled the change in American agriculture from hand power to horse power.[7]

Before the Civil War, canals and railroads had been built to link distant parts of the United States east of the Mississippi. In the North, railroad construction continued even during the war. One result was a decline in freight rates, which made it more profitable for farmers in the Midwest to ship their crops to eastern cities. Crop failures in Europe created demand for American grain, and exporting grain to Europe brought additional profit to American farmers.

Enhanced profitability encouraged even more farmers and immigrants to move to the American Midwest. During the two decades before the Civil War, the production of America's major crops doubled, with the largest growth occurring in the Midwest. In 1860, William H. Seward, a U.S. senator at the time and future secretary of state under President Abraham Lincoln, concluded that "owing to Mr. McCormick's invention, the line of civilization moves westward thirty miles each year."[8]

Ironically, Cyrus McCormick, a southerner by birth who owned slaves and opposed the Civil War, became one of the major contributors to the success of the North during the war. Each reaper sold during the war freed up an estimated two or three farmworkers, many of whom enlisted in the Union cause, contributing an estimated half of the Union's million-man army and navy.[9]

Moreover, despite the loss of farm laborers and the disruption of traditional routes of transportation, grain production swelled by 50 percent in the North during the first two years of the war, thanks in large part to ever-increasing sales of reapers and other labor-saving farm equipment. In fact, the scarcity and high cost of farm labor led to the almost universal adoption of the reaper.[10] Because of the abundance of grain, northern soldiers and sailors were comparatively well fed during the war, as were northern civilians, and no civilian rationing occurred during the war. Just as important, England and France had poor grain harvests before and during the early years of the war and needed a hefty hike in imports from America. Grain exports from northern states jumped during the war, which discouraged England and France from diplomatically recognizing the Confederate states as an independent nation. The two countries needed grain from the North more than they needed cotton from the South—and thus McCormick's reaper again contributed to the ultimate Union victory.

Mechanization's Effects

Farm mechanization continued throughout the nineteenth century. Mechanical mowers, crushers, and windrowers had come into widespread use by the early twentieth century. These inventions revolutionized the speed at which wheat could be harvested and advanced productivity on American farms. Such innovations encouraged conservative farmers to upgrade their farm equipment and expand the size of their planted acreage as well. Larger, more complicated, and more productive farm machinery was marketed. The sale of such equipment rose even more in the twentieth century, when farmers shifted from horse power to mechanical power and tractors; large farm machines mechanized much of American agriculture. Because the equipment was expensive and worked better on flat land, the Great Plains became the epicenter of American grain cultivation.

With mechanization came specialization and standardization. Farmers needed new types of crops and new methods of farming to maximize the profit from the investment in the expensive new equipment. They also needed to produce more to make the same profits, leading to larger and larger farms and, simultaneously, to the decline of the traditional family farm. In 1920, 6.45 million farms were operating in the United States. By 2004, the number of American farms had declined to about 2.1 million. In 1800, 95 percent of the American population was engaged in farming; today less than 2 percent is directly involved in agriculture.

The small farms were eventually replaced by large factory farms. By 1990, 320,000 large farms were producing 77 percent of America's total agricultural production.[11] The amount of food produced by large farms has surged steadily ever since. Many critics charge that large factory farms cause untold damage to the environment and that they destroy local communities. Advocates for large factory farms have argued that the farms produce more food for less money and play an essential role in modern food production.

With more mechanization and hikes in productivity came surpluses, which had to be sold or warehoused. Farms became dependent on regional, national, and international markets, and also, often, on federal subsidies to maintain high production levels.[12]

Postscript

After the Civil War, McCormick's company continued to thrive, until 1871, when the Great Chicago Fire destroyed his factory. Undaunted, McCormick built a new plant outside Chicago, and sales in subsequent years exceeded even his optimistic expectations. In 1884, the year McCormick died, his company sold 54,841 reapers. For his contributions, Cyrus McCormick has been called the Father of Modern Agriculture.[13]

The McCormick family continued operating the company until 1902, when it merged with William Deering's farm-equipment division and several other farm-equipment makers to form International Harvester. International Harvester dominated the manufacture of farm equipment throughout the early twentieth century, but, due to financial losses, the company sold off its agricultural and construction machinery operations in the 1980s. The company was renamed Navistar International Corporation in 1986; today it is the largest manufacturer of medium and large diesel trucks.

Restaurant favored by the smart set (Rupert Hughes, *The Real New York* [New York: The Smart Set Publishing Company, 1904])

6.

A Multiethnic Smorgasbord

WELL AFTER AMERICAN independence, British culinary traditions continued to dominate American home cookery. This began to change in January 1848 as a result of three unconnected events. One was the discovery of gold in the American River near Sacramento, California. The second was the signing of a peace treaty between the United States and Mexico, ending the Mexican-American War. The third was revolution in Europe, particularly in Germany. These nearly simultaneous events thousands of miles apart brought large waves of non-Anglo peoples—Chinese, Mexicans, and Germans—and their cuisines into the United States. These groups—and the millions of immigrants who followed—enticed Americans away from their stolid British culinary roots, introducing a wealth of ingredients, flavors, and dishes from many different cultural, religious, and ethnic traditions that continue to influence the American culinary world today.

Multiethnic Culinary History

The Chinese, Mexicans, and Germans were not the first large groups of non-Anglos to end up in the United States. In addition to Native Americans and enslaved Africans, the United States had acquired thousands of citizens of French heritage when President Thomas Jefferson bought New Orleans and the

Louisiana Territory in 1804. French culinary traditions were adopted by many upper-class Americans, and French food was often served at fashionable dinner parties and restaurants, such as Delmonico's. Yet other waves of immigrants came into the United States from Ireland. Protestant Irish immigrants had been arriving since the mid-eighteenth century, and the pace of immigration picked up during the early nineteenth century. Many Irish immigrants to New York were employed in eating and drinking establishments. In 1814, William Niblo, a self-proclaimed gourmet from Ireland, opened the Bank Coffee House, which was considered one of the best eating establishments in New York. Fifteen years later, he opened Niblo's Garden, featuring a restaurant that quickly became one of the most important eating places in town.[1] The initial trickle of Irish immigrants became an enormous wave after the potato famine began in Ireland in 1845. Hundreds of thousands of Catholic Irish refugees came to America during the next decade, but, surprisingly, they had little impact on American culinary life.[2] Unlike the Irish refugees, other newcomers left lasting influences on American foodways.

Part 1: The Gold Rush

On January 24, 1848, James W. Marshall, a carpenter supervising the construction of a sawmill on the American River forty miles from Sacramento, California, spotted some shiny flecks in the millrace. Making some tests, he found that the flecks were gold. Marshall's employer, mill owner John Sutter, tried to keep the discovery secret, but the news quickly leaked out. Word of Marshall's find reached San Francisco, and the great California gold rush was on.

At the time, California had an estimated population of about 7,000 residents of European descent and some 20,000 American Indians scattered throughout the territory. During the next few years, an estimated 300,000 Americans, Europeans, Chinese, Japanese, Australians, and Hawaiians flooded into northern California. While most of these adventurers eventually left the area, by 1850 California's permanent population, excluding Native Americans, had reached 90,000.

Before the gold rush, few Chinese lived in California. One exception was Chum Ming, a merchant, who arrived in San Francisco in 1847. Hearing about the gold strike in early 1848, he immediately relayed the news in a letter to his cousin, Cheong Yim, in China. Ming then headed for the gold fields. Four months later, a boatload of Chinese miners arrived in San Francisco, and ship after ship soon followed.[3] It wasn't just the lure of gold that enticed Chinese laborers to California; thousands were fleeing civil war and natural disasters in the region around

Canton (Guangdong). An estimated 20,000 to 30,000 Chinese from this area came to California during the gold rush. When the gold eventually petered out, many immigrants returned home or moved elsewhere, but others remained in California.[4]

By 1850, San Francisco had a Chinatown, with five restaurants. Norman Asing, a man of Chinese ancestry who said he was "a naturalized citizen of Charleston, South Carolina," was the proprietor of one, the Macao and Woosung.[5] Other Chinese eating houses, such as the Balcony of Golden Joy and Delight, soon followed. Some seated as many as 400 customers at a time. These restaurants attracted both Chinese and non-Chinese patrons with all-you-can-eat meals at a reasonable price.[6] According to one miner, the Chinese restaurants were the best eating houses in San Francisco.[7] William Kelly, an Englishman who visited California in 1850, found French, Spanish, and American restaurants in San Francisco, but he was particularly impressed with the Chinese restaurants, which he considered excellent: "They served everything promptly, cleanly, hot, and well cooked."[8] To supply these restaurants, as well as Chinese grocery stores in the city, shippers had begun to import quantities of Chinese food from Hong Kong.[9] By the 1860s, sizable shipments of these imported goods, such as dried oysters, were moving from China to San Francisco.[10]

When silver was discovered in Nevada, in 1859, Chinese immigrants headed over the Sierra Nevada mountains and began mining in that territory—and, naturally, they also opened grocery stores and restaurants along the way.[11] Not everyone in Nevada was impressed with the Chinese restaurants. A Virginia City resident, Mary Mathews, considered their restaurants "filthy"; she never knew what she was eating and suspected the meat in the dishes was rat.[12] This was a common view of many Americans confronting Chinese food for the first time. It was caused by racism and wariness of a new cuisine that differed so much from their usual "American" fare.

As part of the construction of the transcontinental railroad, inaugurated in 1863, an estimated 10,000 Chinese laborers helped build the western portion, and Chinese cooks came along to prepare their meals. With the railroad's completion, in 1869, the Chinese population—and the delights of their culinary repertoire—spread eastward across America;[13] midwestern and eastern cities, particularly New York, soon saw the establishment of Chinatowns with Chinese eating places.[14]

Importing food products from Hong Kong proved costly, and many Chinese farmers started to grow Asian vegetables and fruits in California; others established fishing villages along its coast. By 1880, the Chinese population in California alone exceeded 100,000. Nativist fears about Chinese immigration led

Congress to pass, in 1882, the Chinese Exclusion Act. This law sharply curtailed the number of Chinese immigrants entering the country and also imposed new requirements on Chinese immigrants living in the United States.

Hemmed in by racial prejudice and restrictions on employment, Chinese Americans gathered into densely populated Chinatowns in cities across America. These neighborhoods became tourist attractions, in part because of the unusual food served in "exotic" Chinese restaurants.[15] In traditional Chinese fashion, these establishments served large portions of rice, accompanied by stir-fried vegetables and meat flavored with ginger and soy sauce. For their non-Chinese customers, Chinese cooks invented fried rice, chow mein, and Hangtown fry (a kind of oyster omelet).[16] The most famous of these bastardized Chinese dishes was chop suey (possibly a corruption of *jaap sui*, or "bits and pieces").[17] In 1889, Chicago chef and cookbook author Jessup Whitehead wrote that "chop soly" was a savory ragout, the national dish of China. He noted that "its main components are pork, bacon, chicken, mushrooms, bamboo shoots, onions, and pepper. These are the characteristic ingredients; other incidental ones are duck, beef, perfumed turnip, salted black beans, sliced yam, peas, and string beans. No doubt a curious and wonderful compound, but one that may be palatable withal."[18]

By the 1880s, chop suey joints had become popular in New York. A writer in *Leslie's Illustrated* wrote, in 1896, that "an American who once falls under the spell of chop suey may forget all about things Chinese for a while, and suddenly a strange craving that almost defies will power arises" and "he finds that his feet are carrying him to Mott street."[19] Within a few years, there were more than a hundred chop suey restaurants in New York. By the late 1890s, chop suey restaurants had opened in San Francisco, Philadelphia, Chicago, and other cities.[20] By the century's end, the basic menu had become fairly set: chop suey, chow mein, egg foo young, and a noodle soup called yat gaw mein, or "yakaman." Egg rolls probably didn't appear until the 1920s. These dishes, although based on home-style village food, had been relentlessly adapted to American tastes.[21] One description of these chop suey establishments noted that non-Chinese diners found the food "really toothsome and gratifying." But the author of that description, who had traveled extensively in China, also pointed out that the food had little in common with that actually served in China.[22] Chinese Americans rarely ate anything like it, either. After sampling some chop suey in a restaurant, a Chinese American in New York opined, in 1901, that "there is a great deal of pork in it, and it is too greasy. It is made more to suit American tastes."[23] Other Chinese Americans regarded chop suey as "a culinary joke at the expense of the foreigner."[24]

Nevertheless, the Americanized chop suey and other exotic dishes led to the increasing popularity of Chinese food in the United States. By the mid-twentieth century, more restaurants in the United States were serving Chinese-style food than any other ethnic cuisine—and there are today more Chinese restaurants in the United States than there are McDonald's, Burger Kings, and Wendy's combined.[25]

Part 2: The Treaty of Guadalupe Hidalgo

At the time of Marshall's discovery of gold, California was not yet legally part of the United States. Less than two years before the gold rush, California was still part of Mexico, just as Texas had been Mexican territory before 1836. In that year, American settlers in Texas declared independence from Mexico. Although Mexico failed to put down the revolt, it did not recognize Texan independence. It wasn't until 1845 that the United States annexed Texas, but the border with Mexico remained in dispute. President James K. Polk, a southerner interested in extending slavery westward, authorized the U.S. Army to occupy the disputed territory, an action that initiated war between Mexico and the United States. The military engagements in the Mexican-American War ended in September 1847, but it wasn't until February 2, 1848, that the two countries signed the Treaty of Guadalupe Hidalgo.

With the annexation and conquest of Texas, California, and the Southwest, the United States acquired a multicultural empire with culinary traditions significantly different from those of the rest of the country. While visiting San Antonio in the 1850s, landscape architect and designer Frederick Law Olmsted wrote about his meals of tortillas, tamales, and hashed meat.[26] On a walking tour through Texas in 1869, the journalist Stephen Powers noted in markets "long strips of beef, and large quantities of red and green peppers and garlic."[27] Recalling life in the mid-nineteenth century, Fr. Pierre Fourier Parisot, of St. Mary's Church in San Antonio, wrote that tortillas and frijoles were the principal foods of the Mexican ranchero, sometimes supplemented with eggs and chili con carne.[28] Two mid-nineteenth-century travelers, H. F. McDanield and Nathaniel Alston Taylor, reported that the Mexicans in San Antonio lived "principally on hash made of dried beef and rendered fiercely hot with red pepper. With this they eat pods of red pepper, raw onions, and cornbread made into crackers, which have a strong taste of lye. In summer they sometimes appear to live for days together on nothing but watermelons, for which their fondness is remarkable and really child-like and affecting."[29] Stephen Gould, who wrote *The Alamo City Guide* in 1882, described San Antonio's Military Plaza as teeming with

"Mexican lunch tables, where one can get a genuine Mexican breakfast with as good hot coffee as can be found in the city. Those who delight in the Mexican luxuries of tamales, chili con carne, and enchiladas, can find them here cooked in the open air in the rear of the tables and served by lineal descendants of the ancient Aztecs."[30] These stands sold "'chile con carne,' 'tamales,' 'tortillas,' 'chile rellenos,' 'huevos revueltos,' 'lengua lampreada,' 'pucheros,' 'ollas,' with leathery cheese, burning peppers, stewed tomatoes, and many other items," according to U.S. Army officer and diarist John G. Bourke, who had served along the U.S.-Mexican border and carefully examined the lifestyle and foodways of Mexicans and Mexican Americans living along the Rio Grande River in the late nineteenth century.[31]

At first, few Mexican foods caught on in Anglo America. Exceptions included: chili sauce, enchiladas, tortillas, refried beans, Spanish rice, and tamales. On the subject of tamales—beef, pork, or chicken encased in corn dough, tied in corn husks, and boiled or steamed—Harris Newmark, a grocer and early resident of Southern California, confessed that it "took some time for the incoming epicure to appreciate all that was claimed for them and other masterpieces of Mexican cooking."[32]

To better appeal to Anglo tastes, Mexican vendors and later restaurateurs modified the strong flavors, especially in spicy chili-laced dishes. Anglo-Americans, for their part, created new recipes based on traditional Mexican dishes. The recipe for tamale pie, for instance, became popular around the beginning of the twentieth century, reaching its high point in 1956, when a single cookbook published fifteen recipes for it.[33] Dispensing with the laborious procedure of wrapping a filling in cornmeal dough, enfolding it in a corn husk, tying the packet shut, and steaming it, tamale pies consisted of the same ingredients (minus the corn husk) simply layered in a casserole dish. This was covered with a piecrust in its initial versions; later versions were made with a layer of cornmeal mush at the dish's bottom and another on top. As time went on, Anglo-Americans modified the same ingredients into tamale loaf, tamale pudding, and tamale casserole.

Chili con carne was another dish that was adapted to make it more appealing to Anglo-American tastes. The first-known publication of the term *chile con carne* appeared in the title of an 1857 book written by S. Compton Smith, an American observing food in Monterey, Mexico. Smith defined it as "a popular Mexican dish—literally red peppers and meat."[34] It is likely that the dish Smith identified was consumed throughout northern Mexico and the southwestern United States but that the term itself was an Americanization. Other sources reported that the proper Mexican term was *carne con chile*, emphasizing the meat rather than the hot peppers.[35] Whatever the actual name, descriptions of chili con carne appeared abundantly in nineteenth-century travel accounts. John G. Bourke described it as "meat prepared in a savory stew with chili colorado, tomato, grease, and generally, although not always, with garlic."[36] Anglo-Texans adopted the term and hijacked the dish to such an extent that Francisco J. Santamaría, author of *Diccionario general de americanismos*, dismissed chili con carne as "a detestable dish identified under the false title of Mexican" sold in the United States from Texas to New York.[37] By 1939, chili con carne had become closely associated with Mex-Tex cookery,[38] a term that was later reversed to become Tex-Mex. Other regional Mexican American cooking styles emerged: New Mexican cookery,[39] Cal-Mex, which evolved in Los Angeles,[40] and Sonoran cookery, which unfolded in Arizona.[41]

In time, many "Mexican" dishes were concocted to please the American palate. Salsa (which means "sauce") recipes ran the gamut, as sauce recipes do in all great cuisines. Americans, though, came to love *salsa cruda*, an uncooked sauce based on ripe tomatoes or tomatillos, chilies, and cilantro. A salsa craze swept America during the 1980s, and for a time sales of bottled salsa overtook sales of ketchup. Mexicans enjoy tostadas and *totopos* (fried corn tortillas, whole or cut up), but thin, crisp tortilla chips are an American invention; a staple at Mexican restaurants in the United States, they never caught on in Mexico except in tourist traps. When Mexican-food doyenne Diana Kennedy asked the owner of a Mexican restaurant why tortilla chips were served at the meal's beginning, he humbly reminded Kennedy of the market pressures: "I have to do it that way. Our customers expect it."[42]

Another "Mexican" food that burst onto the American snack-food scene, during the 1960s, was the nacho, which likely originated with a restaurant worker in Texas named Ignacio (Nacho) Anaya. As the story goes, one day Anaya was asked to prepare a snack for the wives of American army officers. The cook was out, so Anaya "grabbed a whole bunch of fried tortillas, put some yellow cheese on top, let it heat a little bit, then put some sliced jalapenos on it."[43] Wherever and however they truly originated, nachos quickly spread throughout Texas, finding their way to a concession stand at Dallas's state fair in 1964.[44] Within two decades, nachos were being served throughout the United States at sports stadiums, airports, and fast-food establishments.

Part 3: Revolution

January of 1848 also saw the rise of a revolutionary wave that began in Sicily, spread to France, and quickly engulfed the rest of Europe. None of the uprisings was successful, but particularly devastated were areas of southern and western Germany. Tens of thousands of people were killed and hundreds of thousands of survivors fled their homes in search of a new life. By 1850, an estimated 435,000 Germans had arrived in the United States.

Many arriving German immigrants went into food-related businesses. Some opened saloons and beer gardens, serving mugs of lager with sausages, sardines, herring, ham, pig's feet, and rye bread.[45] Others set up breweries, especially in the Midwest, where Cincinnati, Milwaukee, Chicago, and Saint Louis became the centers of American beer production.[46]

Some Germans, like immigrants from elsewhere in Europe, became street food vendors. Around 1871, Charles Feltman was operating a pushcart at Coney Island in New York, selling sausages on rolls with sauerkraut. By the 1890s, his specialty had come to be called a hot dog, and the rest is history.[47] Two German immigrants, Frederick and Louis Rueckheim, started as street vendors in Chicago, and, in 1896, they invented a caramel-coated popcorn snack they called Cracker Jack. Another German, Nelson Morris, whose parents had lost their property in the 1848 revolution, moved to Chicago in 1854. He worked in the stockyards and became a meat-packer. After the Civil War, he built the largest meatpacking empire in America, Morris and Company.[48]

Other German immigrants opened restaurants that introduced a whole new line of food into American culinary life. Auguste Ermisch's New York City restaurant, for instance, served, beginning in 1873, something called Hamburg steak. A *New York Times* article described it as "simply a beefsteak redeemed from its original toughness by being mashed into mincemeat and then formed into a conglomerated mass. This is very appetizing, but conscience compels us to state that it is inferior to the genuine article, which can also be had here in a very satisfactory condition of tenderness."[49] Over the next twenty years, Hamburg steak, as it became known, took America by storm; by the 1890s, it had evolved into the quintessential American food, the hamburger sandwich, and was sold by street vendors in most cities.[50]

In 1850, another German immigrant, Ferdinand Schumacher, opened a grocery store in Akron, Ohio. His major customers were German and Irish immigrants, and they bought a lot of oats—which, at the time, most Anglo-Americans considered animal feed. Sales were such that Schumacher decided to specialize in oats. In 1854, he set up the German Mills American Oatmeal Factory in Akron. Sales were brisk, particularly to cities with large immigrant populations, so Schumacher opened additional mills to meet the increasing demand. Soon he became the largest oat miller in America, and even professed to be the largest oat miller in the world. For this, Schumacher was dubbed the Oatmeal King.[51]

Still other Germans opened so-called delicatessens, retail stores that sold specialty food items. According to Artemas Ward, chronicler of the nineteenth-century grocery trade, the first delicatessen in America opened on Grand Street in New York City around 1868.[52] At that time, Manhattan's Lower East Side had a substantial German immigrant population. Delicatessens attracted not only German Americans but also passersby who were enticed by the windows displaying foreign and "fancy" foods. During the late nineteenth century, delicatessens filled the gap between butcher shops, which sold mainly uncooked meats, and general grocery stores, which sold primarily generic and packaged goods. Delicatessens quickly spread from New York to other cities. By 1910, they had become common throughout urban America, and ubiquitous in New York City.

The first German American delicatessens sold cooked, ready-to-eat meats, poultry, and fish, as well as specialty products such as cheeses, teas, mushrooms, caviar, olive oil, pickles, and other imported canned goods. Later, delicatessens sold tuna and chicken salad sandwiches as well as vegetable salads, such as coleslaw and potato salad. Originally, customers purchased the prepared foods and took them elsewhere to eat, but as delicatessens thrived and expanded, some made a place for customers to sit down and eat in the store, particularly at lunchtime.

During the 1880s, Jewish immigrants, fleeing political oppression and crushing poverty in eastern Europe, began pouring into New York and other eastern cities. Some of the more entrepreneurial opened delicatessens, similar to German delicatessens. If the shop was kosher, it sold only meat, fish, and pareve (neutral) foods; a typical selection featured chicken soup, corned beef, gefilte fish, lox, knishes, pastrami, chopped liver, tongue, and garlic pickles. If Jewish dietary laws were not followed, the menu might include things like bagels and bialys with cream cheese, herring in cream sauce, blintzes, and cheesecake. Jewish delis also popularized Jewish-style breads, notably rye and pumpernickel.[53]

Delicatessens remain an important cultural component of American cities, but the term is used much more loosely today. As other new groups of immigrants—Italians, Greeks, Puerto Ricans, West Indians, Asians, Russians, and Mexicans—moved into American cities, many found that deli ownership proved an excellent way to enter American economic life. While some delis today still specialize in cured meats, pickled fish, and other old-world specialties, most sell a general line of packaged and prepared foods. Deli owners from newer immigrant groups, though, often include their native favorites; Korean American–owned delis, for example, frequently sell kimchi and other Asian delicacies, and West Indian proprietors offer savory turnovers called patties. Today, there are more delicatessens in America than ever, and several chains now franchise "New York" delis throughout the nation—although they may have little in common with the real thing.

Immigrant Effects

In the 1880s, the pattern of immigration to the United States shifted as people from southern and eastern Europe flooded into the country. The pace of immigration accelerated in the decade from 1901 to 1910, when 9 million people arrived in American cities from abroad. Most immigrants tried to keep their culinary traditions alive, but it wasn't until after World War II that mainstream Americans began to adopt (usually bastardized) versions of ethnic foods, newly enriching the traditional American diet. This trend has continued ever since, and today ethnic foods are readily available in restaurants and grocery stores around the nation.

Mass immigration into the United States continued until the 1920s. By that time, an estimated 5 million Germans—the largest ethnic immigrant group in American history—had come to the United States, with a peak in the years between 1881 and 1885, when 1 million Germans settled here, mostly in the Midwest. Between 1820 and 1930, an estimated 4.5 million Irish entered America. Over 2 million Jews fled the pogroms of the Russian Empire and came to America between 1881 and 1924. During the decade ending in 1920, over 2 million Italians immigrated to the United States, and about 1.5 million Swedes and Norwegians also came to American shores. Anti-immigrant sentiment finally slowed these mass migrations, and, in 1921, the U.S. Congress passed the Emergency Quota Act, followed, three years later, by the Immigration Act of 1924. Both laws restricted immigration. After World War II, however, immigration began to swell again, and by the twentieth century's end, hundreds of thousands of immigrants were entering America—legally or otherwise—every year.

Foreign contributions to the American diet did not come equally from all immigrant groups. Newcomers, in some cases, found it impossible to buy their accustomed foods in America, and they often faced social pressure to conform to American eating habits—a major hurdle on the road to assimilation. Italian foods and dishes, on the other hand, in time reached all levels of society and, at least superficially, all parts of the country. Today, there are more Italian restaurants in the United States than restaurants offering the foods of any other ethnic group. The late twentieth century saw a new wave of Chinese immigration; authentic and regional Chinese foods have taken the place of gold rush–era chow mein and chop suey, and today Chinese food is the third most popular ethnic food in America.

As noted, Mexican culinary influences spread slowly around the United States. Small Mexican American roadside restaurants, often called taco stands, sprang up throughout California and the Southwest. Taco Bell turned Mexican-style snacks into fast food, and the chain quickly expanded around Los Angeles; today there are about 6,700 Taco Bell outlets, generating about $5 billion in annual sales.[54] In addition to such fast-food establishments, there are today more than 7,000 Mexican restaurants throughout the United States. Mexican food is now the second most popular ethnic cuisine in the United States, and it is now a close runner-up to Italian food.[55]

Italians, Greeks, Japanese, eastern European Jews, Chinese, Koreans, and other immigrants introduced or popularized particular fruits, vegetables, seafoods, or traditional dishes while serving as cooks, truck gardeners, fishermen, delicatessen and restaurant owners, vendors, or wholesale food sellers.[56] Many common American dishes—hot dogs, hamburgers, chili con carne, chop suey, gyros, tacos, tamales, bagels, pizza, spaghetti, sushi, pad thai, and Swedish meatballs—to name but a few—owe their origins to immigrants.

The immigrant experience in this country has thus created a cornucopia of ethnic or ethnic-inspired foods that have enriched and expanded the scope of American cuisine. As Donna Gabaccia wrote in *We Are What We Eat: Ethnic Food and the Making of Americans*, "all Americans mingle the culinary traditions of many regions and cultures within ourselves. We are multiethnic eaters."[57]

Postscript

Neither James W. Marshall nor his employer, mill owner John Sutter, profited from the discovery of gold at the mill site. The mill was never completed as the workers headed for the hills in search of gold. Marshall lived out his life in a small cabin surviving on a meager garden. He died in 1885. John Sutter's various businesses failed and he, too, died in poverty, in 1880.

Ferdinand Schumacher joined with other oatmeal manufacturers to create what eventually became the Quaker Oats Company, the largest cereal manufacturing company in the world by the 1890s. He died in 1908.

The Treaty of Guadalupe Hidalgo, signed in 1848 with the Provisional Mexican Government, which had been created by the U.S. military, was roundly condemned by most Mexicans at the time. Mention of the treaty continues to raise hackles among some Mexicans today.

Thanksgiving dinner at the Five Points Ladies' Home Missionary Society of the Methodist Episcopal Church (*Harper's Weekly*, 9 [December 23, 1865]: 804)

7.

Giving Thanks

I N THE 1830s, Alexander Young, a Unitarian minister in Boston, began compiling primary source documents about the Pilgrims. In his research, he ran across a book titled *Mourt's Relation*, which had been published in England in 1622. This work contains a letter from one of the first settlers of Plymouth Plantation, Edward Winslow, in which he wrote that in the autumn of 1621, William Bradford, the governor of the just-established colony, had declared a holiday after the crops were harvested. The English colonists had just made a treaty with the local Indians, ninety of whom unexpectedly showed up to solidify it. According to Winslow, the Indians and colonists feasted for three days in celebration of the treaty. In 1841, Alexander Young republished Winslow's letter in his compilation of early records, *Chronicles of the Pilgrim Fathers of the Colony of Plymouth*. Young added a footnote to Winslow's description of the 1621 event, claiming that this "was the first thanksgiving, the harvest festival of New England. On this occasion they no doubt feasted on the wild turkey as well as venison."[1]

While the Pilgrims did have many days of thanksgiving, they did not view this feast with the Indians as one of them. It was an insignificant event and the Pilgrims took no notice of it in subsequent years. The whole idea that the Pilgrims were the first to celebrate Thanksgiving in America was, in fact, preposterous. Many days of thanksgiving had been celebrated previously by Europeans in the new land. Young's creation of the "first Thanksgiving" myth might have died a quiet death in that obscure footnote had not other New England writers picked up the idea, embellished it, and presented it as ironclad truth.² Twenty-two years after the publication of Young's book, Thanksgiving was proclaimed a national holiday, and the Thanksgiving dinner became enshrined as America's most cherished culinary extravaganza. It remains so today.

Giving Thanks History

Giving thanks for God's blessings is part of the religious traditions brought to the New World by Europeans. Spanish explorers and colonists had been celebrating days of thanksgiving in what is today the United States for decades before the Pilgrims landed in Massachusetts. The English colonists at Jamestown had celebrated days of thanksgiving more than a decade before the Pilgrims landed. Even the Pilgrims themselves had had days of thanksgiving well before the proverbial first Thanksgiving noted by Young. Winslow did not assign the name to the event of the fall of 1621, and William Bradford, the chronicler of early life at Plymouth Plantation, made no mention of a thanksgiving at that time. During the following decades, the Puritans celebrated many days of thanksgiving, but they had nothing to do with food. Local ministers set thanksgivings at any time of the year after a particularly important event—a providential rainfall, a good harvest, or perhaps a military victory. Although thanksgiving dinners had been common in England, the Puritans held days of thanksgiving as solemn holy days. In Puritan New England, a thanksgiving day would have been spent in church, and little evidence has survived indicating that special food was served; indeed, it is unlikely that feasts would have been prepared or served on holy days.

A few references to Colonial thanksgiving dinners have survived, but they are from the southern colonies, not New England. Shortly after the American victory at Saratoga in 1777, however, the Continental Congress declared a day of thanksgiving. When the War for American Independence ended, in 1784, another thanksgiving was proclaimed. President George Washington declared national days of thanksgiving in 1789 and 1795. None of the proclamations establishing these days made any mention of a thanksgiving dinner. By this time, though, thanksgiving dinners were common in many places in America. A participant in a 1784 thanksgiving meal in Norwich, Connecticut, remarked, "What a sight of pigs and geese and turkeys and fowls and sheep must be slaughtered to gratify the voraciousness of a single day."³ William Bentley, pastor of East Church, in Salem, Massachusetts, wrote in 1806 that "a Thanksgiving is not complete without a turkey. It is rare to find any other dishes but such as turkies & fowls afford before the pastry on such days & puddings are much less used than formerly."⁴

An observer in 1817 reported that Thanksgiving dinner consisted of "roasted turkey, a smoking plum-pudding and pumpkin-pies."[5]

Edward Everett Hale, a Unitarian minister and author, remembered the Thanksgiving dinners that his family celebrated in Massachusetts during the early nineteenth century. They commenced with chicken pie and roast turkey, then proceeded to several different types of pies, tarts, and puddings, and ended with dried fruit.[6] A New Hampshire Thanksgiving dinner of the same era began with a ham and a large roast turkey, followed by chicken, duck, celery, plum pudding, pies, and fruit, finally ending with coffee and tea.[7] An 1831 dinner in Geneva, New York, featured turkey, beef, duck, ham, sausage, potatoes, yams, succotash, pickles, nuts, raisins, pears, peaches, pie, tarts, creams, custards, jellies, floating islands, sweetbreads, wines, rum, brandy, eggnog and punch.[8] In 1835, an observer in Maine reported that everyone looked forward to Thanksgiving "with bright anticipations of feast and frolic. For a week preceding, all is preparation for its approach. Our markets are thronged with the various provisions indispensable to a Thanksgiving dinner; and the 'bustling housewife' is busily engaged in preparing them for her expected guests."[9] The writer Harriet Beecher Stowe remembered her childhood Thanksgivings, in Litchfield, Connecticut, replete with turkey, chicken, chicken pies, plum puddings, and sweet pies.[10]

Nationalizing Giving Thanks

Many influences helped nationalize Thanksgiving. New England soil was not the best for farming, and during the early nineteenth century, many New Englanders moved to other parts of the United States in search of better farmland. With the completion of the Erie Canal, New Englanders migrated to New York's central valley and later to the Midwest. Transplanted New Englanders kept the Thanksgiving dinner traditions alive in their new homes and urged their newly adopted communities to celebrate the feast as well. New York was the first state outside New England to declare Thanksgiving a holiday, and midwestern states soon followed. Thanksgiving became widely celebrated throughout America, especially in the North, but by the mid-nineteenth century, it was still a holiday celebrated only at the local or state levels.

The person who made Thanksgiving a national holiday was Sarah Josepha Hale, who was born in 1788 in Newport, New Hampshire. After running a school for five years, she married David Hale, a lawyer, who died in 1822. To support her five children, she turned to writing. In 1823, she published her first book of poetry, *The Genius of Oblivion*, and, four years later, she published her first novel, *Northwood; or, a Tale of New England*, which featured an entire chapter describing Thanksgiving dinner:

there was roasted turkey, beef sirloin, a leg of pork, mutton, a goose, two ducks, chicken pie, stuffing, "innumerable" bowls of gravy, plates of vegetables, plates of pickles, preserves, butter, bread, and "a huge plum pudding, custards and pies of every name and description," but "pumpkin pie occupied the most distinguished niche." There were also several kinds of cakes, and a variety of sweetmeats and fruits. Beverages included currant wine, cider, and ginger beer.[11] *Northwood* established the model for what became the "traditional Yankee Thanksgiving dinner."

Northwood catapulted Hale into literary stardom. She became the editor of *American Ladies' Magazine*, a small monthly published in Boston, and after its purchase by Louis A. Godey, in 1836, Hale became the editor of *Godey's Lady's Book*. Under Hale's management, the magazine prospered: subscriptions went from 10,000 annually in 1837 to 150,000 by 1860, a phenomenal achievement.[12]

At the time, only two national holidays were celebrated in the United States: Washington's Birthday (February 22) and Independence Day (July 4). A few years after the story of the "first Thanksgiving" appeared in Young's book, Hale launched a campaign to make Thanksgiving a national holiday. Beginning in 1846, she wrote regularly to members of Congress, prominent individuals, and the governors of every state and territory, requesting each to proclaim the last Thursday in November as Thanksgiving Day. In an era before television, radio, the Internet, or even the typewriter, this campaign was a daunting task. Hale also wrote editorials in *Godey's Lady's Book* promoting Thanksgiving. Each year, she listed the states that had agreed to celebrate the holiday. Her efforts did receive support and publicity from various quarters. Magazines and newspapers printed Thanksgiving stories, songs, and poems.[13] Even the transcendentalists chipped in: Ralph Waldo Emerson wrote a Thanksgiving poem and Margaret Fuller wrote about Thanksgiving in newspapers and books.[14]

By 1859, Hale was close to success, with thirty states and three territories celebrating Thanksgiving on the third Thursday of November. After the Civil War broke out and she was unable to communicate with many southern states, Hale devised a different strategy. She wrote, in 1863, privately to William Seward, Lincoln's secretary of state and a former senator from New York, requesting that President Lincoln declare Thanksgiving a national holiday.[15] She also wrote directly to President Lincoln, and she may have met with him. Her efforts finally paid off a few months after the North's military victories at Gettysburg and Vicksburg: in the summer of 1863, Lincoln declared the last Thursday in November a national day of Thanksgiving.[16]

Thanksgiving church services continued to be held in the nineteenth century, but the religious content of the day declined as the century progressed. In 1834, a writer remarked that Thanksgiving should be spent in a "house of prayer with our hearts tuned to the sacred service, and the flame of devotion burning brightly in our bosoms," and that Americans "should kneel around the holy altar, and send up from thence the incense of thanksgiving and praise." But she also noted that it was proper that the country's citizens "close the day in an innocent enjoyment of the blessings with which we are surrounded, mingling therewith a solemn sense of that goodness which permits us to partake of them."[17] By the 1870s, this dual view had changed. *Scribner's Magazine* proclaimed, in 1871, that Americans had "almost lost sight of" the religious character of the day. In cities, the author reported, no one considered attending religious services on Thanksgiving a duty, and in the country, women and men attended services, but their attention was really focused on "what has grown to be considered the real event, the raison d'etre of the day, namely, the dinner."[18]

By the nineteenth century's end, the Thanksgiving meal had become an elaborate and abundant feast—and an opportunity for the host and hostess to display their generosity to their families and guests. At the center of the feast, turkey reigned supreme. While many other main dishes had been tried, it was turkey that thrived, mainly because it was less expensive than the alternatives. The turkey also became symbolic, thanks to the myth of the first Thanksgiving. The traditional side dishes—stuffing, gravy, sweet potatoes, succotash, corn bread, cranberries, and pies—were inexpensive as well, so that Thanksgiving dinner was affordable to all but the poorest Americans.

And even the poorest Americans might have a dinner on Thanksgiving as charitable groups sponsored dinners for the homeless and indigent. One such event, held in the notorious Five Points district of Manhattan, was captured in a lithograph in *Harper's Weekly*. The picture showed hundreds of poor children standing at tables eating Thanksgiving dinner. The dinner was sponsored by the Ladies' Home Mission of the Methodist Episcopal Church; it turned into an annual event and was held throughout much of the nineteenth century.[19] There is another *Harper's Weekly* illustration, of a middle class family sharing the leftovers from its dinner with a poor immigrant waif; the lithograph is titled *The First Thanksgiving Dinner*.[20] St. Barnabas House, in New York, served 1,400 pounds of turkey to 1,000 indigent guests. In 1895, Mrs. Frederick W. Vanderbilt sponsored a "turkey dinner" with all the fixings for 400 poor boys of Newport, Rhode Island.[21] Similar events have been held in almost every city in America ever since.

Giving Thanks to the Pilgrims

By 1870, school textbooks had begun telling the tale of the Pilgrim fathers and their first Thanksgiving dinner.[22] A decade later, the Pilgrim-centered story had blossomed in accounts published in magazines, newspapers, and books. Jane G.

Austin, a popular American novelist of the late nineteenth century, wrote a series of books on the Pilgrims. In her novel *Standish of Standish: A Story of the Pilgrims*, she included a full chapter on the first Thanksgiving. In this fictional account, the Pilgrims—less than a year after their arrival in America-—celebrated Thanksgiving at a long table, with bowls brimming with hasty pudding topped with butter and treacle, "clam chowder with sea biscuit swimming in a savory broth… great pieces of cold boiled beef with mustard, flanked by dishes of turnips." Another table, claimed Austin, held a large pewter bowl full of "plum-porridge with bits of toasted cracker floating upon it," and turkeys were stuffed with beechnuts. Then there were "oysters scalloped in their shells, venison pasties, and the savory stew compounded of all that flies the air." Game was caught by hunters, and the Pilgrims and American Indians ate "roasts of various kinds, and thin cakes of bread or manchets, and bowls of salad" and "great baskets of grapes, white and purple, and of native plum, so delicious when fully ripe in its three colors of black, white, and red." The food was downed with "flagons of ale" and "root beer, well flavored with sassafras."[23]

The only foods on Austin's list that the Pilgrims might actually have consumed in the fall of 1621 would have been turkey, venison, corn (maize), and ale. Austin had exercised complete artistic license in describing the meal, which she was certainly entitled to do in a work of fiction. As unbelievable as that mythical first Thanksgiving dinner may sound to us today, at the time it was widely accepted as accurate. A review in *Publisher's Weekly*, for instance, proclaimed Austin's first Thanksgiving scene as "faithfully" portrayed.[24] The story was then adopted by many schoolteachers and incorporated into the history curriculum. Plays and pageants were devised celebrating Thanksgiving, with classes reenacting the first Thanksgiving, complete with children dressed up as Indians and Pilgrims; some schools offered Thanksgiving dinners based on Austin's fictional version of life in Plymouth in 1621.[25] *Standish of Standish* was reprinted several times, and Austin's version of the Pilgrims and that first Thanksgiving became embedded in the country's American history curriculum.[26] In 1919, Austin's novel was adapted as a play for children, and many schools and communities performed it when the three-hundredth anniversary of the first Thanksgiving rolled around in 1921.[27] This curriculum spawned, in turn, a large children's literature celebrating the Pilgrims and the first Thanksgiving.[28]

Thanksgiving dinner and the Pilgrims were enshrined on the covers and inside pages of some of America's most popular magazines. Illustrator Thomas Nast's cartoon, appearing in *Harper's Weekly* in 1869, shows Uncle Sam carving a turkey at a bountifully appointed dinner table, surrounded by men, women, and children of different religions and ethnicities.[29] J. C. Leyendecker's cover for the

November 1907 *Saturday Evening Post* pictures a Pilgrim stalking a tom turkey.[30] American painters also contributed to the myth: Jennie Augusta Brownscombe's painting *The First Thanksgiving*, completed in 1914, appeared in many school textbooks, and Jean Louis Gerome Ferris's *First Thanksgiving* was frequently reprinted in magazines.[31] Other popular works of art and literature have fostered the myth ever since.[32]

Giving No Thanks

Not everyone was happy with the Thanksgiving dinner. In 1835, William Alcott, a physician and vegetarian, stated that he was opposed to the feast on moral grounds as well as for medical reasons. He called Thanksgiving a carnival, "loaded with luxuries not only on the day of the general thanksgiving, but for several days afterward." He was particularly concerned because New England-ers were also beginning to celebrate Christmas, and he claimed that the two feasts had already merged into one long period of overindulgence that caused serious health problems.[33] John Harvey Kellogg, the vegetarian director of the Battle Creek Sanitarium, took up the cause against the Thanksgiving dinner. He believed that the large meal was a tragedy in the making that could cripple diges-tive "organs completely and produce a fatal uremia."[34]

Few Americans paid any attention to Alcott or Kellogg at the time, but dur-ing the past thirty years, vegetarians have shifted their focus from condemning the Thanksgiving dinner to condemnation of its centerpiece—the turkey. Veg-etarians celebrated the holiday; they just eliminated the bird from the feast. Ani-mal rights organizations, such as People for the Ethical Treatment of Animals (PETA), gain visibility for their cause around Thanksgiving. For PETA members, "turkey day" is a time to convince Americans to give up eating meat in general and turkey in particular. PETA has sponsored petitions and published leaflets encouraging a turkeyless Thanksgiving under the slogan Give turkeys something to be thankful for!

Giving Thanks Effects

The rapid adoption of the Thanksgiving myth had less to do with historical fact and more to do with the arrival of hundreds of thousands of immigrants to the United States in the late nineteenth and early twentieth centuries. In the face of this great wave of immigrants from so many lands, the public education system's major task was to Americanize them by creating a common understanding of the nation's his-tory, in particular, an easily understood history of America. The problem was that

Jamestown, which had the greatest claim to be the founding American colony, was where slavery had begun, and after the bloody Civil War—fought, in large part, to free the slaves—that wasn't a message anyone wanted in school textbooks. On the other hand, the absurd Pilgrim fathers, with their floppy hats and mythical blunderbusses, and the newly invented first Thanksgiving dinner, at which colonists and Indians feasted together, were ideal elements for the story of America's beginning. The tale gave legitimacy to the colonists' settlement of the land and suggested friendly relations with the Native Americans.[35] Few educators and textbook publishers could resist the temptation to use these attractive images.

The immigrants, who had celebrated no such holiday as Thanksgiving in their native lands, readily joined in the feast because it demonstrated their loyalty to their adopted country and their belief in American abundance. As they adapted the celebration to their own tastes, the immigrants modified the menu by including their own traditional foods alongside the standard Thanksgiving dishes. The turkey retained its place of honor—after all, it was native to America and a symbol of the nation's bounty.[36] But the newcomers complemented the turkey with their own festive dishes—pasta, fried rice, sauerkraut, refried beans, or pierogis—honoring their own history as well as that of their new home.

Thanksgiving remains one of America's most important holidays. Come November, schoolchildren still reenact the first Thanksgiving, and turkey, gravy, and cranberry sauce predictably appear on school cafeteria menus. Newspapers, magazines, and television programs tell of the Pilgrims and their feast with the Indians. Retailers make relentless commercial use of Thanksgiving as the start of the Christmas shopping season, and parades and other public gatherings are held in cities and towns across America. And the family Thanksgiving dinner holds its place as America's preeminent national culinary event.

Postscript

Alexander Young was a prolific writer who published dozens of biographies and religious tracts during his lifetime. His *Chronicles of the Pilgrim Fathers* went through many editions, and it remains in print today. In 1849, he became the secretary of Harvard's board of overseers and corresponding secretary of the Massachusetts Historical Society. He died in 1854.[37]

Sarah Josepha Hale's literary career flourished. In all, she published nearly fifty books, and she continued to serve as editor of *Godey's Lady's Book* until 1877. She died in 1879. For her efforts to make Thanksgiving a national holiday, Hale is remembered as the Mother of Thanksgiving.[38]

Advertisement for Gail Borden's Condensed Milk (courtesy of Hexion Specialty Chemicals)

8.

Gail Borden's Canned Milk

G AIL BORDEN, an entrepreneur who'd failed miserably at manufacturing dehydrated meat in the shape of biscuits, invented a method of preserving milk by adding sugar, heating it, and reducing it. Basically broke, but with financial help from friends, Borden embarked on his condensed milk project. He felt he'd perfected the process in 1852, but his attempt to manufacture it on a commercial scale didn't work out, and his faithful investors lost their money. Borden tried again in 1858, with yet another partner, opening a plant in Wolcottville, Connecticut. Just as Borden began shipping condensed milk to New York City, *Frank Leslie's Illustrated Newspaper* broke the shocking story of New York's "swill milk trade." In the wake of this nauseating exposé, which went on for months, Borden's canned and pasteurized milk found a ready market.[1] Borden's advertising stressed the fact that his canned milk was safe, and panicked New Yorkers eagerly snapped it up. Encouraged by early sales figures, Borden optimistically began construction of several additional plants. These new factories began operation just as the Civil War began. Although Borden didn't know it, he had just taken a major step toward the industrialization of American food processing.

Canned History

Gail Borden was not the country's first commercial canner. During the early nineteenth century, American commercial food preservation was based largely on the migration of English canners, such as William Underwood, who had served a pickling and preserving apprenticeship with London's Mackey & Company. He migrated to the United States and, in 1819, established the firm later known as the William Underwood Company. By 1821, he was shipping bottled plums, quinces, currants, barberries, cranberries, pickles, ketchup, sauces, jellies, and jams to South America.[2] Other canning operations opened in other cities at about the same time. The main items canned were luxury goods for hotel restaurants and ships' provisions.[3]

Early tin-canning operations were small and labor-intensive because the processing was done entirely by hand. The can's sides and bottoms were cut from sheets of tin and soldered together. Food was placed in the can, and the lid was soldered in place. The can was then placed in a boiling water bath for five hours, with a hole in the lid providing a means for steam to escape. When the water bath was done, the hole was soldered shut and the can sealed airtight.[4] These techniques were not well understood and there were serious problems, such as bursting cans and contamination that sometimes sickened or even killed consumers.

On the eve of the Civil War, canned goods were still specialty items bought by only a select few. The public was leery of both the price and the health risks associated with canned goods. Two inventions changed this. The first was John L. Mason's patent on the self-sealing zinc lid and glass jar, issued on November 30, 1858. This screw-on lid simplified the canning process and made the jars genuinely reusable. It revolutionized fruit and vegetable preservation in the home. As the jars were easy to use and comparatively inexpensive to produce, their popularity soared. By 1860, Mason jars were being shipped throughout the United States.[5] With the invention of the Mason jar, Americans became much more familiar with the canning process. Commercial bottlers used the same screw on cap on their manufactured goods. The second change was that American canners learned to speed up the commercial canning process by heating bottles and cans in a solution of calcium chloride, which shortened the time required for the water bath.[6] This meant faster production and lower consumer prices, leading eventually to the replacement of home canning by commercial canning.

When the Civil War began, the Union faced the challenge of distributing food to its military forces, which were spread out over thousands of miles. Commissary units were set up and an extensive supply system developed. Railroads, riverboats, wagons, and carts were organized into a coherent system to feed the troops. This system worked well with the basics—grains, for instance, could easily be shipped over thousands of miles without difficulty. But fresh fruits and vegetables were another matter. During the summer, they could be bought locally, and, in fact, some military units lived off the land. In the off season, however, fresh produce was simply unavailable. The Union army faced a particular problem with milk, which remained in good supply in the North and Midwest but was scarce in the South, where most Civil War engagements were fought. The Commissary Department came up with a solution: Borden's canned milk.

Gail Borden had been a teacher, land surveyor, inventor, real estate salesman, and editor. In 1848, he invented a "meat biscuit" that he alleged would keep indefinitely; he hoped to sell it for use on long expeditions and sea voyages. At the time, the Great Exhibition at the Crystal Palace in London was the foremost venue for introducing new inventions, and in 1851 Borden displayed his meat biscuits there. Despite his considerable promotional efforts, he found few takers and lost his $600,000 investment.[7]

So, Borden went into the canning of condensed milk. Despite his optimism, his company was just a moderate success, until the fall of 1861, when a customer entered the offices of the New York Condensed Milk Company and asked a few questions of its proprietor. The man was a Commissary Department agent for the Union army, and his first order was for 500 pounds of condensed milk.[8]

The army's Commissary Department was satisfied with that first shipment, and within months sent Borden orders for much more. Canned milk had worked out so well that the federal government gave contracts to other canners throughout northern and border states to supply a variety of canned goods for the land and naval forces, and for the wounded and sick in hospitals.[9] Once the military contracts came through, the future of Borden's enterprise was assured. Contracts also came from sanitary commissions, which had been set up to nurse sick and wounded soldiers back to health. In 1864, the company generated a profit for the first time—a handsome $145,000—and it enjoyed sizable profits thereafter.[10]

Borden's canned milk was so successful that, in 1863, the Commissary Department expanded its contracts for a wide variety of canned goods to feed the northern army.[11] Large wartime orders made it financially viable to build new canning plants, and they sprang up throughout the northern and border states. Their goods were shipped by train, wagon, ship, and riverboat to distant outposts and naval vessels. The federal contracts had primed the pump, and when the war ended, many large canning plants were already operating.

Most soldiers and sailors given these rations were eating canned food for the first time, and they liked what they tasted. (Returning Confederate soldiers, too, had acquired a taste for canned foods, as they'd often raided Union supply trains during the war and carted off what they could.) When soldiers and sailors returned home after the war, civilian demand for canned goods soared.

As the demand for canned goods grew after the war, canneries opened around the country. In Baltimore alone, the number of canneries jumped from thirteen in 1860 to close to thirty by 1867. Some would-be canners paid up to $5,000 to be taught the "secret process" of preserving foods. With time, the quality of these operations improved, as did their efficiency, which reduced costs.[12] Whereas the annual output was 5 million cans in 1860, the figure was six times greater a decade later.[13] By the 1880s, cheap canned goods were commonly available in most grocery stores throughout the nation.

Canning technology took a major leap forward with the invention of the "sanitary can" in the early twentieth century. It built on previous inventions, such as the double-seamed cans first manufactured in 1859 and used in Europe shortly thereafter. A thick rubber gasket similar to that used on Mason jars was placed between the end and body of the can, and the end was crimped to the body by rollers. This method was demonstrated at Chicago's Columbian Exposition in 1893. But the rubber gasket was cumbersome and costly. Charles M. Ams came up with the idea of lining the can's edge with rubber cement, reducing the amount of rubber used and simplifying the sealing process. His invention was dubbed the sanitary can. Ams refined the process and designed a line of commercial machines that eventually revolutionized the canning industry.[14] These machines cut strips of metal into proper lengths, and a mechanical trimmer formed the finished product. In 1901, the American Can Company was formed, and within a few years it had taken over almost the entire can-making business. American Can's annual output reached, by 1914, 3 billion cans.[15]

In the late nineteenth century, the technology of vacuum sealing food in glass containers was also being perfected. Bottlers faced serious problems related to glass durability and capping methods: Heating the filled bottles to temperatures above 200°F, which sterilized the contents, resulted in enormous breakage, so they tried heating the contents first, then pouring the food into hot bottles and corking them. As the contents cooled, the corks shrank and were unable to maintain the vacuum; air was drawn through and around the cork, and the food quickly spoiled. In the early twentieth century, researchers discovered ways of manufacturing glass bottles that were shatterproof at higher temperatures. Researchers also concluded that vacuum sealing was absolutely essential. Covering corks with a metal cap created a closure that effectively sealed the contents from contact with outside air. This type of bottle was especially important in the carbonated-drink industry. Another major advance was the development of the screw cap, which made it possible to reseal bottles after opening.

Despite the spectacular success and rapid expansion of the bottling and canning industries, all was not well in the food-packaging world. Prices continued to drop as a result of cutthroat competition, but quality, on the whole, deteriorated. Many canneries put up inferior goods marked with fraudulent weights; a contemporary report noted that the dry weight of "2-pound" cans of oysters was often as little as eleven ounces.[16] Since the industry's inception, contamination and adulteration had been alarming and chronic problems. These serious concerns became more menacing and more visible as the industry expanded. Fly-by-night manufacturers filled cans and bottles with low-quality products or toxic ingredients, and consumers got sick and some died. These abuses spurred the movement to enact pure food laws in individual states, and, beginning in 1876, an attempt was made to pass legislation in Congress. Federal efforts were not successful until June 1906, however, when Congress passed the Pure Food and Drugs Act. While its passage did not immediately end abuses, there was a sharp decline in unsanitary practices.[17]

For customers, the main problem was that they could not see what was in cans until they were paid for and opened. Large canners concluded that labels were needed to identify the product inside the can. The obvious first step was to illustrate the product inside, such as peas, beans, tomatoes, or peaches. The Campbell Soup Company initiated the idea of using labels and advertising to attract buyers. Campbell's management knew that their customers were women, and that the way to reach them was through "child appeal." The company created the characters later known as the Campbell Kids, plump, rosy-cheeked children, who suggested that Campbell's soups were wholesome and nourishing. Kids first appeared on advertisements in early 1905, and they have continued to represent Campbell's for more than a century.[18] Other canning companies followed Campbell's lead, and other culinary advertising icons, such as the Jolly Green Giant, entered American life through the packaging and promotion of canned goods.

Canned goods were easily transported and could be stored for months—or years—without spoiling. With the rise of the grocery store and later the supermarket, canned goods were widely distributed. Large cans were used in restaurants and institutions. During World War II, metal was rationed, and canned goods were restricted largely to the armed forces. American soldiers carried cans (and can openers) into battle. When the war ended, canned goods proliferated during the heady days of the postwar economic boom. Television made national advertising possible and profitable. By the 1950s, one out of every three products in supermarkets was canned. Today, this has decreased to one in ten, but canned goods remain a mainstay of the American diet.

Canned Effects

Commercial canning made it possible to preserve perishable foods in season and to eat them year-round. Canned foods were also convenient: they were already washed, cut up, and cooked, and, after heating, they were ready to eat. As the cost of producing canned goods declined, canned fruit, vegetables, milk, and meat came to be consumed by all but the poorest Americans. A more varied year-round diet with canned fruits and vegetables undoubtedly transformed the health of many Americans. During the late nineteenth and early twentieth centuries, Americans grew taller and healthier.[19] While there were many reasons for this—better sanitation, pure food laws, and medical advances—a reliable supply of year-round canned produce likely contributed as well.

Even as technological innovations made it possible to produce canned goods faster and more cheaply, the equipment necessary for high-speed processing became more expensive. Consequently, small and medium-sized canneries that served their local areas couldn't afford it, and they were undersold in their markets by national brands. In addition, the Pure Food and Drugs Act required food processors engaged in interstate trade to strictly adhere to proper health and safety procedures. This made it even more difficult for smaller companies to survive, and many closed or were bought out.

Larger canning operations enjoyed economies of scale: By the mid-twentieth century, they had invested in state-of-the-art equipment, ensuring maximum efficiency at the lowest possible price. Some large plants turned out millions of cans or bottles of food daily. During the tomato season in 1935, the Campbell's Soup factory in Camden, New Jersey, produced 10 million cans of soup in one day.[20] Large canners also invested in national distribution networks and extensive advertising campaigns to boost sales. More recently, mighty conglomerates with the scope to expand to foreign markets have come to rule the canning and bottling trade: Heinz, Campbell Soup, ConAgra, Del Monte, Kraft Foods, PepsiCo, Coca-Cola, and Cadbury Schweppes Americas Beverages are some of the largest. Still, some small local canners and bottlers have survived, and many thrive in niche or regional markets, sometimes by returning to centuries-old recipes and methods.

Today, most Americans use canned foods and beverages—either buying them at the supermarket to serve at home or consuming them in restaurants. In 2006, Americans consumed 100 billion cans of beverages and 29 billion cans of food.[21] Annually, Americans buy billions more products in glass and plastic bottles. Cans and bottles have made it possible for many Americans to enjoy foods and beverages that would otherwise be unaffordable.

Postscript

When the Civil War ended in 1865, Gail Borden returned to Texas, where he started several small businesses. He died in 1874, a wealthy man. Borden's company thrived through the late nineteenth and early twentieth centuries. Elsie the Cow, Borden's bovine spokeswoman, appeared on the scene in 1936, and she was popularized at the 1939 New York World's Fair. Elsie also made it into *Life* magazine and the *Saturday Evening Post*, and became the official "spokescow" for Borden during the 1950s. The company faced financial difficulties during the 1990s and began to sell off its subsidiaries. Borden, Inc., sold its dairy subsidiary in September 1997; in 2001, it sold the last of its food lines to the American Italian Pasta Company, H. J. Heinz Company, and Kraft Foods.

"Raising the Old Flag Over Fort Sumter," April 15, 1865 (Library of Congress Prints and Photographs Division)

9.

The Homogenizing War

SOUTH CAROLINA SECEDED from the Union in December 1860, but Fort Sumter, which controlled the entrance to Charleston Harbor—the state's largest port—remained under the control of a small Union army garrison. At the time, the fort was in the process of construction. When the fort was about to be resupplied by the Union navy, the Confederates surrounding the fort gave the Union army's commander, Major Robert Anderson, the choice of surrendering the fort or facing bombardment. He chose to defend the fort. At 4:30 a.m. on April 12, 1861, Confederate batteries around Charleston Harbor directed their fire on Fort Sumter.[1] The cannonade continued until the following day, when Anderson agreed to a cease-fire. As part of the agreement for surrendering the fort, Anderson insisted there be a one hundred gun salute as the American flag was lowered. As the flag was being taken down on April 14, Union cannons fired off, and cartridges accidentally exploded, killing a Union soldier—the only one to die during that engagement. Anderson and his men were transported north by the Union navy, and the first military engagement of the Civil War ended. For the next four years, the nation was engulfed in a bloody conflict that killed an estimated 1 million Americans, North and South. When the war ended, the slaves were emancipated and the Union was restored. In addition to these crucial social and political changes, the Civil War also set in motion agricultural, industrial, and legislative revolutions that shaped the foods Americans ate, decreasing regional culinary diversity and effectively homogenizing American food.

Homogenizing Food South and North

Prior to the Civil War, by far the most interesting regional cuisine had flourished in the South, where southerners enjoyed a varied and complex culinary life. For the poor, putting meat on the table meant fishing, hunting every kind of wild game that ran, crawled, or flew, raising poultry and pigs, growing fruit and vegetables in small gardens, and gathering the abundance of wild plants. The long southern growing season was hospitable to a wide variety of food crops, so vegetables and fruits, rice, and corn were plentiful in the South before the war. For the well-do-do, the antebellum South was a cornucopia of culinary delight. Plantation owners found it financially more lucrative to focus on export crops, such as indigo, cotton, and tobacco, than to raise food crops, but the proceeds from the sale of export crops financed the purchase of the choicest local produce and the importation of staples and luxury items. An elaborate and sophisticated cookery emerged, based largely on slave labor and their skills.

For the slaves, their diet depended on where they lived. Slaves in South Carolina were often given plots of land to plant their own gardens, which supplemented the basic rations provided to them by plantation owners. Many slaves grew vegetables familiar to them from their native Africa, such as okra, cassava, Bambara groundnuts, peanuts, yams, and sweet potatoes, and they raised chickens, Muscovy ducks, and guinea fowl.[2] Because slaves staffed the kitchens on plantations and in the wealthy households of Savannah, Charleston, and other southern cities, these vegetables, and their methods of preparation, became part of a wider southern cookery. Slaves were often assigned duties in the kitchen as children, and they remained there all their lives, becoming expert cooks and kitchen managers. Incorporating luxurious foreign ingredients that their wealthy masters imported, such as wine, sugar, and rare spices, slave cooks invented a sophisticated and elaborate cuisine.

When a slave had surplus produce from his garden patch, he could sell it to the plantation owner, or he might load it onto a homemade mule cart and go into town to sell it on market day. Upon arriving, the mule team was unhitched, the cart tipped up, and the produce stall was open. In Savannah, Georgia, in 1855, a magazine reported, "On certain days of the week, twenty or more of these market-wagons may be counted from the steps of the hotel."[3] With the cash they earned this way, African Americans were able to purchase amenities, such as coffee and tea, otherwise unavailable. And by selling their vegetables and fruits,

African Americans indirectly influenced the diets of poor white southerners, who began to grow, raise, and sell the same crops. The result was the creation of a southern regional cookery shared by many southerners—rich and poor, free and slave.

This new native southern cookery was based on ingredients and cooking techniques that were common in neither England nor New England at the time. It was reflected in some now-classic southern cookbooks, such as Mary Randolph's *The Virginia House-wife, or Methodical Cook* and Sarah Rutledge's *The Carolina Housewife*.[4]

When the Civil War began, President Lincoln declared a blockade of southern ports, with the intent of preventing cotton and tobacco from being exported and military equipment and supplies from being imported from abroad. The blockade, ineffective at first, gradually began to strangle the southern economy. Luxury items, such as wine, coffee, tea, and chocolate, disappeared from the southern table. As more Union ships took up positions around southern ports, blockade runners were captured; southern forts guarding major harbors were systematically taken over by Union forces, and the blockade became much more effective. Soon, imported products—sugar, cooking oil, salt, wheat, and other staples—became scarce.

As familiar foods disappeared from their tables, southerners began to alter their eating habits. Substitutes were devised for foods that could no longer be imported. Rice flour and cornmeal were substituted for wheat flour. Teas were made from herbs. The most unusual food that came to the fore during the war was the peanut, which until then had been considered a food fit only for slaves, children, and animals. Southern housewives substituted peanut oil for lard in bread and pastry, and for olive oil in salad dressings, and roasted peanuts were used to make beverages to replace coffee and chocolate. For decades after Appomattox, many wartime substitutes remained part of the southern diet.[5]

Despite the war's end, the opulent dining habits of the plantations never revived; many slaves who had done the kitchen work migrated away from the South. Mrs. Abby Fisher, who had been a cook on a plantation, brought southern cookery to San Francisco, where her recipes were transcribed and published in a cookbook called *What Mrs. Fisher Knows about Old Southern Cooking*.[6] Other former slaves moved north, where many were employed as professional cooks in restaurants and upper-class households. Writing in 1914, the American historian Gaillard Hunt concluded, "The professional cooks of the country were negroes, and the national cookery came from them."[7]

The Civil War influenced northern dietary patterns in other ways. Those who joined the Union army and navy traveled—many for the first time—far from their farms, hometowns, and home states. In far-flung camps and ports, they sampled foods that were not part of their culinary heritage. When northern armies occupied the South during and after the Civil War, Union soldiers got their first taste of southern foods, which many missed after their return home. Many northern soldiers were first exposed to peanuts, for instance, during the war. In the postwar years, a major trade commenced between southern peanut-growing areas and northern cities.[8] During the decades that followed, many beloved southern foods and dishes, such as fried chicken, barbecue, gumbo, jambalaya, rice, and sweet potatoes, became popular throughout the nation. The distinct local foodways in the North and South began to mingle and meld.

During the war, the Union military helped create the canning industry. After the war, veterans back home who had acquired a taste for the new canned foods craved them; as production snowballed, canned goods became cheaper and safer. Inexpensive canned goods became generally available throughout the United States by the late nineteenth century.

The Union army also contracted with meat-packers, particularly in the Midwest, to supply the troops. One contractor was a German immigrant named Nelson Morris, a small Chicago pork packer. During the war, he shipped 20,000 live cattle to the Union army.[9] At war's end, Morris was the largest meat-packer in Chicago, and with the continued construction of railroads, he was ready to expand sales of meat to population centers in the East.

The mechanization of agriculture, which had accelerated during the war, progressed at an even faster pace during the century's final years, further expanding the national food supply and shifting American eating habits. Mechanization meant that fewer laborers were needed on farms, and after the Civil War came an exodus from rural to urban areas. In the city, new and unfamiliar foods were available, and city life necessitated different food distribution systems, such as chain grocery stores, street vendors, cafés, and restaurants. Different dining schedules also evolved: In rural America, dinner—the heaviest meal of the day—was eaten at two o'clock, forming a break in the workday, and a light supper was served before bedtime. The urban and industrial lifestyle converted dinner into lunch—a smaller meal usually eaten at midday—and dinner became a substantial evening meal. Mechanization also decreased the cost of staples, such as wheat and corn, making them generally available to most Americans.

Homogenizing Legislation

Just as significant for American culinary life were the changes effected by legislation passed during the Civil War. The South's secession eliminated legal opposition to policies that had been debated and defeated for decades. The swift passage of four bills in two months in 1862 had a far-reaching influence on agriculture and what Americans ate.

The first was the Homestead Act, which gave applicants title to 160 acres of undeveloped federal land. Such a measure had been discussed for the two previous decades, but it was opposed by southern legislators, who feared that supporting small landowners would threaten their slavery-based plantation society. When the South seceded, southern congressmen left Washington, D.C., ending the debate. Congress passed the Homestead Act and President Abraham Lincoln signed it into law on May 20, 1862. This made it possible for settlers to establish farms at almost no cost. Few claims were filed under the Homestead Act during the Civil War, but immediately after the war, thousands of new homesteads, mostly in Iowa, Kansas, Minnesota, and Nebraska, were approved. These farms contributed to the growth of America's food supplies and a drop in food prices.[10]

A second piece of legislation created the U.S. Department of Agriculture (USDA). Discussion about the federal government's role in agriculture had been under way since 1790, when President George Washington proposed the creation of an agricultural board to disseminate scientific information to American farmers. Proposals continued to surface for decades, but none was ever accepted by Congress. In 1839, Congress did pass a small appropriation requiring the U.S. Commissioner of Patents to issue an annual report disseminating "agricultural statistics and for other agricultural purposes."[11] In 1852, prominent agriculturalists and congressmen organized the United States Agricultural Society, which lobbied regularly for the creation of a federal department focused solely on agriculture.[12] But southern legislators, concerned with states' rights, firmly opposed it. With southern political leaders absent, Congress passed the bill creating the USDA on May 15, 1862. The USDA rapidly expanded its activities, and appropriations have accelerated ever since.

The third history-making bill was the Pacific Railway Act, passed by Congress on July 1, 1862. This legislation authorized two railroad companies to construct a railroad along the one hundredth meridian.[13] When the transcontinental railroad was completed seven years later, foodstuffs began pouring in from the Pacific Coast to the eastern seaboard; immigrants streamed in the opposite direction, and the country's midsection quickly became populated.

The final one was the Morrill Land Grant College Act, which allotted states 30,000 acres of public land for every senator and representative the state had in Congress. The proceeds from the sale of this land were to be used to create agricultural colleges. This, too, had been under discussion, for fifteen years in this case, and, like the others, this bill had been opposed by southern legislators.[14] The Morrill Act passed with little dissent on July 2, 1862. During the next few years, most states established agricultural colleges. These institutions promoted agricultural education by offering courses in botany, chemistry, zoology, and other subjects related to farming. The second Morrill Act, passed in 1890, gave each state funds to use for specific instruction in agriculture. The effects of these laws were wide dissemination of technology and scientific advancements in agriculture throughout the United States.

Homogenizing Effects

Each of these changes had a major influence on what Americans ate after the Civil War. The railroads created a national distribution system, permitting food to be grown and processed almost anywhere and shipped inexpensively throughout the United States. Canned food was easy to ship and made a wide variety of fruits and vegetables available throughout the year and across the country.

Perhaps the most long-lasting effects related to the USDA's creation. In 1887, Congress passed the Hatch Act, which provided for a subsidy for each state for conducting research into agricultural matters. Experiment stations were set up in almost every state. The act also required the publication of bulletins to disseminate research findings from the work conducted by experiment stations. The impact of agricultural colleges, experiment stations, and bulletins was a heightened productivity in American agriculture.[15]

In 1889, the Department of Agriculture acquired cabinet rank, and today it administers thousands of programs related to food and agriculture. The USDA has sponsored extensive research to help farmers improve their crops. On the other hand, critics have charged that USDA programs have strongly supported factory farms and large commercial concerns at the expense of small, independent farms.

Beginning in 1898, states established agricultural extension services, which were given the assignment of publicizing the latest and best agricultural information to farmers. In 1914, Congress passed the Smith-Lever Act, providing funds for the agricultural cooperative extension services in each state to teach agriculture, home economics, and related subjects to the public.[16] The USDA funded research into common farm crops and animals, upgraded agricultural techniques, and disseminated knowledge about agricultural findings. One result was ever-larger harvests, leading in turn to lower costs, which made staples generally affordable for all Americans.

As Ulysses S. Grant wrote in his *Personal Memoirs*, the Civil War had changed everything: "Prior to the rebellion the great mass of the people were satisfied to remain near the scenes of their birth." But the war, he continued, "begot a spirit of independence and enterprise," and Americans were on the move. As a result, two decades after the war ended, the country had filled up "from the centre all around to the sea," and railroads connected "the two oceans and all parts of the interior."[17] Changes that began during the Civil War contributed to the loss of local and regional foodways and the birth of a national culinary style. Although local specialties have survived here and there, most Americans today eat more or less the same range of processed foods.

Postscript

On April 14, 1865, as part of the Union celebration of victory in the Civil War, Major General Robert Anderson raised the American flag over the battered remains of Fort Sumter. It was exactly four years to the day that he had lowered the flag, surrendering the fort to the Confederates. It was also the day that President Lincoln was shot at Ford's Theatre in Washington, D.C.

Joining the Central Pacific and Union Pacific Lines at Promontory Point, Utah, May 10, 1869; the Union Pacific locomotive is on the right (Library of Congress Prints and Photographs Division)

10.

The Transcontinental Railroad

AT NOON ON Sunday, May 10, 1869, the Central Pacific Railroad locomotive *Jupiter* faced Engine No. 119 of the Union Pacific Railroad at Promontory Summit, Utah. Telegraph lines had been completed just a few days earlier connecting the nation's east and west coasts, and within moments, railroad tracks would do the same. Construction had begun at opposite ends of the proposed route, and where the tracks met, a hole had been drilled so that Leland Stanford, of the Union Pacific, and Grenville Dodge, of the Central Pacific, could tap in the last spike, which was made of seventeen-carat gold from California's gold mines. As Stanford and Dodge took turns striking the ceremonial spike, a photographer snapped pictures, preserving the moment for posterity (the Chinese workers, who had been instrumental in constructing the western portion of the transcontinental railroad, had been asked to step aside, and they do not appear in the historic photograph.) When that task was completed, a telegraph operator transmitted the word "Done" in Morse code: within minutes bells pealed and cannons roared from San Francisco to Washington, D.C., and celebrations commenced throughout the United States—even in the states of the defeated Confederacy. Prior to the transcontinental railroad's completion, it had taken months to travel between New York and San Francisco. Once the "golden spike" had been driven in, however, the trip was reduced to seven days, and the cost dropped from $1,000 by ship to $150 for first class and

$70 for steerage or immigrant class by rail.[1] Within days, produce from California began to travel eastward and processed goods and immigrants westward. The transcontinental railroad's financial success spurred the construction of other railways. New track was laid at unprecedented speed, until all parts of the nation were united through a transportation grid. Food grown or processed in one part of the country could be distributed swiftly to other regions, and the American food supply grew from a local and regional distribution system to a national one.

Rail History

Experimental railroads had been constructed in England and France in the mid-eighteenth century, but the first American line was the Baltimore & Ohio Railroad, connecting the city of Baltimore with the Ohio River. When the steam engine *Tom Thumb* went into operation in August 1830, there were only 23 miles of railroad track in the United States. Within a decade, this had spiked to 2,800 miles. The expansion of the railroads meant that market gardeners and dairy farmers who did not live near a canal or navigable river could nonetheless ship fresh produce into cities daily, and cities that manufactured comestibles, such as flour, sugar, and alcohol, could sell them in rural areas. By 1860, there were more than 31,000 miles of railroads in the nation, the majority in the North and Midwest.[2]

Railroads played a crucial role during the Civil War, permitting rapid movement of troops and helping supply armies deployed over thousands of miles. To feed the Union army, the North contracted with food canners, who shipped their goods by train to distant outposts and naval supply stations. Although there were fewer railroads in place in the South, they were similarly important during the war. In fact, the Union occupation of Atlanta in 1864 and Major General Sherman's march to the sea and then northward targeted southern railroads, sealing the fate of the Confederate army in northern Virginia, which largely depended on supplies brought by train from Georgia and the Carolinas.

In the North, the railroads affected the food industry long after the war's end. Prior to the Civil War, for example, hog packing was a minor industry in Chicago. At the war's onset, the Mississippi was closed to traffic, and railroad lines through Chicago dominated east-west transportation. Hog production more than tripled, and at the war's end, the city was processing one-third of the nation's hog production, surpassing Saint Louis, Louisville, and Cincinnati. Soon Chicago became known as the new Porkopolis of the West, a sobriquet previously bestowed on Cincinnati.[3]

Transcontinental Railroad

The construction of a transcontinental railroad connecting to the Pacific Coast had been discussed since the 1830s, well before railroads were common and before California was part of the United States. After the signing of the 1848 Treaty of Guadalupe Hidalgo, which annexed California and much of the Southwest to the United States, serious proposals were presented in Congress to construct a railway that would connect the nation's eastern and western portions. These proposals snagged, however, on disagreement as to what route such a railroad would take. Southerners wanted a route that connected the South with California; northern legislators lobbied for a central or northern route. With the beginning of the Civil War, southern legislators withdrew from Congress, and opposition to a central route for the transcontinental railroad melted away. Legislators became convinced that the railroad was a necessary defense measure, and also that it would strengthen trade with Asia, via the west coast. Congress passed the Pacific Railway Act on July 1, 1862. This legislation authorized two railroad companies to construct a transcontinental railroad along the one hundredth meridian.[4] At the height of the Civil War, in 1863, construction on the railroad began at opposite ends of its route. The Union Pacific, employing more than 8,000 immigrants—mainly Irish and German—built west from Omaha; the Central Pacific, employing 10,000 laborers—mainly Chinese—built eastward from Sacramento.[5]

The meeting of the construction crews on May 10, 1869 meant the Pacific Coast was connected to the rest of the nation. Within a few months, growers began shipping tomatoes and even bananas eastward from California. Within two years, many other agricultural products—apples, pears, plums, vegetables, and salmon, as well as canned goods, were being shipped from California.[6] By the century's end, large tracts of land in southern California had been planted with large citrus groves, and soon oranges and lemons from the state were available throughout the nation.[7] One serious problem with shipping perishable fruit and vegetables was that passenger trains took precedence over freight trains, which were often delayed by weeks, so that much of the produce spoiled before arriving at its destination. Despite sizable losses, it was nevertheless profitable for farmers to regularly ship their goods long distances by railroad.

Refrigerated Cars

During the 1870s, railroads opened the grasslands of the Great Plains and Texas, heralding a new era in American meat production. Since meat could not be kept fresh in transit, live cattle had to be transported to slaughterhouses. This was costly: live animals took up much more space than dressed meat on trains, and they had to be fed along the way; many cattle died in transit. A thousand-pound steer, when butchered, weighed only 550 pounds, which meant that almost half the animal was discarded.[8] If animals could be slaughtered and butchered in a central location, the dressed meat could be transported from there to cities and the transportation costs reduced since a greater volume of meat could be packed into the same number of railroad cars used for live animals. This system functioned during the cold months but could not be used during the warm seasons. The problem was how to create a cooling system that would permit year-round transportation of dressed beef.

Since the early nineteenth century, ice had been used for commercially preserving food. It was usually cut from lakes in the North and shipped throughout the country in the spring. Lake ice was bulky to transport and required large, insulated storage facilities, and an extensive distribution system. Moreover, lake ice contained impurities and, when it melted, promoted the growth of mold and bacteria, creating unhealthy conditions in the icehouses. When it became possible to manufacture pure ice by machine, meat-packers could store carcasses for short periods so that meat could be pickled or salted before being shipped.[9]

During the mid-nineteenth century, produce was being transported on ice over short distances, but not until 1867, when a southern Illinois fruit grower, Parker Earle, devised a portable ice chest, did refrigerated transportation become a reality. By April 1868, Chicago was receiving fruits and vegetables from as far away as Mississippi via railroads; later, produce was sent from Texas and Florida to Chicago using this ice-cooling method.[10] Likewise, by the 1880s, truck gardeners in Virginia and North Carolina were making use of refrigerated cars to ship produce to New York, and Florida began shipping oranges by train to New York in 1889.[11]

Earle's invention was clumsy and expensive; it worked reasonably well for small consignments of fruits and vegetables, but not for large freight, such as dressed beef. Ice was effective only when in direct contact with meat, and this left an unappealing discoloration on it. In addition, sides of beef were bulky and required much larger shipping containers. Several attempts were made to develop ice-cooled freight cars in the 1860s, but none was successful. In 1867, Michigan Central Railroad's master car builder, J. B. Sutherland, of Detroit, patented a new type of insulated freight car with ice bunkers that held 4,000 pounds of salted ice at each end of the car. Ventilation shafts in the floor permitted a flow of cold air throughout the car. Sutherland was on the right track, but his design needed refinements before it could be economically employed. These modifications were patented the following year by William Davis, also of Detroit.[12] Meat-packer George Hammond of Detroit began sending small shipments of dressed beef to Boston and New York via refrigerated car in 1869.

Several problems prevented the wide adoption of refrigerated railroad cars at this time. The first was the meat-packers had major financial investments in the system as it was: cattle was shipped on the hoof to stockyards and other facilities in cities, and slaughtering, butchering, and packing in a central location would have made the system obsolete.

The railroad companies were not interested in the new system, either. At the time, the railroads were spending lots of money on expanding their rail lines throughout the nation, so they lacked capital to invest in new equipment and facilities. Refrigerated cars were expensive and, unlike cattle cars, could not efficiently be used for other purposes. Also, based simply on cargo volume, the railroad companies stood to lose money shipping dressed beef: the meat from a single steer weighed less than 55 percent of the live animal's weight and occupied far less space. In addition, railroad operators believed that refrigerated cars would make existing stock cars and stockyards, in which they were heavily invested, obsolete. As a consequence, railroad firms charged customers using refrigerated cars for dressed meat much higher prices than they did those sending live animals in cattle cars.[13]

Another problem was that ice in refrigerated cars had to be constantly replenished, making it difficult to go long distances without a substantial ice-making infrastructure. During the early nineteenth century, ice was available only during the winter months. Then, in the 1860s, European inventors devised ways of making ice based on the principles of absorption and condensation. Machines employing these principles could make ice anywhere at any time. During the mid-1870s, the new ice-making machines were introduced into the United States and were soon commonplace. But they were too heavy and bulky to be mounted on railroad cars.

The final obstacle to shipping meat in refrigerated train cars came from East Coast slaughterhouses and butchers; both were understandably opposed to the idea of shipping dressed beef into their communities, which threatened a loss of trade and, potentially, their businesses. Local butchers did everything they could, consequently, to prevent the import of dressed meat from the Midwest. Rumors circulated that meat carried long distances or held in transit for prolonged periods was unsafe to eat, and East Coast consumers became leery of buying dressed beef from Chicago.[14]

A Swift Solution

Gustavus Swift, a native of Massachusetts, had started out selling fresh meat in his brother's butcher shop, and he later ran a large meat market in Clinton,

Massachusetts. He moved to Boston, where he worked in the stockyards as a cattle buyer. Entering into a partnership with James A. Hathaway, who exported frozen beef to England, Swift saw the changes under way in the cattle industry stimulated by railroad transportation. He moved first to Albany, then to Buffalo, where he established facilities for transporting beef to Boston. In 1875, Swift moved to Chicago, where he engaged in buying and selling cattle for the Hathaway and Swift Company. Assessing refrigerated railroad cars and the new ice-making technology, Swift concluded that it should be possible to transport dressed beef anywhere by combining the two. He also believed that such an enterprise would be lucrative. Swift also began sending dressed meat to Boston and started experimenting with refrigerated railroad cars, such as those produced by William Davis. Hathaway wanted Swift to concentrate solely on shipping live cattle, while Swift believed that the future lay in transporting dressed beef. Hathaway and Swift parted ways, and, in 1878, Gustavus Swift opened a slaughterhouse and established Swift and Company.[15]

Swift's three main rivals were Nelson Morris, George Hammond, and Philip Armour. Morris, a German immigrant, had come to Chicago in 1853. He began in the stockyards before opening his own butchering facility, which became Morris and Company. He made a fortune during the Civil War supplying cattle to the Union army. Morris's biggest rival was Philip Armour. Armour had sought his fortune in California during the gold rush but abandoned that and opened a wholesale grocery business in Milwaukee. He went into partnership with a meat-packer, and they incorporated Armour and Company in 1867. Eight years later, Armour moved his operation to Chicago. Meanwhile, Hammond had established slaughterhouses in Detroit and Hammond, Indiana, a few miles from Chicago.[16]

Both Morris and Hammond had been sending dressed beef to the East Coast since the early 1870s. Morris had done so only during the winter; Hammond, using Davis's refrigerated cars, had shipped dressed meat from Detroit to Boston. The problem was that the meat nonetheless spoiled after a few days, because there was no way to refill the ice bunkers along the way. Only fast passenger trains could be used, and this inflated costs, which defeated the purpose of shipping dressed meat in the first place.[17]

Swift requested refrigerated cars from the three railroad lines running through Chicago. When they refused, Swift approached a fourth railroad company, the Grand Trunk Line, which, at the time, did not have much cattle business. The Grand Trunk Line was longer than the others, traversing Canada for part of the way to New York and Boston, but the company was willing to do business with Swift so long as he supplied the refrigerated cars and constructed reicing facilities along the route. This was better than nothing, so Swift agreed. He ordered ten cars from Detroit, and with them he established an integrated system for operating and reicing refrigerated railroad cars. At the time, this was a purely speculative venture. The new cars and the reicing facilities were expensive. There was no guarantee that the sale of fresh meat imported from Chicago would cover the capital outlay. The general belief was still that refrigerated cars could extend the winter season by only a few months, because they did not have enough cooling power to be used effectively in hot weather. Swift's system worked, though, and he is credited with creating the first refrigerated train service delivering fresh meat long distance year-round.[18]

Not completely satisfied with the cars, however, Swift approached a Boston engineer, Andrew Chase, to design a new car. Chase discovered the importance of circulating currents of air in the cars, and he designed a refrigerated car with ice bunkers that could be easily replenished from outside. The new car made the long-distance shipping of dressed meat practical, efficient, and profitable for Swift.[19]

As soon as Swift's deliveries began generating big profits, other meat-packers jumped on board—literally and figuratively—and other railroad companies reluctantly agreed to transport the refrigerated cars. Philip Armour created the Armour Refrigerator Line in 1883. He not only established reicing facilities but also constructed his own refrigerated cars. Armour had the capital to establish refrigerated lines to California, thus abating the problem of fresh fruits and vegetables spoiling in transit, although scheduling problems persisted. Refrigerated cars often took thirteen days from California to Chicago and nineteen days to reach New York, and the produce often arrived in an overripe condition. Despite the problems, refrigerator cars were quickly adopted by railroad companies. By 1900, Armour alone owned 11,000 refrigerated cars for shipping meat and produce.[20]

Because purchasing refrigerated cars and building reicing facilities over thousands of miles required large amounts of capital, the livestock industry became more centralized. The major meat-packers, such as Swift, Morris, Hammond, and Armour, gained control of the industry. By 1890, it was estimated that these companies packed 89 percent of the beef in America. In that year, too, the four companies were charged and found guilty of illegally fixing beef prices. This charge contributed to the passage, later that year, of the Sherman Anti-Trust Act, which prevented any agreements that restrained trade.[21] In 1902, Swift, Armour, and Morris formed the National Packers Association, which popular magazines lampooned as the Beef Trust. The practices of these meat-packers were exposed in a series of articles in the popular *Everybody's Magazine* and in a book by Charles Edward Russell, former managing editor of the *Chicago American*.[22] His articles contributed to the passage, in 1906, of the Meat Inspection Act. The National Packers' Association did not break up until 1920, however.

Rail Effects

Prior to the construction of railroads, commercial dairying, market gardening, and butchering had to be centered around cities because perishable produce could not be transported far. With the construction of railroads, however, perishable foods—fruits, vegetables, milk, and meat—could be shipped from ever greater distances to city markets. As railroads extended into different growing regions, produce that was out of season in the North could be shipped up from the South, or from the sunny Southwest; California's fruit and vegetable crops came eventually to supply most of the country. Railroads also facilitated the consumption of milk and produce, thereby improving the health of many Americans.[23]

The coming of the railroads and the advances in refrigerator-car construction made it feasible for cattle and hogs to be slaughtered and butchered in centralized midwestern stockyards and the dressed meat transported to eastern cities.[24] Chicago, Omaha, and Kansas City became the centers of meatpacking in the United States. The falling cost of railroad shipping accelerated the exchange of agricultural goods. It also made it possible for food processors to be located virtually anywhere in the country and still have access to markets throughout the United States.

The new rail routes made much of the country accessible for farming and ranching, and, also owing to them, the crops grown on this land could easily be shipped throughout the nation.[25] The railroads also created a national distribution grid for processed food, which became available in almost every local community.

The railroads contributed to centralized food processing and production in particular cities. Chicago, for example, a transportation hub with access to the Great Lakes and the Mississippi River complex, rapidly expanded just before the Civil War as its processing of beef doubled and of pork tripled in the eight years between 1852 and 1860.[26] During and after the Civil War, Chicago continued to expand its food-processing and transshipment capabilities.

The railroads opened up local and regional markets to competition. Local producers had difficulty competing with large manufacturers, and many local companies went out of business or merged with other firms producing similar foods. The shipment of dressed beef from the Midwest to eastern cities, for instance, all but eliminated local slaughterhouses and reduced the number of butchers. In 1860, New York City had more than 2,000 butchers; only a few hundred survived in 1900. These butchers had counted on their customers' appreciation of the quality and flavor of their meats, but shoppers readily gave up locally butchered beef and pork for cheaper cuts shipped from the Midwest.

Slaughterhouse waste, which had been a real problem for East Coast cities, became, in the Midwest, an opportunity. With mountains of meat by-products accumulating at his Chicago slaughterhouses, Philip Armour concluded that there was money to be made in converting the waste into usable products. He hired chemists, who were able to find dozens of ways to use the waste products to produce lard, gelatin, soap, glue, glycerin, grease, isinglass, and fertilizer. He later declared that waste was criminal. When asked what parts of the pig he used in his operations, he reportedly replied, "Everything but the squeal."[27]

The twentieth century saw the construction of all-weather roads and, eventually, the interstate highway system. The advent of long-haul trucks with roof-mounted refrigeration systems, in 1948, made it possible for refrigerated and frozen foods to be easily distributed to even the most isolated communities. Trucking also set in motion the decentralization of food processing, enabling processing plants to be constructed where labor costs were lowest and local and state zoning and taxing policies favored business.[28] Finally, the invention of shipping containers and the construction of container ships, begun in 1956, made it easier for many foods—particularly fruits, vegetables, grains, and meat—to be shipped to and from the United States, thus rapidly expanding a global food system that had been under way since before the American Revolution.[29]

Postscript

As soon as the golden spike was tapped in, it was removed. Today, it is on display in the Stanford University museum.

George Hammond died in 1886; Philip Armour in 1901. When Nelson Morris died six years later, his estate was valued at $20 million.[30] Philip Armour's son, J. Ogden Armour, took over his father's firm and acquired what remained of the Hammond Packing Company. Armour also acquired, in 1923, Morris and Company.

When Gustavus Swift died in 1903, his worth was estimated at more than $7 million—a fortune at the time.[31] In 1989, ConAgra acquired Swift and Company and combined it with Montfort, Inc. ConAgra HM Capital Partners LLC and Booth Creek Management Corporation acquired Swift and Company in 2002; they sold it to JBS SA, South America's largest beef processor, in July 2007; today, the combined company, with more than $10 billion in annual sales, is the largest beef products processor in the world.[32]

In slaughterhouses, cattle carcasses were placed on hooks that were moved by a conveyor belt through five stations, each manned by a single worker. Five-man crews could disassemble an average of seventy-five animals per hour, or more than one per minute. William C. Klann, a Ford Motor Company worker, visited a Chicago slaughterhouse; he told Henry Ford about the "disassembly line" and suggested that it might be applied, in reverse, to factory production. Ford implemented the idea and is often credited with the assembly line's invention.[33]

Bird's-eye view of the fairgrounds of the Centennial Exposition, 1876 (Library of Congress Prints and Photographs Division)

11.

Fair Food

THE SOUTH'S DEFEAT in the Civil War hardly put a dent in regional animosities. On the contrary, many southerners harbored desires for revenge and dreams of independence. To maintain control of the southern states and enforce federal law, Union troops occupied the South for more than a decade after the war's end. One attempt to mend the wide national rift was a centennial exposition, scheduled to open in Philadelphia in 1876. The exposition's supporters hoped that both northerners and southerners would come together to celebrate the hundredth anniversary of the nation's founding.

President Ulysses S. Grant opened the Centennial Exposition in Philadelphia on May 19, 1876, and from the first day fairgoers by the thousands flocked to the 236-acre site with its 180 fascinating exhibition halls. When the exposition closed six months later, more than 10 million visitors had passed through its gates. Those who attended the exposition were privileged to glimpse the nation's industrial, commercial, and cultural future, particularly well illustrated by the exposition's culinary exhibits: a wide variety of foodstuffs—many commercially processed—that became mainstays of the American diet and remain so today.

Fair History

The Philadelphia Centennial Exposition was not the first world's fair: that honor goes to the Great Exhibition at the Crystal Palace in London, which opened in 1851. It was at this exhibition that Cyrus McCormick had won a gold medal for his reaper, initiating international sales of his agricultural machinery. When the London exhibition closed, it was disassembled and shipped to New York City, where it was reconstructed. The exhibition opened to the American public in 1853, but it was a financial failure, and it took a number of years before such an international fair was again considered in the United States.

The idea of a centennial exposition was first broached in 1867, but not until 1871 did Congress establish a centennial committee, charged with managing an "international exposition of arts and manufacture." In an effort to avoid the financial problems of the New York fair, the committee planned the selling of stock to cover operating expenses, the stock to be redeemed after the exhibition's close. By 1873, however, few shares had been sold. Worse yet, a financial panic had struck the nation, and its disastrous effects lingered through 1876. The exposition was in serious financial trouble three years before its scheduled opening. The Women's Centennial Committee came to the rescue by selling stock and conducting a series of events to generate funds and heighten visibility, such as concerts, art shows, and bazaars. Eventually, the committee raised more than $126,000, and the Centennial Exposition was placed on a solid financial footing.[1]

Food played an important role at the exposition. As described by Francis A. Walker, the chief of the Bureau of Awards, the exhibition halls were bursting with "barricades of hams, pyramids of canned meats and fruits, stores of pickles, sauces and jellies, assortments of coffees, teas and tobacco." Walker concluded, with something of a flourish: "The display of food products, animal and vegetable, at Philadelphia was enormous in quantity, and almost incomprehensible in variety. After all, it is by food we live."[2]

Many foods showcased at the exposition became American favorites within a few years. The Horticultural Hall, a forty-acre display of tropical plants, featured fig, cacao, pineapple, and banana. Although these tropical fruits had been imported into the United States since the early 1800s, they were known mostly to the inhabitants of port cities. Bananas sold for ten cents apiece outside the Horticultural Hall, and within a few years they became one of America's favorite fruits.[3]

Flavored soda water was a major attraction at the Philadelphia exposition. Philadelphian Charles Lippincott had begun manufacturing soda fountains in 1832, and James W. Tufts had introduced a line of soda fountains in 1862. At the

1876 exposition, Lippincott and Tufts went in together to construct their own building, which was fitted with a thirty-foot soda fountain and dozens of soda dispensers, ready to refresh thirsty fairgoers. Tufts and Lippincott paid $20,000 for the soda concession, plus a $2 daily royalty for each soda dispenser. This totaled an estimated $52,000—an astronomical sum in 1876.[4] But it turned out to be a worthwhile investment: Temperance advocates had banned the sale of hard liquor at the fair, and the summer of 1876 in Philadelphia was an extremely hot one. The soda counters remained crowded throughout the exposition's run.

After the exposition closed, Tufts and Lippincott both made fortunes selling soda fountains to drugstores around the nation.[5] In 1883, James Tufts patented the Arctic soda fountain, which became popular throughout the United States. In 1891, Tufts and Lippincott joined with two other soda fountain manufacturers to create the American Soda Fountain Company. Soon, soda fountains became important social centers, particularly in small towns: By the nineteenth century's end, prohibition had become law in counties and states, and soda fountains took the place of bars and taverns as local meeting places, particularly for the nation's youth. By 1908, there were an estimated 75,000 soda fountains in the United States.[6] A by-product of soda fountains was the variety of new beverages created in them. Within a decade of the exposition, numerous soft drinks had been formulated by enterprising druggists at their soda fountains. Hires Root Beer, Moxie, Dr Pepper, and Coca-Cola came to be manufactured commercially.

Snack foods, such as popcorn and peanuts, were highly visible at the exposition. Such snacks had been sold on the streets of American cities and on trains since the early nineteenth century. One vendor at the exposition was selling red and white popcorn balls at a booth in Machinery Hall. The booth was "crowded all day, and thus showed the attractiveness of the exhibitor's peculiar wares and machinery." I. L. Baker, who sponsored the popcorn booth, paid the steep fee of $8,000 for the exclusive popcorn concession throughout the grounds. Baker set up several of his "curious and attractive furnaces and selling-booths" and sold popcorn for five cents a bag.[7] Outside the exposition, merchants sold wagonloads of peanuts.[8] While there are many reasons for the popularity of popcorn and peanuts, the exposition gave them national visibility, and they remain two of America's most popular salty snacks.[9]

Canned Goods and Hamburgers

Commercial canning had been under way in America since the 1820s, but it had not taken off until the Civil War, when government contracts to supply troops spurred the development of canneries in northern states. The manufacturing of canned goods made solid progress after the Civil War, and it reached its heyday in the 1880s. Many canners were present at the Philadelphia exposition, and most received awards for their products. A small firm from Camden, New Jersey—the Joseph Campbell Preserve Company (later renamed the Campbell Soup Company)—was awarded a medal, and the company was so proud of it that the award was depicted on its soup-can labels.[10]

The Vienna Bakery was one of the most popular food establishments at the exposition. In 1873, Eben Norton Horsford, a founder of the Rumford Chemical Works, in Providence, Rhode Island, was appointed a member of the United States Scientific Commission, which visited the Vienna Exposition in 1873. As part of his work, Horsford concluded that the bread made in Vienna was superior to that made in America, and he wrote up his findings for a government publication.[11] This led to the inclusion of a Vienna Bakery at the Centennial Exposition. The concession for the bakery was acquired by Gaff, Fleischmann & Co., a small firm manufacturing "German pressed yeast." The company was founded in 1868 by European immigrants Charles and Maximilian Fleischmann and by Cincinnati brewer and yeast maker James F. Gaff. Their building at the exposition was "crowded to repletion during every day of the exhibition, hundreds, frequently waiting for the opportunities to obtain a seat at one of the marble-top tables, and a chance at the limited but most excellent bill of fare."[12] Their success at the exposition led the three men to set up Vienna bakeries in New York and Philadelphia. After the exposition ended, Fleischmann bought out Gaff and changed the name to the Fleischmann Company. The Vienna bakeries were never established, but the company became the country's foremost yeast manufacturer.

The household meat grinder was one of many labor-saving kitchen tools featured at the fair. Although improvised models had been used in American kitchens since at least the 1840s, and commercial grinders had been sold since the 1850s, the devices were not common in American households. After its demonstration before the throngs at the exposition, however, the home meat grinder soon became an essential kitchen appliance.

Meat grinders were likely used at the exposition's German restaurant. Its proprietor, Philip J. Lauber, of Philadelphia, paid a hefty $6,000 for the right to open a German restaurant at the exposition, and then he spent the astronomical sum of $56,000 to build it. The restaurant, which could accommodate more than 1,000 customers simultaneously, featured German bands, German beer and wine, and, of course, German food. Tens of thousands of fairgoers ate there, and, according to a contemporary article in the *New York Tribune*, one of the most popular items on the menu was hamburger steak—fried ground beef served as a patty on a plate.[13] Thanks to its popularity at the exposition, within a few years hamburger steak had become a fixture on restaurant menus throughout America. Within two decades, the plated hamburger steak had evolved into the American hamburger sandwich.[14]

For the exposition, the Women's Centennial Committee compiled *The National Cookery Book*. This was not the first charitable cookbook published in America; according to cookbook historian Margaret Cook, the first was Maria J. Moss's *Poetical Cook-Book*, published in Philadelphia for the 1864 Sanitary Fair.[15] Fund-raising cookbooks became popular with churches and civic organizations throughout the nation, with the proceeds going to various charitable causes. The recipes were usually contributed by the women (more often styled "ladies") of the organization, with each donor's name or signature printed below her recipe. *The National Cookery Book* was a charity cookbook on a much grander scale. According to the book's editor, it was intended to address questions often asked by foreigners about America's "national dishes." The book consisted of "purely American recipes," excluding "the receipts common to all nations." To accomplish its end, the committee set up to oversee the project sent a letter requesting recipes to women in all U.S. states and territories. Thousands of recipes poured in, and the committee winnowed the number down to about 950.

Within twenty-five years of the Philadelphia exposition, the homemade foods represented in *The National Cookery Book* were outmoded, due largely to three monumental shifts that rocked the United States. The first two were demographic: an internal migration from rural areas to urban centers, and the huge immigration into American cities by newcomers from southern and eastern Europe. Both groups added new ingredients and cooking styles to America's culinary melting pot, although the changes did not become apparent until decades later. The third big shift was the American industrial revolution, which provided employment for migrants and immigrants arriving in American cities and produced cheap goods for them to purchase. Convenient, highly commercial, and low-cost industrial food came to dominate America's palate during the twentieth century.

The World's Columbian Exposition

The success of Philadelphia's Centennial Exposition inspired other cities to host fairs, and most pre–World War II expositions had some influence on what Americans ate. The World's Columbian Exposition, held in Chicago in 1893, was visited by an estimated 27 million people. The agricultural building housed exhibits by the major meat-packers Gustavus Swift and Philip Armour, and by food processors such as the American Cereal Company, renamed the Quaker Oats Company a decade later. California had shipped thousands of oranges to make a replica of the Liberty Bell. The state also shipped wines, and this was the first time that California wine received national and international visibility. In the same building was an exhibit organized by Wilbur O. Atwater, the director of the U.S. Department of Agriculture's Office of Experiment Stations. Atwater believed that the public demanded scientific information, so the display promoted the USDA's recent nutrition research.[16]

The World's Columbian Exposition provided fairgoers with thirty-five restaurants, lunch counters, and a plethora of vendors. Among the featured eating establishments were the White Horse Inn, the Vienna Café, Louisiana's Creole Kitchen, and the San Antonio Chili Stand. Perhaps one of the most unusual places to eat was the New England Kitchen, which was directed by Ellen Richards, instructor in sanitary chemistry at the Massachusetts Institute of Technology. It demonstrated how a family with an annual income of $500 could eat nutritious meals. Next door to the New England Kitchen was another exhibit, run by Juliet Corson, the principal of the New York Cooking School, which also promoted healthy and nutritious food. Another attraction at the exposition was the "corn kitchen" run by cooking-school director and cookbook author Sarah Tyson Rorer, who demonstrated dishes featuring corn and corn products. She also prepared a fifteen-page booklet titled *Recipes Used in the Illinois Corn Exhibit Model Kitchen*. By the time of the exposition's close in October 1893, an estimated quarter of a million fairgoers had visited the kitchen and a million copies of the recipe booklet had been distributed.[17]

The exposition also offered an array of street food through vendors. Frederick and Louis Rueckheim sold a new treat at the fair—popcorn caramelized with molasses and tossed with roasted peanuts. Following the exposition, the Rueckheims tinkered with the ingredients and, three years later, sure they had a winner, began to mass-produce and market their snack. The Rueckheims called their new snack Cracker Jack, and it became America's first nationally sold commercial snack food.[18]

Fair Effects

Throughout the nineteenth century, many Americans grew a substantial portion of their own food on farms or in garden plots. Small general stores catered to those who lived in small communities or who desired luxuries unavailable locally. Food was sold mainly as a generic product measured out from unmarked barrels, casks, sacks, jugs, and jars. This changed as food production was industrialized. Following the Philadelphia Centennial Exposition, food processors and manufacturers burgeoned as agricultural surpluses flooded the market and technology lowered the cost of production. The result was the rise of large food manufacturers, who needed to persuade consumers of the superiority of branded products over generic groceries. To accomplish this, food companies began advertising their products regionally and nationally through newspapers and magazines, and locally via circulars, billboards, and in-store promotions. Food advertising became a major source of American opinion and action regarding what, when, and how to eat.

Expositions created opportunities for like-minded individuals to meet, and often influential organizations emerged. The Columbian Exposition, for instance, gave impetus to the growing home economics movement. Out of the exposition's Woman's Congress came the National Household Economics Association, which aimed "to promote more scientific knowledge of foods, fuel and sanitation, as well as organizing schools of household science and service." Those involved in the exposition and the association went on to organize themselves under the rubric of home economics at Lake Placid, New York, in 1899. They met annually, and often prominent USDA leaders, such as Charles F. Langworthy, chief of nutrition investigations of the Office of Experiment Stations, and nutrition researchers, such as Wilbur O. Atwater, participated in the meetings. Finally, in 1909, the group created the American Home Economics Association, which has championed nutrition education in America ever since.[19]

According to Robert Rydell, author of *All the World's a Fair*, more than 100 million people visited the American fairs between 1876 and 1916, and millions more visited the fairs between the two world wars. But Americans did not have to attend the fairs to be affected by them. Newspapers and magazines regularly covered events at the fairs, and these accounts were avidly read throughout the nation. Postcards were sent, fliers were distributed. Souvenirs—spoons, plates, and table settings, to name a few—were brought home and displayed for years afterward. When a fair closed, the exhibits were often institutionalized in museums around the nation. In an era before radio and television, fairs served as gigantic display windows where the new industrialized foods could gain visibility. In the process, expositions promoted mass consumption of commercial goods.[20]

The national and international fairs and expositions inspired those displaying merchandise and fair attendants to see the world in different ways and instilled ideas that changed the way Americans ate. Health advocate and vegetarian John Harvey Kellogg set up a small exhibit on health at the 1876 Centennial Exposition, and he came away with ideas from other exhibits that he later employed in his Battle Creek Sanitarium in Michigan.[21] Entrepreneurs displayed their wares, sized up the competition, and met their customers. Fairgoers saw the latest products and techniques, and many went on to establish food businesses. Ferdinand Schumacher exhibited flour at the Centennial Exposition and acquired ideas about rolling oats, and Henry Crowell got ideas at the exposition about promoting food products; years later, Schumacher and Crowell teamed up to create what became the Quaker Oats Company. Joseph Campbell, who won a medal for his canned foods, went on to found the Campbell Soup Company. While visiting the Columbian Exposition, a Pennsylvania caramel maker named Milton S. Hershey saw a German chocolate machine, which he ordered on the spot and used to manufacture America's first chocolate candy bars (although it took him years to get the formula right).[22] From this acquisition, the Hershey Chocolate Company was created. Fairs gave entrepreneurs ideas that changed the way Americans ate in the late nineteenth and twentieth centuries and that continue to influence the way Americans eat today.

Postscript

Many other national and international fairs were held in the United States before World War II. Some of the more important include Buffalo's Pan-American (1901), where President William McKinley was assassinated, thereby elevating Theodore Roosevelt to the presidency; Saint Louis's Louisiana Purchase Exposition (1904), where the waffle ice cream cone, Dr Pepper, and puffed wheat were popularized; San Francisco's Panama-Pacific International Exposition (1915), which celebrated the completion of the Panama Canal; and Chicago's Century of Progress International Exposition (1933), where Kraft's Miracle Whip was introduced. The 1939 New York Fair assisted in the revival of French restaurants in America.

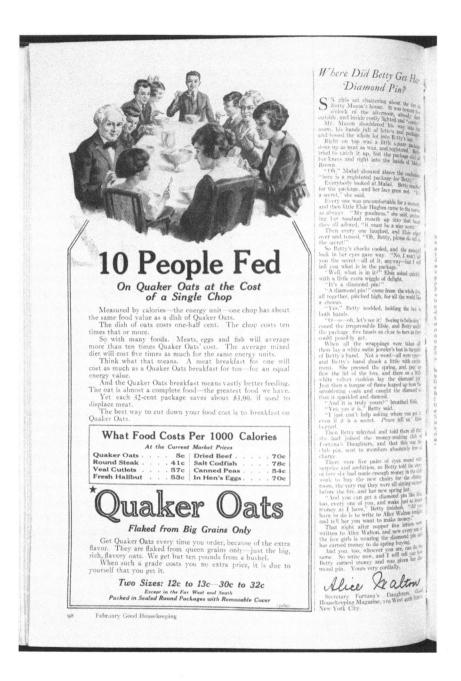

Quaker Oats advertisement, 1919 (*Good Housekeeping Magazine*, vol. 68, February 1919)

12.

Henry Crowell's Quaker Special

AT 6:45 A.M. on April 12, 1891, a fifteen-car freight train filled with Quaker Oats left the station in Cedar Rapids, Iowa, and headed for Portland, Oregon, where it arrived ten days later. This train, dubbed the Quaker Special, then turned south and made its way down the Pacific coast to San Francisco. Along the way, advance men, sent ahead into cities along the train's route before its arrival, briefed newspaper editors about the Quaker Special, bought advertising space, inserted additional puff pieces into the papers, and hired local boys to distribute free samples of Quaker Oats. When the train arrived in a town, its engine, topped with a man dressed as a Quaker, was frequently mobbed by thousands of people.[1] The Quaker Special was the brainchild of Henry Crowell, president of the Consolidated Oatmeal Company, who revolutionized food advertising and marketing in the United States.

Food Advertising

In Colonial times, signs and symbols were used to identify and promote inns, taverns, and coffeehouses. By the early eighteenth century, broadsides, leaflets, and newspapers were advertising imported or specialty goods, such as cheese, chocolate, codfish, coffee, molasses, sugar, tea, and wine. Until the mid-nineteenth century, however, staple foods were sold generically, out of unmarked containers. Since they were sold in bulk—from a peddler's cart or out of a barrel, crock, or box at the general store—there was little need to promote them.

With the advent of canned goods in the mid-nineteenth century, however, came the need for an appealing brand name, attractive labeling, and a memorable trademark or icon. Food manufacturers, competing for market share, needed to persuade Americans of the superiority of their branded products over generic goods. Perceiving the potential of advertising campaigns, food companies timidly publicized their products regionally through newspaper and magazine advertisements, and locally via circulars, billboards, and in-store promotions.

Nevertheless, food advertising was insignificant compared with the promotional schemes for other products, such as patent medicines. Makers of these products rolled out major publicity efforts: They had signs painted in enormous letters on barns and buildings, printed broadsides, advertised in newspapers and magazines, and hired agents and salesmen to promote their products. Patent medicine makers also issued booklets extolling the purported benefits of their products, and these publications often took the form of almanacs with stories, recipes, calendars, historical information, and testimonials from satisfied users, giving the booklets long life as household reading material. As effective as these techniques were, no one had yet applied them to food products.

Quaker Oats

Enter Henry Crowell, the son of a Cleveland grocer. In 1876, aged twenty-one, he visited the Philadelphia Centennial Exposition. Crowell was impressed with the exhibits, but he was particularly taken with the promotion and marketing of the commercial products displayed there. Eager to apply some of these ideas to his father's business, he returned to Cleveland. Unfortunately, soon after Crowell returned home, he suffered a heart ailment and had to put his plans on hold. By 1881, Crowell had recovered; his uncle, Joel Parsons, a wholesale grocer in Cleveland, suggested that his young nephew buy an oat mill in nearby Ravenna, Ohio. The operation had been started by Henry Seymour and William Heston, who knew little about running a mill. Facing financial difficulties, the pair sold the business to Warren Corning, a distiller operating out of Peoria, Illinois. Corning was more interested in distilling than in grinding oats, however, so he put the mill on the market.[2]

Crowell visited the Ravenna mill and decided that it had good potential, largely because the latest technology had already been installed. The former owner, William Heston, had worked for Ferdinand Schumacher, the foremost oat processor of the time. While in Schumacher's employ, Heston had devised a way of processing oats that made it possible for them to be cooked in much less time than whole or steel-cut oats. Schumacher installed this new technology in his mills, making them the most efficient in the country, and began producing a new product—rolled oats. He branded it Rolled Avena (*avena* being the Latin word for oats), and it was an immediate success upon its introduction into the market in 1883.³ Although the patent rights to the invention had been assigned to Schumacher, Heston had negotiated a proviso that allowed him to install this new technology in any mill in which he had an interest. Thus, Heston and his partner, Henry Seymour, had built their own mill in Ravenna incorporating the new technology.

Yet another asset of the Ravenna oat mill was a trademark: the figure of a man dressed in old-fashioned Quaker garb, holding a scroll bearing the word "pure." It is not known for certain why Seymour and Heston selected this symbol, but they thought it important enough to trademark it, and, in 1877, it became the first registered trademark for a breakfast cereal. After purchasing the Ravenna mill in 1879, Warren Corning began using the Quaker image on his whiskey bottle labels, but perhaps the sober Quaker was not the man for the job, because Corning relinquished the trademark to Crowell when he sold the mill. Crowell liked the trademark and promptly changed the company's name to Quaker Mill.

Although Henry Crowell had no experience running a mill, he worked feverishly to make a go of it. He believed that his success depended on packaging his oatmeal in a novel way, and he initially focused his attention on that. Crowell was particularly interested in what had happened with packaging in the canning industry. After the Civil War, demand for canned goods had escalated, but canners faced a serious problem: how to inform customers of what was inside the can. The solution was to paste on colorful labels. And since there were thousands of canners, labels also helped identify the manufacturer, and brand loyalty began to develop among customers for particular companies. Crowell wanted to do something similar in the oatmeal industry. Rather than selling his oatmeal as a generic product shipped in barrels, as other millers did, he decided to sell it in cardboard cartons. At the time, this was cutting-edge technology: the machines that made the cartons had been patented in 1879 by Robert Gair, a Brooklyn-based manufacturer of printed grocery and flour bags. Thus the box itself became an advertisement. To make his packaging difficult and expensive to duplicate, thereby avoiding counterfeiting, Crowell had the box emblazoned with a four-color image of a benevolent, well-fed gentleman in Quaker garb—a reinvented version of his trademark.⁴

Making the box was one thing; filling it was another. One of Crowell's partners invented a machine that could automatically fill twenty boxes per minute;

it could also automatically insert spoons and other items into the box along with the oatmeal. These premiums so enhanced sales that other food companies soon followed suit; premiums continue to be packed into food boxes today.[5]

A packaging solution had been found, but selling oatmeal was something else again. At the time, oats were a generic commodity, so there was not much to advertise. Most companies hired sales representatives who went from city to city pressuring grocery-store owners to carry their products, but grocers did not particularly care who supplied their oats. Hence, competition in the small oat market was cutthroat. Crowell's colorful cartons featuring the cheerful Quaker image represented a new approach to marketing, and this began to change the way grocers and consumers viewed oats—and, eventually, the way Americans viewed food products.

Henry Crowell was a pioneer not only in packaging but also in other aspects of oat manufacturing and marketing. The late nineteenth century saw a dramatic growth in trusts—large groups of manufacturers who banded together to set prices on core products so that everyone in the trust profited at the expense of consumers. Crowell concluded that cooperation was better than cutthroat competition, so he pulled together twenty oat mill operators to create, in 1885, the Oatmeal Millers Association. Ferdinand Schumacher at first refused to join, but he quickly came around when his Jumbo mill, in Akron, burned down. When he did join, he finagled it so that he became the association's president. Schumacher's autocratic rule alienated members, and six months later he was ousted. Several mill owners quit the association after Schumacher's departure, but the remaining mills merged their assets and elected Crowell president. The association also changed its name—first to the Consolidated Oatmeal Company and later to the American Cereal Company.

Under Crowell's leadership, the American Cereal Company began to focus on perfecting and exploiting the Quaker Oats brand name. Crowell had been working on branding since the early 1880s, and his theories evolved over the following decades. His four-color box with the image of a Quaker established the Quaker Oats brand, and there was additional room on the box to include other material. As many Americans had no idea what to do with oatmeal other than boil and eat it for breakfast, Crowell decided to print recipes on the box. Once the carton with the trademark image and content had been perfected, he began an advertising campaign based on what would later be called the theory of constant exposure.[6] Crowell initially adapted the advertising techniques perfected by America's patent medicine purveyors and the successful methods of P. T Barnum, the famed nineteenth-century showman and creator of the circus he titled the Greatest Show on Earth. Crowell printed and tacked handbills onto telegraph poles; painted signs on buildings and barns; widely distributed posters; gave out blotters and calendars to customers; paid wagons and streetcars to carry signs promoting Quaker Oats; and saturated newspapers, church bulletins, cookery booklets, and magazines, such as *Ladies' Home Journal*, *Harper's*, *Scribner's*, and *Atlantic Monthly*, with advertising. In an effort to retain customer allegiance, the company also offered coupons. Customers collected a given number of them and redeemed them for specific prizes, such as agate ware, china, fireless cookers, or double boilers.[7] His company also used customer testimonials and endorsements from alleged nutrition experts, scientists, and other prominent individuals. Crowell also paid for so-called story-line advertisements—narratives that worked the product into the plot—and "puffing" stories—thinly disguised ads presented as features in newspapers and magazines.

New advertisements were disseminated regularly. In one, parents were informed that "children fed on Quaker Oats will develop strong, white teeth." Another featured a woman who had filed for divorce because her husband had failed to bring home a package of Quaker Oats on four consecutive occasions.[8]

The American Cereal Company exhibited at as many local, regional, and national food fairs as possible. In 1891, for instance, at the Boston Food Exposition, the company had the most prominent and centrally located booth, as it did at the New York food show the following year. The attendants at the booths, dressed as Quakers, handed out free one-ounce samples of Quaker Oats.[9] Visitors were also given postcards and pictures with the Quaker image.[10] At the Chicago Columbian Exposition, in 1893, the American Cereal Company erected a large, ornate building to promote its products.[11]

Crowell's promotional techniques added new dimensions to product sales. Traditionally, companies focused on the supply side, usually hiring drummers to encourage groceries and general stores to carry their products. Crowell's techniques, on the other hand, focused on the demand side. They were aimed at appealing to customers, who then pestered store owners to carry Quaker Oats products.[12]

Throughout Crowell's promotional campaigns for Quaker Oats, Ferdinand Schumacher insisted that the American Cereal Company continue to support equally his F. S. brand. Every package of F. S. oat products announced: "The trademark F. S. stands for Ferdinand Schumacher, who is probably better known than any other man in the country as a manufacturer of Pure Food Products. The brand F. S. on a package of flour or cereal is a guarantee to the purchaser that the quality is the *best* that can be had in the market." When sales for F. S. products declined, Schumacher insisted that prices for his products be reduced below those of similar Quaker Oats products. Even with the price break, however, the

F. S. brand continued to lose market share. In the end, Schumacher lost a proxy fight and was tossed out of the company for good; his brand, one of the most famous in the nineteenth century, died before he did in 1908.[13]

Special Effects

Prior to the debut of Quaker Oats, grains, cereals, and flours were generally sold from generic barrels, casks, jars, and other containers. Leading other food manufacturers to develop their own containers and trademarks, the Quaker Oats cardboard box revolutionized food packaging. And packaged foods offered a benefit beyond advertising and marketing. Since the bulk containers often sat open in the store, their contents could become dusty and dirty. They could also become home to flies, worms, mice, rats, and other vermin. Such unwholesome conditions were unappetizing at best and illness causing at worst: the shift to packaging goods transformed food sanitation.

Promotional tactics similar to those employed by Henry Crowell were soon taken up by other food manufacturers, beginning, in 1898 with the National Biscuit Company's promotional campaign for Uneeda Biscuits. The success of Quaker Oats and Uneeda Biscuits inspired the creation of other innovative food products, which in turn employed similar advertising methods—ones that are still in use today: trumpeting grandiose slogans and asserting the healthful qualities of products. Starting in the 1920s, branded foods came to be advertised on radio. From the manufacturer's standpoint, radio's immense power lay in its broad audience potential and its relatively low cost. When radio entertainment programs became popular in the 1920s, food companies commissioned on-air personalities to promote their products. Among the earliest food companies to reap the rewards of radio advertising were cereal makers. In 1926, Wheaties was the first advertiser to produce a singing commercial for radio. Later, television expanded the reach of advertisers to influence millions of Americans at once.

Crowell's advertising concepts changed forever what Americans bought at the grocery store.[14] As observers have pointed out, the modern American diet is largely a result of the advertising and marketing industries.[15] Billions of dollars are spent each year on advertising, which has become the major source of American opinion and action regarding what, when, and how to eat.

Postscript

Ferdinand Schumacher, the Oatmeal king, died nine years after he was ousted, in 1899, from the board of the American Cereal Company. Henry Crowell took the company's presidency, and, under his leadership, the Quaker Oats Company was formed in 1901. Crowell became chairman of the board in 1922 and remained in that position until one year before his death, in 1943. Crowell expended much of the fortune he earned on the Moody Bible Institute Colportage Association. In 1927, he established the Henry Parsons Crowell and Susan Coleman Crowell Trust, which promoted (and continues to promote) the doctrines of evangelical Christianity.

Wilbur Atwater's calorimeter, 1904 (*U.S. Department of Agriculture Yearbook* 1904)

13.

Wilbur O. Atwater's Calorimeter

WHEN GROVER CLEVELAND was elected president in 1892, Edward Atkinson, a socially minded industrialist and amateur nutrition buff, pressed Julius S. Morton, the new secretary of agriculture, to create food laboratories connected with the agricultural experiment stations funded by Congress in 1888.[1] To mollify a friend of the president, Morton sent Congress a special request for a $15,000 appropriation to establish the labs around the nation, never expecting that it would be funded. Congress had never before funded a pure research program and, at the time, the nation's economy was in a tailspin. Much to everyone's surprise, Congress authorized the expenditure of $10,000 for nutrition research, and the funds were disbursed in 1894.[2] An agricultural chemist named Wilbur O. Atwater was charged with coordinating food research at sixteen experiment stations, as well as with investigating the foods consumed by different ethnic groups in various regions of the country. Atwater used a portion of the funds to complete a human respirator apparatus and America's first calorimeter, devices used to measure the number of calories in food.[3] Atwater's research and that of his successors reconceptualized views of food and diet; as a result of their work, Americans have been counting calories ever since.

Nutrition History

During the nineteenth century, German scientists, such as Justus von Liebig, were at the forefront of food-related research. Liebig had discovered that living tissue consists of carbohydrates, fats, and proteins. Although this division would later prove incomplete, it was a revolutionary concept at the time. Beginning in 1844, Liebig published several articles and books; one of the most important was *Researches on the Chemistry of Food*, which was translated and published in England in 1847. His books and articles provoked interest in the new field and inspired other researchers to examine the nutritional qualities of food.

By the mid-nineteenth century, German scientists were in the vanguard of nutrition research, and many American scholars interested in nutrition studied at German universities.[4] Agricultural chemist Samuel W. Johnson, for example, studied under Liebig in the 1850s. Upon his return to the United States in 1857, Johnson became a professor of analytical chemistry in Yale University's Sheffield Scientific School. Five years later, Johnson served as an adviser to President Lincoln in setting up the U.S. Department of Agriculture. Another American who studied in Germany at this time was Wilbur O. Atwater. In 1869, Atwater completed his doctorate in agricultural chemistry at the Sheffield Scientific School, where he had studied under Johnson. Following in Samuel Johnson's footsteps, Atwater then traveled to Germany to study with physiologist Carl Voit, who had been a student of Liebig, and with Max Rubner, one of Voit's students. Voit and Rubner had completed extensive food research, and both later developed instruments for measuring food calories. While in Germany, Atwater also studied the organization of German agricultural experiment stations, a topic about which he would publish an article a few years later; he would also lobby for the establishment of similar stations in the United States. When Atwater returned to the United States in 1875, he was appointed professor of chemistry at Wesleyan University, in Middletown, Connecticut, a position he held for the remainder of his life.[5]

Meanwhile, Atwater's mentor, Samuel Johnson, had been lobbying the Connecticut legislature for funds to establish an agricultural experiment station at Yale. His main argument was that the operation could examine fertilizers used by farmers and that such systematic study would improve fertilizer quality and crop management and thus enhance crop yields. Despite eight years of lobbying, Johnson was unsuccessful in his efforts. Around this time, a wealthy minister named Orange Judd, who also published agricultural journals and books, entered the scene. In 1874, Judd donated funds to Wesleyan for the construction of a building for laboratory science. The following year, he offered the Connecticut legislature a deal: he would provide start-up money for an experiment station at Wesleyan, and Atwater would contribute his time, if the legislature agreed to fund the operation for two years. It agreed and appropriated $5,600 for the nation's first agricultural experiment station; Atwater became its first director.[6] At the end of the two-year trial, the Connecticut legislature decided to continue funding an agricultural experiment station, not at Wesleyan but at Yale, under the direction of Samuel Johnson.

Atwater was puzzled by this shift in support, but he nonetheless began a new phase of his work—conducting studies of different fish species and their food values. Atwater solicited funds and hired assistants to help carry out this new research, which he expanded to include many different foods. For six months in 1882 and 1883, he returned to Germany, where he studied the food research methods employed by Carl Voit and others. Atwater was particularly impressed with the scientific instruments that Germans researchers had devised for measuring food values. Atwater returned to Wesleyan in 1883 and implemented the knowledge he had gained in Germany;[7] his research eventually analyzed more than 1,300 different foods. Atwater also began collecting data directly from the foods served at family dinner tables and analyzing it.[8] Beginning in May 1887, he commenced publishing his findings in a series of five articles in the popular *Century Magazine*. Atwater's underlying argument was that the poor could be fed inexpensively by using low-cost vegetable protein sources. The articles made Atwater one of the best-known scientists in the country.[9]

Beginning in 1885, Atwater and Johnson served as advisers to Congress and President Grover Cleveland. The two men urged Congress to fund the creation of agricultural experiment stations throughout the United States. As a result of their lobbying, Congress passed, in 1887, the Hatch Act, which gave $15,000 to each state for the establishment of agricultural experiment stations. As a result, a second agricultural experiment station was established in Connecticut, at the Storrs Agricultural College (oddly, it was required it be directed by Atwater, who lived thirty miles away, at Wesleyan). In addition, the Hatch Act established the U.S. Office of Experiment Stations, and Atwater was selected as its first chief, a position he held until 1891. Rather than resign his position at Wesleyan, or the directorship of the new agricultural experiment station at Storrs, Atwater retained all three posts while working in Washington by hiring excellent deputies and making frequent trips to Connecticut.

As the first chief of the U.S. Office of Experiment Stations, Atwater established the *Experiment Station Record*, which reported on the studies conducted by all stations around the country. Without formal authorization, he built nutrition studies into each experiment station. After completing his assignment in Washington, Atwater installed his protégé, Alfred C. True, as director of experiment stations, and he created a position for himself, as the USDA's special officer in charge of nutrition investigations.[10]

Atwater again traveled to Europe, with funding from the USDA, and examined various devices used by European scientists to measure food values. German scientists had overcome one of the most serious measuring problems in nutrition studies by inventing a calorimeter. Upon his return to Wesleyan, Atwater was determined to construct his own calorimeter.[11] After a year of work, he concluded that he needed public funds to complete it, as well as to launch a theoretical research project on human nutrition. Congress understood the need to give practical advice to farmers about proper fertilizers, engage in soil analysis, recommend crop and husbandry options, or better methods of production, but funding pure scientific research into nutrition was just not in the legislative cards. It hadn't been done before, and, at the time, the nation's economy was in shambles and a budget-conscious Congress intended to cut programs, not start up new ones.[12] Atwater soldiered on, however, as he could, and his *Farmer's Bulletin* article on "Foods: Nutritive Value Costs" offered Americans the first easy-to-understand account of what science had to say about food and diet.[13]

At this point Edward Atkinson, a wealthy New England cotton mill owner, insurance executive, philanthropist, inventor, and prolific writer, arrived on the scene. Atkinson's interest in nutrition stemmed from the need to feed the poor, particularly immigrants then flooding into America, and his concern with the labor unrest that hit America beginning in the 1880s. Atwater's work in nutrition interested Atkinson, and the two became professional friends for the remainder of their lives.[14]

Atkinson's interest in nutrition came to the attention of Ellen Richards, a chemist and one of the founders of the home economics movement. Richards convinced Atkinson to provide financial support for a venture called the New England Kitchen, which was intended to develop inexpensive methods for educating and feeding the poor. When the kitchen opened, in 1890, Richards used Atwater's research into calories, proteins, and fats to develop its menu, which offered inexpensive, nutritious takeaway food for the poor. Richards and Atkinson believed that immigrants could assimilate faster into American society by eating inexpensive, nutritious American food, rather than the foods they had known in their countries of origin.

Richards also used the operation for her nutrition studies by collecting information from the people who visited the New England Kitchen for their meals. Specifically, she required that the Kitchen's customers fill out self-report survey forms about what they ate. Similar kitchens were established in New York and other cities. To promote the idea of good nutrition across the nation, Richards and Atkinson set up a New England Kitchen at Chicago's Columbian Exposition of 1893. Visited by 10,000 people during the exposition, it featured a wholesome meal consisting of nutritionally balanced broths, stews, baked beans, and Graham bread, all for only thirty cents. Unfortunately, by the time the exposition closed, the kitchens had been declared failures, and the New England Kitchen closed in 1899.[15] It nevertheless provided a model for other social service centers then opening in immigrant areas of large cities. It was the model, for instance, for Jane Addams's Hull-House Kitchen, in Chicago, with its public kitchen for the poor.[16]

Despite the failure of the New England Kitchen, Atkinson, an armchair economist, was hooked on the idea of feeding the poor wholesome yet inexpensive food. Particularly concerned with the evils of undercooked food, he devised a slow-cooking oven made from a soap box placed on a metal table. The oven had a heat-resistant lining and used an oil lamp as a heating element; it could cook a meal unattended in a few hours. Atkinson believed that this device, which he called the Aladdin Oven, was perfect for providing workers with hot meals: they could put in the food and light the lamp upon arriving at work and have a hot meal ready by lunchtime. Atkinson was so excited by the idea that he funded the oven's manufacture, distribution, and promotion. Despite his best efforts, though, the Aladdin Oven did not work well, and it disappeared from the market.[17]

Although his Aladdin Oven was a failure conceptually and financially, Atkinson remained a strong supporter of nutrition research. He was also a prominent supporter, as well as a friend, of Grover Cleveland, who was reelected president in 1892. After Cleveland took office, Atkinson wrote to Julius S. Morton, secretary of agriculture, and encouraged him to create a series of food laboratories similar to the New England Kitchen. He hoped that these labs would be connected with the agricultural experiment stations funded by Congress in 1888. Atkinson also published his views in a USDA bulletin titled *Suggestions for the Establishment of Food Laboratories in Connection with the Agricultural Experiment Stations in the United States.*[18] To the amazement of its proponents, Congress authorized the expenditure of $10,000 for nutrition research and continued funding until 1914, when the effort was subsumed under a new Office of Home Economics in the USDA.[19]

Edward Rosa, a professor of physics at Wesleyan, was the lead builder of the human respirator apparatus and the calorimeter, although Atwater received much of the credit.[20] With the designs of Voit and Rubner as their foundation, Rosa and Atwater built an airtight chamber large enough that human subjects could live in it for days, engaging in various activities while researchers carefully observed and measured food intakes and bodily outputs, including respiration. In this way, the researchers were able to determine food values and systematically calculate and tabulate the caloric composition of carbohydrates, proteins, and fats in different foods. This research eventually involved 300 studies with more than 10,000 men, women, and children. The study was so large and comprehensive that it has never been duplicated. In 1896, based on their findings, Atwater and a graduate student, A. P. Bryant, published food tables that listed the minimum, maximum, and average values of the known nutrients of American food.[21]

Atwater used the results of his studies to stress what he believed was a cheap, wholesome, and efficient diet for the poor, with protein from legumes rather than from meat. He considered fruits an unnecessary extravagance. He also believed that Americans ate too much and exercised too little—ideas that loom large in today's continuing debates about nutrition and obesity.

Atwater suffered a heart attack in 1905 and died two years later. The nutritionist Francis Benedict and other researchers continued down the path Atwater had blazed, using the calorimeter to further measure metabolism and other bodily processes.[22] Benedict studied the varying metabolism rates of athletes, students, vegetarians, Mayans living in the Yucatán, infants born in Massachusetts hospitals, and ordinary adults. He even constructed a calorimeter large enough to hold twelve Girl Scouts for an extended period of time. His biggest innovation was the invention of portable field respiration calorimeters. Based on these studies, Benedict published a metabolic standards report with extensive tables based on age, sex, height, and weight.

The studies conducted by Atwater and his associates influenced many other researchers. The application of these new findings to the daily diet and home cooking was championed by Ellen Richards, whose *Chemistry of Cooking and Cleaning: A Manual for Housekeepers* became a defining work, going into several editions. Richards is considered the founder of the home economics movement in America, and food chemistry became an important component of the curriculum at the Boston Cooking School, run by Fannie Farmer, the Philadelphia Cooking School, under the direction of Sarah Tyson Rorer, and other schools. Nutrition also became an important component of Fannie Farmer's *Boston Cooking-School Cook Book*, first published in 1896, and most other cookbooks. Dietitians applied the principles of nutrition in hospitals, military installations, public schools, and other institutional settings. Dietitians also rose to prominence in the home economics movement, and a group of them founded the American Dietetic Association in 1917. Nutrition studies conducted by Atwater and others also influenced food processors, who, beginning in the 1920s, began to change their methods of manufacturing food in hopes of strengthening its nutritional content.

Caloric Effects

The results of Atwater's calorimetry studies influenced many areas of American life. The calorie was an easily understood concept used by the scientific community as well as the public. It did not take long for calorie counting to become part of the American culinary life. In 1918, Dr. Lulu Hunt Peters, a Los Angeles physician, published *Diet and Health, with Key to the Calories*, which was based on the work of Atwater and his successors.[23] As Americans became increasingly concerned with weight and diet, the calorie became the focal point of many weight-control programs, such as today's Weight Watchers. Such diet plans base many of their food recommendations on the research conducted by Atwater and his protégés.

Although only a few are given mention here, many scientists and researchers contributed to a better understanding of nutrition in the United States. Wilbur O. Atwater, a pioneer in nutrition studies in America, inspired others to continue working to define the nutritional content of food. Prior to Atwater's work, most scientists had conducted their research on animals. Atwater's work, however, emphasized human nutrition. Atwater directed the first agricultural experiment station in the United States, served as the first chief of the USDA's Office of Experiment Stations, conducted huge nutritional studies, and constructed devices critical to our understanding of nutrition. Atwater set the nutritional standards of his day, and the researchers he trained continued his work after his death. While many contributed to our understanding of nutrition, it is Atwater whom scholars today identify as "the father of American nutrition."[24]

Postscript

Nutrition studies also prompted the U.S. government to encourage manufacturers to enrich their products with vitamins and minerals. During the 1920s, "vitamania" hit the United States, and many Americans concluded that all the nutrition they needed could be supplied by a pill packed with synthesized vitamins.[25] During World War II, the Food and Nutrition Board, a committee of the National Research Council, devised and disseminated nutritional standards—called recommended dietary allowances (RDA)—for energy, protein, and eight essential vitamins and minerals. These were considered the levels of nutrients required by the average adult for good health. During the war, the USDA also promoted the "basic seven," a special modification of the RDA guidelines to help Americans deal with wartime food shortages. This was modified after the war to the "basic four," which stressed dairy products, meats, fruits and vegetables, and grains. As new research demonstrated additional requirements, RDAs were eventually replaced, in the late 1990s, with standards called dietary reference intakes (DRI). In the interest of promoting better eating habits among Americans, the Department of Health and Human Services and the Department of Agriculture jointly disseminated the Dietary Guidelines for Americans. First published in the 1980s, the guidelines have been regularly updated ever since. Because of an increase in heart disease in America, in 1992 the USDA unveiled a new food pyramid, which broke from the recommendations of the previous food charts to emphasize consumption of more grains and less animal protein, fat, and sugar.[26]

Cracker Jack advertisement, circa 1916 (*The Cracker Jack Story* [nl: Borden, 1987]; courtesy of COSI Columbus)

14.

The Cracker Jack Snack

POPCORN VENDORS Louis and Frederick Rueckheim worked the streets of Chicago in the early 1880s, but they spent their spare time experimenting with new products to sell. One of their better efforts combined popcorn, molasses, and peanuts, and the crowds flocking to the exhibits at the 1893 Columbian Exposition seemed to like it. In fact, no matter how much of the confection the brothers made, demand always exceeded supply. In trying to expand production, however, the Rueckheims confronted several stumbling blocks: Working with small batches, it was possible to spread the sticky confection on large pans, then stir it together when it was cool and dry. In large batches, though, the molasses-covered popcorn and peanuts melded together into irregular blobs. This old low-volume, time-consuming method had to change. Louis Rueckheim solved the problem in late 1895 by creating a quick-drying process for the popcorn mixture that permitted swift and continuous packaging. With this solution in place, the Rueckheims invested in new equipment, enabling them to boost their productivity.[1] But before they could advertise their product—and in the 1890s, advertising was essential—the Rueckheims needed to come up with a catchy brand name. Legend has it that John Berg, one of their salesmen, sampled the new confection and exclaimed, "That's a crackerjack!"[2] The name stuck and Cracker Jack was off the ground, and so was a new category of commercial snack foods—today, a multibillion-dollar global industry.

Snack History

Prior to the twentieth century, many Americans considered eating between meals an unhealthy habit. Even though snacking was common in nineteenth-century America, many medical practitioners spoke out against the practice, averring that eating between meals promoted indigestion, dyspepsia, and many more serious maladies.[3] Later, snacking was condemned because it ruined the appetite for meals, which consisted of more nutritious and healthful food.[4] Snack opponents included Sylvester Graham and his followers, and health-food guru John Harvey Kellogg, who considered eating between meals "extremely harmful." The snacks that Kellogg was referring to were not like the high-sodium, artificially flavored snacks of today; popular at the time were fruits, nuts, flour-based products such as biscuits and cookies, and cheese.[5]

Despite warnings from medical professionals and nutrition experts, by the mid-nineteenth century, pretzels, peanuts, candy, popcorn, and related products such as popcorn balls were being sold at fairs, circuses, sporting contests, amusement parks, and other venues. They were usually made at home and sold at small kiosks or stands, or by street vendors from carts or wagons.

One ambitious popcorn vendor was Frederick W. Rueckheim, who had immigrated to Illinois from Germany in 1869 and worked on a farm outside Chicago. With $200 he had saved from his farm wages, Rueckheim relocated into the city after the Great Chicago Fire, searching for work. Soon after his arrival, he met a man named William Brinkmeyer, whose popcorn stand had burned down in the fire. Brinkmeyer convinced Rueckheim to become his partner and invest in his popcorn specialties business.[6]

Catering to those rebuilding fire-ravaged Chicago, Brinkmeyer and Rueckheim operated out of a rented room. Their business prospered, and a year later Brinkmeyer sold his share to Rueckheim, who sent for his brother back in Germany to help run the operation. When Louis Rueckheim arrived, the business was renamed F. W. Rueckheim & Brother. The two operated out of a back-room kitchen equipped with only one hand popper and a single molasses kettle.[7] Not until 1884 did the brothers acquire steam-powered machinery. The Rueckheims experimented with sugarcoating different products; they tested various sweeteners with different combinations of marshmallows, nuts, and other ingredients before devising a confection composed of popcorn, molasses, and roasted nuts. In 1893, they decided to go with peanuts—the least-expensive nut they could find.[8]

The story of salesman Jack Berg coming up with the name for the product is likely apocryphal. At the time, the term "cracker jack" was common slang for something first-rate. Whatever the truth might be, the Rueckheims began using the name Cracker Jack for their confection on January 28, 1896, and applied for a trademark on February 17, 1896. Thirty-six days later, the U.S. Patent Office issued the trademark.[9]

Shortly thereafter, the Rueckheims commenced a promotional and marketing blitz in Chicago, followed closely by campaigns in New York and Philadelphia. Three different advertisements appeared in the July 13, 1896, issue of Philadelphia's *Grocery World*. These promotions announced that Cracker Jack was a new confection, not yet six months old, that had "made the most instantaneous success of anything ever introduced." The Rueckheims called their new product the 1896 sensation. Cracker Jack advertisements also contained the phrase "the more you eat the more you want." To meet the orders generated by this aggressive marketing, the company produced four and one-half tons of Cracker Jack daily. Inspired by the 1891 Quaker Oats advertising campaign, the Rueckheims sent a special train with fourteen railroad cars filled with Cracker Jack to New York City and Philadelphia. Drummers stirred up interest, and samples were given out at stops along the way. In Philadelphia alone, four carloads were distributed within ten days of the train's arrival.[10]

At first, Cracker Jack was sold in large cardboard boxes, but the Rueckheims discovered that it was hard to keep the product crisp, even under the best conditions. After the box was opened, humidity turned the snack soggy. Henry G. Eckstein, the former general superintendent of a Chicago confectionery company and a friend of the Rueckheims, proposed a new packaging system to keep out moisture and maintain crispness: seal the Cracker Jack boxes with wax. But this did not succeed in keeping out moisture. So Eckstein visited Germany in search of new packaging techniques. He found one that used waxed paper, and he paid the inventor $500 to teach him how to manufacture it. Back in Chicago, Eckstein tinkered with the new packaging material, finally enclosing the Cracker Jack in waxed paper and two other protective layers. The packaging problem was finally solved.[11] The small package was just right for a single serving, and it could easily be marketed through street vendors, kiosks, drugstores, grocery stores, and, eventually, movie theaters. It was evidently first served at baseball games before 1907. The following year, the lyricist Jack Norworth and composer Albert Von Tilzer immortalized the product in their song "Take Me Out to the Ball Game":

> Buy me some peanuts and cracker-jack—
> I don't care if I never get back.

Neither Norworth nor Von Tilzer had attended a baseball game prior to composing the song, but presumably both had consumed Cracker Jack.[12]

The Rueckheims touted Cracker Jack as the "greatest seller of its kind." The campaign was so successful with children that, by 1908, Cracker Jack began to appear in elementary school textbooks.[13]

The Rueckheims advertised in *Billboard* (then a magazine for professional vendors, not a music-industry publication) just to promote the new packaging. The ad promoted Cracker Jack as "a delicious Pop Corn Confection, packed in moisture proof packages, that keep it fresh for a long time." It was "a quick seller" and "a money maker for the concessionist."[14] Sales soared, thanks mainly to the advertising and the new packaging.

Cracker Jack remained a singularly popular confection primarily because of extensive national advertising. Another reason for its success was the premiums in each box. Like Quaker Oats, beginning in 1910, every box contained "a valuable premium coupon.". The coupons could be redeemed for over 300 "varieties of handsome and useful articles, such as Watches, Jewelry, Silverware, Sporting Goods, Toys, Games, Sewing Machines, and many other useful Household articles." In 1912, the company shifted from coupons to a small toy in every package. More than "500 varieties of handsome and useful articles" were inserted into the boxes.[15] The toy gimmick worked: throughout the early twentieth century, the company grew and grew, grossing, in 1928, its largest pre–World War II profit—$716,659.[16]

During the Depression, many snack foods disappeared, simply because Americans had less disposable income. The Cracker Jack Company, however, weathered the Depression remarkably well. Its premier product was inexpensive; at just a nickel a box, it was something that most Americans could afford. To boost sales, the company began purchasing sophisticated prizes from Europe and Japan to put into its packages.[17]

Two major reasons for the company's solid profits were steadily improved marketing and increasingly efficient operations. Automation permitted Cracker Jack to undersell its competition while making a profit. The confection cost about one cent per box to produce and the packaging about two cents more. Grocers and vendors paid $0.0325 per box, leaving the company a profit of $0.0025. This may seem a tiny sum, but consider the volume: Cracker Jack sold millions of boxes per year. Cracker Jack's competitors charged $0.035 per box, so grocers and vendors profited more by selling Cracker Jack, which encouraged retailers to stock Cracker Jack rather than competing brands. As a result, sales soared, even during the Depression. By 1937, the Cracker Jack Company declared itself the producer of "America's Oldest, Best Known and Most Popular Confection."[18]

Sales of Cracker Jack slid during World War II because of sugar rationing and reduced capacity to manufacture toy prizes. After the war, sales rebounded. By

1947, annual sales had reached 100 million packages, worth more than $3 million. By 1970, Cracker Jack was being enjoyed in 41 percent of American households. It had retained its dominance of the ready-to-eat popcorn category for decades. Reportedly the largest user of popcorn in the nation, the company processed twenty-five tons of popcorn per day. The company also expanded abroad. Cracker Jack had been introduced into the United Kingdom in 1897 and into Canada in 1901. By 1976, Cracker Jack was being sold in fifty-three countries.[19]

Snack Attack

Cracker Jack was, of course, not the only snack food in America. Commercial sweet snacks had been sold in the United States since the eighteenth century, but they did not become popular until the price of sugar declined in the mid-nineteenth century. By the late nineteenth century, there were more than 300 candy manufacturers in America. Many more companies were started during the twentieth century. Most of them manufactured hard candies, usually sold in bulk to stores, which displayed them in large glass jars and sold them for a penny apiece.

Chocolate making in America also began in the eighteenth century. One early company was begun by James Baker, who initially produced chocolate for drinking. During the nineteenth century, European confectioners determined how to convert chocolate, previously served mainly as a beverage, into a confection. Companies specializing in making chocolate were established, such as Cadbury and Rowntree, in England, and Nestlé and Tobler, in Switzerland. American chocolate makers learned from Europeans how to manufacture milk chocolate and then turn it into different kinds of candy.

The Stephen F. Whitman Company, founded in Philadelphia in 1842, created America's first packaged confection, Choice Mixed Sugar Plums. The company produced its first "sampler," consisting of chocolate-coated candies, around 1912. Inside the box's lid was a chart for identifying each chocolate. Many chocolate companies were incorporated during the nineteenth and early twentieth centuries. Ghirardelli's, in San Francisco, began producing handmade chocolates in 1852. In 1921, Charles See opened a candy shop in Los Angeles. See used the image of his wife, Mary See, as his store's icon. See's Candies expanded throughout California. Candy salesman Russell C. Stover opened a candy store in Denver, where he also began manufacturing candy and slowly expanding his operation. Today, Russell Stover candies are sold tin 40,000 retail stores throughout all fifty states.

All chocolates were made by hand until Milton S. Hershey, a caramel maker in Lancaster, Pennsylvania, began producing chocolate candies by machine. He acquired the machinery in 1894 and, during the next six years, experimented with making milk chocolate, which he used to produce, around 1900, the chocolate bar. The Hershey Company dominated chocolate candy production in the United States for the next fifty years, and it remains the largest American chocolate producer today.

Although Hershey's chocolate bar was cheap—five cents—it was not an immediate favorite. Only after World War I did chocolate become popular. During the war, the U.S. Quartermaster Corps ordered forty-pound blocks of chocolate for the American army in France. Soldiers returning from the war demanded chocolate. Between the two world wars, an estimated 30,000 different candy bars were sold.[20]

Chocolate makers learned how to make milk chocolate from Hershey and began producing chocolate bars. The Standard Candy Company, of Nashville, Tennessee, produced, in 1912, the first combination candy, called the Goo Goo Cluster, by coating caramel, marshmallow, and roasted peanuts with milk chocolate. The Clark Bar, composed of ground roasted peanuts covered with milk chocolate, was the first nationally marketed combination candy bar, and its success encouraged other companies to produce new combination bars. The Baby Ruth candy bar was released in 1916 and was extremely successful, due mainly to the promotional activities of its originator, Otto Y. Schnering. He chartered an airplane and dropped the bars by parachute over the city of Pittsburgh. He later expanded his drops to cities in more than forty states. At the same time, the company began a national promotion campaign using national magazines. An advertisement in *Collier's* magazine in 1926 heralded the Baby Ruth as the "Sweetest Story Ever Told" and asserted it to be "the world's most popular candy."[21]

Mars, Inc., founded by Frank Mars, introduced the Milky Way in 1923 and 3-Musketeers bars in 1932. Mars's Snicker bar, released in 1930, quickly became the most popular chocolate bar in America and has retained that title ever since. M&M Company, founded in 1940 by Forest Mars, Frank Mars's son, introduced M&Ms in 1940, and it has been the nation's most popular candy since the 1950s.[22]

Salty snacks, such as popcorn and peanuts, were being sold by vendors by the early nineteenth century. They had particular appeal to children, and both were connected with children's holidays, especially Halloween and Christmas. Planter's Peanuts, formed in 1906 in Wilkes-Barre, Pennsylvania, became the first successful commercial peanut manufacturer and seller. Its creation of the memorable Mr. Peanut character ensured their long-term success.[23]

During the late nineteenth century, potato chips joined the list of commercial salty snacks, but they didn't catch on. They were sold out of barrels, and as soon as the barrels were opened, the chips began to deteriorate. Exposed to air and humidity, they often went stale long before they were sold. During the early twentieth century, manufacturers began experimenting with cans, waxed paper, glassine, cellophane, and other materials for packaging individual portions. The customer could see the product through the packaging, and the new materials kept the food fresh until opened.

Once this new packaging technology had been established in the 1930s, potato chip sales took off. One potato chip manufacturer was Herman W. Lay, of Nashville, Tennessee. In 1932, he was hired by Barrett Foods, an Atlanta snack-food firm, to sell peanut butter sandwiches in southern Kentucky and Tennessee. He was an aggressive businessman and began acquiring distributorships. When Barrett's founder died in 1937, Lay bought the company's factories in Atlanta and Memphis. His potato chips were the first product to bear the Lay's brand name.[24] During World War II, the sale of potato chips surged, in part because of sugar and chocolate rationing. By the war's end, the firm had become a major regional producer of snack foods. After the war, Lay automated his potato chip manufacturing business and diversified its products: In 1945, he met Elmer Doolin, manufacturer of Frito Corn Chips in San Antonio. Doolin and Lay teamed up to produce and sell Fritos. This was the beginning of a beautiful relationship that came to include other products. Cheetos, for instance, invented by the Frito Company, were marketed by Lay beginning in 1948. Two years after Doolin died, in 1959, the two companies merged, creating Frito-Lay, Inc. The merged company continued to grow. Six years later, Frito-Lay merged with Pepsi Cola Company, creating PepsiCo. By the end of the 1960s, Frito-Lay had become the dominant company in the snack world, and it remains so today.

Snack Effects

Snacking between meals was strongly opposed by both medical professionals and diet reformers in the nineteenth century. With the growing availability of commercial snack foods in the early twentieth century, Americans began to change their eating habits. Natural whole foods were replaced with commercially branded foods. By aiming directly at America's sweet tooth and salt-loving taste buds, commercial snacks changed the negative attitude toward eating between meals.

The initial success of snack foods can be attributed to their low cost and association with happy occasions, such as holidays, fairs, circuses, and sporting events. From their earliest appearance, snack foods quickly charmed their way into American life. The rapid growth of grocery stores and supermarkets made it easy for Americans to buy their favorite snack foods and sodas, and advertising campaigns competed to tell them which ones to buy. Advertising became even more important and effective with the invention of radio and television, which offered remarkably efficient new means of snack-food marketing. With the end of Prohibition, in 1933, bars reopened and began offering free salty snacks to help drum up drink orders. The interest in salty snacks swelled even more during World War II, when rationing left sugar, candy, and chocolate in short supply; salty snacks, based on corn, potatoes, and peanuts, suffered no shortages in America during the war years.[25] The hefty expansion in disposable wealth in the United States during the twentieth century meant that most Americans could afford snack foods just about anytime they got the craving for them.

Since World War II, the sale of both sweet and salty snacks has soared, abetted by television advertising. As the twentieth century progressed, the quantity and diversity of sweet and salty snack foods proliferated, until every grocery store, kiosk, newspaper stand, and corner shop in America was heavily stocked with bags and packets of candies, chips, chocolates, crackers, pretzels, and much more. Thousands of snack foods are now manufactured in America. Collectively, these products today constitute a market niche capable of generating $26 billion in annual sales.[26]

Postscript

In 1963, the Cracker Jack Company was sold to Borden, Inc, based in New York City. By the late 1970s, Cracker Jack's commanding lead in the confectionery field slipped abroad and rapidly declined at home. This can be attributed to the rise of stiff competition. For sweeteners, competitors utilized maple syrup, sugar, and caramel, which sugar-loving Americans may have favored over the less-sweet molasses that Cracker Jack continued to use. Franklin Crunch 'n Munch outsells Cracker Jack, and Screaming Yellow Zonkers and Poppycock are fast catching up with the market leaders.

Borden went on a buying spree in the 1980s that resulted in the purchase of twenty-three companies. With the further acquisition of Laura Scudder's snack-food company, of Anaheim, California, and the Snacktime Company, in Indianapolis, Indiana, Borden became the nation's number two seller of snack foods, behind Frito-Lay, then a subsidiary of PepsiCo. But during the early 1990s, Borden went into serious financial decline. In 1997, Borden sold Cracker Jack to Frito-Lay, America's largest snack-food business and a subsidiary of PepsiCo. Borden itself went out of the food business.

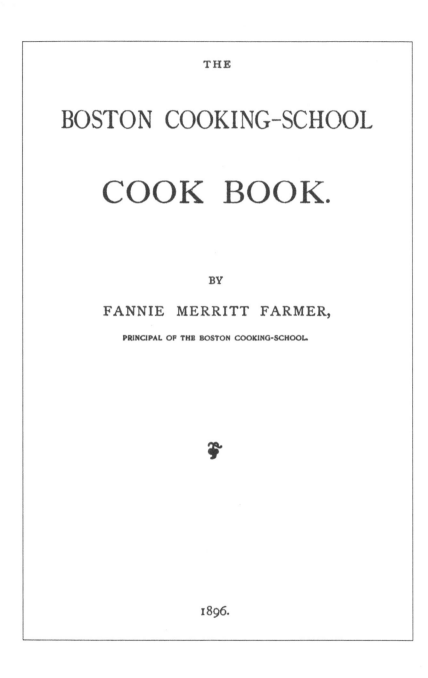

THE

BOSTON COOKING-SCHOOL

COOK BOOK.

BY

FANNIE MERRITT FARMER,

PRINCIPAL OF THE BOSTON COOKING-SCHOOL.

1896.

Cover of the *Boston Cooking-School Cook Book* (Fannie Merrit Farmer, *Boston Cooking-School Cook Book* [Boston: Little, Brown, 1896])

15.

Fannie Farmer's Cookbook

WHEN MARY J. LINCOLN was appointed principal of the Boston Cooking School in 1879, it had no written curriculum, so she set about collecting the recipes used in the classes and writing a text around them. Her popular *Mrs. Lincoln's Boston Cook Book*, published in 1884, became the text used in the school. When Fannie Merritt Farmer took over as principal in 1893, she decided that the book was due for a revision. After finishing a new edition, she approached the Boston publisher Little, Brown and Company, which had published *Mrs. Lincoln's Boston Cook Book* and the works of other Boston women. Farmer believed that they should publish her work as well, but the editors at Little, Brown didn't see it that way. Lincoln's cookbook had been reprinted annually since 1884 and was still in print and selling well. While Mrs. Lincoln was famous for her frequent lectures and published articles, Fannie Farmer was unknown outside Boston. Lincoln was also cofounder of *New England Kitchen Magazine*, the most popular cookery periodical of the day.[1]

Undaunted, Fannie Farmer persisted, and Little, Brown finally consented to publish her book, but they required she fund the first printing herself, making the book, in today's phraseology, a vanity publication. Farmer agreed to the terms. She defrayed some printing expenses by publishing eighteen pages of paid advertisements tucked into the cookbook's end pages. She also wrote a promotional cookery booklet for the Rumford Chemical Works, a baking powder company, which likely generated some income as well as visibility. As it turned out, no doubt to Little, Brown's surprise, Farmer's cookbook was a success. It had a ready-made local audience—the students at the cooking school and the hundreds of attendees at her lectures. And that was just the beginning. Her *Boston Cooking-School Cook Book*, published in 1896, became one of the largest-selling cookbooks in American history and eventually the model for American cookbooks.

American Cookbooks and Culinary Schools

British cookbooks had been published in the American colonies beginning in 1742, but not until 1796 did the first cookbook *written* by an American appear in print. Even then, Amelia Simmons's *American Cookery* reflected mainly English culinary practices, and many of Simmons's recipes were borrowed from earlier British works. *American Cookery* did, however, contain many New World ingredients and some non-English-derived recipes, and its publication spurred other Americans to write cookbooks. Mary Randolph's *Virginia House-wife*, published in 1824, signaled the first real departure from British cookery practices and represented a breakthrough for American cooking.

After the Civil War, upper-middle-class America was swayed by the influx of French chefs into the United States. One popular food authority of the period was Pierre Blot, a Frenchman who had immigrated to the United States around 1855 and lectured on the culinary arts. In 1863, Blot published his first cookbook, *What to Eat, and How to Cook It*. At the time, European chefs considered haute cuisine an art form, and the recipes in their cookbooks were suggestive rather than directive. They believed that cookery needed to be learned through a long apprenticeship under a professional chef. But Blot decided to break from this training system and create a school for students interested in fine cooking. In 1865, he opened the Culinary School of Design, in New York, styling himself professor of gastronomy, but the project failed. With financial assistance from the daughter of Commodore Cornelius Vanderbilt, Blot subsequently opened the New York Cooking School, which catered mainly to wealthy women and their cooks who were interested in studying a simplified version of the techniques of French cookery.[2]

Although Blot's school survived only a few years, it inspired others to create similar institutions—although for different purposes and designed for different audiences. Juliet Corson opened the New York Cooking School in 1876. Unlike Blot, Corson targeted her teaching at both middle-class women and their children and poor and working-class women. She hoped that the latter, upon completion of their course work, might find employment as domestics. Based on her lectures, Corson penned the *Cooking School Text Book and Housekeepers' Guide*, which simplified cooking and promised that anyone who could follow simple directions could become a cook in "twelve easy lessons."[3]

A similar school opened in Boston. The Women's Education Association (WEA) sponsored, in 1878, the Boston Cooking School.[4] Founded in 1872 to serve as a catalyst for educational opportunities for women, the WEA offered a laboratory chemistry course for women at the Massachusetts Institute of Technology (MIT). Its teacher, Ellen Richards, was the first woman to graduate from MIT. Richards had worked in the areas of nutrition, food adulteration, and general issues related to home economics. Her book *Chemistry of Cooking and Cleaning: A Manual for Housekeepers*, became a defining work for the food-science movement. Richards's views influenced the curriculum of the Boston Cooking School. When Mary J. Lincoln became its principal in 1879, she incorporated the work of Richards and her colleagues into the school's operations. Lincoln's cookbook included many recipes taught in the Boston Cooking School[5] and also some of Richards's ideas about nutrition and cookery.

Lincoln resigned as principal in 1889, and she was replaced by Fannie Merritt Farmer, a former student at the school. While in high school, Farmer had been struck down with an illness, probably polio.[6] Farmer eventually regained her ability to walk, but she retained a pronounced limp for the rest of her life. While recovering from her illness, she had worked with her mother in their kitchen. Unable to attend college because she hadn't graduate from high school, the thirty-one-year-old Farmer decided to enroll in the Boston Cooking School. After only a year of training at the school, Farmer was asked to serve as assistant principal. Four years later she became principal.[7]

Early in her tenure, Farmer decided to rewrite Lincoln's comprehensive teaching manual, perhaps at the suggestion of Mrs. William Sewall, the president of the school. Farmer dedicated the cookbook to Sewall "in appreciation of her encouragement and untiring efforts in promoting the work of scientific cookery, which means the elevation of the human race."[8]

Farmer's work, titled the *Boston Cooking-School Cook Book*, incorporated a condensed account of the progress made during the previous decade by scientists, which "rightfully should demand much consideration."[9] The cookbook opened with a superficial commentary on food science, with chemical formulas and discussions of protein, carbohydrates, and fats. In addition to incorporating some basic food science into her cookbook, Farmer made significant stylistic changes to Lincoln's original. In many of her 1,849 recipes, she listed ingredients first and then offered simple, step-by-step instructions, so that virtually anyone could prepare a dish with a reasonable chance of success. This organization also helped the reader to be sure she had all the ingredients on hand before starting to cook. Farmer was not the first to use this format, but she employed it more systematically, and her pattern became the standard for American cookbooks. Where Fannie Farmer made a marked departure from her predecessors was in the section of the cookbook titled "Measuring Ingredients." In earlier cookbooks, ingredient measurements had been casual and variable: "knob of butter the size of an egg," "a rounding coffee-spoonful," "a heaping teacup," or "a sufficient amount." Farmer, like the exacting instructor she was, stressed *level* measurements: "a cupful is measured level," and "a tablespoonful is measured level. A teaspoonful is measured level." These were phrases she also used in her lectures and written articles. For these unusually specific instructions, Farmer became known as "the mother of level measurements."[10]

Upon its publication in 1896, Farmer's book received widespread attention in a number of newspapers and magazines. The *New England Kitchen Magazine*'s review was, understandably, rather cool, pointing out that Farmer had not mentioned the contributions of her predecessors, such as Mary Lincoln, at the Boston Cooking School. Boston's *Literary World* was more upbeat, identifying Farmer's cookbook as "specially appropriate for the graduates of our public schools." The reviewer was especially taken with Farmer's comments "on correct proportions of food, combinations of ingredients" that "state clearly and concisely the principles of nutritive values," which distinguished this book from others of its era.[11]

Since Farmer had paid for the first print run of her cookbook, she retained control of the copyright. She stood to lose her investment if she could not sell the copies but to profit handsomely if it sold out. Even at a price of two dollars—more than other cookbooks at the time—the entire first printing of 3,000 copies sold out. The book was reprinted twice in 1897 and regularly reprinted almost every year thereafter. The cookbook's financial success was beyond anyone's wildest estimates.

Many reasons have been proposed for the early success of Fannie Farmer's cookbook. Its original title made clear its connection with the Boston Cooking School, a popular and respected institution at the time. Farmer herself, although virtually unknown prior to the book's publication, was a clear writer and an excellent lecturer. After the cookbook's publication, she lectured throughout the United States and wrote numerous articles for popular magazines. In 1896, Farmer helped launch the *Boston Cooking-School Magazine of Culinary Science and Domestic Economics*, later renamed *American Cookery*, which quickly became America's most important cookery magazine, maintaining that status until World War II, when it went out of business.

In addition, broader societal shifts created conditions that contributed to the success of the *Boston Cooking-School Cook Book*. Historically, women had learned cookery from their mothers. During the late nineteenth century, there was a mass exodus from rural America to the cities, and for many mothers and daughters the traditional kitchen-table linkage weakened. At about the same time, many American cities were inundated with immigrants, German and Irish immigrants beginning in the mid-nineteenth century and expanding by the turn of the century to include southern and eastern Europeans. Immigrant women thus lost their culinary connections with their mothers and grandmothers. City women consequently turned more and more to cookbooks, trustingly following the step-by-step directions.

The ready availability of new kitchen equipment in the early twentieth century also changed the nature of cooking. Gas stoves, for instance, made it possible to more carefully control cooking temperatures; oven thermostats further refined the process. The introduction of standardized measuring cups and spoons made it possible to follow recipes more accurately. Clocks and timers became necessary items of kitchen equipment, because published recipes specified precise cooking times. These innovations helped create a new kitchen science and way of cooking among women who, traditionally, would have cooked by instinct.

Farmer Effects

Cookbooks and cooking schools carry changes in food fashion to wide audiences. Fannie Farmer's *Boston Cooking-School Cook Book* popularized scientific cookery, a perspective that remains a part of American cookbooks today. The idea that cooking is a science should rightfully be credited to Ellen Richards and others in the home economics movement, but it was Fannie Farmer who popularized it. Most recipes in American cookbooks, magazines, and newspapers came subsequently to be organized in a manner consistent with Farmer's presentation, and the idea that cookery was an art form disappeared from most American households.

Farmer published a revised edition of the *Boston Cooking-School Cook Book* in 1906. It, too, was a success, enjoying almost annual reprints. By 1915, more than 360,000 copies of the book had been sold. That's just the beginning of the story, however. Farmer's cookbook sold tens of thousands of copies annually for years after her death. Revised editions were published beginning in 1924,[12] and by 1930, more than 1.4 million copies had been printed. Revised editions continued to appear on a regular basis, many of them edited by Wilma Lord Perkins, Fannie Farmer's niece. In 1965, the cookbook's name was changed to *The Fannie Farmer*

Cookbook. California-based cookbook author Marion Cunningham edited the twelfth and thirteenth editions, and in 1996, *The Boston Cooking-School Cook Book* was reprinted in facsimile in honor of its one-hundredth anniversary. More than 4 million copies of the original work and its successors have been printed, making it one of the best-selling cookbooks of all time.

Fannie Farmer's success encouraged others to write cookbooks. Irma Rombauer's *Joy of Cooking*, first published in 1931, had sold 6 million copies by the time Rombauer died in 1962. The *Better Homes and Gardens Cookbook* had done even better, with estimated sales, by that year, of more than 11 million copies. About 4,000 new cookbook titles are released annually by commercial publishers in the United States, and cookbooks outsell every other category in the publishing industry.

Despite the continued impressive sales of cookbooks, as of 2008, Americans prepare only 32 percent of their evening meals from scratch. The remainder are purchased at restaurants or are ready-to-eat foods purchased at supermarkets.[13]

Postscript

Fannie Farmer's other cookbooks, *Chafing Dish Possibilities* and *Food and Cookery for the Sick and Convalescent*, also sold well. The Boston Cooking School closed shortly after Farmer left it, in 1902. Farmer promptly created Miss Farmer's School of Cookery, which survived until World War II, when most of its potential students were employed for the war effort. Farmer died in 1915 a very wealthy woman.

One graduate of Miss Farmer's School of Cookery was Ruth Lockwood, who worked for WGBH, Boston's noncommercial broadcasting service, in the early 1960s. Because of her culinary knowledge, she became the associate producer of Julia Child's PBS program *The French Chef*.

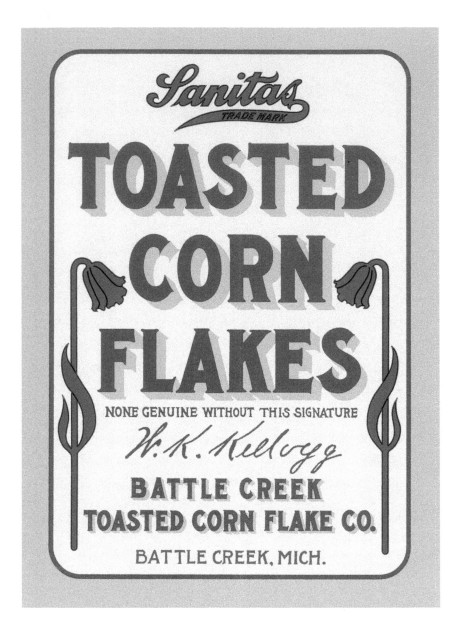

Sanitas Toasted Corn Flakes box, circa 1906, later renamed Kelloggs Corn Flakes (courtesy of the Kellogg Company)

16.

The Kelloggs' Corn Flakes

HEALTH ADVOCATE Dr. John Harvey Kellogg and his younger brother, Will Kellogg, invented a new way of processing corn: they steamed and softened the kernels, added flavorings, and then flattened it by feeding it through two steel rollers. The resulting flakes were then baked in an oven. This process created a cereal they called toasted corn flakes, which the Kellogg brothers served at their sanitarium in Battle Creek, Michigan. To sell their products to former sanitarium patients and health-food advocates, the brothers established the Sanitas Nut Food Company, with Will Kellogg as president and John Harvey Kellogg as the major stockholder. They began selling Sanitas Toasted Corn Flakes in 1898. Dr. Kellogg was opposed to advertising and marketing on principle, believing that all funds generated by sales should support the Battle Creek sanitarium, so the Kelloggs' new product didn't get much attention outside the health-food community. When the manufacturers of other cereals, such as Quaker Oats, Grape-Nuts, and Shredded Wheat, enjoyed spectacular sales as a result of their aggressive advertising campaigns, Will Kellogg began chafing at his brother's restrictions, knowing they were losing out on a huge financial opportunity. Acquiring sole rights to Toasted Corn Flakes in 1906,[1] Will Kellogg converted the health-food corn flakes into a mainstream consumer product, and cold cereals have dominated the American breakfast ever since.

Breakfast History

In Colonial times, breakfast was eaten immediately upon rising or a few hours later, after the earliest chores had been completed. For most Americans, the meal usually consisted of some kind of gruel or porridge. In more affluent households hearty breakfasts might have included such things as lamb chops, tripe, clams, broiled salmon, beefsteak, liver, kidneys, bacon or ham, smoked fish, codfish cakes, poultry, muffins, waffles, pancakes, potatoes, fried, boiled, or scrambled eggs, corned beef hash, mush, grits, hominy, bread, rolls, and seasonal fruit.[2]

Nineteenth-century medical professionals were greatly concerned about breakfast. Hydropathist and health reformer Thomas Low Nichols reported, in 1864, that it wasn't the number or type of dishes that was a problem as much as the way the food was prepared. He reported that a "common breakfast" offered twenty dishes: "But butter and lard are so cheap that they are used with great profusion, and the best viands and vegetables are rendered indigestible. Hot bread made with lard and strong alkalies, and soaked with butter; hot griddle cakes covered with butter and syrup; meats fried in fat or baked in it; potatoes dripping with grease; ham and eggs fried in grease into a leathery indigestibility—all washed down with many cups of strong Brazil coffee."[3]

The vegetarian Sylvester Graham proposed a shift to a simple cereal-based breakfast, but his advice was little heeded at the time. Graham's successors, however, sold cereal products associated with Graham. Hydropathist James Caleb Jackson, owner of Our Home on the Hill Side, in Dansville, New York, began, in the 1860s, supplementing the breakfast menu with biscuits made from Graham flour, oats, and cornmeal. Thinking the wider public would appreciate a healthful breakfast food, he baked wafers made of Graham flour, crumbled them, and then baked them a second time. He dubbed his invention Granula and sold the cereal through the Our Home Granula Company. It was so hard, however, that some people called it wheat rocks, and it was necessary to let it soak in milk or water overnight before trying to eat it.[4] This proved to be a weakness in later years when housewives demanded ready-to-eat cereals. Jackson may well have changed the formula, for in the 1880s he touted in advertisements that Granula was "ready for immediate table use."[5] Whatever its formula, Jackson's Granula became America's first commercial breakfast cereal.

John Harvey Kellogg

Ellen G. White, a leader and prophetess of the Seventh-Day Adventists, and her husband, James, visited Jackson's Our Home in 1864. She was delighted with the regimen but disapproved of some of its activities, such as card playing, dancing, and other entertainments. She pondered whether the Seventh-Day Adventists should have an institute of their own, but nothing came of the idea upon her return home to Battle Creek, Michigan.[6] White declared she had had a vision enlightening her on health reform, and, based on the vision, she wrote an essay, "Health or How to Live," which contained similar ideas to those espoused by Jackson.[7] White and her husband returned to Dansville in 1865, and after her return home this time, she launched the Western Health Reform Institute, which opened in September 1866. As its director, she selected a doctor who had worked at Our Home. The institute emphasized the water cure and a simple culinary regimen centering on bland vegetarian food; cards and dancing were not allowed. The institute was incorporated separately from the Seventh-Day Adventist Church and had its own board, on which James White and other Adventists served.[8] To gain visibility and promote the ideals espoused by White, the institute began publishing a monthly journal called the *Health Reformer*. Despite support from the Seventh-Day Adventist community, during its initial ten years, the institute barely limped along.

In the 1870s, Ellen White set her hopes on a local teenager, John Harvey Kellogg, born in Tyrone, Michigan, in 1852. Kellogg's parents subscribed to Russell Trall's *Water Cure Journal*, which served as the main communications medium for those interested in hydropathy. Kellogg was raised on the culinary recommendations that appeared in that journal. He went to work as a copy editor for the Seventh-Day Adventist's publication, *Review and Herald*, at the age of twelve. Like Sylvester Graham, Kellogg suffered from serious childhood illnesses, and these may have led him to read the works of Graham, the hydropaths, and other health reformers. At the age of fourteen, he became a vegetarian, due largely to his readings. Still in his teens, Kellogg taught at a local high school and planned to become a teacher. He enrolled at the Michigan State Normal College, in Ypsilanti, where he survived on a "diet of vegetables, nuts, fruits, and graham bread for an average of six cents a day." In the fall of 1872, with encouragement from Ellen and James White, Kellogg studied medicine for six months at the Hygeio-Therapeutic College, in Florence Heights, New Jersey, which was directed by Russell Trall, by then a friend of the Whites. Trall was short on staff, so he hired Kellogg as a part-time instructor in chemistry. Kellogg had read Justus von Liebig's works and taught the class creditably, but Trall and Kellogg had different ideas on medicine, and Trall removed Kellogg from his position. Kellogg survived the six-month ordeal and was surprised to find a diploma in the mail after his departure. For the next two years, Kellogg attended the College of Medicine and Surgery at the University of Michigan. Then, with a thousand dollar loan from the Whites,

Kellogg undertook studies at New York's Bellevue Hospital Medical College. In 1875, he returned to Battle Creek, where he was elected to the medical staff of the Western Health Reform Institute. In the spring of 1876, he left Battle Creek and visited Philadelphia's Centennial Exposition, where he set up a small exhibit on health and temperance. He then traveled to New Jersey, where he planned to engage in research and write.[9]

However, that summer the Whites asked Kellogg to become the institute's physician in chief, which he did on October 1, 1876. He remained in that post for the next sixty-seven years. At the time he became the chief physician, the institute was still just a minor clinic with several small buildings and twenty patients, eight of whom left shortly after Kellogg's arrival. Kellogg renamed the institute the Battle Creek Sanitarium and took charge of *Good Health*, the Adventist health journal. With Kellogg in firm control, White sanctioned the construction of a new, large building. In 1878, the five-story Medical and Surgical Sanitarium was completed, and Kellogg began building the sanitarium's infrastructure. Kellogg and the Whites had disagreements, and, in 1880, Kellogg forced James White off the sanitarium's board. When the sanitarium was rechartered in 1897, Kellogg made sure that it was completely divorced from the Seventh-Day Adventist Church.[10]

Kellogg enforced a vegetarian regimen at the sanitarium and sought to develop new vegetarian products. He was also a strong believer in the importance of thorough mastication. Patients with tooth problems, however, had difficulty chewing hard foods like zwieback, then a mainstay on hospital menus. To make such foods easier for these patients to manage, Kellogg ground zwieback and other hard breadstuffs into small pieces or granules. He called this product Granula.

Although he opposed advertising campaigns, Kellogg was not averse to making money on his creations, and in 1877 he put his Granula on the market.[11] To avoid legal problems with James Jackson, who had been selling his own Granula since the early 1860s, Kellogg altered its makeup by grinding up a three-grain biscuit, thus creating the prototype of today's Grape-Nuts, and changed the name to Granola, which seemed to satisfy Jackson. Kellogg's wife, Ella, devised recipes using Granola, and these were regularly published beginning in 1885.[12] Kellogg went on to develop countless Granola variations, serving them at the sanitarium. As a service to former patients, Kellogg made these health foods available to them through the mail. The problem was that the cereal still tended to be hard, even after being saturated with water or milk. Dental problems were epidemic in the nineteenth century, and many Americans had few or no teeth. Patients with dental problems found it difficult to chew the hard cereal, while others broke their teeth trying to do so. So in the early 1880s, Kellogg set up a lab at the sanitarium and began experimenting with softer alternatives made from cereal grains, which he eventually began serving at the sanitarium.[13]

Kellogg was not the only health-food advocate experimenting with dried cereals. An inventor and businessman named Henry D. Perky had invented a machine that flattened cooked wheat between two steel rollers, similar to the apparatus used for rolling oats. In addition, however, he added devices that shredded the wheat flakes and then formed the shreds into biscuits. He acquired patents for its components and began manufacturing a shredded wheat biscuit–making machine, which he planned to lease to others. Perky's Cereal Machine Company had few takers, and sales of the biscuits he produced himself were dismal—mainly because his archetypal shredded wheat, unlike today's product, was not completely dried when sold, and it spoiled quickly. Unhappy grocers sent the spoiled biscuits back to Perky. Seeking technical advice and a potential partner, Perky visited John Harvey Kellogg in Battle Creek, where he also may have met Charles W. Post, a businessman who, at the time, was setting up his own health institute there. Perky showed Kellogg his shredding machine and discussed his plans for manufacturing and leasing it. Kellogg was intrigued and visited Perky in Denver a few months later, offering to buy the rights to the shredding machine. Both men agreed on a price of $100,000—but then Perky abruptly backed out. He did agree to send Kellogg a machine, but after Kellogg threatened to make a shredding machine of his own, Perky reneged on his offer.[14]

In the fall of 1894, Perky moved to Massachusetts, where he established a factory to produce his improved biscuits, using high heat to ensure thorough drying. The Shredded Wheat we know today was manufactured first in Roxbury, a Boston suburb, and later in a factory set up in the industrial town of Worcester, Massachusetts.[15]

Even before the Cereal Machine Company had begun mass production, Perky had been promoting both biscuits and machines. He exhibited them at a booth at the 1893 Columbian Exposition in Chicago, where he sold small quantities of biscuits. With his Roxbury factory in operation, Perky debuted his products at the October 1894 Boston World's Food Fair, sponsored by the Boston Retail Grocers' Association. Perky's company had purchased two exhibition spaces at the fair, and he designed the display himself. To the thousands of grocers and members of the general public visiting the exhibition, the company gave away free packages of Shredded Wheat, advising them to serve it with cream and sugar. The biscuit's novel pillowlike shape created excitement, and the product drew wide attention, especially from health-food advocates. As a result of the Boston fair, Perky began selling Shredded Wheat directly to grocers, who found a ready market for it.[16] At last Perky concluded that his company should be selling biscuits and not machines, and he renamed the Cereal Machine Company the Natural Food Company.

As early as 1894, references and recipes using Shredded Wheat biscuits began appearing in a variety of cookbooks.[17] In 1897, Perky began publishing cookery booklets with dozens of recipes using Shredded Wheat—everything from main dishes for breakfast, lunch, and dinner to desserts. Hundreds of thousands of these booklets were distributed free of charge during the following decade.[18] By 1899, Perky had again changed the name of his business, this time to the Shredded Wheat Company. In 1901, he relocated the firm to Niagara Falls, New York, where he constructed the world's largest cereal factory.[19] At the Pan American Exposition, held in nearby Buffalo the same year, Perky constructed one of the finest pavilions, which competed successfully with the displays of Quaker Oats and those of other cereal companies.

Another display at the fair was one created by Charles Post, a former patient at Kellogg's sanitarium. After serious financial reversals in the late 1880s, Post, a Fort Worth businessman, suffered a series of breakdowns. In 1891, hoping to strengthen his health, Post and his family moved to Battle Creek, which was little more than a village at the time. The family lived in a small cottage near the sanitarium, and, according to legend, each day for nine months, Post's wife, Ella, pushed him in his invalid chair up to the sanitarium, where he underwent his treatment regimen. When his health did not improve, Post decided to leave, but by this time Dr. Kellogg had already told Ella that her husband did not have long to live.[20]

Ella learned that a Mrs. Elizabeth Gregory, who lived in Battle Creek, might be able to assist her dying husband. Gregory was a Christian Scientist, and she insisted that Post had the power to heal himself. Encouraged to give faith a try, Post moved into Gregory's home, where he ate food she prepared for him and read *Science and Health*, the textbook of Christian Science, written by the church's founder, Mary Baker Eddy. Miraculously, Post recovered his health and almost immediately began formulating plans for a clinic based on his new-found knowledge. On March 23, 1892, he began buying property (with his wife's money) on which to build a health institute of his own. He named it La Vita Inn, and charged lower rates than did Dr. Kellogg. Post also wrote *I am Well!* which told of his miraculous recovery and the importance of "natural suggestion," or what later came to be called the "power of positive thinking." Post's book quoted heavily from Henry Ward Beecher and other prominent ministers.[21]

With his institute doing well, Post concluded that the time was right to start manufacturing health foods. He particularly liked the "caramel coffee" served at the Kellogg sanitarium. At some point, Post offered to go into business with Kellogg to market it, but Kellogg refused—or so the story goes. Post decided to create and sell his own version. He hired a Swiss chemist to create a healthful drink similar to the coffee substitute served at the sanitarium. Post wasn't pleased with the results, so he began experimenting himself.[22] In late 1894 he perfected a cereal-based coffee substitute consisting of wheat berries, glutenous bran, and New Orleans molasses; he called it Postum and began manufacturing it in his barn at La Vita Inn. Post advertised in the local Battle Creek newspaper, but he also visited local grocers and offered them a deal: they didn't have to pay for the new product until they sold it. Then he made another unusual offer—he'd supply free sample cups of Postum in hopes that customers would like it and buy some on the spot. The free sample ploy, unusual at the time, brought droves of customers into the stores; Postum quickly sold out and frantic grocers had to reorder more just a week later. In its first year alone, it generated a profit of $174,000, an unheard-of amount for the time. In 1896, Post incorporated the Postum Cereal Company to manufacture and sell his grain-based coffee substitute.

Post's timing was impeccable. Medical professionals had been warning about the dangers of drinking coffee, and Post claimed his beverage was just the thing for "jangled nerves." Also helpful was Post's Battle Creek address, which led Americans to believe that his operation was somehow connected with Kellogg's sanitarium.

Post seized the moment and began experimenting with other products. In January 1898, he started marketing Grape-Nuts, made from wheat and malted barley, which served to sweeten the cereal. Grape-Nuts was a variation on Jackson's Granula and Kellogg's Granola, made by the same method. Post's advertisements touted Grape-Nuts as a "scientific health food" containing "vitalizing" elements, and health-food advocates promptly endorsed it. Specifically, advertisements avowed that Grape-Nuts cured a wide range of illnesses—rickets, malaria, rheumatism, brain problems, heart disease, consumption, and appendicitis—to name but a few.[23] Packed inside each carton was an eight-page booklet titled *The Road to Wellville*, replete with Post's philosophy along with advice to eat Grape-Nuts at breakfast, lunch, and dinner.[24] When *Collier's Weekly* refused to publish Grape-Nuts advertising because of its inflated and outrageous claims, Post spent $150,000 for an advertising campaign against the magazine, charging that the editors were vilifying him because he had refused to advertise in *Collier's*. In response, *Collier's* said Post was a "faker" and that his published statements against *Collier's* were lies.[25] *Collier's* sued Post for libel and won a $50,000 judgment against him.[26]

Kellogg was not pleased with Post's promotional efforts, either. Put off by Post's tawdry advertising campaigns, Kellogg made an ethical decision to market his products only through *Good Health* and other Seventh-Day Adventist publications.[27] Kellogg believed that the promotional efforts of other manufacturers, particularly Post, were disingenuous, and he felt that the profits from sales of his health food should be used to support the sanitarium, not for advertising his corn flakes. Kellogg regularly announced that his sanitarium had no connection with Grape-Nuts "or any other of the numerous nostrums made or sold by parties advertising from Battle Creek. The prestige of Battle Creek as a health center has made this an attractive place for the operations of various charlatans, and not the least pretentious and predatory of these are the numerous food charlatans who, posing as experts and discoverers, have reaped a rich harvest from the credulity of a confiding public and to some extent at the expense of the Battle Creek Sanitarium, because the profession and the public are generally unacquainted with the facts above stated."[28]

Meanwhile, Kellogg had been pursuing his own product development ideas, some stemming from his meetings with Henry Perky in the spring of 1894. Kellogg stayed away from the shredded cereal concept, but he did use Perky's idea of rollers in his experiments. By mistake, Kellogg one day fed wheat that had been cooked and tempered through two steel rollers. Examining the resulting flakes, he believed they had distinct possibilities. (He also put nuts through the rollers, producing the first commercial peanut butter.) John Kellogg and his brother, Will, continued experimenting, and before long they had developed their first flaked cereal—Granose Flakes. Although they had used some of Perky's ideas, Kellogg promptly applied for patents beginning in May 1894. Granose was first marketed in 1895, and by the year's end, more than fifty tons of Granose had been manufactured and sold.[29] In 1898, Kellogg separated the manufacture of food products from the sanitarium itself by establishing the Sanitas Food Company, with Will installed as president and manager. They sold their new flaked cereal by mail, mainly to other health institutes.

Other companies manufacturing cereal were soon established in Battle Creek. They imitated the Kelloggs' process and had no scruples about commercializing and advertising their products. Profits rolled in, and new manufacturers opened factories in any building they could find—even in tents, if necessary. During the early 1900s, "Battle Creek was in the midst of a wheat flake boom comparable to a Texas oil strike or the Florida real estate boom of the 1920s," revealed Horace Powell, Will Kellogg's biographer. By 1902, thirty-two manufacturers of flaked cereals were operating in Battle Creek, a city of just 30,000 residents, and twelve more companies were situated in the surrounding county. According to a contemporary account in the *New York World*, the factories were running night and day—even on Sundays—to keep up with the orders pouring in.[30] In 1903,

Kellogg's patent on flaked cereal was declared invalid, and even more companies jumped into the burgeoning market.[31]

With imitators duplicating their Granose, the Kelloggs experimented with other flaked cereals, focusing particularly on corn. They had had some success in 1898 with a product they called Sanitas Toasted Corn Flakes. John's wife, Ella, published recipes using Toasted Corn Flakes as an ingredient in her cookbook *Healthful Cookery*, published in 1904.[32] But as the Kelloggs soon discovered, because of corn's high oil content, the flakes quickly turned rancid, so their cereal was not viable as a commercial product. Nevertheless, the Kellogg brothers forged ahead and eventually solved the corn oil problem. Will added sugar to the mixture, over the objections of John, who believed that sugar was potentially more a danger to health than eating meat. But sugar made a better-tasting product, and Will was interested in making sales.[33]

By late 1905, the corn flake business was booming and other cereal manufacturers had gotten into this line. In January 1906, Charles Post introduced a new one, which he called Elijah's Manna. It was his version of the corn flakes made at the Battle Creek Sanitarium. After Bible Belt ministers complained that the name was a sacrilege, Post rechristened the cereal Post Toasties.[34]

To successfully compete with Post and the other flaked-cereal manufacturers, Will Kellogg believed that a full-bore promotion and distribution effort was necessary, which meant removing John Kellogg from his position of control. At the time, John Kellogg needed money. The sanitarium had burned down in 1902, and he had amassed debts while reconstructing it, and these hefty loans were coming due. This gave Will an idea. He approached a Saint Louis insurance executive who had been a patient at the sanitarium, Charles D. Bolin, and asked him to invest funds in a new company that would manufacture corn flakes. Bolin liked the idea and agreed to give Will $35,000 in cash and $180,000 in loans in exchange for stock in the new company. Will used the funds to launch the company and to buy the rights to Sanitas Toasted Corn Flakes from his brother. In February 1906, Will Kellogg set up the Toasted Corn Flakes Company, and the following month the company officially acquired the rights to Sanitas Toasted Corn Flakes.[35]

With the new company safely in his hands, Will Kellogg began advertising Sanitas Toasted Corn Flakes on a large scale beginning in the fall of 1906. Ads and promotional offers were featured in magazines such as *Ladies' Home Journal*, *McClure's*, *Scribner's*, and the *Boston Cooking-School Magazine*, with the slogan "It won its favor through its flavor." The company's ads featured an attractive young woman along with the suggestive slogan "Wink at the grocer, and see what you will get." Attractive women were used to advertise corn flakes at food exhibitions, contests were held to pick the most beautiful "cornflake baby," and sandwich-sign men dressed as ears of corn paraded through towns; the company also offered various premiums and prizes.[36]

In 1907, Will Kellogg changed the name of the product from Sanitas Toasted Corn Flakes to "Kellogg's Toasted Corn Flakes," and his signature appeared on the cereal box to guarantee the product's authenticity. He later alleged that he had done so because a man named Blanke began, in 1906, advertising Toasted Corn Flakes, and Kellogg wanted to avoid confusion. It was nonetheless clear that Will Kellogg had made the change to take advantage of the Kellogg name, which at the time was synonymous with health food. The name change upset John Kellogg, who did not want his name associated with a commercial product. In retaliation, he renamed Granose Kellogg's Toasted Wheat Flakes. John Kellogg proclaimed them to be the only legitimate flaked cereal and began marketing his newly named product through the Sanitas Food Company. This was too much for Will, and the two brothers moved from strong personal disagreements to the court. Will won the case, and Dr. Kellogg was forced to change the name of his product. The brothers were soon back in court on other matters, and for years they tried unsuccessfully to resolve their differences through the legal system.[37]

Cereal Effects

By the early twentieth century, many Americans were increasingly concerned about the connection between food and health, in part due to muckrakers like Charles Edward Russell and Upton Sinclair. Breakfast cereals were associated with the Battle Creek Sanitarium, and many cereal companies effectively used the health theme in their promotions. As the century progressed, health became a major selling point for cereals as well as for other processed foods. Another advantage of cereals was their convenience. The typical full-fledged nineteenth-century meal would have taken hours to prepare, while cold cereals took just seconds. Finally, commercial cereals succeeded because of advertising and promotion—a lesson quickly learned by other food manufacturers.[38]

As more women entered the workforce during the twentieth century, cereal makers touted the fact that children could prepare their own breakfast cereal without the need of mother's help. According to medical authorities of the day, cereal was good for children, so this was a double win for busy working mothers. With children as an important market, manufacturers added sugar to seal the deal. After World War II, with sugar rationing a thing of the past, cereal makers upped the ante by adding even more sugar to their products. Kellogg's introduced Sugar Pops in 1950. Frosted Flakes, also manufactured by Kellogg's, was first produced in 1952. Its first mascot was a kangaroo; later, Tony the Tiger assumed the role. Kellogg's also bought the licensing rights for Superman, who appeared on Frosted Flakes boxes during the 1950s. Today, Frosted Flakes is the second-largest-selling cereal in America.

General Mills introduced Trix, which contains 46 percent sugar, in 1954. Its advertising slogan, "Trix are for kids," was introduced in the 1960s. John Holahan, then vice president of General Mills, invented Lucky Charms in 1963. The cereal, its child appeal based on pastel marshmallow shapes, has changed regularly over the years, acquiring new shapes and flavors. The Lucky Charms mascot is a leprechaun, which first appeared in advertisements in 1964. In 1979, General Mills rolled out a sugar- and honey-coated version of Cheerios called Honey Nut Cheerios, which is among the top-selling cereals.

Today, ready-to-eat breakfast cereals, many produced by the Kellogg Company, are served in nine out of ten American households. Americans buy 2.7 billion packages of breakfast cereal each year. We consume about ten pounds, or 160 bowls, of cereal per person each year. In terms of dollar value, breakfast cereals are the third-most popular product sold at supermarkets. Annually, the industry uses 816 million pounds of sugar, or almost 3 pounds of sugar per capita. More than 1.3 million cereal commercials air on American television each year, and most of them target children.[39] Ironically, these breakfast cereals, which started as health foods, are now considered major contributors to excess sugar in the American diet, especially in the diets of children.

Postscript

Henry Perky sold his shares in the Shredded Wheat Company in 1904 and died two years later. In 1928, the firm merged with the National Biscuit Company, later known as Nabisco.

Charles W. Post died in 1914, a likely suicide. His daughter, Marjorie Merriweather Post, inherited her father's estate and continued to build the Postum Cereal Company. In 1929, the company acquired Clarence Birdseye's General Seafoods and was renamed the General Foods Company.

John Harvey Kellogg wrote thousands of articles for journals; he eventually published more than fifty books and many achieved wide distribution. Dr. Kellogg toured the country, lecturing to thousands of people, and later delivered lectures in Europe. The Medical and Surgical Sanitarium flourished under Kellogg's guidance, and among the rich and famous who flocked to it were Henry Ford, J. C. Penney, Thomas Edison, and President William Howard Taft.

Less well known but a frequent visitor to the sanitarium was Mary Frances Holbrook, the maternal grandmother of M. F. K. Fisher. Holbrook lived with the Fisher family and enforced John Harvey Kellogg's culinary philosophy on the family's dining regimen. Fisher completely rejected Holbrook's culinary bent and went in the opposite direction, expressing her sensual relationship with food in her poetic and insightful books, beginning with, in 1937, *Serve It Forth*. She wrote: "Without my first eleven years of gastronomical awareness when Old Mrs. Holbrook was in residence, I probably would still be swimming in unread iambics instead of puzzling over the relationship between food and love."[40]

John Harvey Kellogg and Ellen White had their differences. In the 1890s, White charged him with selfishness, pride, and other sins. He was expelled from the Seventh-Day Adventist Church in 1907. After the schism, White expanded the Seventh-Day Adventist–sponsored Loma Linda Sanitarium in California into an educational facility to train "medical missionaries."[41] White died in 1915, aged eighty-seven.

After the disputes with his brother, John Kellogg retired from product development. His chief interest was his sanitarium. By 1935, it had treated more than 300,000 patients, and Dr. Kellogg had influenced millions of others through his books, lectures, and the products he had invented. Like so many other businesses during the Depression, the sanitarium began to lose money, and it closed in 1942. Kellogg died the following year at age ninety-one. His influence on America's breakfast table is still felt today; he would likely be dismayed to know that the onetime health food is now a major factor in the overconsumption of sugar, especially among children.

Will Kellogg served as president of the renamed Kellogg Company until 1929. By then, the company had sold more than 50 million boxes of Corn Flakes.[42] The company continued to produce new cereals, such as Rice Krispies, Frosted Flakes Gold, and Special K. In 1930, Kellogg established the W. K. Kellogg Foundation, which today supports sustainable agriculture and many other worthy causes. Will Kellogg lived until 1951, when he died, like his brother, at the age of ninety-one.

Poster of Upton Sinclair's *The Jungle* (Library of Congress Rare Book and Special Collections Division)

17.

Upton Sinclair's Jungle

I N OCTOBER 1904, Upton Sinclair traveled to Chicago, where, for seven weeks, he toiled in the stockyards, interviewing workers, labor leaders, and journalists. Upon returning to his home near Princeton, New Jersey, Sinclair set to work on a novel about his adventure. Even before he completed it, in the summer of 1905, a serialized version began appearing in the *Appeal to Reason*, a socialist publication. The series was widely acclaimed for its vivid portrayal of the meatpacking horrors. Sinclair approached several book publishers with the completed novel, but they either declined or asked Sinclair to remove portions they deemed offensive. Sinclair refused to change his novel. Finally, Doubleday, Page & Company agreed to publish the work uncensored.[1] On February 28, 1906, Upton Sinclair's *The Jungle* was released, and overnight the book became an international cause célèbre. Magazines and newspapers throughout America reported its publication and its revelations. Within a matter of months, Congress passed the Pure Food and Drugs Act and the Meat Inspection Act. Pure food became the law of the land, and the quality and safety of America's food supply improved as a result; however, the debate about what constitutes pure food and how the food industry should be regulated continues to shape what Americans eat today.

Jungle History

Upton Sinclair was a most unlikely person to start a revolution in the way Americans ate. In 1904, he was an obscure twenty-eight-year-old hack writer who barely made a living cranking out dime novels. He had written twenty-one such novels prior to *Manassas: A Novel of the War*, which was published by Macmillan in the summer of 1904. He had grandiose notions for *Manassas*, hoping it would be the first of a trilogy about the Civil War, but when sales proved disappointing, he abandoned his plan. Just when things seemed bleakest, though, Sinclair's life took an amazing turn.

He had joined the Socialist Party in 1902. When the meat cutters' and butchers' union went on strike in the Chicago stockyards in July 1904, Sinclair published an article in the socialist magazine *Appeal to Reason*, supporting the workers. The article was subsequently released as a broadside, and 35,000 copies were distributed by the striking workers in Chicago.[2] In September 1904, the strike failed, and the defeated and demoralized workers went back to work, but Sinclair did not forget their strike. Neither did the strikers forget their champion.

Fred G. Warren, the editor of the *Appeal to Reason*, liked Sinclair's article on the strike. He wrote to Sinclair congratulating him on the publication of *Manassas* and inviting him to write a novel on "wage slavery," a socialist term referring to work done for meager wages. Sinclair agreed, but he needed to come up with a good angle. With the meatpacking strike still on his mind, Sinclair proposed an investigation into working conditions in Chicago's stockyards. Warren gave Sinclair $500 for the first serial rights to the proposed novel.[3]

After his arrival in Chicago in October 1904, Sinclair interviewed the socialist Ella Reeve Bloor (a.k.a. Mother Bloor), who supplied him with investigative material. Another socialist, Algie Martin Simons, gave Sinclair a copy of a pamphlet he'd written, "Packingtown," the name of Chicago's stockyards. Sinclair also read the journalist Ernest Poole's articles about the meat strike in the summer of 1904 and articles about Lithuanian workers in the stockyards, which had appeared in the *Independent* in July and August 1904. Sinclair also met Adolph Smith, an English doctor who had published a series of articles in the *Lancet*, a British medical journal, in which he called Packingtown "foul and abominable."[4] While Sinclair was influenced by many previously published works, his depictions of the conditions and events that ended up in *The Jungle* were not borrowed: he either witnessed them firsthand or, more likely, heard about them from the workers he interviewed.

After seven weeks of interviewing and poking around, Sinclair returned to his home near Princeton and, on Christmas Day 1904, began writing the novel.

Even before finishing the book, in the summer of 1905, the first installments of the serial had begun to appear in the *Appeal to Reason*. The book was also serialized in a smaller journal, *One-Hoss Philosophy*, beginning in April 1905. Although the subscriptions to these publications was limited, Sinclair's articles received widespread attention, and his readers were shocked and disgusted by what they learned from his stories.

While the work was still being serialized, Sinclair began revising and refining his work. Macmillan had agreed to publish the series in book form, but when he presented the revised version to its editors, they demanded that parts of the text be removed—particularly the graphic descriptions of slaughterhouses. Sinclair refused and left Macmillan, offering the book to four other publishers, all of which turned it down.

Determined to reach the broadest possible audience, Sinclair decided to self-publish his work. Another socialist, author Jack London, asked readers of the *Appeal to Reason* for donations and subscriptions to help Sinclair publish the book. Heeding the call, readers sent in more than $4,000. (Sinclair later said that this was more money than he had made in the previous five years.) While the manuscript was being typeset, Sinclair offered the work to yet another publisher, Doubleday, Page & Company. Before it agreed to publish the work, Doubleday sent an employee to Chicago to check on the scenes depicted in the novel. When he returned with confirmation of Sinclair's shocking stories, Doubleday agreed to publish the account uncensored,[5] and the book came out on February 28, 1906. *The Jungle* was reviewed—not always positively—in newspapers across the country and in Europe; William Randolph Hearst serialized the story in his newspapers, and the book became an overnight best seller.[6]

Upton Sinclair believed that capitalism in the United States had reverted to the law of the jungle; for him, the horrifying conditions at meatpacking plants were but one example of a more widespread problem. He hoped his novel would generate sympathy for the working class and particularly for the immigrants toiling in Chicago's Packingtown. Sinclair described the conditions at the packing plants in nauseating detail, telling of dead rats and their feces being ground into sausage and inspectors who looked the other way when diseased animals unfit for human consumption were slaughtered and sold as meat. Publication of *The Jungle* sparked widespread public outrage—not so much about the workers' ill treatment, as Sinclair had hoped, but about the spoiled, tainted, and adulterated meat products coming out of Packingtown.

The Jungle was immediately attacked by the meatpacking industry. A series of articles appeared in the *Saturday Evening Post* under the byline of J. Ogden Armour, the son of the late Philip Armour and the owner and president of Armour and Company, one of America's largest meat companies. The articles denied the accuracy of the novel's depiction of the working conditions in the stockyards. Sinclair responded with an article in *Everybody's Magazine* giving evidence of the truth of his depictions and pointing out the factual inaccuracies in Armour's articles. Armour's writings received extensive coverage in other newspapers and magazines, but they showed disturbingly little interest in Sinclair's response. Sinclair concluded that the popular press was afraid of losing the meat-packers' advertising revenue and therefore would not publish negative articles about the industry, which was most likely true.[7]

While Sinclair was delighted with the lavish attention his book had received from the press, and overjoyed with the resulting royalties, he was disappointed by the public's response to his novel. In October 1906, he wrote in *Cosmopolitan*, "I wished to frighten the country by a picture of what its industrial masters were doing to their victims; entirely by chance I had stumbled on another discovery—what they were doing to the meat-supply of the civilized world. In other words, I aimed at the public's heart and I hit its stomach."[8] Perhaps he should not have been surprised at the lack of interest in workers' rights considering his vivid picture of diseased animals, rotten meat spiked with chemical preservatives, tubercular workers, and rat-infested meatpacking factories.[9]

The Jungle cannot be given sole credit for the passage of the pure-food legislation that followed its appearance; there were many other factors in play. Perhaps the most important was the strong support of President Theodore Roosevelt. Doubleday had sent Roosevelt a prepublication copy, which he promptly read. He was sensitive to the issue from his service in the American military during the Spanish-American War. There was an incident involving soldiers' being sent "embalmed meat," heavily treated with preservatives, and they refused to accept it. The U.S. Army held hearings on the meat and other provisions sent to the military during the war, and Roosevelt had testified about its poor quality. Nonetheless, he did not trust Sinclair's account, so, in early April, Roosevelt sent Charles P. Neill, commissioner of labor, and James Reynolds, a New York lawyer, to Chicago to inspect the meatpacking factories. Even though the plants had been partially cleaned up, Neill and Reynolds still found revolting conditions, and their disclosures convinced Roosevelt to support the legislation. When the meat-packers attacked the accuracy of Sinclair's observations, Roosevelt released the Neill-Reynolds report, which substantiated the stories in *The Jungle*, fueled a public outcry, and generated a landslide of public support for the proposed legislation.

Sinclair was not alone in his criticism of the meat industry. Popular journalist Charles Edward Russell, for example, went inside the "beef trust." At the same time Sinclair's articles were running in the *Appeal to Reason*, *Everybody's Magazine* was serializing Russell's story, titled "The Greatest Trust in the World." His non-fiction book of the same name had been published in 1905—months before *The Jungle*'s release. Evidently both men were unaware they were working on similar stories. Russell's book, however, never achieved the fame of *The Jungle*.[10]

Sinclair's and Russell's books were not, to be sure, the first to focus on food safety. It had been a topic of discussion before the Civil War, and a steady, if muffled, drumbeat of concern and alarm had been audible ever since. State legislatures in Massachusetts, Illinois, New York, New Jersey, and other states began passing pure-food laws in 1857, although the laws were often not enforced.[11] In 1879, Italy restricted importation of American pigs, and during the 1880s, other European countries followed suit on the grounds that American meat was diseased. To combat these export problems, pure-food bills were introduced into Congress every year beginning in 1879, but they failed despite a growing public awareness of and concern with industrialized food. Opposition to federal legislation came from agricultural interests fearful of losing domestic markets, food processors opposed to federal control, and political conservatives opposed to governmental interference in the marketplace. These powerful opponents were buyers of advertising space in newspapers and magazines, so many periodical publishers showed no support for pure-food legislation and rarely printed articles exposing food adulteration. Most Americans were consequently abysmally ignorant of problems in the nation's food-supply system.

Yet another force behind pure-food legislation was Harvey W. Wiley, who had earned his M.D. degree from Indiana Medical College and then studied at Harvard and in Germany. In 1874, he accepted an appointment as the first professor of chemistry at the newly founded Purdue University, in Lafayette, Indiana. He was subsequently appointed to the position of Indiana state chemist, and, in this capacity, he conducted studies of food and beverage adulterations for the State Board of Health.[12]

In 1883, Wiley was appointed chief chemist in the U.S. Department of Agriculture. With characteristic thoroughness, he concentrated on the wholesomeness of the nation's food. From this national position, he conducted studies of food adulteration and contamination. Wiley was also a persuasive writer and speaker, and he believed that part of his responsibility was to educate the American public about his findings. His evangelical zeal led him to speak at many gatherings, of both laypersons and scientists. He inspired Alice Lakey, of the Consumers' League, to support a national food law and formed coalitions with the General Federation of Women's Clubs and the Association of Official Agricultural Chemists, which established, in 1897, a committee on food standards, chaired by Wiley.

Bowing to pressure generated by Wiley and his coalitions, the Senate, in 1899, began hearings on pure-food legislation. Although the Senate again failed to pass the legislation, the hearings contributed to a growing surge of agitation in the nascent pure-food movement.[13]

At the time of the Louisiana Purchase Exposition in Saint Louis in 1904, a pure-food congress was held simultaneously with the annual meeting of the National Association of State Dairy and Food Departments. At these two meetings, food reformers from around the country and some international representatives came together to discuss pure-food issues. At the exposition, a booth was set up next to the exhibit hosted by manufacturers of preserved foods to lend visibility to the pure-food movement. The booth displayed over 2,000 adulterated products manufactured in the United States, each with a chemist's seal attesting to its noxious contents. Adulterated items came from every state.[14] Food manufacturers considered getting an injunction against the display but decided that legal action would only give the pure-food movement more publicity.

The display was the brainchild of Robert Allen, the food and drug administrator in Kentucky. Allen had met Wiley in 1902, and the two had become fast friends. The following year, Allen was elected secretary of the National Association of State Dairy and Food Departments, a position he held for the next seven years. Under Allen's influence, the association endorsed national pure-food legislation that had been proposed by Wiley. In February 1905, a committee of six supporters, headed by Allen, met with President Teddy Roosevelt to solicit his support of pure-food legislation. Roosevelt listened to what the delegation had to say and asked them to return in the fall. At their fall meeting, Roosevelt told them he would ask Congress to consider pure-food legislation. In his annual message to Congress, he recommended that a "law be enacted to regulate interstate commerce in misbranded and adulterated foods, drinks, and drugs."[15]

The agitation for state and national pure-food legislation disturbed food manufacturers across America. Business leaders worried about the potential elimination of preservatives such as carbolic acid, borax, boric acid, salicylic acid, benzoic acids, and the benzoates, which gave their products a long shelf life and increased profits. They formed the Association of Manufacturers and Distributors of Food Products, based in Boston. The association asserted that it stood for honest labeling of all food products and that members guaranteed that their products were "wholesome and free from deleterious, objectionable or unhealthy ingredients." By 1903, the Joseph Campbell Preserve Company, Curtice Brothers, P. J. Ritter Conserve Company, Williams Brothers, and thirty other businesses had become members. Despite its public statements, the association remained opposed to the elimination of many preservatives, believing them to be safe and outside the purview of federal government regulation.[16]

Walter H. Williams, president of Williams Brothers, in Detroit, was a leader of the opposition to pure-food laws. He believed that preservatives were a necessary ingredient in many canned and bottled foods. He was opposed to national food legislation mainly because he presumed that Wiley would administer the law, and Wiley was opposed to the use of any and all chemical preservatives in prepared foods. In 1901, Williams hired E. O. Grosvenor, former food commissioner for Michigan, to lobby against pure-food legislation and otherwise protect the interests of manufacturers.[17]

Initially, Wiley and other pure-food advocates only wanted manufacturers to identify preservatives and colorings on their product labels. In a speech to the Household Economic Association in November 1904, Wiley asked simply that foods be honestly labeled: "Then if people want to eat dyes and poisons, they alone are responsible." Again, at the Retail Grocers' Association meeting in Philadelphia in February 1905, Wiley stated that adulterations need not be abolished, only "honestly labeled."[18] Labeling laws were eventually passed in many states. Under these laws, commissioners could declare that products were misbranded if chemical analysis proved preservatives had been used in the product but not listed on the label. Despite this shift, the food and drug bill did not make it out of the Senate in 1905, leading the *Nation* to charge, in an editorial, that the failure to pass the food bill was "a capital illustration of the Senate's treasons, stratagems, and spoils."[19]

Jungle Effects

Harvey Wiley was the stalwart, immutable force behind pure-food legislation, but, despite his unflagging support for it, beginning in 1882, no new laws had been passed by Congress. The main difference in 1906 was the timely publication of Upton Sinclair's *The Jungle*, which outraged the American public and convinced President Roosevelt to intervene in support of the legislation. Good as Sinclair's intentions were in writing *The Jungle*, it had a tremendous impact on American food in the form of the Pure Food and Drugs Act and the Meat Inspection Act. Neither was expected to make it through Congress, but pass they did. A front-page article in the *New York Times* proclaimed that the Meat Inspection Act's passage was "the direct consequence of the disclosures made in Upton Sinclair's novel, 'The Jungle.'"[20]

Judging by public comment at the time, and according to historians in subsequent decades, the publication of *The Jungle* was the reason the legislation passed.[21] Most surprisingly, however, Sinclair opposed the bills. He believed the watered-down Meat Inspection Act would benefit meat-packers and not improve working conditions. In his prediction, Sinclair was right: the Meat Inspection Act and the Pure Food and Drugs Act indeed assisted large packers, who could more easily meet the new federal standards, and the passage of these laws convinced many Americans that commercial meat and canned goods were safe; as a result, working conditions for laborers did not make the national agenda for decades.

With regard to issues raised in *The Jungle*, the Meat Inspection Act empowered federal inspectors to examine animals before and after slaughter, to be present when diseased animals were destroyed, and to inspect processed products for dangerous chemicals, preservatives, or dyes. In addition, no meat that had not been inspected could be shipped across state lines. The Pure Food and Drugs Act established a regulatory body to set and enforce safety standards for thousands of different foods to prevent their adulteration or mislabeling. It also mandated truth in labeling. Despite its flaws, this law did establish the federal government's responsibility in preventing abuses perpetrated by businesses. The surprise effect of the legislation's assurance of a safe and wholesome food supply was that, as Americans became more confident that meat and processed foods were safe, sales of these foods soared. The two acts boosted sales of processed foods and the profitability of the large food companies, which could more easily comply with the legislation's requirements, and many small companies went out of business.[22]

Postscript

Upton Sinclair used the windfall royalties from the sale of his book to create a socialist commune in Englewood, New Jersey. But the commune's buildings burned down in 1907, and Sinclair, again penniless, returned to writing novels. He eventually wrote close to a hundred, but none ever came close to the popularity, influence, or financial success of *The Jungle*, which has rarely been out of print since it was first published.

Sinclair left the Socialist Party during World War I, when the party refused to support the war effort. Sinclair settled in California, and, during the Depression, unsuccessfully ran for governor of the state. Somewhat ironically, his candidacy was strongly opposed by William Randolph Hearst, who had serialized *The Jungle* in his newspapers in 1906. Sinclair died in 1968.

As a result of his support of food-safety legislation, Harvey Wiley became the first chief of the newly created Bureau of Chemistry, which was responsible for enforcing the Pure Food and Drugs Act. Under Wiley's direction, the real work of cleansing the nation's food supply of contaminants and impurities began. With Wiley's guidance, standards for food safety were established. The Bureau of Chemistry had the power to bring criminal charges against violators and confiscate adulterated, contaminated, or mislabeled food. In 1930, the Bureau of Chemistry was renamed the Food and Drug Administration (FDA).

Packing Bird's Eye frozen food (Library of Congress Prints and Photographs Division)

18.

Frozen Seafood and TV Dinners

I N 1912, Clarence Birdseye, an Amherst College dropout, headed north to become a fur trader in Labrador, Canada. While there, he later alleged, he made a discovery—that "foods frozen quickly in the dead of winter kept their freshness as long as they were kept at a very low temperature."[1] When he returned to the United States, in 1915, as a hobby he began experimenting with ways to quick-freeze food. As he later told the story, he began his experiments with seven dollars' worth of equipment, salt, ice, and an electric fan. By 1924, he had perfected the process and, with three partners, founded the General Seafoods Company, in Gloucester, Massachusetts. Thus Clarence Birdseye helped create a new industry that has reshaped what Americans eat at home and in restaurants ever since.

Frozen History

Clarence Birdseye was not the first person to freeze food as a way of preserving it. People have understood the principles of the process for centuries. In Colonial America, cool, underground cellars were known to be the best place to preserve food. By the late eighteenth century, Americans were using ice to cool cellars wherever local conditions permitted. A flourishing ice trade began in the early nineteenth century, and by 1830, New Englanders were harvesting blocks of lake ice during the winter and spring for shipment to insulated icehouses along the nation's coasts and navigable rivers. Ice was thus obtainable in large cities year-round.[2]

For those who could afford it, ice was also used for making frozen drinks and ice cream, which became fashionable in the early nineteenth century. Frozen poultry was sometimes shipped by wagon and boat to eastern cities from the Midwest, but only during the winter months, and ice was occasionally used to freeze fish on ships at sea as well. After the Civil War, the ice trade expanded to include foreign markets.

Ice cooling had its limitations, however. Ice was bulky and expensive to transport; storing and distributing it required insulated buildings and a well-organized system of ships and ice wagons. Lake ice contained impurities, so it could not be used for human consumption. Even after machines had been invented that could manufacture pure ice, problems persisted: Melting ice generated moisture that fostered the growth of mold and bacteria, creating unhealthy conditions in the ice box or ice room. As important, ice was effective for chilling or freezing only when in direct contact with food. In a room or cabinet, ice could not, even when combined with salt, lower the temperature of food much below the freezing point.

Mechanical cooling systems based on absorption and condensation were devised in the 1870s. These systems could lower the temperature of food well below freezing, making them much more efficient than ice boxes. By the 1870s, therefore, frozen meat was being shipped from the United States to the United Kingdom.[3] The new technology made freezing food a viable option and encouraged the growth of the frozen food trade. Livestock, for example, could be slaughtered and butchered close to where it was raised, then shipped in refrigerated train cars to cities hundreds or thousands of miles away. Since this system required large amounts of capital, it also contributed to the centralization of the livestock industry, and it was during this period major meat-packers, such as Swift and Armour, emerged.

The availability of frozen foods offered a number of advantages to both food suppliers and consumers. Among them was its encouragement of regional specialization; that is, fruits and vegetables could be grown in a particular area but then frozen and shipped anywhere, hundreds or even thousands of miles to market. Since frozen foods could be stored for longer periods, farmers and distributors could sell their products when they would obtain the highest price. Freezing also expanded consumers' food choices, making produce available well beyond its local growing season. Moreover, consumers benefitted from the greater stability of food prices resulting from the possibility of freezing food. Frozen foods were particularly useful for restaurants: they enabled a small kitchen to supply a diverse demand and permitted restaurant chains to centralize their cooking, thereby lowering costs.

Frozen foods did have major drawbacks, however. Manufacturers had to educate a skeptical public about their products. Many people believed that frozen foods were unhealthful; others did not like the taste or smell of thawed food; and still others complained about the cost of frozen food. These complaints were justified during the industry's early years, when the process of freezing, storing, and transporting frozen food was still in its infancy. Some companies froze inferior-quality food, knowing that it would be impossible for consumers to tell the difference between good and bad food at the point of sale. Some retailers thawed or refroze foods before selling them, thus speeding deterioration and spoilage. There were few trucks equipped with the proper equipment for keeping the food frozen while traversing the distance from the point of manufacture to the point of sale.

Corporate laboratories and the U.S. Department of Agriculture eventually took steps to deal with such problems. They made recommendations on such matters as the rapidity with which foods needed to be frozen, freezing methods, storage temperatures, dehydration, and the length of time frozen foods could be stored without spoilage. Still, doubts about frozen food did not disappear entirely, and the industry engaged in mass promotional efforts to win over consumers. Package design also became important—both to prevent dehydration during storage and to attract shoppers. Some technical problems associated with frozen foods were solved during the 1920s, a period that also witnessed a drop in the cost of frozen foods and the more widespread use of home refrigerators with small freezers.

Clarence Birdseye

One strand in the history of frozen food in America can be traced to Clarence Birdseye, a field naturalist and taxidermist. While a student at Amherst, he worked for the U.S. Geological Survey (USGS) during the summers, before moving to Labrador in 1912. When he returned to the United States in 1915, he went back to work for the USGS. In 1918, he served as an administrative assistant for the U.S. Fisheries Association. These positions enabled him to support his growing family while pursuing his interest in experimenting with freezing seafood. Early on, Birdseye had concluded that quick-freezing fish in the Arctic created small ice crystals that left the cell structure, taste, and texture of the fish intact; he began experimenting with ways to duplicate this flash-freezing process in the laboratory using multiple metal plates. In 1922, he went into the frozen fish business with a group of investors, but they couldn't make a go of it. Rather than give up, however, Birdseye borrowed funds on his life insurance policy and tried again with new partners. In 1924, they formed, in Gloucester, Massachusetts, the General Seafoods Company.[4]

Birdseye's contribution wasn't limited to the process of freezing seafood, however; more important was the moisture-proof cellophane packaging he devised, which permitted food to be frozen faster and kept it from disintegrating when thawed.[5] Birdseye also championed the use of the freshest-possible food in the freezing process. But the public knew little about frozen foods at the time, and it was years before home freezers were common. Most stores were not equipped with freezers, either, and Birdseye was unable to establish a distribution system for his products. He approached the Postum Company, makers of Grape-Nuts and Bran Flakes. They began working with Birdseye and saw the potential of frozen foods. The Postum Company, renamed General Foods, made an offer to Birdseye. In June 1929, a few months before the October stock-market crash that marked the beginning of the Great Depression, Birdseye sold the General Seafoods Company—and its 168 patents—to General Foods for $22 million.[6] Despite his millionaire status, Birdseye continued working with General Foods to improve the process of freezing food.

Even as the Depression deepened, General Foods invested the capital necessary for promoting and marketing frozen food. They trademarked the name Birds Eye and began a broad promotional effort. Sales were insignificant until the mid-1930s, largely because of the unwillingness of grocery stores to invest the thousand dollars needed to purchase a small freezer, which held relatively little product. As other companies entered the market, however, such freezers became more common, and, by 1941, Birds Eye Food had sold 100 million pounds of frozen food.[7]

Before World War II, the main frozen foods available were peas, beans, corn, spinach, berries, cherries, apples, and peaches. During the war, canned foods were in short supply on the home front because the armed forces needed canned goods for the war effort since they were less perishable and more easily shipped overseas. Frozen foods containing meat were rationed, but frozen fruits and vegetables, which did not require metal in their packaging, became more widely available during the war. Consequently, many Americans tried frozen foods for the first time during this period.

Frozen prepared foods, such as chicken à la king, first came on the market in 1939, but they did not become popular in the United States until after the war. The makers of Breyers Ice Cream took an exotic tack, marketing frozen chow mein and chop suey with vegetables under the brand name Golden Pagoda.[8] After the war, an avalanche of new frozen foods hit the market, such as Sara

Lee cakes, Quaker Oats waffles, Swanson chicken potpies, and Birds Eye fish sticks. Sales of frozen foods reached at this time 1 billion pounds, an impressive development that encouraged fly-by-night outfits to enter the market with poor-quality products that gave frozen foods a bad name.

Frozen Dinners

During World War II, the Naval Air Transport Service flew planes long distances over the Atlantic. Some flights lasted as many as six hours and required food service. At first, the service operators brought fresh food on board and prepared meals in flight, but it soon became apparent that it would be easier to bring frozen food on board and just heat it up. They contracted Maxson Food Systems, a division of W. L. Maxson Corporation, of New York, to produce frozen food for in-flight meals. Called Strato-Plates, these first frozen in-flight meals offered a portion of meat—ham, breaded veal cutlets, or beef stew—and two vegetables, such as potatoes, sweet potatoes, french fries, beans, or peas. Maxson cooked each food individually to the point where the entire meal would require only fifteen minutes to finish cooking. The partially cooked food was then dished onto processed-paper plates with three compartments, quick-frozen, and shipped to the airport. On the plane, the meals were heated and served on the same plates. The company also invented the Maxson Whirlwind oven, which blew hot air through the box to heat the frozen meals in fifteen minutes.[9] Commercial airliners, such as Pan Am, also used Maxson's frozen meals and ovens on long flights. After the war, the company changed the name to Sky Plates and marketed an expanded line to the public, but they did not catch on. The Sky Plates were too complicated to manufacture, too expensive, and they proved unprofitable. Maxson pulled out of the frozen-food business.[10]

Other companies took up where Maxson had left off. In 1947, Philadelphian Jack Fisher formed FrigiDinner, Inc., which sold ten "variety platters"—frozen dinners in aluminum trays—for bars, railroad dinning cars, and airlines. Pittsburgh brothers Albert and Meyer Bernstein started Frozen Dinners, Inc., in 1949. It sold frozen dinners on aluminum trays under the trademark One-Eyed Eskimo. The Bernstein brothers formed the Quaker State Food Corporation in 1952, and within two years, they had sold more than 2.5 million frozen dinners. Stouffer's, in Cleveland, Ohio, began producing frozen dinners in early 1953. Nevertheless, frozen meals had yet to capture the public imagination, and, to tell the truth, they didn't taste very good.[11]

What did appeal to Americans was frozen orange juice, which was first marketed, unsuccessfully, in the 1930s. Experiments eventually demonstrated that removing much of the water from the orange juice before freezing enhanced the taste. Frozen orange juice concentrate went on sale in 1945, and less than a decade later, it accounted for 20 percent of the entire frozen-food market.[12]

Another slice of frozen-food history began with Carl A. Swanson, a Swedish immigrant who had come to the United States in 1896, at the age of seventeen. Swanson worked on a farm in Blair, Nebraska, for a while and then moved to Omaha, where he worked in a grocery store during the day and took courses in accounting at night. While working at the grocery store, he met John O. Jerpe, who owned a small commission company. The Jerpe Commission Company bought eggs and cream from local farmers, processed the eggs, made butter from the cream, and sold these products to distributors, charging a commission to the farmers. In 1899, Swanson invested his savings and became a partner in Jerpe's company. With Swanson on board, the company began to expand, selling chicken, turkey, and other meats. Swanson did well in the business, and, in 1928, he bought the company from Jerpe. Swanson's sons, Gilbert and W. Clarke, joined the business, and, in the 1940s, the company's name was changed to C. A. Swanson and Sons.[13]

Among many other products, the Swansons specialized in poultry. In 1935, Birds Eye Foods, then a division of General Foods, selected the C. A. Swanson company as their supplier of frozen turkeys. Birds Eye leased the needed patented freezing technology to the Swansons, who thus learned the frozen food business. That first year, the Swansons packed a modest 60,000 pounds of food.[14]

Birds Eye wanted more, so Carl Swanson leased a large Colorado warehouse and converted it into a cold-storage facility, which allowed him to create a sizable turkey-processing operation. In 1936, Swanson guaranteed farmers in February that he would purchase their turkeys in September. As this was at the depth of the Depression, when many families were struggling just to keep their farms, Swanson also advanced funds in the spring to help pay for feed and other expenses; the farmers would repay him in the fall when he bought their turkeys. This system worked well during times of scarcity as well as in times of plenty: In the spring, when turkeys were in short supply, Swanson could get them at a guaranteed price from his farmers while other processors had to pay more. In the fall, when turkeys were plentiful, Swanson froze them to sell in the spring, when the supply was limited. By 1942, Carl Swanson had become the nation's largest turkey processor, and *Fortune* magazine dubbed him the Turkey King of the country.[15]

During the late 1940s, Swanson began a poultry-buying spree, purchasing millions of chickens and turkeys from California to Minnesota. Now the question was what to do with all the frozen poultry not purchased by Birds Eye. Swanson's sons believed that the company should get into the heat-and-serve food business using Birds Eye's quick-freezing technology and packaging. When Carl Swanson died in 1949, his sons began manufacturing frozen oven-ready chicken and turkey potpies in aluminum trays. These proved an instant success, and, by 1951, the potpies were being distributed through most U.S. supermarkets. No matter how many potpies the Swanson plants produced, they had a hard time keeping up with demand. At the peak, the company was turning out 250,000 pies per day.[16] This phenomenal success encouraged the Swansons to consider other possible frozen foods and meals.

About this time, Gerry Thomas, a Swanson company executive, visited Frozen Dinners, Inc., in Pittsburgh. Frozen Dinners was one of Swanson's distributors; it prepared in-flight food for Pan Am's overseas flights. These airline meals were packed in aluminum trays that could be heated in on-board convection ovens. Maxson had tried selling such frozen meals in supermarkets, but it had been unsuccessful. The meals gave Thomas an idea, though. He took a three-compartment aluminum tray back to Omaha and proposed that the Swansons fill it with frozen sliced turkey and side dishes for serving at home.[17]

The brothers liked the idea, and Gilbert Swanson began work on the production end while the company's food technologist, twenty-two-year-old Betty Cronin, started in on the technical issues. The production crew came up with a prototype consisting of a rectangular aluminum tray with three compartments: a large one for a turkey entrée with giblet gravy and stuffing and two smaller compartments for side dishes—whipped sweet potatoes and green peas with a pat of butter. The tray was sealed with aluminum foil. Twenty-five minutes in the oven at 425°F, and the meal was ready to eat. Several thousand of these meals were test marketed in cities from Omaha to Chicago. They were initially called the Television Dinner, piggybacking on the popularity of the exciting new technology that was just entering mainstream American life. Clarke Swanson spearheaded marketing, distribution, and sales. A Chicago-based advertising firm, Tatham Laird Company, designed a six-color package featuring a television set. At the time, most frozen-food packaging was printed in two colors, so Swanson's Television Dinner was sure to stand out in the grocery store freezer case.[18]

It was a risky venture. Historically, turkey was eaten mainly during the fall and winter, around Thanksgiving and Christmas. No one knew if Americans would eat it other times of the year. In addition, frozen foods had not yet been completely accepted by the American public. Although many people had tried them for the first time during and after World War II, there was still little consumer enthusiasm for them in the early 1950s. Moreover, there were still obstacles related to frozen-food processing, marketing, and storage, and large freezers remained uncommon in grocery stores as well as homes.

The test marketing of Swanson's Television Dinners proved successful, however, and the company expanded the line to include chicken and beef entrées as well as different side dishes. The Swansons invested heavily in promotion, and they shortened the product's name to TV Dinner.[19] The new dinners were officially rolled out for food editors in October 1953, and two months later the product hit the national market.[20] By 1956, the Swanson company was selling 13 million TV Dinners annually. This phenomenal feat can be attributed in part to the product's name, TV Dinner, which suggested to purchasers that the meals were meant to be eaten in front of a television set.[21]

The TV Dinner's packaging was also a factor in its success. The six-color, laminated parchment box "was the wonder of the industry because it reproduced the contents with such stunning, lip-smacking fidelity." The design itself imitated the appearance of a television set, with simulated knobs and a wood-grain finish.[22] Finally, at ninety-eight cents apiece (Swanson's cost was only twenty cents), TV Dinners were a cheap alternative to a home-cooked meal.[23] Swanson may not have been the first company to market frozen dinners, but it was certainly the one to popularize and cash in on them.

Frozen Effects

In postwar America, consumers were increasingly interested in faster, more convenient meal preparation. As culinary historian Warren Belasco has noted, "Underlying all such dishes was impatience with traditional, labor-intensive cooking."[24] The success of frozen dinners was assured as women, the traditional home cooks, increasingly went into the workforce. Simultaneously, the 1950s were the height of the postwar baby boom, and these working mothers came home to hungry young children. Women simply did not have the time they once had for preparing traditional meals for their families. Food manufacturers had come to recognize this by the 1950s, and they set about making heat-and-eat meals common American fare.[25] Today, frozen food—whether Salisbury steak or mac and cheese, soy burgers or enchiladas—is most frequently reheated in the microwave, shaving minutes off the already short preparation time.

Frozen dinners were convenient and easy to prepare and came in disposable dishes. The kids were happy with them and so were overworked mothers, who usually prepared the meals after a hard day's work. Along with frozen dinners came inexpensive folding trays that were "perfect for TV dining," and soon it was not unusual to find the whole family eating in front of the television set—instead of at the traditional dining table.[26]

Frozen dinners also made it possible for each family member to eat a different meal at the same—or a different—time. This further eroded family conversation and communication, especially when the TV was on. The tradition of eating family meals together at the table began to disappear in the late 1950s, partly because of frozen dinners. Today, the average American family eats fewer than five meals together per week. The end of the family meal also meant changes in "family relationships, cultural identity, ethnic diversity," which were traditionally linked to preparing and consuming meals together.[27]

As the volume of sales of frozen foods escalated, prices dropped, and lower prices allowed more people to purchase packaged dinners. Less than two years after the TV Dinner's introduction, twenty-five companies were producing complete frozen dinners, and the frozen food industry had reached $1.5 billion in annual sales. Many new companies entered the field. In 1954, Campbell's Soup released a line of frozen soups, concluding that frozen foods were the culinary wave of the future. The following year, Campbell's purchased C. A. Swanson and Sons and expanded its line of frozen foods to sixty-five items. By 1959, a quarter of a billion TV dinners had been sold. At the time, more than 1,000 frozen-food processors were generating collectively annual sales of $2.7 billion—a 2,700 percent increase since 1949.[28] By 1965, the total sales of frozen food had reached $5.2 billion, and the industry has continued to grow ever since. As of 2007, Americans directly consume $25 billion worth of frozen-food products annually, and additional billions of dollars' worth of frozen foods are served in restaurants, fast-food chains, cafeterias, hospitals, schools, military installations, and other outlets.

Postscript

Clarke Swanson died in 1961; Gilbert died seven years later;[29] Gerry Thomas died in 2005.

The General Foods Company, owners of the Birds Eye brand of frozen food, was acquired, in 1985, by Philip Morris. Four years later, General Foods and Kraft were combined to create Kraft General Foods. Today, Kraft Foods is one of the largest food companies in America.

The success of the frozen TV Dinner encouraged others to jump into the market, and thousands of similar products have since been created. Swanson's TV Dinners slowly lost market share to their varied competition. Pinnacle Foods Corporation acquired Swanson in 2001 and, in 2004, celebrated the TV Dinner's fiftieth anniversary.

Interior of Piggly Wiggly (Library of Congress Prints and Photographs Division)

19.

Michael Cullen's Super Market

IN THE MIDST of the Depression, Michael J. Cullen did something unusual: While everyone else in the country was just trying to hold on to their jobs, he quit, in 1930, his at the Kroger Grocery and Baking Company. Even more surprising, while other grocery stores were going under, he opened a new one, in Jamaica Estates, New York. His store, called King Kullen, was larger than was common at the time, and he filled it with an unprecedented variety of products. By increasing sales volume, Cullen was able to cut prices and stimulate profits. King Kullen's newspaper and radio ads asked, "King Kullen, the world's greatest price wreckers, how does he do it?" Customers were willing to travel farther to take advantage of his low prices. Soon other entrepreneurs were opening even larger stores, called supermarkets.[1] Today, supermarkets supply most of the food Americans eat at home; what's sold—and not sold—at supermarkets has a huge influence on what we eat.

Super History

For almost 300 years, public markets had been the primary retail and wholesale food source for urban Americans. Financed and regulated by municipalities, public markets were originally scheduled events held in the streets one or two days a week, and vendors would come with wagons or pushcarts to offer their wares, often products they had grown, raised, or made themselves. Later, permanent indoor markets were set up where vendors could rent stalls. In small towns, or communities without public markets, general stores supplied merchandise. As American cities grew larger, specialization emerged. Small grocery stores selling both perishable and nonperishable foods appeared, and, by the mid-nineteenth century, family-owned grocery stores far outnumbered public markets.

The family owners of such grocery stores were startled when the Great Atlantic Tea Company was founded by George F. Gilman and George H. Hartford around 1860. Gilman, the owner of a leather company, also dabbled in shipping interests. He imported small consignments of tea, which he sold to wholesalers. Hartford, his assistant, convinced Gilman that they would make more money if they cut out the middlemen and retailed the tea themselves. Gilman, with Hartford, subsequently opened a retail tea store in New York City, and they also began selling tea through the mail. Three years later, they named their business the Great American Tea Company. Sales were good enough that Gilman and Hartford started buying tea in bulk, allowing them to lower their expenses even further and undersell other grocers. They expanded their line to include coffee and other luxury products. By 1865, the partners had five small stores in New York City, thus creating America's first grocery chain. The completion of the transcontinental railroad, in 1869, made it possible for the company to receive shipments of tea and other specialty goods from Asia via San Francisco, and then ship them by train throughout the country. Hartford and Gilman began opening stores across the nation, and they changed the name of their new, bicoastal company to the Great Atlantic and Pacific Tea Company, subsequently shortened to A&P. Over the next few decades, the A&P stores gradually augmented their inventory to include a full range of groceries.[2]

The early success of A&P was condemned by independent grocers, who attacked the company for its predatory pricing and destruction of small family-owned businesses. Despite such criticism, A&P built more stores and expanded its product lines. By 1925, A&P had more than 14,000 stores across the United States.[3]

Other entrepreneurs, impressed by A&P's success, started their own grocery chains. The Jones Brothers Tea Company was founded in Scranton, Pennsylvania, in 1872 by Cyrus, Frank, and Charles Jones When the brothers expanded their chain into New York, they changed the name to Grand Union Tea Company, soon shortened to Grand Union. In 1883, Bernard H. Kroger began a chain store operation in Cincinnati. Two German immigrants, brothers Charles and Diedrich Gristede, opened their first grocery store, in New York, in 1891. In Los Angeles in 1906, Charles Von der Ahe opened a store that came to be known as Von's.

In Boise, Idaho, Marion Skaggs started the Skaggs Cash Stores chain in 1916. Ten years later, it merged with another grocery chain to create the Safeway stores.

Albert Gerrard and his brother Hugh opened a butcher shop in downtown Pomona, California, in 1900. Within fourteen years, they had expanded it to a small grocery store called the Triangle Grocerteria. As at most grocery stores of the time, Grocerteria's clerks would take the customer's shopping list and scurry about the store collecting the items. When the Gerrards moved their store to a larger building, in 1915, they decided to let the customers pick up their own merchandise. They placed a sign in the window: "We know you will like our system— Wait on yourself, No Clerk." To make it easier for customers to find what they wanted, the Gerrards positioned each product in alphabetical order. To capitalize on their novel concept, they named their stores Alpha Beta Food Markets.[4]

In 1916, Clarence Saunders established the first King Piggly-Wiggly grocery store, in Memphis, Tennessee. It was the first store to call itself self-serving, and clerks served only as cashiers. Able to run the store with minimum staff, Saunders could lower prices and undersell his competition. Within eight years, Saunders had a chain of over 1,000 self-serving stores. But then other grocery store chains began to follow his example. Saunders had to borrow money to keep up, and he eventually lost control of the business.[5]

The term "supermarket" was first used in the grocery trade in Southern California, in the 1920s. Around Los Angeles, where land was relatively inexpensive, chains such as McDaniel's, Ralph's Grocery Company, and Alpha Beta constructed warehouselike stores organized into departments, and some had parking lots. These self-service warehouses were about ten times larger than normal grocery stores at the time and had a far greater selection of foods. They also had parking lots, so they were more convenient for suburban customers, who got into the habit of stocking up in a single weekly bout of "one-stop shopping."[6] City shoppers continued to make the rounds of small local stores on a daily basis, but suburbanites preferred a weekly shopping trip—even more so when larger refrigerators and home freezers became available in the late 1940s, which allowed them to stock up on months' worth of chilled and frozen foods when they were on sale.

Management of smaller corporate chains and affiliated independents at first ignored the success of the early Southern California supermarkets, believing these oversized stores were just a passing phase. Two developments changed their minds, however. The first was engineered by Michael J. Cullen, founder of the King Kullen grocery chain. Cullen began as a clerk working in the A&P grocery store in Newark, New Jersey. He moved up in the A&P hierarchy and became the company's regional superintendent. Cullen left A&P and worked for other grocery store chains in the Midwest, and, by 1930, when he launched the King Kullen chain, in Jamaica Estates, New York, he knew much about the grocery business.[7] Cullen sold more than 1,000 basic food products at a lower cost than was that offered by local grocery stores. He offered free parking in lots adjacent to the store, and customers with cars flocked to his store. When his first store proved a success, he quickly opened more, so that, by 1936, fifteen stores were serving Long Island and the Bronx. King Kullen's success encouraged others, and a display-space race commenced. In 1932, the Big Bear store, in Elizabeth, New Jersey, was set up in an abandoned automobile factory with 50,000 square feet. It attracted 200,000 customers with gross sales of $90,000 every week. Other, small retailers saw the writing on the cash register and opened similar operations in abandoned factories and buildings. Their goal was to generate a small profit on each sale, undercutting traditional chain and independent grocery stores by at least 10 to 15 percent but making up the difference with a much larger sales volume.[8]

In the New York area alone, these new supermarkets generated annual sales in excess of $15 million, which may not seem like a lot today, but it was a small fortune during the Depression. With this kind of cash in play, no problem was too big to be resolved by the new supermarkets. When local communities restricted the distribution of supermarket fliers, supermarkets hired blimps to promote their establishments. When two biscuit suppliers refused to sell to a certain supermarket, citing the low price the store offered, the supermarket began buying biscuits in bulk and packaging them in an operation adjacent to the store.[9] Suppliers got the message and lowered their prices. Grocery store chains and independent grocers got the message, too, and scrambled to catch up.

The second reason why supermarkets took off was the Depression, which hit America just as Michael Cullen was opening his first supermarket. Price became the all-important factor in where consumers chose to shop, and supermarkets offered much lower prices than small stores. Shoppers were willing to forgo the pleasant atmosphere and personal attention of a small grocery store for the chill, cavernous supermarket with its lower prices. Beginning in the mid-1930s, many grocery chains closed their smaller stores and opened large supermarkets. Independent grocers were unable to follow suit, and tens of thousands went out of business during the late 1930s and early 1940s.

World War II slowed the growth of supermarkets as wartime restrictions halted construction, foods were rationed, and many food processors concentrated on military contracts. Before the war, almost all grocery clerks had been young men; as they enlisted and left their jobs, women filled their places. When the war ended, women continued to work in supermarkets. The postwar period also saw a tremendous growth in the number of supermarkets, from 10,000 in 1946 to 17,000 in

1953.[10] Their capital resources gave them a head start in the rush to construct new, suburban markets as they abandoned the less-lucrative, inner-city stores.

Large supermarket chains continued to press their advantage over smaller stores. The same sort of cost savings made possible by mass production applied to mass distribution. Supermarket chain managers were better able to control overhead costs and employ profit-saving devices. They could hire buyers who specialized in certain product lines, thereby maximizing volume purchasing and reducing unit costs. Supermarket chains also developed the most efficient ways of routing food items from centralized warehouses to retail stores; hub-warehouse operations saved both time and money. Some supermarket chains sold their own product lines that undercut brand-name prices; by relying on the store's own reputation, house brands obviated the need for expensive advertising campaigns. Chains also were able to promote themselves through premiums, special sales, and coupons, which were important sales builders in the mid-twentieth century.

Chains usually had better insurance than smaller operations, so if catastrophe struck—a fire or a flood, for instance—they were more likely to survive and rebuild. Chain operators could close financially troubled stores while keeping more successful locations open, thus making the corporation as a whole better able to survive economic hard times and shifts in local demographics. They also had the wherewithal to analyze and select the best sites for stores, and to continually establish new outlets. With the advent of television advertising, large chains gained a tremendous advantage in their ability to finance regional and then national ad campaigns.[11]

Finally, large supermarket chains had enormous purchasing power, which usually generated price breaks from manufacturers.[12] Purchasing power gave supermarkets tremendous power over food companies. Store management could add or eliminate a thousand items every year, depending on consumer response and sales. Large chains could threaten to discontinue particular products if the manufacturers or wholesalers would not offer sufficient discounts. This advantage made it difficult for small local and regional producers and manufacturers to compete with national and international operations.[13]

Still, America's supermarket chains developed symbiotic relationships with both their suppliers and their customers. Factory farms, which today supply most of the produce, meat, and poultry in the United States, found it easier to sell their products to a few large companies than to deal with many smaller operations. Manufacturers supported large supermarket chains because of the high volume they generated. Consumer groups supported the big chains because they offered lower prices than the independents.[14]

Over the past fifty years, the selection of products offered in supermarkets has grown substantially. In the 1940s, an average supermarket carried 3,000 different items; by the late 1950s, this had doubled. By the 1970s, supermarkets were stocking more than 10,000 items. Larger and larger stores have been constructed to house these products: the average supermarket is now about 30,000 square feet, and the very largest stores stock as many as 90,000 products in spaces of 50,000 square feet or larger. The seemingly unlimited variety of items in today's supermarkets is arranged in long rows of bright, attractive packages, with catchy names intended to attract shoppers and enhance sales. And it works. In 2007, the Food Marketing Institute reported that Americans expend $535.4 billion annually in supermarkets.[15]

Super Challenges

Supermarkets owe much of their success to changes in American demographics. As women entered the workforce during and after World War II, they were less willing or able to spend as much time shopping or cooking. As the twentieth century neared its end, however, other changes had a negative effect on supermarkets. In families with two employed parents, eating out and bringing home take-out meals came to replace a significant proportion of home-cooked dinners. Simultaneously, new competition arose for supermarkets. First there was the return of the public market, though in a more modern form. Since the 1970s, green markets, or farmers' markets, have sprung up in many urban areas, offering fresh produce, artisan breads, farmstead cheeses, and small-batch preserves. Many people appreciate the opportunity to buy directly from local farmers, who benefit tremendously from the direct sales.

A second significant challenge has been the rapid rise of small convenience stores. Neighborhood delis, bodegas, mom-and-pop shops, fruit stands, and roadside chains, such as 7-Eleven and WaWa stores, have proliferated during the past three decades. These stores typically stock everyday staples as well as a wide variety of snack foods. Although their prices are higher than those at supermarkets, people are willing to pay extra for the convenience, weighing the price of gas for a drive to the supermarket against a few cents extra for a quart of milk. Supermarkets have faced a third major challenge from new, upscale chains, such as Trader Joe's, Whole Foods, Fiesta Mart, and Central Market, which have cut into the sales of the more profitable "gourmet" and specialty products traditionally sold in supermarkets.

A third challenge arose when large retail general-merchandise chains such as Costco and Wal-Mart began selling grocery items. Founded in Seattle, Washington, in 1983 by James Sinegal and Jeffrey Brotman, Costco initially sold mainly packaged foods in large "economy" sizes, but it has since expanded into fresh produce, meats, seafood, baked goods, and liquor (where permitted by state or local laws). Wal-Mart Stores, started in 1962 in Bentonville, Arkansas, by Sam Walton, began as a discount department store. Expanding aggressively in the United States and then abroad, it had become, by the 1990s, the largest retail chain store in the world. In that same decade, Wal-Mart began selling bulk-purchased groceries at reduced prices. Wal-Mart's Supercenters and their volume division, Sam's Club (the latter, like Costco, a membership outlet), have been highly efficient in selling goods at reduced prices. Wal-Mart had virtually no sales of food in 1993; by 2001, it was the second-largest food retailer in America. Today the company is the largest seller of groceries in the world. Wal-Mart went from selling $66.5 billion of groceries in 2004 to $135 billion four years later, which was more than the next three chains combined. Kroger—the nation's second-largest chain, at $60.5 billion, was followed by Safeway, at $40 billion, Supervalu, at $33 billion, and Ahold, at $22 billion.[16]

Traditional supermarket chains have scrambled to meet these challenges. During the past few decades, many have added delis and are now selling more prepared items, bulk foods, and fresh-baked breads. Supermarkets also have diversified their product lines and installed new departments with organic, vegetarian, and ethnic foods, such as the Taquerias in Fiesta Marts, which sell Mexican food. Today, most supermarkets also issue membership or club cards that give shoppers additional discounts and ensure customer loyalty.

Supermarkets have also tried to meet the challenges by reducing their costs, particularly employee wages. Wal-Mart and some other supermarkets are non-union operations, so their employees have little bargaining power, but many other chains do have unionized workforces. A major expense in grocery operations is staff, but cutting costs by keeping down wages or cutting employee benefits inevitably creates labor problems. Over the years, strikes have occurred at many supermarket chains.

Super Effects

Supermarkets reshaped the marketing of processed food in America. Impulse or unplanned buying has been attributed to the rise of supermarkets. One study has suggested that as many as three-fourths of all supermarket purchases are unplanned. Banking on the trend, manufacturers have repackaged their products in attractive designs and colors to catch the attention of the impulse buyer, and supermarkets have been designed to force customers to walk all the way to the back of the store for the most commonly purchased staples, such as milk and bread. Shoppers thus pass by many more products and likely pick up some along the way.[17]

The growth of the American supermarket has resulted in some unintended consequences, however. As more and more products became available, shoppers had a harder time making intelligent choices, even after unit pricing became standard and nutrient information was required on packaged foods. Shoppers were more influenced by advertising and promotion, and today food companies as a category are one of the largest advertisers in the country. Foods that were not advertised disappeared; those that were promoted, thrived.

As for fresh foods, to satisfy a steady demand for fruits and vegetables year-round, suppliers have to ship produce from hundreds or thousands of miles away. Many varieties, too fragile to ship when ripe, must be picked unripe, packed, then ripened days or weeks later at the supermarket. The search for varieties best able to survive handling has resulted in a consistent decline in the taste, texture, quality, and appeal of many fresh foods. In addition, canned and packaged foods have intentionally been made sweeter, saltier, or simply blander, "to offend the fewest people."[18]

Despite the imposing variety of foods available on supermarket shelves, the average shopper buys relatively few of them. The biologist and anthropologist Lyall Watson believed that the products sold in supermarkets that blanketed the country and swept away local culinary differences resulted in dull commercial conformity. He identified a "supermarket syndrome," characterized by the following symptoms: "an increasing unwillingness to prepare one's own food, an ignorance of the techniques involved, a reliance on an ever-dwindling variety of foods, an offhand attitude to the whole question of eating, and a loss of curiosity about foods that had never before been tried."[19]

By the beginning of the twenty-first century, food had become a global business. U.S. supermarkets have set the standard for the rest of the world, and American food corporations continue to expand overseas. Foreign countries have likewise invested in American supermarket chains. Helped by the North American Free Trade Agreement, the World Trade Organization, and various free-trade agreements with countries such as Chile, it is likely that supermarkets will widen their range of products even more in the future.

Postscript

George F. Gilman remained president of the Great Atlantic and Pacific Tea Company until 1879; he died in 1901. George H. Hartford became president in 1879 and remained in that position until his death in 1915. At that time there were more than 3,000 A&P grocery stores. Hartford's sons took control of the business and expanded the number of stores even further. Gilman's and Hartford's efforts ensured that A&P would be the largest grocery store chain for more than fifty years.

When Michael Cullen died in 1936, just six years after opening his first store, the chain included fifteen supermarkets. King Kullen, the company he founded, is one of the few supermarket chains to remain in family hands. Although there were earlier—and larger—grocery stores, Cullen's chain popularized the idea of the supermarket, and the Smithsonian Institution recognizes King Kullen as America's first supermarket.[20]

Cover of first issue of *Gourmet*; drawing by Henry Stalhut, January 1941 (courtesy of Condé Nast Publications)

20.

Earle MacAusland's *Gourmet*

THERE'S AN OLD adage in the publishing world that there's no good time to launch a magazine. But January 1941 must have seemed like a particularly bad moment to do so—especially a magazine called *Gourmet* and subtitled *The Magazine of Good Living*. For the previous decade, the world had been in the throes of the Great Depression, and millions of unemployed Americans found themselves reduced to standing in bread lines. *Gourmet*'s intended audience was, of course, the well-to-do, who'd gotten a taste for fine food and wines while traveling abroad. But in September 1939, Europe went to war, and the annual vacation trip to Paris or Rome or London was an impossibility. The pleasures of haute cuisine, fine wines, and exotic foreign travel—precisely the focus of the new magazine—would soon be replaced by concerns about food rationing, scrap-metal drives, fuel conservation, travel restrictions, and war. Worse still, *Gourmet*'s founder, Earle R. MacAusland, knew little about food and had scanty funding for his shaky enterprise. The new publication was starting off with no subscribers and no advertisers, and just to make things a little more difficult, there was soon to be a paper shortage. Yet, the magazine survived and fostered the cult of fashionable food in America.

Culinary Magazines

Since the early nineteenth century, newspapers, journals, magazines, and almanacs had been publishing recipes and occasional articles about food, and with the advent of women's magazines, such as *Godey's*, "food departments," with recipes and articles, became common. Magazines devoted to mainly culinary matters surfaced in the late part of the century. Publications such as the *American Kitchen Magazine*, the *Boston Cooking-School Magazine* (later renamed *American Cookery*), and many others were popular during the late nineteenth and early twentieth centuries. These magazines, published for women, offered practical information about food preparation with plenty of practical recipes, old-fashioned kitchen wisdom, and no-nonsense articles filled with the latest information about food, health, nutrition, and the domestic sciences. Most of these magazines, however, went out of business well before World War II. Magazines such as *Good Housekeeping*, *Better Homes and Gardens*, and *Women's Day* published recipes and food articles, but food was not central to them, as it would be for *Gourmet*.

Just before the United States entered World War II, authors such as M. F. K. Fisher and James Beard had interested sophisticated Americans in culinary matters. Fisher's poetically written works and Beard's practical cookbooks began to create an audience for a new kind of food writing. Yet, until Earle MacAusland started publishing *Gourmet*, no American food magazine had capitalized on this interest.

MacAusland was born in Taunton, Massachusetts, in 1891. Although his Scottish immigrant parents were not wealthy, they did live in a private house on Boston's Beacon Hill. MacAusland studied (without much success) at both the Massachusetts Institute of Technology and Harvard. In the 1920s, he moved to New York and went into publishing, eventually holding executive positions at the Butterick Publishing Company, which published books and magazines about women's fashions as well as the occasional cookbook. MacAusland first attempted to publish a magazine of his own in the early years of the Depression; it failed, leaving MacAusland, in 1932, bankrupt. He was then hired by the *National Teacher-Parent Magazine*, later renamed *Parent's Magazine*, as vice president in charge of advertising, and he rose to become the magazine's editor and publisher.[1]

Nonetheless, MacAusland never gave up his dream of launching his own magazine. When he saw a catalog from S. S. Pierce, the esteemed Boston-based source for imported and domestic fancy foods, MacAusland had an idea: why not publish a magazine targeting the same upscale audience? He spent two years searching for investors, but whenever he explained his idea, people thought he was crazy. When the money didn't materialize, MacAusland approached his parents and brother, who agreed to fund the printing of the first issue.[2] Since

MacAusland had little knowledge of culinary matters, he sought others willing to write for his new venture. One writer who signed on was Pearl Metzelthin, author, in 1939, of a very successful work, *The World Wide Cook Book: Menus and Recipes of 75 Nations*. Metzelthin joined the new magazine as its editor.[3]

MacAusland also attracted Louis De Gouy, a Frenchman by birth, who had been a pupil of Auguste Escoffier, the famed French chef and restaurateur. De Gouy had supervised the kitchens of several royal families and had been a chef at restaurants in both Europe and the United States. In 1931, De Gouy had opened the Institute of Modern and Practical Cooking, in New York City, and, six years later, he began publishing cookbooks. De Gouy became *Gourmet*'s "gourmet chef," a position he held until his death, in 1947.

A third collaborator was Samuel Chamberlain, an artist, writer, and photographer whose illustrations and writings had appeared in more than forty books. Chamberlain and his wife, Narcissa, had gone to live in France in 1922 and stayed there until 1934, when they moved to Boston. While in France, he contributed material to *Vogue*. During their time in France, the Chamberlains attended a gastronomic fair in Dijon and became interested in culinary matters. They began collecting recipes, ending up with twenty boxes of them, which they brought along when they moved back to the States. When MacAusland approached Chamberlain about joining the staff of *Gourmet*, Chamberlain was hesitant to commit himself to a venture with, in his view, so little chance of success. Nevertheless, he agreed to work with the publication and eventually became *Gourmet*'s associate editor. For the first issue, Chamberlain wrote a column titled "Burgundy at a Snail's Pace," which took the form of a trip through the birthplace of France's most famous wines.[4]

The first issue of *Gourmet*, printed in December 1940 but dated January 1941, was forty-eight pages long and contained no advertising. Another writer for the magazine, Clementine Paddleford, a columnist for thirty years who wrote about inexpensive food and shopping for readers of the *New York Herald Tribune*, turned to the finer things in her articles for *Gourmet*. In her first *Gourmet* column, titled "Food Flashes," she noted that "imports of European delicacies" had dwindled; still, she reassured readers, America had "battalions of good foods to rush to appetite's defense."[5] The first editorial, explaining *Gourmet*'s mission, gushed that "there had never before been an American magazine that took such an adventurous interest in food."[6]

MacAusland began making the rounds with copies of the inaugural issue to drum up advertising accounts; he also sent sample copies to wealthy and prominent individuals. His efforts at attracting support paid off: He signed up a few advertisers, but more important, he secured two backers. One was Ralph

Reinhold, of Reinhold Publishing, which later emerged as the Van Nostrand Reinhold Company. The other backer was Gladys Guggenheim Straus, the granddaughter of the wealthy Swiss-born philanthropist Meyer Guggenheim. In addition to being considered cofounder of *Gourmet* with Earle MacAusland, she also served as vice president and assistant editor. Despite his initial support, MacAusland had to sell advertising during the day and work on the magazine at night in an attempt to make a go of *Gourmet*.[7]

The magazine's second issue featured the first installment of a column titled "Clémentine in the Kitchen," written by Samuel Chamberlain under the pseudonym Phineas Beck (a pun on the French *fin bec*, or "epicure"). The Clémentine of the column was a fictionalized composite of two women who had cooked for the Chamberlain family in France; one a Burgundian cook named Clémentine Bouchard, who accompanied the family when they returned to the United States. The columns (with recipes by Chamberlain's wife, Narcissa) were collected and published in book form in 1943; *Clémentine in the Kitchen* remained in print for decades (most recently as a Modern Library paperback released in 2000). After the World War II, MacAusland sent Chamberlain back to France for a gastronomic tour that yielded several articles, collected and published in *Bouquet de France*, a hefty tome illustrated with Chamberlain's own drawings and photographs, and with recipes by Narcissa. Published by *Gourmet*, the book accompanied many Americans on their tours of France in the 1950s and for decades afterward. The Chamberlains were subsequently commissioned to create two similar volumes, *Italian Bouquet* and *British Bouquet*, for *Gourmet*.[8] MacAusland continued to seek out the best food writers of the day to contribute to his magazine. He was foresighted enough to hire James Beard, who had just published his first cookbook, *Hors D'oeuvre and Canapés, with a Key to the Cocktail Party*; M. F. K. Fisher, whose *Serve It Forth* appeared in 1937; and chef Louis Diat, whose book *Cooking à la Ritz* was published in 1941 (he is also credited with creating vichyssoise).[9] Other contributors to *Gourmet* were such popular writers as Ray Bradbury, Jane Grigson, Joseph Wechsberg, Elizabeth David, and even F. Scott Fitzgerald, who was published posthumously.[10]

That *Gourmet* magazine ever published a second issue is amazing enough, but its survival the next five years was nothing short of a miracle. In December 1941 the United States entered the war, and for the following four years, rationing and transportation restrictions limited what Americans could eat. Yet, years later, MacAusland concluded that the war was the reason for his magazine's early success: during the war, "there were no domestic servants, so women had to go into the kitchen and do their own cooking."[11] Perhaps more to the point, for wealthy folks who had eaten at the finest restaurants in France before the war, and for those hoping to do the same someday, *Gourmet*'s articles supplied a vicarious taste of haute cuisine, and its recipes enabled readers to prepare the dishes at home (assuming the ingredients were available). As culinary historian Anne Mendelson has written, "Hardship (and later the war) fostered a taste for images of a happier past and perhaps a happier future."[12] Shortly after the war's end, MacAusland moved the operation into a penthouse in New York's plush Plaza Hotel.[13]

Gourmet celebrated its ten-year anniversary in 1951 with the publication of *The Gourmet Cookbook*, with Earle MacAusland credited as author. Food critic Charlotte Turgeon reviewed the book in the *New York Times* and praised it as "the first of its kind to be brought out in this country! Ten years ago a group of people conceived the felicitous idea of publishing a magazine devoted to good food, telling the tale of eating around the world with a variety of ideas and authors that would please the palates and pocketbooks." She also praised the cookbook and the magazine: "Never compromising with short cuts or substitutes, Gourmet Magazine has weathered war and rationing without lowering its standards and is celebrating its first successful decade with the publication of a splendid volume."[14] *The Gourmet Cookbook* was the first of several published by the magazine.[15]

By its second decade, *Gourmet* had become an important contributor to the American food scene, particularly with regard to entertaining, and an arbiter of taste. The magazine had its largest subscription base in Washington, D.C., where it doubtless supplied the diplomatic community with ideas for their parties, dinners, and receptions.[16] Over the next three decades, *Gourmet* continued to focus on haute cuisine, wine, travel, and entertaining stories about the good life. For its first decade or so, the magazine's main focus was on French food, but as the years went by, the articles and recipes broadened to cover cuisines from all over the world.[17]

Fashionable Success

Gourmet's success created an audience for other food magazines in the United States. In 1955, two retired advertising executives in Chicago began sponsoring a magazine they called *Bon Appétit*, which at first was usually found as a giveaway in liquor stores. The magazine was later acquired by Pillsbury, which, in 1975, sold it for about $30,000 to Cleon Knapp, of Knapp Communications, in Los Angeles. To distinguish his magazine from *Gourmet*, Knapp targeted medium-income readers, and the magazine caught on quickly. Knapp pumped millions into promoting *Bon Appétit*, and by 1980, it had a circulation of 1.1 million subscribers—more than any other food magazine at that time.[18]

Other food magazines soon appeared on the newsstands. *The International Review of Food and Wine* was first published in 1978. The brainchild of Michael Batterberry, his wife, Ariane, and three others, *Food and Wine* had been under development since the early 1970s. The Batterberrys and their associates eventually convinced the principals of the Kenyon Company, an international advertising firm, to become publishers of the new venture. A search for investors netted solid support. The most important investor was Playboy Enterprises, which put up half of the funds for the magazine and helped initially with circulation, printing, and public relations. Playboy's publisher backed out of the deal after only a few issues had been published, but the magazine continued with other investors. *The International Review of Food and Wine* targeted men and was intended to compete with *Gourmet*. Like *Gourmet*, it published popular writers, such as George Plimpton and Wilfred Sheed. Michael Batterberry, who served as the magazine's editor in chief, described the magazine as taking "food seriously but not pompously."[19]

Many other food magazines were launched during the decades that followed. In 1972, *Sphere, the Betty Crocker Magazine*, devoted mainly to cooking and crafts, first appeared as a free publication. Five years later, it was acquired by Forum Communications, which changed its name to *Cuisine* and shifted the focus solely to cooking. By 1980, *Cuisine* had a paid circulation of 800,000. Another publication, *Cook's Magazine*, begun in 1980 by Christopher Kimball, who came from the direct-mail marketing field, focused on cooking techniques.[20] *Cuisine* and *Cook's Illustrated* (as it was retitled) were followed by numerous other magazines.[21]

Newspapers got in on the act as well and began hiring food columnists. Professional food journalism took off when the *New York Times* hired its first food columnist, the Mississippi-born food critic and writer Craig Claiborne, who had trained at the Swiss Hotelkeeper's Association, in Lausanne, Switzerland. Other newspapers followed the *New York Times*' lead, and soon a cadre of authoritative newspaper food writers helped attune millions of Americans to the finer points of good food and cooking. Today, most newspapers in the nation have food sections—many of them appearing on Wednesdays—that help keep Americans abreast of the latest developments in the culinary world. With the advent of the Internet, there are now numerous food blogs, Web sites, and listservs catering to an ever widening group of food enthusiasts.

Fashionable Effects

From the beginning, Earle MacAusland was interested in "good living," accessible through fashion, entertaining, dining, and leisure. Being a gourmet, as the magazine repeatedly affirmed, had nothing to do with money, class, or social status. It meant that the food you cooked and ate should be lovingly prepared and eaten with congenial company, and these could be enjoyed by everyone.[22] Decades before the culinary illuminati began raising concerns about junk food and fast food, *Gourmet*'s editorial policy stressed using fresh ingredients and cooking from scratch—no shortcuts or simplifications allowed. Yet, *Gourmet* was read mainly by well-heeled people who wanted to be sophisticated about food, not by those who actually cooked or cleaned up after the fashionable meal. *Gourmet* was for those who wanted to enjoy a delicious, congenial meal with dazzling conversation in fashionable surroundings. It was also for those could only imagine such occasions, whose trips to Paris, Rome, and London began and ended between the covers of a magazine.

Today, because of limitations of time, money, kitchen space, or energy, many Americans experience the pleasures of fine food only through the written word. Through *Gourmet*, upwardly mobile Americans have been able to acquire an understanding of the good life, and even cook a decent meal if so inclined. In turn, *Gourmet* created a market for upscale food; food magazines, food columns in newspapers, specialty products, and upscale restaurants followed in the magazine's wake—as did other food magazines, which exploited the culinary fashion established by *Gourmet*.

Postscript

One avid reader of *Gourmet* was the newlywed Julia Child, then living in Washington, D.C., with her husband, Paul, who was assigned to the State Department. She believed that Paul wanted a sophisticated wife who knew how to cook a fine meal. In fact, she did not learn how to cook well until Paul had been reassigned to France, in 1948.

Earle MacAusland died in 1980, but *Gourmet* continued publication, eventually being acquired by Condé Nast, publishers of *Vogue*. At the time of MacAusland's death, about a hundred recipes were appearing in each issue, often complicated affairs not easily made by home cooks.

Condé Nast also acquired *Bon Appétit*, in 1993. To promote sales of *Gourmet* and *Bon Appétit* and to take advantage of a new online market, Condé Nast uploaded, in 1994, a culinary Web site (www.epicurious.com). Its importance has soared since it was rejuvenated in 2004. With its blogs, videos, articles, and archive of more than 100,000 recipes, Epicurious.com is one of the largest culinary Web sites. During the past few years, it has attracted more than 5 million visitors every month.

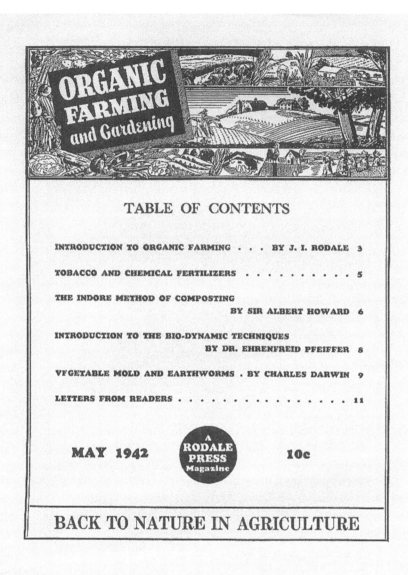

ORGANIC FARMING and Gardening

TABLE OF CONTENTS

MAY 1942   A RODALE PRESS Magazine   10c

BACK TO NATURE IN AGRICULTURE

Cover of first issue of *Organic Farming and Gardening*, May 1942 (used with permission of Rodale Inc.)

21.

Jerome I. Rodale's *Organic Gardening*

I N LATE 1942, in the midst of World War II, Jerome I. Rodale began publishing a magazine titled *Organic Gardening*. Wartime is not a good time to begin publishing any magazine, but Rodale's was a publication that singularly suited the zeitgeist. The war effort swelled food production, and the federal government encouraged Americans to grow fruits and vegetables in backyard victory gardens. An estimated 80 percent of the population responded, and, in 1943, these gardens produced 40 percent of the fresh produce consumed in America.[1] There was little synthetic fertilizer available during the war—the nitrates used for petrochemical fertilizer were needed to make munitions—and so it was an opportune time to promote chemical-free gardening. After the war's end, however, American interest in organic food declined, and for the next sixteen years, Rodale's magazine, renamed *Organic Gardening and Farming*, ran in the red. Any other publisher would have given up on such a proven loser, but Rodale continued to pour money into the publication. Decades later, organic food was rediscovered by millions of Americans, and organics are one of the fastest-growing food sectors in America today.

Inorganic Food History

Organic fertilizers, such as animal waste, and crop-rotation systems, such as growing beans in alternate years with corn, were known and used in Colonial

America, but in the land-rich new nation, many farmers didn't worry about depleting their farmland—they simply moved elsewhere, usually farther west. In an ever-expanding nation with plenty of unoccupied land, this system worked well.[2] But when fertile farmland was no longer there just for the taking, farmers had to make their acreage produce year after year. They turned to fertilizers—natural and manufactured—for productivity gains on their farms.

The German scientist Justus von Liebig argued for replacing organic manure with synthetic fertilizers. Liebig concluded that only a few components in the manure provided fertility. Add nitrogen, potassium, and phosphorous to the soil, and plants would flourish, even in depleted soil.[3] Despite Liebig's pronouncement, in 1840, synthetic fertilizers were little used in America until after World War I.

From the chemists' point of view, the difficulty in making synthetic fertilizer was how to fix nitrogen, which required nitrogen atoms to be split and then combined with oxygen atoms. A German chemist, Fritz Haber, figured out, before World War I, how to do this, but it was Carl Bosch who realized how to commercialize Haber's discovery. Synthetic fertilizer made according to the Haber-Bosch formula was sold in the United States prior to World War II, but its use did not become almost universal until after the war.[4]

At the same time that American farmers began feeding their crops synthetic fertilizers, they also started to spray their fields with immense amounts of chemical pesticides and herbicides. Naturally occurring poisons, such as nicotine sulfate (extracted from tobacco leaves), had been used as insecticides since colonial times, and they remained in use well into the twentieth century. A few chemical pesticides had been manufactured in the early twentieth century, but the event that changed American agriculture for decades to come was the discovery, by Paul Müller, a Swiss chemist, that DDT, a new synthetic contact insecticide, was devastatingly effective. Shortly after World War II, chemical manufacturers began producing large amounts of DDT and other synthetic pesticides and herbicides, and in the following decades, their use became common among American vegetable and fruit gardeners and farmers.

Synthetic fertilizers became the standard after World War II, when large factories that had produced munitions shifted to fertilizer production. This infusion of petrochemical fertilizers, pesticides, and herbicides, along with the application of antibiotics and hormones, prevented disease and insect damage in plants and maximized yield in crops and animals raised for meat, milk, or eggs. Farm mechanization and the use of irrigation also became widespread, and large farms began to specialize, growing a single crop or raising one type of animal, thus abandoning the tradition of animal and plant diversity that had characterized the American farm for generations. Each of these changes required major financial investments on the part of farmers, but once these costly shifts had been made on large farms, food production costs dropped, and, in turn, the market value of crops and herds declined. Many small farmers, unable to compete with the large producers, sold out to big corporate operations.

During the postwar years, commercial food processors began using a dizzying array of additives and stabilizers, which lengthened product shelf life and reduced losses from spoilage. Some additives, such as vitamins and minerals, offered health benefits to consumers; too often, though, the substitution of a synthetic (such as vanillin for pure vanilla) simply saved the processor money. During the decade from 1949 to 1959, 400 new additives were incorporated into processed food products. Some additives were emulsifiers, colorings, preservatives, or flavoring agents; others prevented the fat in food from turning rancid.[5]

Rodale and the Organic Farming Movement

Even before the postwar expansion in the use of pesticides, herbicides, petrochemical fertilizers, antibiotics, hormones, preservatives, and additives, an entrepreneur named Jerome I. Rodale was championing its opposite—organic gardening. One of eight children of an immigrant grocer on New York's Lower East Side, Rodale had read about and followed the health regimen espoused by physical culture promoter Bernarr Macfadden. Rodale had set up, in 1923, an electrical equipment business with his brother,[6] and during the Depression, they moved from New York to Emmaus, Pennsylvania. As the business prospered, the Rodales branched out into publishing.

In 1940, Rodale read a compelling book, *An Agricultural Testament*. Its author, Sir Albert Howard, a British agronomist who had worked in India, extolled organic farming and discouraged the use of chemical fertilizers. Rodale wrote to Howard, and the two corresponded regularly. Impressed with Howard's views, Rodale bought a farm and promptly put into practice Howard's ideas of composting as well as his own nutrition-related beliefs. Rodale declared his efforts at organic farming a success, and he set about encouraging others to follow in his footsteps. In May 1942, he started a magazine, *Organic Gardening*, and for a time, Howard, who lived in England, served as its associate editor. The magazine stressed composting, soil building, and biological control of pests as the fundamentals of organic agriculture. Rodale became so upset about the use of synthetic fertilizers and insecticides, especially the recently introduced DDT, that he wrote a book, *Pay Dirt*, strongly condemning their use. Howard fully supported Rodale's views and wrote the book's introduction.[7] Neither Howard nor Rodale, however, convinced many at the time of the correctness of their views.

Organic Gardening proved, for its first sixteen years, to be a money loser; however, other Rodale publications, such as *Prevention*, helped them pay their bills until the concept of organic gardening caught on, in the 1960s. Until then, the readership of *Organic Gardening and Farming* had consisted mostly of small-town and suburban backyard gardeners. Meanwhile, the agricultural establishment dismissed Rodale as a quack, a crank, a gadfly, and a manure-pile worshipper.[8]

Organic farming, according to Rodale, was best practiced on a small scale, and it thus challenged the idea of corporate agriculture and the American food distribution system, which was growing increasingly centralized and dependent on long-distance transportation. Organically grown foods were often more perishable, so they could be distributed only locally. Ideally, farmers and customers would deal directly with each other in farmers' markets, and the middlemen—shippers, brokers, wholesalers, supermarket owners—would be eliminated.

Rodale retired in 1960 and died eleven years later, but he left intact a publishing empire that continued to flourish. Rodale's passionate belief in organic gardening might well have remained a fringe view had it not been for a set of unusual circumstances. The potential dangers of additives and pesticides became apparent—and were made known to the public at large—during the 1960s. Writer William F. Longgood, in *The Poisons in Your Food*, questioned the safety of additives in processed food that had invaded the daily diet of Americans. Two years later, Rachel Carson, a biologist and nature writer, exposed the evils of DDT, first in a series of articles and then in her book *Silent Spring*. Although Rodale had condemned DDT beginning in 1944 and Rodale and Carson corresponded from time to time, there is no evidence that his views influenced hers.[9]

Organic gardening complemented other antiestablishment activities, including opposition to the Vietnam War, the promotion of civil rights, the rise of the women's movement, the hippie subculture, and New Age spirituality. These coalesced into the so-called counterculture. Besides opposing other mainstays of the establishment, countercultural advocates revolted against the mainstream American food industry, with its factory farms, concentrated animal-feeding operations, chemical-laced canned goods, and corporate lobbying.

Rodale's *Organic Gardening and Farming* offered an alternative: a food system free from the domination of corporate agribusiness. At first, those adopting his organic methods were small communal operations based on a utopian agricultural model of a simpler, more "natural" lifestyle. For city dwellers, it was sometimes possible to establish organic gardens on vacant city lots, in parks, and at botanic gardens—as long as the soil had not already been poisoned with the toxins of urban life. Subscriptions to *Organic Gardening* leaped tenfold, from 60,000, in 1958, to more than 600,000, in 1970.[10]

To make organic foods available to a wider audience, some advocates established food co-ops, self-run by members who each contributed a certain amount of time to the project. Initially, these co-ops were no-frills sources of chemical-free staples, such as brown rice, whole-grain breads, herbal teas, nuts, seeds, beans, dried fruits, honey, bean sprouts, and soy products. As they became more commercial, the co-ops began offering natural cheeses, yogurt, organically grown fruits and vegetables, pure juices, granolas, oils, and vitamin and mineral supplements. By the 1970s, there were an estimated 5,000 to 10,000 food co-ops in the United States.[11]

By the late 1960s, vegetarianism had become ingrained in the counterculture as a health-promoting measure and as a means of fighting hunger in America and around the world. The popularity of this view can be attributed, in part, to dietitian-turned-social-activist Frances Moore Lappé. Discouraged by an unrewarding career in social work, Lappé turned, in 1969, to the field of ecology. In her studies, she read about the immense quantity of farmland devoted to growing feed grains for livestock, learning that 21.4 pounds of feed-grain protein was required to produce 1 pound of beef protein. She also encountered the theory of protein complementarity—that specific combinations of legumes, seeds, grains, and dairy products in the daily diet could easily supply a person's protein requirements without resorting to ecologically wasteful meat. Lappé's groundbreaking book, *Diet for a Small Planet*, sold over 3 million copies. The book explained that, by feeding vegetable protein to animals rather than directly to humans, Americans were wasting scarce protein resources at a time when much of the world was going hungry or suffering from serious nutritional deficiencies. This inefficient process required, she argued, disproportionate amounts of land and water as well as fertilizers, pesticides, and herbicides. Lappé pointed out that, if Americans ate their protein directly in the form of plant products, these wasted agricultural resources would be available to produce food for the hungry. Lappé recommended "getting off the top of the food chain" as a way of transforming consciousness, reintegrating mind and body, and embracing social responsibility.[12]

By the mid-1970s, the countercultural food movement had reached the wider population. Food companies responded by ridiculing food reformers, calling them lunatics, faddists, quacks, or health nuts while lining their own views with such reassuring words as "knowledgeable," "scientific," "constructive," "generally recognized," "responsible," and "the best scientific judgment attainable." Many mainstream Americans had nonetheless become concerned about the issues raised by the counterculture. In response to market pressures, food companies slowly began to alter their labeling and advertising slogans, which soon abounded with such claims as "additive-free" and "all natural." Eventually, even the large food companies began decreasing or eliminating the additives in many of their products.

The American public became increasingly confused by the new jargon and mixed messages coming from the food industry, medical establishment, government, and self-appointed nutrition experts. Wooed by spokesmen for the food manufacturers and warned by advocates of health foods, repeatedly alarmed by gloomy stories of a chemical-laden food supply only to be reassured by industry-hired academicians, the public was driven into a fog of uncertainty about food and food choices.

Organic Effects

The countercultural food movement spurred interest in food and nutrition. More and more Americans grew distrustful of food companies and the Food and Drug Administration, which many believed was controlled by the food industry. There arose a clear need for independent research and the dissemination of easily understood, accurate public information about food. This concern led to the founding, in 1971, of the Center for Science in the Public Interest (CSPI), in Washington, D.C. Michael Jacobson, one of its founders, had a doctorate in microbiology from the Massachusetts Institute of Technology, and he had long been researching food additives and the nutritional composition of processed foods. By 1977, the CSPI was focusing almost exclusively on food issues, publishing eye-opening nutritional analyses and critiques of fast foods and convenience foods. Jacobson's *What Are We Feeding Our Kids?* and *Marketing Madness* helped raise public awareness of food and nutrition. The CSPI also established, and continues to publish, *Nutrition Action Healthletter*, the largest-circulation newsletter reporting on nutrition, diet, and related health issues.

Many enterprises founded in the 1960s and based on counterculture ideals have survived and thrived. Erewhon (named after Samuel Butler's 1872 novel about an imaginary country where illness is a punishable offense) was founded as a co-op in 1966 to supply food to Boston-area followers of macrobiotic gurus Michio and Aveline Kushi. It later opened retail shops in the Boston area, and then on the West Coast. Celestial Seasonings, begun in 1969 in Boulder, Colorado, offered additive-free herbal teas made from organically grown or wild plants. Erewhon, after acquiring the venerable cereal company U.S. Mills, in 1986, has become one of the largest retailers, manufacturers, and distributors of natural foods in the United States. Celestial Seasonings, sold to Kraft in 1984, became independent again in 1988 and is now the country's largest purveyor of herbal teas.

Some of America's most famous restaurants also emerged from the counterculture food movement. As a student at the University of California, Berkeley, in the 1960s, Alice Waters had been involved in the Free Speech Movement. In 1971, she opened the groundbreaking restaurant Chez Panisse, an outgrowth of the home-cooked meals she had been preparing for free-speech activists. Waters stressed the use of fresh, local, seasonal ingredients. Moosewood Restaurant, in Ithaca, New York, founded by Mollie Katzen and other co-op members in 1973, started out as a communal operation, with all decisions made by the entire staff. Improvised daily, the all-vegetarian menu featured a variety of ethnic dishes and plenty of whole grains—a Lappé-inspired example of how to live well without wasting the earth's protein resources. Both Waters and Katzen wrote cookbooks that have become modern classics: Waters's initial effort was *The Chez Panisse Menu Cookbook*, while Katzen's was *The Moosewood Cookbook*. Both women also wrote children's cookbooks (*Fanny at Chez Panisse*, by Waters, and, from Katzen, *Pretend Soup, Salad People*, and *Honest Pretzels*). The efforts by Alice Waters, Mollie Katzen, and many others of their generation to change the way Americans eat led to a revolution in American cookery that stresses fresh ingredients and locally grown food.

The counterculture food movement also effected a renaissance in vegetarianism in the United States. The North American Vegetarian Society was founded in 1974, and several vegetarian and vegan magazines, such as *Vegetarian Times* and *VegNews Magazine*, now boast large subscriber bases. Lappé continues her work through the Food First Institute for Food and Development Policy, in San Francisco, and she and her daughter, Anna Lappé, have published a follow-up book, *Hope's Edge: The Next Diet for a Small Planet*.[13] In 2006, there were an estimated 7 million vegetarians in the United States, and even fast-food outlets have added vegetarian options to their menus.

Another impact of the counterculture food movement was a burgeoning interest in organic gardening. In concert with this interest, which has grown further in the past few decades, there has arisen a movement to preserve the farm by connecting consumers in cities with small farmers in surrounding areas. One such effort led to the growth of urban farmers' markets, where local growers truck in their produce and sell it directly to customers, thus eliminating the middlemen and establishing a direct connection between city dwellers and farmers. A remarkably successful example has been New York City's Greenmarket, started, in 1976, by Barry Benepe. Today there are twenty Greenmarket sites in the city, and Benepe's efforts have served as a model for hundreds of other urban farmers' markets around the nation.

Another attempt to connect farmers to consumers is Community Supported Agriculture (CSA). Begun in Japan in the 1960s, CSA programs first appeared in the United States in the mid-1980s. In a CSA, farmers and community members work together as partners to create a local food system in which the farmers produce vegetables, fruits, meats, and related products and sell them directly to community members, who, at the start of the growing season, must commit to purchasing produce at a specific price. By doing so, the consumers share the risks of production with the farmers. Today, there are, according to the Biodynamic Farming and Gardening Association, more than 600 CSAs in America.

The 1990 Farm Bill passed by the U.S. Congress contained the Organic Foods Production Act, which set national standards for how organic food must be produced, handled, and labeled. Organic foods could not, for instance, include synthetic fertilizers or pesticides. The bill also established the National Organic Standards Board, which issues a list of prohibited substances, such as synthetic fertilizers and antibiotics, that cannot be used in organic foods. After twelve years of work by the National Organic Standards Board, the National Organic Program (NOP) took effect, in October 2002; it is administered by the U.S. Department of Agriculture (USDA). The NOP covers in detail all aspects of organic food production, processing, delivery, and retail sale. Under the NOP, farmers and food processors wishing to use the word "organic" in reference to their businesses and products must be certified organic by the USDA. Producers with annual sales not exceeding $5,000 are exempt from the rule and do not require certification. However, they must still follow NOP standards, keep proper records, and submit to a production audit if requested, but they cannot use the term "certified organic."

Much interest in organic food has sprung from health-food stores. By 1970, more than 300 health-food stores and restaurants had opened in Southern California alone.[14] This was just the beginning. Thousands more appeared in other communities across America. In 1978, college dropout John Mackey and his girlfriend, Renee Lawson, opened a health-food store with the tongue-in-cheek name Safer Way, in Austin, Texas. Two years later, Mackey merged his store with another retailer's to create Whole Foods. Then a small operation with a staff of just nineteen, the store featured organic and other quality foods. By 1984, Whole Foods had become so successful that it began opening additional stores and acquiring other grocery chains. It now has almost 200 natural-food supermarkets around the nation. It is currently the preeminent distributor of organic food in America—although other grocery stores are expanding their organic offerings and may surpass Whole Foods in the future.[15]

As conceived by Jerome I. Rodale and those who followed in his footsteps, the ideal system of food production centers on small farmers growing and selling their own fruits and vegetables directly to consumers. During the past decade, however, large factory farms have taken up organic foods, and nationwide big box discount chains, such as Wal-Mart, have begun selling it. The rise of "big organic" was not what Rodale expected. Yet, his ideas have shaped what some Americans eat today—and what more Americans will likely eat in the future. Although less than 3 percent of the food and beverages Americans buy today is organic, this is expected to grow in the coming decade.[16]

Postscript

Jerome I. Rodale and Sir Albert Howard, often considered the father of modern organic agriculture, continued their correspondence until Howard's death in 1947.[17] In 1971, Rodale was invited as a guest on *The Dick Cavett Show*. While filming the interview, Rodale boasted to Cavett that, thanks to the food he ate and the life he led, he was so healthy that he "expected to live on and on." He had "no aches or pains" and he was "full of energy." Minutes later he died of a heart attack.[18]

Despite the highly publicized circumstances of his death, Rodale's work has continued its impact. In addition to *Organic Gardening* and *Prevention*, Rodale Press publishes popular magazines on health and wellness. In addition to the commercial company, Rodale also established the Soil and Health Foundation, the forerunner of the Rodale Institute, which, in its own words, "champions organic solutions for the challenges of global climate change, better nutrition in food, famine prevention and poverty reduction."[19]

Microwave World®

Vol. 6, No. 1
January-February 1985

What We Were. What We Are

Cover of *Microwave World*, 1985 (*Microwave World* 6, no.1 [International Microwave Power Institute, Canada, 1985])

22.

Percy Spencer's Radar

I N 1944, Percy Spencer, an engineer at the Raytheon Manufacturing Corporation, of Waltham, Massachusetts, leaned close to a tube emitting microwaves, part of a radar system he was working on, and was amazed to find that a candy bar in his shirt pocket instantly melted. Suspecting he was on the brink of a most interesting discovery, Spencer concluded that microwaves could heat food. When he placed a bag of unpopped popcorn in front of the radar-emitting device, the kernels exploded and popcorn flew all over the lab. The following day, Spencer placed an egg in front of it and wowed observers when it blew up, splattering them with its contents. Based on these experiences, Spencer told Elmer J. Gorn, Raytheon's chief patent attorney, that he thought he could make a device that would cook "food faster and more efficiently than any conventional cooker." "Do you think you can get me a patent on the idea?" Percy asked Gorn. After Spencer explained his idea more fully, Gorn agreed to help him apply for a patent. Spencer's first patent application was submitted to the U.S. Patent Office in 1945. The application described two parallel magnetrons heating food on a conveyor belt. In 1947, William M. Hall and Fritz A. Gross, two of Spencer's coworkers, applied for a patent for a microwave heating device enclosed in an oven. It consisted of two microwave-generating magnetron tubes packed in a metallic box with a timer and a means of controlling the power of the microwaves.[1] Spencer and his colleagues had solid reasons to expect a quick commercial success, but, as it turned out, it took more than two decades before the technology and microwaveable frozen food revolutionized food preparation at home and in restaurants.

Microwaveable History

The microwave heating device was the culmination of the work of many individuals during the previous decades. In the mid-1930s, British scientists had begun experimenting with pulse radio waves, which bounced off close objects, such as nearby ships and airplanes, before returning to a receiver. Based on military needs, the British government made sizable investments in developing this technology, soon to be called radar. A serious challenge facing these early researchers was developing more powerful radio waves that could bounce off distant objects and remain strong enough to return to the receiver. In an attempt to meet this challenge, British physicists John Randall and Henry Boot, of Birmingham University, decided to place a cavity resonator, which allows the oscillation of electromagnetic waves at certain frequencies, around a cathode ray tube. This combination was found to boost the power of the microwaves.[2] On February 21, 1940, Randall and Boot discovered a revolutionary way to generate microwaves by having them pass through cavity magnetrons. This made it possible to send out a stream of microwaves, which would then bounce back after striking a ship or plane. This early-warning radar system was just what Great Britain needed as war with Germany loomed.

As the Battle of Britain raged in 1940, the war-strained British electronics industry found itself unable to develop and produce the quantity of magnetrons, essential components of radar equipment, that the war effort required. The British government thus decided to share technological secrets with the United States, which was not yet at war, and ask American electronics companies, such as General Electric and Raytheon, to mass-produce magnetrons. British scientists had brought a magnetron with them when they visited Raytheon one Friday in the summer of 1940. Percy Spencer took the top-secret magnetron home over the weekend, and, by the following Monday, he had figured out how to mass-produce the devices. Production soon accelerated from 17 tubes per week to 2,600 per day. By war's end, Raytheon was producing 80 percent of all magnetrons in use by the Allied Forces. For his services, Spencer was awarded a Distinguished Service Medal, the U.S. Navy's highest civilian honor.[3]

Six months before the end of World War II, Raytheon's president, Laurence Marshall, brought together senior employees to thrash out what directions the company should take after the war ended. If Raytheon was to survive in the postwar world, it would have to convert to commercial projects. At the time, it was generally known that magnetrons generated heat from the vibration of molecules in reaction to the frequency of the microwaves. Spencer understood this phenomenon and suggested applying it for heating food.

After the war, General Electric, Westinghouse, RCA, and Raytheon explored magnetron heating applications. At the time, the scientific and professional prognosis for commercial microwave heating, particularly for food applications, was unpromising. Still, some scientists were hopeful and took practical steps toward its realization.[4] While other manufacturers were exploring commercial applications, primarily in industry, Raytheon's effort was directed toward developing a microwave oven.

A few months after Raytheon employees Hall and Gross submitted their patent application for a microwave device in an oven, Spencer filed a patent application for a method of preparing food in a "microwave oven." Spencer proposed that Raytheon exploit the discovery, playing the major role in getting Laurence Marshall interested in such a device. Raytheon spent an estimated $100,000 to construct a prototype microwave oven, which was placed in Marshall's home kitchen in 1946. After trying out the new oven, Marshall was highly enthusiastic about its potential. He "foresaw a complete revolution in furnishing piping-hot food to large volumes of people." Marshall ordered "engineers to develop an oven with inside trays on which cold sandwiches could be heated and served almost without interruption." Raytheon held a contest to name the new oven, and the winner was Raydar Range. This was soon changed to Radar Range, and, finally, the two words were merged, giving Radarange.[5]

The first commercial Radarange manufactured by Raytheon was a freestanding, white-enameled unit operating on 220 volts of electricity and requiring an internal water-cooling system. This early model was first bought by a Cleveland restaurant in 1947. Because the drop-down door was a potential nuisance in small kitchens, subsequent Radaranges incorporated sliding vertical doors. The price tag on the Radarange was $3,000, so initial sales were limited mainly to restaurants, railroads, cruise ships, and vending-machine companies.[6] Despite its high price, hotels and restaurants installed the oven because it was convenient and saved time.[7]

Development of the microwave oven continued in the 1950s, with Raytheon dominating the field of commercial microwave ovens and heating applications. It was the only manufacturer of microwave ovens for restaurants and the principal manufacturer of the magnetrons used in the ovens. After further experimentation with the Radarange, Raytheon developed, in January 1952, an experimental model for home use. The oven was powered by a water-cooled magnetron, which required plumbing connections. The magnetron and related components were located below the oven, and the entire structure stood five and a half feet high. It was a large, bulky device weighing 750 pounds, and it thus proved impractical for domestic use.[8]

Raytheon concluded that the home market was just not ready for microwave ovens, so it licensed Hotpoint, Westinghouse, Kelvinator, Whirlpool, and Tappan to develop consumer models. Raytheon furnished each company with power supplies, magnetrons, and basic oven design data. The Tappan Company, a manufacturer of conventional ovens, was the most interested in microwave ovens. What was needed was a magnetron requiring less power and a heat-dislocation system that could replace the bulky water-cooling mechanism. Tappan engineers designed a cabinet with an air-cooled system, and eventually they relocated the magnetron and related components behind the oven. Relocating the magnetron meant microwaves were fed directly into the oven cavity. In October 1955, Tappan introduced the first commercial microwave oven for the domestic consumer market. Designed to fit within the space occupied by a standard forty-inch range or for built-in use, the unit had a stainless steel exterior and aluminum oven cavity with a glass shelf. The oven featured dual cooking speeds, a browning element in its top, an oven timer, and a recipe card file drawer. The oven retailed for $1,295 and was marketed as an "electric range."[9]

The Hotpoint division of General Electric, which also had done research in microwave cooking, unveiled its own electronic microwave oven the following year. Although both the Tappan and Hotpoint ovens generated unprecedented enthusiasm and interest, sales were dismal. The price was still too high for the average consumer, and the technology for producing microwaveable food products was not well understood. Not many food processors took the technology seriously, and few microwaveable foods were produced. Looking back, microwave scientist Robert V. Decareau recalled that it was "extremely doubtful if the microwave-oven business came close to breaking even during those first ten to fifteen years."[10]

Tappan continued tinkering with its microwave oven. By 1965, the company had introduced the first "microwave cooking center," with a microwave oven mounted above a conventional range. However, the unit retailed for well over $1,000, still too expensive for the average consumer. Even so, an estimated 10,000 households in America owned a microwave oven by 1966. While many industry observers anticipated high sales of built-in and countertop microwave ovens, little evidence supported their rosy predictions.[11]

Two events, however, turned the microwave industry around. The first was the invention, in the early 1960s, of a compact, low-cost magnetron by Keishi

Ogura, of the New Japan Radio Company—40 percent of which was owned by Raytheon. The second was Raytheon's acquisition of Amana Refrigeration, Inc., in 1964. Amana's president, George Foerstner, was a microwave visionary. Amana appliance engineers teamed up with Raytheon experts to design a household Radarange. In August 1967, Amana introduced its first microwave oven, which operated at 115 volts and sold reasonably for under $500. The unit was well received by the public, and Foerstner predicted that the company would sell 50,000 ovens per year. His estimate turned out to be low, and its remarkable success brought a trail of imitators in its wake.[12]

Manufacturers still had problems to solve, however, before the microwave oven could be more widely accepted. For one thing, they needed to convince the public that microwave ovens were safe. Doubts about microwave oven safety were unleashed by the passage, in 1968, of the Radiation Control for Health and Safety Act. The act initially concerned radiation emitted by color television sets, but it was later expanded to include microwave ovens. On January 4, 1970, the U.S. Department of Health, Education and Welfare published the results of microwave oven radiation tests. The tests revealed that microwave ovens sold before 1970 leaked radiation at levels that might be harmful to human health. The federal government set new standards and required design changes for safer microwave ovens.[13] With these changes, public apprehension slowly abated.

Another crucial challenge facing manufacturers was convincing food processors to repackage their products in order to make them more suitable for microwave ovens. Aluminum foil blocked microwaves and damaged ovens. Traditional frozen foods contained too much water for microwave ovens, so water content had to be adjusted. But food processors were not interested initially in working with microwave oven manufacturers, primarily because the market for microwaveable foods was simply too small. By the 1970s, however, more than 10 percent of all American homes had microwave ovens, and ovens were in wide use in vending businesses and in restaurants. And the number was growing steadily. Once major food processors noticed the trend, they promptly invested in the development of food products that could be microwaved. Cookware companies introduced specialized dishes for microwave ovens. By 1975, microwave ovens were selling at over 1 million units annually, outselling gas ranges, and the demand for microwaveable foods spiraled up accordingly.[14]

Pillsbury, the Minneapolis-based consumer food giant, became interested in microwave ovens, mainly to service their vending business. In 1971, Pillsbury hired James D. Watkins, a University of Minnesota graduate who had used the microwave oven there in his student days. Pillsbury had Watkins evaluate the company's line of microwaveable products. Under the tutelage of Mike Harper,

Pillsbury's director of research and development, Watkins began developing new microwave products. Beginning in 1976, the company started marketing products intended specifically for microwave ovens.[15]

During this period, Pillsbury went through numerous shakeups, due, in part, to successive mergers and acquisitions. When Pillsbury purchased Green Giant, in 1978, it decided to let that company handle microwaveable foods, and Pillsbury only reluctantly supported its own line of these foods. Pillsbury failed to understand the importance of the superior packaging James Watkins and his team had created, which afforded better heat dispersal. As a consequence, the company squandered its early lead in microwaveable products.[16] Other companies jumped into the void left by Pillsbury, developing everything from ground-beef dinners to cake mixes.

Simultaneous with the development of microwaveable products, consumer publications were helping home cooks learn how to use their microwave ovens. Microwave recipes and how-to articles appeared in magazines, and cookbooks brimmed with practical information on how to cook in microwave ovens. Virtually all manufactures of the commercial ovens produced cooking booklets and books for their customers. In addition, beginning in 1972, dozens of popular microwave cookbooks appeared. They covered everything from preparing ethnic foods—Japanese, Chinese, Mexican, Italian, and French—to cooking all types fruits, vegetables, and meats.

An explosion in the consumption of fast foods and casual-food restaurants rocked America in the late 1970s, and the microwave oven helped make that possible. Sit-down restaurants, from coffee shops to family-friendly chains, also took advantage of the microwave's versatility. Where speed and convenience count, microwave ovens have had a major impact on commercial food preparation. Food can be prepared in conventional ovens in a central kitchen and flash frozen. The frozen dishes can then be distributed to chain outlets, where they are popped into a microwave oven when ordered. Microwaveable foods have made it possible for restaurants to offer a wide variety of dishes that can be prepared and served quickly with minimal staff. By the 1980s, the increase in the number of microwaveable foods on the market was accelerating, and a revolution in food preparation was under way in American home and restaurant kitchens.

Microwaveable Effects

The microwave oven has contributed to America's gulp-and-go culture. It is one of the most widely used appliances at home; an estimated 90 percent of American households have one. As Mona Doyle, president of the Consumer Network, in Philadelphia, observed in 1989, "With the microwave you just reach into your freezer and pop it into the oven, and zap! It's done."[17] The main use of home ovens is to reheat food, such as leftovers and coffee, heat precooked frozen commercial products, or make popcorn.

The primary advantages of the microwave over the traditional oven are speed and convenience. Precooked frozen foods can be kept in freezers up to the point of service and then cooked to order. This results in fresher food, less waste, less preparation time, and lower costs, since less labor is required to prepare the food. Today, microwaves are particularly important in small and medium-sized restaurants, bars, cafeterias, snack bars, hospitals, coffee shops, convenience stores, vending areas, fast-food outlets, on airplanes, and for hotel room service and mobile service carts. With the dramatic improvements in the quality of frozen foods and the expanded services provided by several nationwide distribution companies such as Sysco and U.S. Foodservice, even dishes served at upscale restaurants may be frozen items that have been microwaved before serving.

Postscript

For his achievements, Percy Spencer was elevated to senior vice president and, subsequently, member of the board of directors at Raytheon. He eventually acquired hundreds of patents—but none more significant than the patent for the microwave oven. At the time of his death, in 1970, half of Raytheon's commercial profits were generated from the sale of Radaranges.[18]

First home of what would become the Culinary Institute of America (courtesy of The Culinary Institute of America)

23.

Frances Roth and Katharine Angell's CIA

DURING WORLD WAR II, with millions of Americans in the military and millions more working in war-related industries, restaurants faced a serious shortage of trained chefs and culinary professionals. Restaurateurs in New Haven, Connecticut, began to think about creating a school for training potential employees. But, the war ended before their plans were put into effect. After the war, the labor problem shifted: there were plenty of potential workers, but few had experience or training to work in the food-service industry. Working with New Haven restaurants, Frances Roth, a lawyer and former city assistant district attorney, and Katharine Angell, the wife of the president emeritus of Yale University, formed the New Haven Restaurant Institute to educate returning soldiers, sailors, and airmen for work in restaurants. Sixteen students showed up for the first courses, which began in May 1946. Student enrollment grew slowly, and a few years later, the school changed its name to the Culinary Institute of America (CIA). No one knew at the time that the culinary school Roth and Angell created—and its competition—would professionalize America's culinary world and change the foods Americans ate.

Cooking School History

The New Haven Restaurant Institute was not America's first cooking school. Beginning in the eighteenth century, traveling experts had offered cooking lessons to students in their homes—usually to young women, whose chances for marriage were enhanced by culinary proficiency. The shift from such private lessons to public courses was made by Elizabeth Goodfellow, a pastry cook and confectioner who, in the early nineteenth century, began offering cookery lessons in her Philadelphia pastry shop. Another cooking school, established in the mid-nineteenth century, was that of Pierre Blot, a French immigrant who lectured on culinary arts. The school lasted only a few years, but it inspired the next phase of American cooking schools, which taught new immigrants and the poor.

A New York librarian named Juliet Corson volunteered, in 1873, to work at the Women's Educational and Industrial Society, which offered free courses in sewing, bookkeeping, and the like to poor women in hopes of helping them find work. Believing that cookery instruction would prepare women for domestic employment, the society's managers asked Juliet Corson to teach a cooking class. Her work at the society attracted the attention of her well-to-do acquaintances, who encouraged her to open her own cooking school. Corson did just that, in 1876. She also wrote several books based on her lectures, including *Cooking School Text Book and Housekeepers' Guide to Cookery and Kitchen Management*, a textbook that was adopted by cooking schools in other cities. Following Corson's lead, similar schools opened in Philadelphia, under the direction of Sarah Tyson Rorer, and in Boston, first under the direction of Mary J. Lincoln and later under Fannie Merritt Farmer. When Farmer left the school in 1902, she opened Miss Farmer's School of Cookery, which operated until 1944.

Another type of cooking school was based at colleges and universities. These schools were originally intended to prepare women for life as homemakers, but they later became vocationally directed. The first-known cookery program at a college was at Iowa Agricultural School, in Ames (later Iowa State University). The school began offering a course in domestic economy in 1876. Similar programs were instituted at other colleges and universities around the nation. The course work usually included topics such as dietetics, household science, bread making, and many others. A number of graduates of these college programs went on to teach in public schools, and many also became leaders in the home economics movement. Other university programs, such as Cornell's School of Hotel Administration, which opened in 1922, offered courses for students studying hotel restaurant management.

The CIA

Sarah Tyson Rorer—the founder of the Philadelphia Cooking School and author of almost a hundred popular cookbooks—first recognized the problem that would confront the food-service industry for decades to come: the lack of trained culinary professionals. In 1914, she predicted correctly that the lack of labor would create a need for cooking specialists, who would "command big salaries because they can direct a large staff of workers."[1]

Historically, many cooks and other restaurant workers in the United States were immigrants. When Congress began restricting immigration during the 1920s, this source of cheap labor disappeared. Although labor was not a problem during the Depression, it did became a serious issue, especially for restaurants, during World War II, when 25 million American men and women went into the military and millions more went to work for businesses directly related to the war effort. At the time, there was no system for training culinary professionals in the United States. This left restaurants with few professional workers or executives in their kitchens.

The New Haven Restaurant Association, with 300 restaurateurs and fifty wholesalers and suppliers as members, took on the problem of the wartime labor shortage. The association's founder, Richard Dargen, and the executive secretary, Charles Rovetti, thought up an unusual solution for at least part of their labor problem. In 1943, they approached William Cronin, the war manpower commissioner in New Haven, and, a few months later, area restaurants were declared an "essential industry," which meant that all employees were frozen in their positions. The restaurant labor force in New Haven was thus stabilized, but there was still a shortage of trained professional chefs.[2]

To solve this second problem, Dargen and Rovetti discussed the possibility of opening a school for training culinary professionals. What gave impetus to the idea was the passage, in June 1944, of the Servicemen's Readjustment Act. This unprecedented law, also known as the G.I. Bill, permitted returning servicemen to attend college at government expense. If the New Haven Restaurant Association's cooking school could get accredited, returning servicemen could take its courses for free while the federal government picked up the tab.

In late 1945, the association leased a building to house both its offices and a new cooking school, which was initially called the New Haven Restaurant Institute. Frances Roth was selected to be the school's director. She formed a partnership with Katharine Angell, who was made president and chair of the board. Angell sought funds to support the fledgling institution. Roth called on Alonzo Grace, the Connecticut commissioner of education, who helped get the institute accredited so that returning servicemen could qualify for financial assistance under the G.I. Bill. The New Haven Restaurant Association, the City of New Haven, and the New Haven Civic Association all helped fund the renovation of the building, and manufacturers of kitchen equipment supplied the latest professional-grade appliances.[3]

Before the school opened, Roth and Angell made an important decision: they incorporated the institute as a not-for-profit educational organization, rendering it independent of the New Haven Restaurant Association. Roth selected a board of directors, hired staff, and created a program with both hands-on cooking classes and professional restaurant management. The institute's doors opened in May 1946 with sixteen students, but the second class, entering in the fall of that year, doubled to thirty-five. In anticipation of larger and larger classes, the school bought a mansion in 1947 and transferred its operations there. The same year, the school completely severed its connections with the New Haven Restaurant Association and changed its name to the Restaurant Institute of America. In 1951, the name was changed once again, this time to the Culinary Institute of America. By 1965, the CIA had 300 students. Roth's and Angell's successors upgraded the faculty, established a core curriculum, and began publishing a manual, *The Professional Chef*, which was revised several times and served as the school's bible for many years.[4]

It wasn't long before increasing enrollment had outgrown the New Haven mansion, and in 1971, the institute purchased a former Jesuit seminary in Hyde Park, eighty miles north of New York City. After its move from Connecticut, the CIA acquired a charter from New York State permitting it to award associate's degrees, thus becoming the first culinary school in America to offer a degree. The large Hyde Park campus also permitted the construction of dormitories, and the CIA became the first culinary school to offer a residential program. Courses at the relocated CIA began in September 1972, and by 1980, the school had 1,300 students and an annual budget approaching $3 million. In 1993, the CIA began offering a bachelor's degree. Two years later, the institute opened a second campus, north of San Francisco, at Greystone in the Napa Valley.[5] In 2001, the CIA had assets of more than $164 million. By 2007, more than 37,000 students had graduated from the CIA, and many of its graduates have made their careers as professional cooks.

The Competition

The CIA's success—and a growing interest in culinary matters generally—brought a wave of new cooking schools to America. Celebrity chefs, such as

James Beard and Dione Lucas, opened cooking schools that flourished for years. Peter Kump's New York Cooking School, which opened in 1978 in a cramped brownstone kitchen, evolved into the Institute for Culinary Education, which each year enrolls about 23,000 students in full-time and avocational programs. The French Culinary Institute, in New York, was started by Dorothy Cann (later Hamilton) in 1984; she had been impressed and inspired on a visit to a culinary school in France.[6] On its faculty was Alain Sailhac, formerly of Le Cirque, Jacques Pépin, the respected cookbook author and television celebrity, and André Soltner, longtime chef at New York's restaurant Lutèce. Jacques Torres, another Le Cirque alumnus, became dean of the school's pastry program.[7]

The CIA's main competition, however, was the culinary program at Johnson & Wales, a college founded as a business school in Providence, Rhode Island, in 1914. In 1963, the school was accredited to offer associate's degrees in the arts and sciences, and in 1970, its program was expanded to award baccalaureate degrees.

However, Johnson & Wales faltered due to a lack of students, and, in 1972, entrepreneur Morris Gaebe purchased it and became the university's chancellor. The following year, Gaebe initiated what became the College of Culinary Arts, which offered degree programs in the hospitality and food-service fields. Gaebe hired former CIA instructors and recruited CIA graduates to get the culinary school off the ground, and it soon became the CIA's first real competitor. In 1984, Johnson & Wales established a campus in Charleston, South Carolina, and schools were also set up in other cities across America and eventually in other countries as well. In 1988, the school's name was officially changed to Johnson & Wales University. Thousands of students have graduated from its culinary arts program, including the famed chef and television star Emeril Lagasse, who graduated in 1978. By 2007, Johnson & Wales had become the largest food-service educator in the country.

With the success of the CIA and Johnson & Wales, culinary schools have become big business, and several large chains, such as Laureate, Le Cordon Bleu, and the Art Institutes have opened in many cities across the United States.

Professional Results

Culinary schools helped foster respect for the culinary profession by elevating standards through education. Graduates of culinary schools such as the CIA and Johnson & Wales serve as chefs and restaurant managers, and they run thousands of culinary operations behind the scenes. Some opt to work with large commercial food operations, such as CIA graduates Christopher Martone, the executive chef at Subway Restaurants; Steve Ells, the founder of Chipotle Mexican Grill; and Dan Coudreaut, the director of culinary innovation for McDonald's.

While cooking schools helped professionalize the culinary field, television has enhanced the appeal of a culinary career. Julia Child's pioneering TV program, *The French Chef*, was followed by dozens of others, culminating in the launch, in 1993, of the Food Network. Such programs made it possible for a number of chefs—including many CIA and Johnson & Wales graduates—to become television stars. The author and television personality Anthony Bourdain graduated from the CIA, as did restaurant and TV chefs Cat Cora, Charlie Palmer, Rocco DiSpirito, and Todd English. Johnson & Wales's Emeril Lagasse has hosted several Food Network programs, such as *Emeril Live*, which reached more than 90 million homes daily.

Culinary schools sprang up in cities across the nation, educating future chefs and culinary professionals. Most programs are similar to those offered by the CIA and Johnson & Wales. By 2001, there were 162 schools awarding degrees in culinary arts. In addition, small private schools continue to offer cooking classes, as do department stores, supermarket chains, restaurants, and hotels. Recreational cooking classes are popular throughout the United States; classes for children and teenagers, for couples, and for groups are offered nationwide. Enrollment in cooking classes in the United States had reached unprecedented levels by the beginning of the twenty-first century.

Postscript

Frances L. Roth remained as the CIA director until 1965. Of her, Craig Claiborne wrote: "All of the world's great chefs have been men, but the one individual who has probably done more than any other to give fine cuisine a foothold in the United States is a woman. She is Mrs. Frances Roth, a kind and intelligent gem of a person, with a seeming inexhaustible capacity for getting her own way."[8] Katharine Angell retired as president and chair of the CIA board in 1966. Today, the CIA's culinary library is named after her.

Ray Kroc's first restaurant in Des Plaines, Illinois, 1955 (courtesy McDonald's Corporation)

24.

McDonald's Drive-In

LIKE THE RESTAURATEURS in New Haven, Connecticut, Southern California restaurant owners Richard and Maurice McDonald confronted similar problems of locating cooks after World War II. Rather than open a school to train culinary professionals, however, they decided to create an efficient, self-service hamburger stand modeled on the assembly line, where unskilled workers could be given simple tasks to perform with little needed training. They reduced their menu to a few items and eliminated carhops, so customers had to walk up to an outside window to order their food. When the McDonald brothers' octagonal drive-in opened in 1948, it served inexpensive fast food. Within a decade, the company the brothers had started and the model they had created had changed American eating habits, an influence that continues to this day.

Fast Food History

"Eat and run" is not a twentieth-century phenomenon: from the earliest years of America's history, the speed with which Americans eat has appalled European observers. Apparently Americans have long believed that there are more important things to do than waste time preparing food, eating, and cleaning up afterward. In 1794, an English textile manufacturer visiting America reported in his journal that, within a half hour of eating, "every person had quitted table, to go to their several occupations and employments, except the Frenchmen and ourselves; for the Americans know the value of time too well to waste it at the table."[1] In 1819, English visitor Adam Hodgson reported that, in a tavern, "everyone rises as soon as he has finished his meal; and the busy scene is usually over in ten minutes."[2] Another English traveler, Captain Basil Hall, having his lunch at the Plate House, in New York, in 1827, noted that, within seconds of giving his order, waiters brought the dishes. In the twenty minutes he was in the restaurant, two sets of diners had been served.[3] A visiting Russian observed, in 1857, that Americans bolted everything down. About this same time, other travelers reported that Americans took less than four minutes to eat their meals.[4]

In 1841, an English visitor declared the American dinner was "hurried over" and treated with "irreverence." He noted further that "all manner of good things are set before you, but no time for reflection or selection is allowed—promptitude of decision is your only chance." Or, as he summed it up, "Gobble, gulp, and go" is the order of the day. Commenting about women eating in this manner, he lamented that "to behold the fairest of the fair adopt the bolting system is really awful."[5] Clearly, fast food arose in America long before the fast food industry—indeed, fast food chains simply tapped into what had become an ingrained American trait.

Burger History

Hamburg steak—chopped beef formed into a patty—was introduced to the American public by German immigrant restaurateurs in the 1870s. Thrifty, simple fare that customers could garnish with whatever condiments they liked, it was an immediate hit. Hamburg steak swept across America, and within a decade, it was commonly served in restaurants and cafés throughout the country. By the 1890s, street vendors were selling "hamburger steak" patties on buns, thus creating the hamburger sandwich. Unscrupulous vendors purportedly mixed fillers and adulterants into the chopped beef, and for the next three decades or so, the hamburger sandwich suffered from an unsavory reputation.[6]

One early-twentieth-century hamburger sandwich vendor was a short-order cook in Wichita, Kansas, named J. Walter Anderson. In 1916, Anderson bought a partly refurbished shoe repair store and opened up his own hamburger stand, selling the sandwiches for five cents apiece, a price almost anyone could afford. Aware of the negative reputation of hamburgers, Anderson had fresh beef delivered twice a day and designed his stands so that customers could watch their hamburgers being prepared. In 1921, he went into business with Edgar Waldo

"Billy" Ingram. The partners repackaged Anderson's hamburger stand, creating a new architectural design for new drive-ins, complete with crenellations, a tower, and a fresh coat of paint, and they changed its name to White Castle.[7] The ultraclean appearance of their drive-ins and the workers' crisp, white uniforms helped restore the hamburger's wholesome image—and made a great deal of money for the owners.

White Castle's success spurred the development of other hamburger chains, often with similar-sounding names, such as the White Mama diner, in Worcester, Massachusetts, White Tavern Hamburgers, in Amsterdam, New York, White Tower, in Milwaukee, and White Mana, in Jersey City, New Jersey. Within a decade, the hamburger had been transformed from a working-man's low-class lunch to a highly popular food served in cheerful drive-ins across America. By the 1930s, most medium-sized cities in America had fast-food hamburger outlets, and many drive-ins, roadside stands, diners, and coffee shops also served hamburgers.[8]

During World War II, hamburger chains faced serious shortages of both labor and beef, which was rationed during the war. Sugar was also rationed, so soft drinks were in short supply. As a result, many chains closed or reduced their number of franchises. After the war, rising crime rates and suburban flight brought additional problems to inner-city hamburger chains, such as White Castle and White Tower.[9]

The Brothers McDonald

Richard and Maurice McDonald moved to Los Angeles from New Hampshire in 1930, hoping to find work in the movie business. They were hired to push sets around sound stages before leaving to open a movie theater in Glendora, California. When the theater proved less successful than hoped, they opened a small hotdog stand. In 1940, they left the hotdog business and opened a stand selling hamburgers and barbecued chicken, in San Bernardino, a community about a hundred miles east of Los Angeles. Their drive-in employed twenty young women as carhops to take orders, serve the food, and collect payment from customers. After noting that 80 percent of its sales were hamburgers, the McDonald brothers dropped the chicken, which also took much longer to cook. After World War II, the McDonalds became convinced that their target audience was suburban families, so they designed a new environment that would attract that clientele.

The McDonalds also wanted to reduce expenses and increase profits through greater efficiency. They adopted, therefore, as a central feature of their operation, the assembly-line model popularized by auto pioneer Henry Ford, whose techniques had previously been adapted for use in food service in cafeterias, Automats, and other settings. According to the model, work was divided into simple tasks that could be performed with a minimum of training. This meant that employees were interchangeable and easily shifted from one task to another. The system also provided customers with fast, reliable, and inexpensive food. In exchange, customers had to wait in line, pick up their food from the counter, eat quickly, clean up their own trash, and leave without delay, making room for those next in line.

To accommodate the new assembly-line system, the McDonald brothers redesigned their restaurant, installing larger grills and machines, called Multimixers, that made six milk shakes simultaneously in metal containers. After the milk shakes were made—eighty or more were mixed in advance—they were poured into paper cups and held in a refrigerated case, thus speeding up the process of filling orders. Their model created a militarized production system based on a workforce of teenage boys, who were responsible for simple, easily learned tasks: some cooked the hamburgers, others packaged the sandwiches or poured the soft drinks and shakes, and still others placed the orders in paper bags. The McDonald model did away with indoor seating and streamlined the menu to a few items in addition to fifteen-cent hamburgers and nineteen-cent cheeseburgers. The hamburger patties weighed only 1.5 ounces, and all burgers came with the same condiments: ketchup, chopped onion, and two pickle slices. The other items were dime fries, twenty-cent shakes, and large and small sodas. In the new "self-service" restaurant, customers placed their orders at a walk-up window and ate in their cars. All food was served in disposable paper wrappers and paper cups, eliminating the need for washing dishes as well as the problems of breakage and theft.[10]

French fries were not on the menu at first. But after their drive-in opened, the brothers decided to add them. There was no space in their efficiently designed stand for the frying kettles, however, so they added on to their building, installing a "hot sink for rinsing the potatoes, cutters and peelers."[11] Adding french fries to their menu was a wise decision—potatoes were cheap and freshly fried potatoes went perfectly with hamburgers and sodas. McDonald's french fries would become one of the most profitable items on the menu.

The McDonald Brothers Burger Bar Drive-In was an octagonal building, which was not unusual for Southern California at that time. When the renovated drive-in opened in 1948, it got off to a rocky start: customers honked their horns, expecting carhops to come out and take their orders, as at other drive-ins. Eventually, customers figured out the new system and came back again and again for the low prices, fast service, and good hamburgers. The McDonald brothers aimed to have their employees serve a customer a full meal—hamburger, fries, and a beverage—in only twenty seconds. As customers steadily grew, profits rose. In 1951, the restaurant grossed $275,000 and netted $100,000. Within three years, profits had exceeded $300,000. Reports of the brothers' phenomenal success raced across the nation, and, in July 1952, *American Restaurant* magazine ran a cover story on the "McDonald's New Self-Service System." The McDonald brothers realized they were ready to franchise their operation, so they began advertising in magazines in search of interested participants.[12]

As radical as their new model of food preparation and service was, the McDonald brothers believed they could make it even more efficient by changing the restaurant's layout. They also wanted a more distinctive design, one that could be spotted from the road, something to make their drive-in stand out from the hundreds of other fast-food establishments around the nation. Their restaurant was constructed with a forward-sloping glass front, making its workers visible as they performed their tasks. The walls were painted in red and white candy stripes. Richard McDonald came up with the idea for the golden arches that bisected the roof. The floor consisted of white tile, signifying cleanliness, and the walls had lots of glass, which made food preparation visible to all.[13]

Even before the McDonald brothers had completed construction on their new restaurant in San Bernardino, they had begun selling franchises based on the new design. Franchise holders paid the brothers a relatively small fee and a percentage of sales. Unlike other franchisors, the McDonalds demanded that every outlet be built exactly like their model, with exactly the same food prepared in precisely the same way. There was to be no indoor dining; customers were expected to eat in their cars. A couple of inexpensive concrete benches and tables were provided outside for walk-up customers or for those who preferred to eat outside their automobiles. This overall design and operating plan gave McDonald's an advantage over other emerging fast-food chains because it promised consistency and predictability. Many potential franchise takers, unable to make use of already existing buildings, were unhappy with the constraints. By the end of 1953, the McDonald brothers had sold only twenty-one franchises, a mere ten of them eventually going into operation. Compared with other food chains at the time, McDonald's was hardly a success.

The new McDonald's drive-in in San Bernardino, however, attracted large crowds. Many entrepreneurs visited the site and were impressed with what they saw. Drive-in owners Keith G. Cramer and Matthew L. Burns visited McDonald's in 1952; the following year, they opened Insta-Burger King, in Jacksonville,

Florida, which later became Burger King.[14] After a visit to McDonald's in 1952, restaurant owner Carl Karcher, of Anaheim, California, decided to launch a fast-food chain of his own, which he did in 1956, calling it Carl's Jr.[15] Restaurateur Glen Bell, of San Bernardino, studied the McDonald's operation in developing something similar, only serving Mexican-style food instead of hamburgers. He eventually started the Taco Bell chain.[16] James A. Collins, chairman of Collins Foods International, paid a professional visit to the McDonalds' San Bernardino restaurant and, about a year later, opened a Kentucky Fried Chicken franchise based on the brothers' assembly-line design.[17] Other entrepreneurs opened McDonald's clones, and, by the mid-1950s, there were many fast-food places based on the McDonald brothers' model.[18]

Another visitor to McDonald's in San Bernardino was Ray Kroc, the owner of a Chicago company manufacturing the Multimixers the brothers had installed in their restaurant. Kroc had seen advertisements promoting McDonald's franchises and was surprised to find that the brothers had purchased eight of his company's Multimixers. In 1954, he visited the drive-in and was astounded by the crowds flooding the restaurant. It was entrepreneurial love at first sight—and Kroc immediately foresaw a glowing future for the chain. Kroc met with the brothers and promptly proposed an agreement allowing him to sell McDonald's franchises nationwide. The brothers agreed, with the proviso that all franchises adhere exactly to their model, a concession Kroc readily accepted.[19]

In the mid-1950s, franchising consisted mainly of assigning territories to franchise holders for huge up-front fees. Kroc wanted to control McDonald's operations, so he avoided territorial franchises by selling one store franchise at a time, thereby controlling the number of stores a licensee could operate. He also required strict conformity to operating standards, equipment used, menus, recipes, prices, trademarks, and architectural designs.[20]

In 1955, Kroc created McDonald's System, Inc., and sold himself the first franchise, which opened in Des Plaines, Illinois, in 1955. It was intended to be a model operation that would attract potential franchise purchasers. And it did: by the end of 1959, there were more than a hundred McDonald's operations around the nation. Despite this success, Kroc went through numerous legal and personal disagreements with the McDonald brothers along the way. For one thing, Kroc wanted to innovate, but his agreement prevented him from doing so. Kroc finally solved the impasse with the McDonalds by buying them out, for $2.7 million, an astronomical sum in 1961.[21]

Within a decade of his first encounter with the McDonald brothers, Ray Kroc had revolutionized fast-food service far beyond the brothers' wildest expectations. Kroc founded Hamburger University to train managers and company executives, and the graduates went forth and multiplied McDonald's operations throughout the world.[22] By 1963, McDonald's was selling 1 million burgers a day, and this was only the beginning. The company began advertising nationally in 1966, the same year it was first listed on the New York Stock Exchange. By 1973, McDonald's was so popular that *Time* magazine did a cover story on the McDonald's "Hamburger Empire," subtitling it "The Burger That Conquered the Country."[23]

Ray Kroc's successful franchise system was the prototype for other fast-food chains, which readily adopted the McDonald's model. When other chains introduced innovations, McDonald's made the necessary changes to keep up with its competition. In 1967, Burger King's debut of a newly designed restaurant with indoor seating challenged one of basic tenets of McDonald's: customers eat in their cars. By the 1960s, however, the novelty of eating in the car had worn off, in part because it was uncomfortable on hot and humid days and on cold winter days as well. Indoor eating areas permitted comfortable dining year-round, and, from the response at Burger King, customers seemed to appreciate the new inside seating. McDonald's countered with a new store design featuring indoor seating as well; the design was inaugurated in 1968. The new design also challenged another of the early McDonald's dogmas—that the chain would stay out of cities. Since that time, thousands of McDonald's franchises have found success in urban areas.

Yet another shift was the invention of the drive-through window. In 1948, In-N-Out Burger installed a two-way speaker box for customer orders at its first outlet, in Baldwin Park, California. The innovation sped up ordering and serving. Other fast-food operations, including Jack in the Box and Burger King, experimented with drive-through service, but not until 1969, when Wendy's installed drive-through windows at its franchises, did the new format find success. Customers in cars appreciated being able to order at the drive-through window rather than park their car, stand in line, order, and then return to the car. McDonald's answered the demand by installing, in 1975, its first drive-through window. Today, take-out and drive-through sales account for about 60 percent of the fast-food income in America.[24]

McCriticism

Criticism is endemic to McDonald's, in part because of the company's enormous success—and its huge influence around the world. To many environmentalists McDonald's is a culinary atrocity contributing to rain forest destruction and global warming. For many nutrition advocates, McDonald's sells junk food and contributes to the problem of obesity. Other observers see McDonald's as a symbol of culinary homogenization undermining local and regional cuisines.

While the company has been criticized on a variety of fronts, it has occasionally responded positively to such criticism. In the 1960s, when the company was taken to task for the lack of African American managers in its restaurants, McDonald's made an effort to recruit more black franchise holders. When charged with promoting junk food in the 1980s, the company began selling salads, reduced the fat content of its hamburgers, and changed the way its french fries were cooked.[25] When criticized, around the same time, for causing harm to the environment, specifically for its use of polystyrene foam in coffee cups and food containers, McDonald's responded by creating an alliance with the Environmental Defense Fund to make the company more environmentally friendly. The company also switched from polystyrene to paper products and encouraged recycling. The Environmental Defense Fund has estimated that, since 1989, McDonald's has saved 150,000 tons of waste through the improved packaging it now requires of its suppliers. In addition, the company has purchased more than $4 billion in recycled materials for its own operations. As a result of these programs, McDonald's has received a good deal of positive press coverage.[26]

McDonald's has also been criticized for its influence on suppliers. The logic is simple: McDonald's is the largest purchaser of beef in the world, and, as such, it bears some responsibility for the practices of its suppliers. Criticism has focused on suppliers in developing countries, specifically Central America and Brazil, for their role in destroying tropical rain forests to clear land for cattle raising.[27] In response to these concerns and a potential public relations nightmare, McDonald's stopped buying beef from operations in rain forests or recently deforested lands, and it has also made substantial contributions to groups working to save the environment.[28] Attacks have also come in connection with the conditions in the feedlots and slaughterhouses of its various suppliers. Journalist Eric Schlosser, in his book *Fast Food Nation*, maintains that, as a result of practices followed at McDonald's and other fast-food chains, meatpacking is the most dangerous job in the United States. Schlosser has written that negligent practices by meat-packers "facilitated the introduction of deadly pathogens, such as *E. coli* 0157:H7, into America's hamburger meat."[29] When McDonald's required that ground beef be demonstrably safe, the company's suppliers acquired equipment that allowed for better testing.

McDonald's has also been charged with adversely affecting local cultures and businesses around the world. The chain's success abroad has caused deep resentment among many non-Americans, who see the company as a threat to local culinary traditions. In France, for example, José Bové, a French farmer and leader of the antiglobalization movement, demolished a McDonald's restaurant that was nearing completion.[30] Similar actions have occurred in other European countries. McDonald's has responded to such attacks by pointing out that many of its non-American operations are locally owned and that most products used in McDonald's operations are produced in the host country.

McEffects

Although fast-food chains had been around since the 1920s, the McDonald brothers and Ray Kroc carried the concept of quick service and low prices to its ultimate realization. The application of efficiency to food production championed by them has been refined by fast-food chains over the last sixty years. Some chains use conveyor belts and assembly lines to ensure standardization. Employees clad in identical uniforms are trained to greet and serve customers in the same specific way. The kitchens are filled with buzzers and flashing lights that tell employees what to do next. The computerized cash registers issue their own commands. The surprising consequence has been how quickly fast food claimed such a large proportion of the American diet.

George Ritzer, author of *The McDonaldization of Society*, has argued that the fast-food industry has pursued efficiency to the detriment of other important values. The industry's focus on efficiency has, according to Ritzer, homogenized American life—and, thanks to the globalization of fast food, is now homogenizing the lives of people around the world.[31]

Today, more than 46 million people per day eat at a McDonald's restaurant around the world; in America, fast food is one of the main forms of the American culinary experience, with an estimated 60 million customers visiting a fast-food establishment every day. Owing in large part to fast-food chains, Americans now spend more of their food dollars eating outside the home than in it.

McPostscript

When Ray Kroc began franchising McDonald's, he envisioned an eventual total of 1,000 outlets in the United States. When he died, in 1984, at the age of eighty-one, there were 7,500 McDonald's restaurants worldwide. Today, the chain has more than 30,000 restaurants in more than one hundred countries.[32]

There was no love lost between Ray Kroc and the McDonald brothers. After Kroc bought the McDonald's chain, he built a new McDonald's restaurant across the street from the brothers' fast-food operation in San Bernardino, and later gleefully reported that he "ran 'em out of business."[33] When their original

McDonald's restaurant burned down in 1976, it was demolished, and thereafter Kroc regularly blazoned that his operation in Des Plaines was the first real McDonald's hamburger outlet; it was later converted into a museum. The only surviving restaurant franchised by the McDonald brothers is in Downey, California, and it also operates as a museum.

Ray Kroc's autobiography, *Grinding It Out: The Making of McDonald's*, alleges that Ray Kroc "at age 52 founded the McDonald's hamburger chain and built it from a single restaurant in Des Plaines, Illinois, to an international operation with more than $3 billion in annual sales." When Richard McDonald saw this, he dryly commented: "Up until the time we sold, there was no mention of Kroc being the founder. If we had heard about it, he would be back selling milkshake machines."[34]

Maurice McDonald died in 1971, in Riverside, California, aged sixty-nine; his brother, Richard, died in Manchester, New Hampshire, in 1998, aged eighty-nine.

Julia Child in *Julia's Breakfasts, Lunches, and Suppers* (New York: Knopf, 1999; copyright 1999 by Julia Child)

25.

Julia Child, the French Chef

SOON AFTER *Mastering the Art of French Cooking*, by Simone Beck, Louisette Bertholle, and Julia Child, rolled off the press, in September 1961, sales were good. But the publisher had put minimal funds behind promoting the cookbook, and it was unlikely sales would continue to grow unless there were more promotion. Here fate intervened in the form of Beatrice Braude, whom Julia Child and her husband had met when Braude worked in cultural affairs at the American embassy in Paris in the early 1950s. Graylisted during the McCarthy era, Braude was let go by the embassy and later moved to Boston, where she became a production assistant for Henry Morgenthau's *Prospects of Mankind*, on Boston television station WGBH. The Childs invited her to dinner one evening, and she urged Julia to publicize her book on WGBH's *I've Been Reading*, hosted by a Boston College English professor, Dr. P. Albert Duhamel. At the time, WGBH was a fledgling educational station. Although she didn't own a television set and rarely watched TV, Julia Child agreed to give it a try.

Although Duhamel had not previously interviewed cookbook authors, he was a connoisseur of fine food and readily agreed to interview Child. Rather than just talk for half an hour, Child decided to take her hot plate and a pan and teach Duhamel how to make a French omelet—her first televised cooking demonstration. WGBH's Russell Morash, the future director and producer of *The French Chef*, recalled Child's interview with Duhamel: "I thought to myself: Who is this madwoman cooking an omelet on a book-review program?"[1] The madwoman was about to teach America, through the medium of public television, how to cook, and, in the process, she became the country's first television food celebrity.

American Fascination with French Cookery

Well before Julia Child debuted on television, there was a certain amount of interest in America in French cooking. America's well-to-do had long enjoyed classic French food. For almost 200 years, there had been restaurants in the country offering French fare. Especially during the Gilded Age and Prohibition, wealthy Americans traveled to France, where they dined at the world's finest restaurants; magazine writers and novelists had conveyed the joys of dining in France to stay-at-home Americans, who could vicariously enjoy haute cuisine. After World War II, many more Americans visited France, and a number sojourned there for years. Some first saw France while in the military, while others went there on assignment for the Foreign Service. Still others—the newly affluent upper-middle class—took advantage of the strong U.S. dollar and vacationed in France, where they often discovered simple but excellent food at modest prices in provincial restaurants, superior produce at outdoor markets, and a dazzling array of cheeses and wines they had never heard of back home.

One American who lived in France and fell in love with its food was a tall, no-nonsense, middle-aged woman, born Julia McWilliams. Raised in Pasadena, California, she graduated from Smith College in 1934 and worked as an advertising assistant for the New York City furniture company W. & J. Sloane. In 1938, she returned to Pasadena, where she became the advertising manager for Sloane's Beverly Hills branch. In this position, responsible for an advertising budget of $100,000, McWilliams planned advertising campaigns and wrote copy. Four months after taking the position, she sent out unedited advertising copy, and was fired.[2]

During World War II, McWilliams joined the Office of Strategic Services (OSS), the forerunner of the Central Intelligence Agency. She was posted to Ceylon (Sri Lanka), where, in the summer of 1944, she rose to the important position of head of registry.[3] There, she met New Jersey–born Paul Child, also in the OSS, who was ten years her senior. Paul Child was cosmopolitan, literate, and European in manner. He had lived in France before the war and become something of an epicure. They were both assigned to Kunming, China, at the war's end, and there they enjoyed seeing the sights and talking about the food. After the war, Julia returned to Pasadena, and Paul to Washington, D.C. Believing that Paul favored sophisticated women, Julia thought she could impress him by becoming an accomplished cook. She took cooking classes from two British women, Mary Hill and Irene Radcliffe, at their Hillcliff School of Cookery, in Beverly Hills. The results were often disastrous: "Her béarnaise sauce congealed because she used lard instead of butter; her calves' brains in red wine fell apart; her well-larded wild duck set the oven on fire."[4] Despite months of effort, Julia was no less befuddled by cooking, but, as she later commented, Paul saw in her other redeeming qualities, and, in 1946, they were married. At the time, Paul was working for the State Department, so the newlyweds settled down in Washington, D.C. Julia subscribed to *Gourmet* and acquired a copy of Irma Rombauer's *The Joy of Cooking*, through whose recipes she struggled for years.[5]

Two years into their marriage, Paul was assigned to the American embassy in Paris. From Julia's first meal in France (en route from Le Havre to Paris, they stopped for dinner in Rouen), she fell in love with French food. After they'd settled into their new apartment in Paris, Julia enrolled in the Cordon Bleu cooking school. The class she was in was for former American military on the G.I. Bill, and she was its only female member. She began experimenting with French dishes at home, serving them to her husband, members of the diplomatic corps, and her French and American friends. She also took courses from Claude Thillmont, pastry chef at the Café de Paris. By March 1950, she had quit the class and begun studying independently with Cordon Bleu instructor Chef Max Bugnard, then in his seventies, who had worked under Auguste Escoffier, the famous French chef and restaurateur. Julia took her exams at the Cordon Bleu in April 1951 and received a certificate of attendance.[6]

At a reception for a Marshall Plan executive, Julia met Simone Beck, who told her about the Cercle des Gourmettes, a women's culinary club dedicated to French gastronomy. The Gourmettes met bimonthly for lunch at the home of one of its members or, occasionally, at a restaurant. In January 1951, Julia began attending meetings, and four months later she was asked to join. Beck introduced Julia to Louisette Bertholle, who, having been raised by an English nanny, spoke English. The three women decided to start their own cooking school, which they called L'École des trois gourmandes; the school opened in January 1952. It was targeted at American women living in Paris, and Julia's aim was to make the classes informal and friendly but with a high standard of professionalism. While teaching at the school, which was in fact located in Julia's home kitchen, she continued her private instruction with Chef Bugnard, who also advised her on recipes and menus for the school's curriculum. Julia typed up the recipes for each class, along with a detailed lesson plan. As Julia's biographer Laura Shapiro has pointed out, these classes were the template for all Julia's teaching, writing, and television programs.[7]

Bertholle, while on a visit to New York in 1951, tried to convince Sumner Putnam, an editor at Ives Washburn, Inc., to publish a comprehensive French cookbook. Putnam was interested, but he wanted to test the waters with a much smaller book that would serve as a teaser for the larger work. Bertholle and Beck wrote fifty recipes, in French, and Putnam assigned Helmut Ripperger, a successful cookbook writer and freelance editor, to translate and edit them for the American market. The sixty-three page spiral-bound booklet, titled *What's Cooking in France*, was released in 1952. It received positive mention in the *New York Times*, where the reviewer reported that the small work was the "hors d'oeuvre to a larger work in preparation by the same authors."[8] It was successful enough for Putnam to agree to publish the larger work.

Bertholle and Beck sent Putnam a 600-page collection of recipes. Putnam again turned them over to Ripperger, who was to fashion it into a publishable manuscript, tentatively titled "French Cooking for All." But Ripperger bailed out of the project in the summer of 1952. Putnam then asked Bertholle and Beck to rework the manuscript themselves. They, in turn, asked their new American friend, Julia Child, to review the manuscript, which she did. Julia concluded the recipes were far beyond the abilities of the average American cook. The recipes, she believed, needed to be clarified, simplified, made more concise and more instructional. With encouragement from Bertholle and Beck, Julia jumped into the project, overhauling the work by organizing it around fundamental principles, adding technical instructions, converting the French into readable English, and testing and revising the recipes. Julia sent a revised sauce chapter to Putnam for review, but, by early January 1953, "les trois gourmandes" had heard nothing from the publisher.[9]

Enter Avis DeVoto. In November 1951, Avis's husband, Bernard DeVoto, wrote a piece about kitchen knives for his column "The Easy Chair," in *Harper's Magazine*. Avis had convinced her husband, a prominent writer and historian, to write about how their American-made stainless steel cutlery might be rust-free but could not hold an edge. Julia read the article and sent Bernard a fan letter—along with two French carbon steel knives. His wife, Avis, responded to Julia's letter, and the two began a correspondence that matured into a friendship that was conducted almost exclusively by mail. Julia mentioned their troubles with Ives Washburn and sent Avis a copy of the sauce chapter she'd sent to Putnam. Avis read the revised manuscript and began testing the recipes. She liked them and recommended sending a proposal with recipes to Houghton Mifflin, her husband's publisher. Houghton Mifflin was pleased with the proposal, so the three would-be cookbook writers ended discussions with Putnam and signed a contract with Houghton Mifflin, receiving a small advance. The cookbook, now named "French Home Cooking," was scheduled for release in 1954.[10]

Julia tested and rewrote the recipes, making sure that an average American cook could make them and yet keeping them true to their French origins. Over the next several years, Paul was posted to Marseilles, then Bonn, Washington, D.C., and later to Norway, which slowed the writing process. Bertholle lost interest in the project and backed out of active work on the manuscript, but Beck and Julia continued testing recipes and revising, expanding, and correcting the manuscript. Julia inserted modern equipment where appropriate, and substituted common American ingredients for French products then unobtainable in the United States. All this took time. The manuscript was finally completed on February 24, 1958, but Houghton Mifflin rejected it: the editors felt the book was too big, too complicated, and too confusing for the average American cook. The authors had no choice but to set about revising the manuscript yet again. The reworked manuscript was submitted a year later, but Houghton Mifflin again rejected it, and this time their decision was final.

In the interim, Avis had become a talent scout for Knopf. When she heard that Houghton Mifflin had rejected the manuscript, she sent a copy to Alfred Knopf, who sent it on to Bill Koshland, a vice president at Knopf and an amateur cook. Koshland, in turn, gave the manuscript to Judith Jones, a Knopf editor. She had traveled to Europe on a vacation in 1948 and remained in Paris, where she had fallen in love with the food, and with Evan Jones, her future husband. In 1951, the newlyweds returned to the United States and eventually Judith Jones ended up at Knopf. She was knocked out by the manuscript: its genius, she realized, was in the details of its master recipes and their variations. She, Koshland, and Angus Cameron, who had worked on *The Joy of Cooking* many years before, began testing the recipes and found that they worked. Jones wrote to Julia, exclaiming the manuscript was "revolutionary and we intend to prove it and to make it a classic."[11]

Despite Jones's enthusiasm, Alfred Knopf, the founder of the company, was not excited about the manuscript, even though he hadn't actually read it. The company had just released *Classic French Cuisine*, by Joseph Donon, a chef who had trained under Escoffier. Knopf didn't think the company needed to publish another French cookbook anytime soon. In addition, the manuscript was voluminous, and it would be expensive to print. Perhaps the biggest obstacle, as Jones later wrote, was that the cookbook was written by "three totally unknown ladies with no particular credentials."[12] After extensive internal discussion, Knopf grudgingly agreed to publish it.

Julia and Beck spent an additional year working on the manuscript, and it was finished in August 1960. Jones didn't like the titles proposed by the authors, so she came up with one of her own: *Mastering the Art of French Cooking*. The official release date was set for October 16, 1961, and Beck came over from France to join the festivities.[13]

Chances were slim that *Mastering the Art of French Cooking* would be a hit. It was just one of many French cookbooks published in the United States since World War II, authored by French chefs and professional culinary writers.[14] Written by three unknowns, the book clearly didn't have the built-in high profile visibility of many other works. True, Beck and Bertholle were identified as "well known Parisian hostesses and expert amateur cooks."[15] As for the third coauthor, she was the forty-nine-year-old wife of a retired State Department official. Yes, she had studied French cookery at the Cordon Bleu in Paris and had done some teaching with Beck and Bertholle, but she had never published anything of importance.

Nonetheless, *Mastering the Art of French Cooking* was different from the cookbooks that preceded it, which assumed readers were already familiar with the fundamentals of French cookery. As these basics had been unknown to Julia when she began learning French cooking, she could empathize with American cooks and their mystification by the recipes in other French cookbooks. So, *Mastering the Art of French Cooking* assumed nothing. Julia had taken the French recipes collected by Beck and Bertholle and broken them down step-by-step, so that even a novice cook could succeed with them. The work's ten-year gestation period gave birth to a cookbook with "breadth, thoroughness of explanation, culinary authenticity, distinctive authorial voice . . . and reliability," as food writer David Kamp declares in his book *The United States of Arugula*.[16]

For promoting the 726-page tome, Knopf allocated limited funds for a few advertisements in newspapers and magazines. The book's chances for success were minimal, it was thought, so why waste precious marketing dollars on it? On the other hand, without promotion, such a cookbook was unlikely to find its audience. Then Judith Jones had an idea. A few months before the book was to be published, she called Craig Claiborne, the *New York Times* food columnist, asking him to review the book. Claiborne proposed a deal: if Jones and her husband would host a cookout for him on their Manhattan terrace, he would review the book once it was out. The Joneses upheld their end of the bargain, and, a few days after *Mastering the Art of French Cooking* was released, Claiborne's review raved that it was "the most comprehensive, laudable and monumental work" on French cookery and that it would likely "remain as the definitive work for nonprofessionals." It was "not a book for those with a superficial interest in food, but for those who take fundamental delight in the pleasures of cuisine." "It is written in the simplest terms possible," he added, "and without compromise or condescension. The recipes are glorious."[17]

Claiborne's review gave the cookbook solid credentials and maximum visibility. It generated enough buzz that the authors were asked to conduct a cooking demonstration on the *NBC Today* show, hosted by John Chancellor. Before an estimated 4 million viewers, and working over a single-burner hot plate, Beck cooked up a perfect omelet. The following day, Beck and Julia did a demo at Bloomingdale's. Then they were interviewed on the *Martha Deane* radio program. *Vogue*, *Life*, and *House & Garden* mentioned or reviewed the book, and the food editor of *House & Garden* declared it an "amazing piece of work" and asked Julia to write an article on French cookery.[18]

At their own expense, Beck and the Childs began a promotional tour to Boston, Detroit, Chicago, San Francisco, and Los Angeles. Using their hot plate and some additional equipment they brought with them on the train, they engaged in cooking demonstrations in department stores and were interviewed on local radio and television programs. On December 15, Julia and Beck returned to New York, where they met James Beard, then the "king of gourmets," who had set up a luncheon with food editors, including Poppy Cannon, then of *House Beautiful*. At the luncheon, Beard strongly endorsed *Mastering the Art of French Cooking*, gushing to the authors before the assembled editors, "I love your cookbook—I just wish I had written it myself."[19]

The French Chef

These promotional activities paid off. During its first four months, the book sold 10,000 copies, and Knopf ordered a print run of another 10,000. These were respectable sales figures—especially for a complex and lengthy cookbook written by three unknown authors. Still, without additional publicity, likely sales would gradually have declined and Julia Child would have drifted into obscurity.

After the interview and omelet demonstration with Duhamel on WGBH, twenty-seven viewers wrote to the station—all more or less praising the show. Now, twenty-seven fan letters may not seem a lot by today's standards, but for WGBH in 1962, it was a phenomenally high number. As Julia's biographer Noël Riley Fitch later wrote, sometimes the station wondered if there were as many as twenty-seven people tuned into their programs.[20] With such a resounding success, WGBH proposed to Julia that she do three half-hour pilot programs on cooking. Julia agreed and wrote and rewrote her scripts, practiced making the dishes, checked her timing, and memorized her first lines.[21] Russell Morash was selected to direct the pilots, and, since he knew nothing about food, he was assisted by Ruth Lockwood, a graduate of Fannie Farmer's School of Cookery.[22] Three programs ("The French Omelette," "Coq au Vin," and "Soufflés") were taped in June 1962, and the first was broadcast on July 28 of that year.

The odds were against the show's success, based on the history of TV cooking shows that had come before it: James Beard, a trained actor, had hosted a series of fifteen-minute programs called *I Love to Cook!* for NBC, in 1946; they aired after a variety show, *Elsie Presents*, introduced by a puppet version of Borden's Elsie the Cow. None of Beard's programs have survived, but Beard was reportedly awkward and ill at ease in front of the camera. Regardless of Beard's lack of telegenic skills, television programmers liked the idea, and other shows soon followed. Dione Lucas, an expat English cooking teacher and founder of the Dione Lucas Gourmet Cooking School, in New York, hosted the first national thirty-minute cooking show, on CBS, in 1948. Her programs, *To the Queen's Taste*, followed by *Dione Lucas's Cooking Show*, focused on French food, but her stern and somewhat forbidding presentation made French cookery seem complex and difficult. Many local television stations had experimented with cooking shows, but none had stirred up much public interest.[23]

Julia Child seemed ill-suited to television as well. As many observers have pointed out, she was too tall—six feet two inches—hardly a beauty, her voice warbled, and she often gasped midsentence when she spoke on television. On the other hand, Julia had much to recommend her: She was highly intelligent, energetic, organized, entertaining, authentic, and, as her husband remarked, she was a natural clown in front of the camera. She had an imposing physical presence. Her honesty, folksy manner, and natural charm came through to the television audience. Her manner was both serious and instructional and yet lighthearted and often hilarious.[24]

Unlike other TV cooking show hosts, Julia was a good teacher—her goal was to make French cookery so easy to understand that even average American cooks could serve a respectable French meal based on ingredients acquired from the local supermarket. At the start of most episodes, Julia would describe what was to be accomplished, offer background information, then proceed, step-by-step, to demonstrate how to make the dishes, while offering practical advice, potential variations, and surprising antics along the way to avoid pedagogical boredom. Episodes climaxed with the serving of the tempting dishes. The show had a simple and obvious enough organizational format by today's standards, but one she and her associates at WGBH had to develop from scratch in the 1960s. As she explained it, "What I was trying to do was to break down the snob appeal. There was the great mystery about it, and you didn't tell people what was going on. What I tried to do was to demystify it."[25] In doing so, she popularized French cookery as many Americans gained, through her and her program, some under-standing and appreciation of it.

WGBH was pleased with the results of the three pilot programs, and it agreed to tape a twenty-six-part series. It took three months for the station to line up sponsors, but then *The French Chef* went into full production. The first episodes were filmed in January 1963, and the first program aired on February 11 that same year. Julia wrote an article for the *Boston Globe*, which appeared on the cover of "Boston Globe TV Week" a few days before the series aired. Each program was based on fundamental lessons focusing on a particular dish that many Americans were at least familiar with. The series started with boeuf bourguignonne and ended with crêpes suzette. It was a success almost from the first episode. By March, WGBH had received 600 fan letters—a remarkable number in 1963 by any standard.[26]

Julia's energy, pedagogical abilities, sense of timing, informal, chatty manner, and her humor all contributed to the program's success. When Julia made mistakes on the air, she seized them as what are now called teachable moments. When she flipped a skillet-sized potato pancake and part of it ended up on the stove rather than back in the pan, she reassembled the pieces and assured viewers, "You can always pick it up if you're alone in the kitchen. Who's going to see?" This quickly became part of the cooking lore associated with Julia Child—although the story's particulars often changed in the retelling.[27] Her "failures and her *faux pas* are classic," declared *Time* magazine in 1966.[28]

Another important advantage was the program's WGBH time slot. Earlier, most commercial network cooking programs had been broadcast during the day. *The French Chef* aired during prime time on educational television, which was watched by more affluent, educated, and sophisticated viewers—many of them men—who were already predisposed to be interested in French cookery. Because WGBH was noncommercial and Julia did not endorse products or kowtow to advertisers, she gained credibility in the eyes of her viewers and the American public at large. With very little advertising outside Boston, *The French Chef* became a word-of-mouth sensation throughout the United States. By the beginning of 1965, sixty-six public television stations were carrying her program; by that year's end, ninety-six were doing so.

Julia was paid little for the shows—a few hundred dollars plus expenses—but she did cash in on sales of *Mastering the Art of French Cooking*. When the Book-of-the-Month Club (BOMC) picked it as an alternate book dividend selection, sales through BOMC alone reached more than 65,000 copies.[29] Initially, the authors of *Mastering the Art of French Cooking* were listed in alphabetical order; as a reflection of Julia's growing popularity, however, her name appears first on the cover and title page of the BOMC edition, and it would so appear in all subsequent editions. Store sales rose to 600 copies per month in the summer of 1963; by October 1964, sales had jumped to 4,000 copies per month. By March 1969, the cookbook had sold 600,000 copies. In 1974, the *New York Times* reported that sales had reached 1.4 million, and *Mastering the Art of French Cooking* became one of the century's best-selling cookbooks.[30]

Many reasons have been offered for the tremendous success of *The French Chef*. The low-budget production values perversely enhanced viewer appreciation, particularly when compared with the slick programming on commercial television. Its timing was ideal. Since World War I, well-to-do Americans had been falling in love with France, and this appreciation extended to the upper-middle class after World War II. In January 1961, John F. Kennedy and his Francophile wife, Jacqueline Bouvier Kennedy, moved into the White House; a few months later, they selected René Verdon, who had been executive chef at Essex House, in New York, as the White House chef. By 1962, French cookery had become trendy, but it was still out of reach for most Americans—at least until Julia Child came along. She understood classic French cookery and had the ability to communicate her understanding to a wide American audience, through her writings as well as her television programs.

The French Chef catapulted Julia Child into culinary stardom, and for the next forty years, she was a towering figure in the American food world. In 1965, the George Foster Peabody committee, which issues awards for distinguished achievement in television and radio, gave an award to *The French Chef*. A few months later, the series received an Emmy for best educational television program—the first Emmy ever given to a program on educational television. In October 1966, *Life* magazine touted Julia Child as "the Master Chef," although she never considered herself a chef. On November 25, 1966, Julia's photo appeared on the cover of *Time* magazine, which gave her enormous satisfaction; it also gave the culinary community a feeling that gastronomy had finally achieved legitimacy.[31]

Chef Effects

The French Chef became one of the longest-running programs in the history of public television, and its 200 episodes were still being broadcast more than forty years later. *Mastering the Art of French Cooking* and *The French Chef* introduced an accessible version of French cooking to American homes, and Julia Child's TV sign-off, "*Bon appétit!*" entered the American vocabulary.[32]

Julia Child influenced not only her readers and viewers of her television program, but also the writers and chefs who came after her. Narcisse Chamberlain, daughter of Samuel and Narcissa Chamberlain and a cookbook author and editor in her own right, said, "*Mastering* put good authors on notice that cookbooks had to be honest. As an editor, I admired the volume." Paula Wolfert, the author of authoritative books on Mediterranean cookery, wrote, "Just as it's been said that all Russian literature has been taken from Gogol's overcoat, so all American food writing has been derived from Julia's apron."[33] Patric Kuh, author of *The Last Days of Haute Cuisine: America's Culinary Revolution*, has expressed the opinion that what made *Mastering the Art of French Cooking* a "groundbreaking book was not so much that it was an authentic French cookbook as much as that it was an authentic cookbook that happened to be French. It was understanding the food that allowed its author to go into raptures over a butter-infused serving of fresh peas with pearl onions and just cooked Boston lettuce quarters."[34] As culinary historian and food writer Betty Fussell has noted, "We didn't want to be professional chefs. We wanted to be artists, and Julia was there to show us how cooking could be elevated to art."[35]

Jacques Pépin, a chef born and trained in France, was impressed with *Mastering the Art of French Cooking* in its coverage of the basic techniques an aspiring French cook would learn while serving the traditional three-year apprenticeship. The authors had simply codified it, he noted, broken it down into simple steps. In his 2003 memoir, Pépin wrote, "I was a little jealous. This was the type of book I should have written."[36] He had written several successful cookbooks and hosted a popular television series for KQED, in northern California. Pépin went on to do other television series, including one with Julia Child, *Julia and Jacques: Cooking at Home.* [37]

Over the years, the relationship between Julia Child and Jacques Pépin expanded beyond their television series: they championed the American Institute of Wine and Food, the James Beard Foundation, and the Culinary Trust (the philanthropic arm of the International Association of Culinary Professionals), and the food studies program at Boston University. Some observers attribute the rise of the academic field of food studies in part to Julia's various efforts.

Following Julia's lead, other chefs, restaurateurs, and food personalities— Joyce Chen, Graham Kerr, Jeff Smith, Justin Wilson, and Martin Yan, to name a few—took to the airwaves, and cooking shows debuted on both commercial and newly emerging public television stations. Their perennial popularity culminated, in 1993, in the creation of the Television Food Network. The techniques and format invented by Julia Child and her associates at WGBH for *The French*

Chef established the organizational template for subsequent cooking shows, and they remain the standard today.

Postscript

Louisette Bertholle went on to publish several cookbooks in French that were widely acclaimed throughout Europe. Two subsequent cookbooks by Simone Beck, *Simca's Cuisine* and *New Menus from Simca's Cuisine*, did well in the United States, but they never achieved the success of Julia Child's later books; Beck didn't understand that one major reason for Julia's success was television. Julia herself went on to star in other television series and continued publishing books.[38] She died in 2004, but her legacy survives through her cookbooks, and her TV programs—particularly *The French Chef*—continue to be enjoyed by devoted fans and new audiences alike.

New Yorker Jean Nidetch celebrates her twenty years as head of Weight Watchers, the organization she founded, with a special-ingredient birthday cake during a party in London, England, on April 18, 1983. (AP photo)

26.

Jean Nidetch's Diet

AT THE AGE of thirty-five, Jean Nidetch, a Queens, New York, house-wife, stood five feet seven inches tall and weighed in at 214 pounds. She had tried every diet imaginable, but nothing had worked. In 1961, desperate to lose weight, she enrolled in the obesity clinic run by New York City's Department of Health and was put on a diet championed by Dr. Norman Jolliffe. After losing twenty-one pounds on the diet, she began to lose confidence she could continue. Thinking there might be strength—and moral support—in numbers, she called six overweight friends and asked them to join her in the diet program. The women gathered at Nidetch's house and, borrowing techniques from Alcoholics Anonymous, sat in a circle and took turns speaking about their weight problems and giving each other moral support. One member of the group was Felice Lippert, who, over a period of one year, lost fifty pounds. Nidetch herself lost seventy-two pounds, and the others each lost considerable weight as well. In May 1963, Jean Nidetch, along with Felice Lippert and her husband, Albert Lippert, a garment executive, incorporated Weight Watchers International.[1] Weight Watchers was just one of dozens of diet programs popular in America at the time, but over the years, it has proven to be one of the most successful. By the early twenty-first century, hundreds of such programs had attracted millions of Americans, and millions more overweight Americans have struggled to lose weight on their own, without participating in formal diet programs.

Diet History

Dieting—a regimen of eating and drinking designed to diminish weight—has been part of American life for almost two centuries. Sylvester Graham believed that an abstemious diet of his own devising would make people robust and energetic, yet temperate.[2] Graham was not alone in advocacy of dietary restraint. Other medical professionals believed that gluttony caused indigestion, which in turn led to illness. Graham and his followers believed that gluttony, rather than inadequate nutrition, was "the greatest source of disease and suffering and premature death to man!"[3] But this was a minority view: at the time, corpulence was considered neither unappealing nor unhealthful. This began to change in the late nineteenth century, when fashion magazines and women's clothing manufacturers began to promote slenderness as desirable.[4]

Dr. John Harvey Kellogg picked up where Sylvester Graham had left off, offering a regimen of low-calorie, high-bulk (that is, high-fiber) food at his sanitarium in Battle Creek, Michigan. Like Graham, Kellogg considered overeating and obesity to be more serious evils than intemperate drinking. Kellogg's goal was to reduce his patients' body fat, thereby "reenergizing" them. Kellogg kept up-to-date on scientific research in nutrition, and he was familiar with the work of Wilbur O. Atwater, the scientist who created the calorimeter and developed calorie tables for common foods. In 1904, he began including calories per portion on the sanitarium's menus.[5]

Upton Sinclair, author of *The Jungle*, had visited Battle Creek Sanitarium in an attempt to lose weight, but, in the end, he was dissatisfied with the results. In 1910, he wrote an article, published in *Cosmopolitan*, preaching that his fasting regimen was a cure for both obesity and emaciation. He had lost fourteen pounds in two weeks, he trumpeted, and had never felt better. The article received so many letters that the editors of *Cosmopolitan* asked him to write another one. His sensational assertions led to the creation of fasting clubs in several cities; it also led to a book deal. Sinclair's *The Fasting Cure* hit the stands in 1911 and promptly disappeared.[6] Despite his age-old advice, few Americans were interested in fasting. A new approach to weight loss was needed and it soon emerged.

In the late nineteenth century, chemist Wilbur Atwater began measuring the caloric values of food, and his data became the basis of many subsequent diets. Russell Chittenden, a chemist at Yale University, applied the idea of calories to the question of the amount of energy burned during exercise. The problem was how to translate this new knowledge into a readily usable method for managing food intake. In 1906, Yale professor Irving Fisher delineated an easy way to estimate calories by dividing food into hundred-calorie portions. His book, *How to Live: Rules for Healthful Living*, went through nine printings in less than a year after it was first published, in 1915.[7]

It may have been Dr. Robert Hugh Rose who first advocated counting calories as a way to lose weight. In his book *Eat Your Way to Health*, he argued for a simple diet and offered a system for estimating food values. In the second edition, published six years later, Dr. Rose boasted that his method was a "scientific system of weight control." But it was a Los Angeles physician, Dr. Lulu Hunt Peters, who, in her witty and whimsical book *Diet and Health, with Key to the Calories*, popularized calorie counting as a method of weight reduction. Using the system, Dr. Peters had lost fifty pounds. Her approach began with a period of fasting and then worked up to 1,200 calories per day. Her book was released in the midst of World War I, while Dr. Peters was in Bosnia with the Red Cross; consequently, she didn't find out until her return what a huge success her book was. It enjoyed the endorsement of governmental agencies and went through at least fifty-five printings and several editions, the last released in 1939, and the book eventually sold more than 2 million copies. Calorie counting has been a part of most weight-loss diets ever since.[8]

The 1930s saw the appearance of a variety of fad diets, some fairly sensible and others decidedly strange. Dr. Stoll's Diet-Aid, the Natural Reducing Food was a liquid diet, consisting of one teaspoon each of milk chocolate, starch, whole wheat, and bran, mixed with one cup of water, to be consumed for breakfast and lunch. The diet was promoted through beauty parlors. The grapefruit diet appeared in the early 1930s.[9] It was credited to William H. Hay, who believed that starches, proteins, and fruits should be consumed separately. His diet was limited to a few select vegetables, protein sources, and grapefruit, which Hay announced supplied a fat-burning enzyme. The grapefruit diet, renamed the Hollywood Diet, reemerged in the 1970s, with the new rationale that the fruit's low glycemic index helped speed up the body's metabolism to burn fat.

After World War II, slimness became something of an obsession. Individual stories of successful weight loss were published in women's magazines—a tradition that persists to the present day. It became a commonplace belief that individuals who were unable to control their weight lacked "willpower." Being overweight was seen as a sign of moral or psychological weakness. In the 1950s, physical fitness guru Jack LaLanne first appeared on television promoting weight loss through exercise; as a lucrative sideline, he sold exercise equipment, vitamins, protein wafers, LaLanne Instant Breakfast, other diet foods, and a cookbook. By 1964, more than 8 million Americans—mainly women—were tuning in to watch him exercise, and, by 1965, sales of his weight-loss products and equipment had hit $4 million.[10] Since then, countless others, such as Richard Simmons, have followed in LaLanne's footsteps.

Diet Organizations

America's first national organization focusing on weight loss was Take Off Pounds Sensibly (TOPS), started, in 1948, by Esther Manz, an overweight housewife from Milwaukee. She modeled her program on Alcoholics Anonymous, believing that peer support was the key to successful weight loss. A nonprofit organization, TOPS conducts meetings that "emphasize nutrition and exercise education focused on supplementing members' efforts to manage their weight." After three years, TOPS had 2,500 members in six states. Today, it has 10,000 chapters and more than 200,000 members.[11] The second national weight-loss program, the religiously oriented Overeaters Anonymous (OA), which, today, hosts thousands of meetings in sixty-five countries, was launched in Los Angeles in 1960 by one Rozanne S. and two other women. OA is a 12-step recovery program for overeaters based on the principles established by Alcoholics Anonymous: like AA, OA is a not-for-profit organization.[12]

Jean Nidetch's Weight Watchers, founded in 1963, was a success from the beginning. Unlike TOPS and OA, Weight Watchers was a for-profit business, and within the next three years, it had generated $160,000 in gross sales; within seven years, it had generated $8 million. In 1967, Albert Lippert went to work full-time for Weight Watchers. He oversaw the sales of branded products, such as cookbooks, videotapes, low-fat foods, and a television program. By 1977, the company's annual revenues had surged to $39 million.[13]

Nidetch led Weight Watchers groups and trained leaders, while Lippert handled the business end, which sold franchises and diet products. Many participants who'd found success with the program bought franchises, and, after training, opened Weight Watchers programs in their own communities. The program stressed portion control, balanced meals, and exercise. Nidetch and the Lipperts took the company public in 1968. In 1973, Nidetch published the *Weight Watchers Program Cookbook*, which sold more than a million copies. Five years later, the partners sold Weight Watchers to the H. J. Heinz Company. Since then, Weight Watchers International has continued to expand. Today, it has more than 1 million members attending 29,000 meetings in twenty-seven countries. It boasts 25 million graduates and annual gross revenues of more than $1 billion from food products, books, and magazines.

Diet Products

To support organized weight-loss programs and do-it-yourself diets, manufacturers have produced tens of thousands of ready-to-eat packaged foods. Weight-loss tonics, drugs, and foods with ingredients such as laxatives, purgatives, Epsom salts, arsenic, and even strychnine were first marketed to the public in the 1890s. Saccharin, the first artificial sweetener, was discovered in 1879. It was 500 times sweeter than sugar. Several companies commercialized it, including a small firm called Monsanto Chemical Works, in St. Louis. From its beginning, medical professionals had recommended saccharin as a sugar substitute, but its sales were modest until World War I, when sugar was rationed. Monsanto advertised saccharin as a sugar substitute in 1918, but sales remained fairly slow until the Cumberland Packing Company began, in 1957, marketing Sweet'N Low.[14] Sales again increased during World War II due to sugar rationing. After the war, small packages of saccharin were commonly supplied in restaurants as a non-caloric sweetener for coffee and tea. Saccharin was also added to diet foods, and, by 1984, Americans were consuming on average thirteen pounds of saccharin every year.[15]

Sugar-free products had been manufactured for diabetics since the 1920s. But not until the 1950s did the market for diet products mushroom. Tasti-Diet Foods, for instance, the first such line, was started in 1951 by Tillie Lewis; the canned fruits the company packed were sweetened with saccharin. Diet beverages are a multibillion-dollar business today, but the first diet soda was not marketed until 1951. A Russian immigrant, Hyman Kirsch, owned a soft-drink business in Williamsburg, Brooklyn, and later became vice president of the Jewish Sanitarium for Chronic Disease. For the institution's diabetic and cardiovascular patients, Kirsch developed a sugar-free soft drink sweetened with the artificial sweetener calcium cyclamate. The first diet beverage was No-Cal ginger ale, followed by lime, black cherry, root beer, and cola. Hoping to sell around 100,000 cases, Kirsch sold over 2 million in New York and Washington, D.C., alone. Within a few years, other soda bottlers began producing diet beverages. In 1958, the Royal Crown Cola Company introduced Diet-Rite Cola, which was sweetened with both cyclamates and saccharin. By 1959, fifty companies had sold some 15 million cases of low-calorie soft drinks; by 1963, sales had hit 100 million cases.[16]

A 1963 study estimated that 28 percent of Americans were dieting. In the same year, the Coca-Cola Company introduced Tab—a diet cola sweetened with saccharin. The name "Tab" was a play on words, meant to suggest consumers were "keeping tabs" on their weight. Tab sold well, and in 1967, it was joined by Fresca, a no-calorie grapefruit-flavored soda. In 1970, 7-Up began selling Sugar-free 7-Up, renamed Diet 7-Up in 1979. Sales of diet drinks took off in the late 1970s in response to a widespread attack on sugar by nutritionists, who alleged that sugar caused many health problems, including diabetes, heart disease, and obesity. By 1980, diet drinks had come to account for about 20 percent of the soda market. In

1982, Coke and Pepsi both released diet colas—Diet Coke and Diet Pepsi—each supported by a huge national advertising campaign. By the late 1980s, a considerable variety of diet drinks was available. Diet Mountain Dew, for example, made its debut in 1988.

Another kind of diet drink was the meal-replacement beverage, touted as complete, low-calorie nutrition in a can. Mead Johnson Nutritionals, known for its baby formulas, initially advertised, in September 1959, their measured-calorie product for adults, Metrecal, to the medical profession, launching a major advertising campaign positioning Metrecal as a powerful new weight-loss product. They sold $40 million of Metrecal in the first year, and by 1961, sales had exceeded $100 million. Not long after Metrecal's success, forty similar canned or powdered products entered the race.[17]

A different type of diet product emerged in 1969, when Weight Watchers introduced calorie-controlled frozen dinners. Highly successful diet programs NutriSystem and Jenny Craig followed with complete lines of preportioned packaged foods coordinated with their diet plans. In addition to diet products produced by weight-loss programs, such as Smart Ones, from Weight Watchers, commercial spin-offs included Stouffer's Lean Cuisine and Healthy Choice lines of frozen meals.

In the 1970s, hospitals began offering a new kind of weight-loss regimen: an inpatient program in which obese patients were put on low-calorie liquid diets. Two milk-based products, Slim-Fast and Nestlé's Sweet Success, were created in response to the popularity of these liquid diets. A 200-calorie "milk shake" was meant to replace each of two of the dieter's daily meals. Thousands of food products purporting to be diet foods are now on the U.S. market. In fact, an estimated 50 percent of all food products sold in this country are labeled diet, low calorie, reduced fat, or no fat. Even premium ice cream manufacturer Häagen-Dazs has introduced a line of low-fat ice creams, and Oreos are available in reduced-calorie versions as well. Nabisco has introduced SnackWells, a line of cookies with less fat that resemble their high-fat counterparts. Frito-Lay has introduced low-fat, baked potato chips, and Pringles now offers fat-free versions of its snacks. Fast-food purveyors saw the change in the market and began offering lower-fat meals, but not all have been well received. The McDonald's McLean burger, for instance, was discontinued due to lack of interest. Fast-food salads were more successful. A fat replacement called olestra (trade name Olean) was approved by the U.S. Food and Drug Administration (FDA) for use in savory snacks in 1996, and it soon appeared as an ingredient in several new products, including Frito-Lay's potato chips Wow and Max. Products containing olestra generally contained half the calories of similar products without olestra. Reports surfaced, however, that olestra gave some consumers stomach cramps and intestinal problems; products containing it were withdrawn from the market just a few years later, but some have since returned.[18]

The safety of most artificial sweeteners has also been called into question. Calcium cyclamate was discovered by a graduate student at the University of Illinois in 1937. It was commonly used during the 1950s in diet foods and drinks but was banned as a potential carcinogen by the FDA in 1970. Cyclamates were generally replaced by saccharin, but, following an inquiry in 1977, when toxicological studies suggested the substitute might cause bladder cancer, the FDA took it off the market for a time. The agency placed a moratorium on saccharin use pending further study. The ban was lifted in 1991, but by then diet-soda bottlers had switched to aspartame (trade names NutraSweet and Equal), a sweetener discovered in 1965 and approved for sale in 1974. Numerous allegations have been made against aspartame, but none has been conclusively proven. Recently, other sweeteners, such as sucralose (marketed as Splenda), have come into growing use. In 2005, the Coca-Cola Company introduced a new version of Diet Coke sweetened with sucralose, the same sweetener used in Diet Pepsi. The company also brought out Coca-Cola Zero, sweetened with a blend of aspartame and acesulfame potassium (trade names Sunett and Sweet One).

Drugs have been used for weight loss since the early twentieth century. One early diet drug was discovered in the 1930s, when observers noted dramatic weight loss in obese men working in ammunition factories where a chemical called dinitrophenol (DNP) was being used. Physicians started prescribing DNP, and, by 1935, over 100,000 people had taken it. DNP, used to make explosives as well as dyes and pesticides, sends the human metabolism into overdrive, rapidly burning fat. Concerns about dangerous side effects led to its withdrawal from the market in 1938.[19] But amphetamines—Benzedrine and Dexedrine, which act as moderate appetite suppressants—were widely substituted. By the 1940s, dieters were employing a variety of pills, diuretics, and laxatives to lose weight as effortlessly as possible.

When reports of their abuse surfaced, the FDA required that amphetamines and similar drugs be available only by prescription. This did not put an end to abuse, however. The FDA estimated that a few thousand doctors annually prescribed more than 1 billion pills per year to 5 to 10 million patients, although there was little evidence that such drugs engendered long-term weight loss while extensive evidence accumulated about their dangerous side effects, including strokes, heart attacks, convulsions, insomnia, and addiction.[20]

In the 1970s, phenylpropanolamine (PPA), a decongestant, stimulant, and appetite suppressant, began to be employed in a variety of over-the-counter drugs, such as Dexatrim. In 2000, in response to reports of hemorrhagic strokes among its users, the FDA issued a public health advisory against PPA and requested that all drug companies discontinue its use.[21] In 1993, a prescription drug called fen-phen, a combination of fenfluramine and phentermine, was highly touted as an appetite suppressant and a new solution to obesity. Within just a few years, however, it was proven to cause heart-valve problems and possibly brain damage; it was withdrawn from the market in 1997.[22] "Herbal" supplements based on ephedrine, a plant-derived stimulant, became popular among dieters and bodybuilders in the 1990s, but, following an investigation into the deaths of high-profile athletes and widespread adulteration, ephedrine-based weight-loss drugs were banned.

Yet another category of weight-loss products is diet books. In the past forty years, thousands of diet books have been published in America every year. Many have been fabulously successful from a financial standpoint. In the 1930s and 1940s, Victor Lindlahr's *Eat and Reduce* sold more than 1 million copies; and his *You Are What You Eat* topped 3 million. In the 1950s, Adelle Davis's *Let's Eat Right to Keep Fit* and her other health and diet books sold 7 million copies. Joe Bonomo's *Calorie Counter and Control Guide*, published in 1951, eventually sold 17 million copies.[23]

Some diet books were by medical professionals. Dr. Irving Stillman's *The Doctor's Quick Weight Loss Diet* sold, in 1960, more than 5 million copies. Dr. Robert C. Atkins's *Dr. Atkins' Diet Revolution*, published in 1972, and his other diet books eventually sold 10 million copies, and Dr. Herman Tarnower's *Complete Scarsdale Medical Diet*, released in January 1979, went through twenty-one printings during its first year. Atkins's and Tarnower's programs were both based on the theory that too many dietary carbohydrates prevent the body from burning fat; they allowed unrestricted amounts of protein, while starchy or sugary foods were prohibited. After an interval during which complex carbohydrates were promoted and accepted in the United States as the foundation of a healthful diet, regimes stressing animal protein returned with a vengeance—in, for example, Barry Sears's *The Zone* and Michael R. Eades's *Protein Power*. These diets were criticized for including far too much saturated fat and cholesterol, thereby increasing the risk of heart disease. In 1979, Nathan Pritikin's *Pritikin Program for Diet and Exercise* proposed the weight-loss solution of a very-low-fat diet combined with exercise. Cardiologist Dr. Dean Ornish, whose diet/exercise/meditation program for reversing heart disease was delineated in his 1993 book, *Eat More, Weigh Less*, advised reducing fat intake to less than 10 percent of daily calories as the best route to normal weight and heart health.

In 2002, Gary Taubes's *New York Times Magazine* cover story, "What If It's All Been a Big Fat Lie?" questioned the view that fat consumption is the main reason for the spiraling obesity rates in the United States and suggested that carbohydrates were the true culprit.[24] Almost immediately, the Atkins diet became wildly popular again, although its critics pointed out that calories *do* count in weight control: fat contains twice the calories of either protein or carbohydrates. Another cardiologist, Dr. Arthur Agatston, recommended a more moderate path for heart health and weight loss: reducing carbohydrates (bread, rice, pastas, and fruits) and increasing high-fiber foods, lean proteins, and healthy fats. His book, *The South Beach Diet: The Delicious, Doctor-Designed, Foolproof Plan for Fast and Healthy Weight Loss*, was a best seller, and his diet plan swept the nation.

Diet Effects

Today, dieting is almost as ubiquitous in the United States as obesity, and millions of Americans are counting their calories or carbs or fat grams. At any given time, an estimated one in three women—three times the number of men—are dieting.[25] As of 2007, diet foods, drugs, books, devices, and programs were a forty-billion-dollar industry. Nevertheless, Americans have continued to gain weight. There is little medical evidence that diets work for most people and growing evidence that the effects of extreme diets, particularly yo-yo dieting—losing weight and then regaining it—may be harder on the body than remaining overweight. The sad fact is that when most people go off a diet or regimen, they gain back the weight they've lost.

Despite all the dieting, diet books, weight-loss programs, and diet products, today an estimated 61 percent of Americans are judged overweight and 34 percent are obese.[26] An even more ominous statistic indicating that this may get worse is that the percentage of children and adolescents who are obese has doubled in the last twenty years. Today, 17 percent of American youth are classified as obese.[27] This should come as no surprise since sugary, high-fat, high-calorie foods are heavily marketed to America's youth.[28]

Postscript

Jean Nidetch continued to serve as a consultant to Weight Watchers International after it was acquired by H. J. Heinz. She is still alive. Albert Lippert died in 1998 and his wife, Felice, in 2003. Heinz sold the diet operation of Weight Watchers International to the European investment firm Artal Luxembourg in 1999, but

Heinz retains control of Weight Watchers frozen food. By 2007, Weight Watchers had retail sales exceeding $4 billion.

Ninety-six-year-old Jack LaLanne is still alive and actively promoting his exercise regimen.

Chez Panisse (copyright Alice Waters)

27.

Alice Waters's Chez Panisse

O N OCTOBER 1, 1976, chef Jeremiah Tower created a menu composed solely of local foods from the San Francisco Bay Area: Spenger's
Tomales Bay bluepoint oysters; cream of fresh corn soup, Mendocino-
style; Big Sur Garrapata smoked trout, steamed over California bay leaves;
Monterey prawns; preserved California geese; Monterey Jack cheese; and fresh
caramelized figs.[1] At the time, Tower was the chef at Chez Panisse, a Berkeley,
California, restaurant opened by Alice Waters in 1971.[2] No one paid much attention to the menu at the time, but, twenty-five years later, food critics would hail
it as one of the great switching points in American gastronomy.[3]

Waters History

Alice Waters was an unlikely person to launch an American culinary revolution.
When she opened Chez Panisse, she had had no formal culinary training, had
never worked in a restaurant kitchen, and had never managed anything. A native
of New Jersey, as a child she had preferred Wonder Bread.[4] As a teenager, Waters
moved with her family to Indiana, where she worked for a time at local drive-ins.
When she was seventeen, the family moved to Van Nuys, California. After high
school, she attended the University of California, Santa Barbara, but in the spring
of 1965, she transferred to Berkeley to major in French cultural studies. Waters

spent that summer in France as a part of an academic travel program, and there she began her love affair with French food.

After returning to Berkeley, in the fall of 1965, Waters was swept up in the Free Speech Movement and became deeply involved in the congressional campaign of journalist Robert Scheer, who ran unsuccessfully in the Democratic primary for the U.S. Congress. During this period, Waters began cooking in the French fashion and giving small dinners for her friends. After graduating from Berkeley, in 1967, she became an assistant teacher in a Montessori school and also wrote a column called "Alice's Restaurant" for the *San Francisco Express Times*, an alternative newspaper. Waters later published more than thirty recipes from her column.[5] In late 1968, she traveled to London to study at the International Montessori Center; she took various odd jobs, including waitressing at a pub. While in London, Waters visited a cookware shop owned by the renowned English food writer Elizabeth David, who became a major influence on Waters's culinary views. After leaving London, Waters spent a year traveling around France.

On returning to the United States, she decided to open a restaurant. Armed with Elizabeth David's *French Country Cooking*, and with the support of friends, she opened, on August 28, 1971, a small place in Berkeley. She called it Chez Panisse, after the fictional character Panisse, an old Provençal sailmaker, who appeared in a trilogy of books—*Marius, Fanny*, and *César*—by the French writer Marcel Pagnol.[6]

With Chez Panisse, Waters hoped to create a place where her friends could discuss politics and enjoy good food. After the restaurant's opening, she attended a few cooking classes in San Francisco.[7] But Waters had no training in restaurant management, and for the first several years of its operation, Chez Panisse was in financial difficulty. Her true talent seemed to lie in selecting good chefs, cooks, bartenders, and waiters, and one of the people she hired early on was Jeremiah Tower.

At the time, Tower also seemed an unlikely candidate to launch a culinary revolution. Prior to his arrival at Chez Panisse, he had been a semivagabond, with a master's degree in architecture from Harvard. In 1972, Tower answered a classified ad calling for someone who could compose menus and cook five-course meals à la Elizabeth David. Tower had no formal culinary training, but he adored food and loved to cook. What's more, he had read David's *French Provincial Cooking*, and he needed the money. Despite Tower's lack of experience, Waters hired him, and he began preparing meals at Chez Panisse based on Elizabeth David's recipes and culinary philosophy.

Waters soon realized they couldn't make the dishes served at Chez Panisse taste exactly as they would in France, simply because the local ingredients in the

Bay Area were different. The flavors of fruits and vegetables—whether lettuce, beets, tomatoes, or pears—reflect the soil, water, and air that nourish them, and Berkeley just wasn't Provence. But Waters turned that drawback into an asset by focusing on the rich variety of local produce. She roved the Bay Area in search of the finest seasonal fruits, vegetables, and herbs, locally raised meats, and farmstead cheeses, and served them at Chez Panisse. She also encouraged local farmers to grow herbs and vegetables for chefs, and fostered the development of a network of organic farmers and ranchers around the San Francisco Bay Area. Waters was the first restaurateur to create the position of forager, a person whose job it is "to seek out the best local ingredients and establish working relationships with farmers and suppliers."[8]

The emerging culinary credo of fresh ingredients, simply prepared and presented, pioneered by Waters, was also espoused by Richard Olney, an American cook and food writer who had lived in southern France for most of his adult life. Waters devoured Olney's first book, *The French Menu Cookbook*; his views on the importance of seasonal ingredients and on the sequencing of courses to make a delicious whole strongly influenced her.[9] When Olney came to San Francisco in 1974 to promote his latest book, *Simple French Food*, Waters and Tower went to visit him and invited him to dine at Chez Panisse. He so impressed both Waters and Tower that he became another mentor for the restaurant, and Olney was equally impressed by Chez Panisse. Encouraged by Olney's support and inspiration, both Tower and Waters visited him in France the following year.[10]

Although simple, flavorful food was the norm, on special occasions Chez Panisse offered grandiose, Francophile menus, generated largely by Tower. For the hundredth birthday anniversary of Gertrude Stein, for instance, Tower composed a menu based on recipes from *The Alice B. Toklas Cookbook*.[11] For the third anniversary of Chez Panisse's opening, Tower created individual pizzas he called *panisses*, topped with goat cheese and red-ripe Sonoma beefsteak tomatoes. In one stroke he'd started three enduring food trends—gourmet pizza, goat cheese, and an insistence on the finest local ingredients.[12]

Although Chez Panisse was popular among Bay Area cognoscenti, it remained generally unknown to the rest of the country. Hoping to bring some media attention to the restaurant, Marion Cunningham, then a food writer for the *San Francisco Chronicle*, brought James Beard to Chez Panisse for dinner. Although Beard recorded in his date book that the meal was "delightful," he was not overly impressed, and nothing came of the visit in terms of publicity.[13] Finally, though, restaurant critic Caroline Bates featured Chez Panisse in the October 1975 issue of *Gourmet*. The floodgates had opened, and soon Alice Waters and Chez Panisse had been elevated to national prominence.[14]

Using French techniques, and his own genius for improvisation, Tower created a series of extravagant dinners at Chez Panisse. In 1975, he featured the dishes of important French chefs such as Auguste Escoffier; Prosper Montagné, the author of *Larousse gastronomique*; and Charles Ranhofer, chef, in the late nineteenth century, at the famed Delmonico's restaurant, in New York. Tower also celebrated the culinary works of French gastronome Maurice Edmond Sailland, whose nom de plume was Curnonsky. In 1976, Tower offered a series of dinners honoring various French provinces, including Alsace, Bretagne, and, especially, Provence.

Wondering what culinary innovations to feature next at Chez Panisse, Tower noted, in March 1976, that the Four Seasons restaurant, in New York, was offering a First Annual California Vintners Barrel Tasting Dinner, featuring California wines—but not California food. Then, while researching a meal to celebrate the contributions of Charles Ranhofer, the 19th century chef at Delmonico's, Tower noted that Ranhofer's magnum opus, *The Epicurean*, contained a recipe for a soup called cream of green corn à la Mendocino. Mendocino, of course, is a county that lies less than one hundred miles north of San Francisco. Ranhofer's recipe also reminded Tower of a menu he'd once seen in a nineteenth-century English magazine for "a California banquet." The object of that event, held at the California Hotel, in San Francisco, "was to prove the possibility of making up an extensive menu solely from the products of the State" of California.[15] These sources gave Tower an idea: rather than turning out French food week after week, why not create a menu made up entirely of northern California foods and wines?

With the growing national visibility Chez Panisse enjoyed at the time, it's surprising that Tower's Northern California Regional Dinner, offered at the restaurant in October 1976, did not receive more attention. Nevertheless, from that point on, Chez Panisse Americanized its food. The restaurant's menus were written in English rather than French, and they featured the finest of California's local and seasonal foods. Tower saw the Northern California Regional Dinner as the turning point in the restaurant's evolution, and he believed that the meal "changed the face of American dining."[16]

Tower left Chez Panisse in January 1977 and eventually opened his own hugely successful restaurant, Stars, in San Francisco, in 1984. Tower also published several cookbooks, including *Jeremiah Tower's New American Classics*, which received the James Beard Award in 1986 for best American regional cookbook. Ten years later, Tower won the Best Chef of the Year award from the James Beard Foundation. He went on to host a PBS series, *America's Best Chefs*, in 2002, and published, the following year, a cookbook of the same name. Tower's memoir, *California Dish: What I Saw (and Cooked) at the American Culinary Revolution*, was published in 2003.

After Tower's departure, Chez Panisse and Alice Waters continued to grow and flourish. Waters hired superb chefs and gave them space to do what they wanted. In addition to Tower, some of the most celebrated Chez Panisse chef alumni are Lindsey Shere, Jean-Pierre Moullé, Mark Miller, Judy Rodgers, Deborah Madison, Jonathan Waxman, Joyce Goldstein, and Paul Bertolli. Waters also continued to innovate. In 1980, wanting to offer a casual alternative to the formal downstairs dining room, she opened an upstairs café equipped with a wood-burning brick oven for making pizzas, an innovation inspired by the oven at Tommaso's pizzeria, in San Francisco's North Beach neighborhood.[17]

In collaboration with Chez Panisse chefs, Waters has written or coauthored eight cookbooks, ranging from *The Chez Panisse Menu Cookbook* to *The Art of Simple Food*.[18] Food and restaurant critic Craig Claiborne credited Waters with "revolutionizing American cooking in the 70s and 80s," and he put *The Chez Panisse Menu Cookbook* on his "essential cookbook list." Widely admired, the cookbook sold 90,000 copies. It has been heralded by some commentators as a major "statement on American food."[19]

Waters Effects

As Chez Panisse matured, becoming a touchstone of American cuisine, Waters found willing partners in her mission of promoting local, fresh, seasonal ingredients. She joined fine cooking with community activism, supporting local farmers, organic food, sustainable agriculture, and other causes. Cooking is, in her view, a product of agriculture as well as a part of culture. To help change the culinary culture, Waters created, in 1996, the Chez Panisse Foundation. Part of its mission is to help fund a program called the Edible Schoolyard, which involves schoolchildren in planting gardens and then harvesting, cooking, and enjoying what they've grown.

According to Joan Reardon, one of Waters's biographers, Waters "tried to change the trends toward 'the nationalizing and homogenizing of American food, tastes and habits.'"[20] James Beard wrote, "What Alice has done from the beginning is to create a style entirely hers that broke away from the formal French restaurant. You can't call it *nouvelle cuisine*. I think it's Alice Waters Cuisine." Caroline Bates, who had first reviewed Chez Panisse for *Gourmet* in 1975, concluded twenty-six years later that the restaurant had "changed how we eat."[21] Journalist R. W. Apple Jr., of the *New York Times*, wrote that Waters's "credo—fresh, local, seasonal, and where possible organic ingredients–is followed by hundreds of farmers' markets, thousands of restaurants, and millions of home cooks."[22] Thomas McNamee, another biographer, lauded the way in which Waters "transformed the way Americans eat and the way they think about food."[23]

To describe the style of cooking epitomized by Waters and Chez Panisse, food writers began to talk about a California cuisine. Reflecting Waters's heartfelt endorsement of small-scale, local food production, such operations gained new respect. Artisans milking their own herds to make goat cheese, or stoking wood ovens to bake hearty peasant breads, as well as farmers growing heirloom tomatoes and subtly flavored strains of basil were celebrated for their accomplishments. Upscale farm stands and city shops specializing in fine local foods proliferated around the country. Waters championed organic farms, humane animal husbandry, and sustainable fisheries, and they too became common throughout the United States.[24] As California cuisine spread eastward, chefs in other regions created their own interpretations of what had begun at Chez Panisse, and eventually this became known as the New American cooking.[25]

Of course, Alice Waters was not the only force in this culinary revolution. Before Chez Panisse even opened, the counterculture had already set the stage for many of the innovations for which Waters was later credited, including "growing your own" and favoring simple dishes. After Chez Panisse, many other restaurateurs made their mark in the movement, including Austrian-born, French-trained Wolfgang Puck, chef at Ma Maison, in Los Angeles, and then at his own restaurants, including Spago, in Hollywood.

Postscript

Chefs from Chez Panisse, Stars, and Spago have gone on to launch their own restaurants, and many of them have contributed to the surging new wave in American cooking. But it was Alice Waters—assisted by Jeremiah Tower—who sparked an American food revolution that exploded in the 1980s. Her efforts have been widely recognized and rewarded. In 1992, the James Beard Foundation named Waters the Best Chef in America and identified Chez Panisse as the nation's Best Restaurant. Waters won the James Beard Humanitarian Award in 1997, and, in 2000, *Bon Appétit* magazine gave her a lifetime achievement award. Not to be outdone, *Gourmet* magazine identified, the following year, Chez Panisse as the best restaurant in the nation. Still presiding over Chez Panisse, Waters remains an American culinary icon.

Food Network Best of the Best of ... by Jill Cordes and Marc Silverstein (New York: HP Books, 2004)

28.

TVFN

A T 6:00 P.M. on November 23, 1993, cohosts Donna Hanover Giuliani, then wife of mayor-elect Rudy Giuliani, of New York City, and David Rosengarten, an experienced actor, went on the air with *Food News and Views*, the first live program broadcast on the Television Food Network (TVFN).[1] At the time, the new network reached only 6.8 million cable subscribers—and there wasn't much evidence that those who could watch the programs actually did: TVFN's 1994 first-quarter Nielsen ratings were "barely detectable," at a whopping 0.3.[2] Few observers outside the Providence Journal Company, which had launched the new cable network, thought it had much chance of survival in what was then a crowded cable television field.

Channeling Food

The idea of a channel devoted solely to food and cooking had been bouncing around for almost two years before TVFN actually made its debut. During the 1980s, "narrowcasting"—developing programs and channels aimed at specific, definable audiences—was the buzzword in the cable world. The idea was not to reach everyone—as "broadcasters" tried to do—but to reach a small but significant group that would appeal to advertisers interested in niche marketing. When cable guru Trygve Myhren was named president of the Providence Journal

Company in December 1990, he arrived with an agreement from the other members of the board stating that he could develop programming for the cable TV business, including the company's cable subsidiary, Colony Communications. Myhren called together Colony's leadership and asked for programming ideas. His plan was to launch channels that could be totally ad supported, would appeal to a recognizable niche audience, and could be programmed with relatively inexpensive shows. He believed the idea would come from a genre that had a robust magazine or publishing business but had not yet been featured on television. The most fertile niches would not only support a cable channel but also provide the platform for building brands that could be exploited through sales of related products and services. While they were considering the options, their solution walked in the door. Ken Levy, the director of external relations for Johnson & Wales University, in Providence, Rhode Island, had an idea: why not broadcast cooking shows using the chefs and students from the university's renowned culinary school? Levy made the suggestion, in part, because the university was considering purchasing a large building in downtown Providence that had previously housed the local NBC affiliate. Since the building already had studios and equipment, it seemed to Levy and his associate, Richard G. Carriere, that some space could be dedicated to taping cooking shows, which could then be broadcast to the market surrounding Providence.

To help think through the concept, Levy and Carriere set up a meeting with Joe Langhan, one of the executives at Colony Communications. Acting on Myhren's directive, Langhan was already considering new networks, and, after hearing the idea of televising cooking shows throughout the state, he began warming to the idea of a cooking network. He discussed the concept with others at Colony, including Jack Clifford, the head of the Providence Journal Company's electronic-media empire. Clifford also liked the idea, but, upon reflection, he concluded that setting up a network with just cooking shows wasn't enough. He believed the company should set up a channel showing other food-related programs as well as cooking shows. This could be done by acquiring the rights to existing cooking programs and also developing some new programs. Langhan, the Colony management team, Clifford, and his assistant, Andrew Thatcher, presented the idea to Myhren, who liked it as well—in part because Clifford and Langhan were so enthusiastic about it, and because initial research indicated that the food category enjoyed enormous book sales and magazine-advertising support. The problem was how to make the concept of a cooking channel a reality. No one at the Providence Journal Company, except Myhren, had any experience producing cable TV programming, and everyone already had a full-time job, so it was unlikely that a new network could be set up with the existing personnel.

Myhren wanted to find a consultant and, after interviewing several candidates, chose Stephen Cunningham, previously a consultant to Time Warner's cable systems subsidiary. Myhren was also convinced that, if the network were to succeed, they needed an entrepreneurial cable programming operator to get it off the ground. The right man for the job was Reese Schonfeld, cofounder of CNN with Ted Turner, who had met Myhren when Myhren was serving on the Turner Broadcasting board. Schonfeld came on board in late 1991.

Cunningham, Schonfeld, Clifford, and Langhan began work on a business plan for what was tentatively being called TVFN, the Television Food Network, named by Jack Clifford.[3] This planning group conducted numerous interviews and examined several possible models for a cooking channel. The good news was that cooking shows—colloquially referred to as "dump and stir" programs—were relatively inexpensive to make and formulaic in their construction; many successful programs had already appeared on commercial broadcast networks, cable networks, and PBS. While this type of program was fine for daytime TV, the group believed it would not draw an audience during prime time. Eventually, the group agreed with Clifford that a primary focus on cooking, as initially proposed by Johnson & Wales, was too limiting. The focus needed to be expanded to include *food* more generally. The new channel would therefore feature cooking programs but also offer lifestyle shows to attract a broader audience. Meanwhile, research for the business plan confirmed that food was one of the largest consumer categories—estimated at $500 billion in annual sales, with an estimated $50 billion in annual advertising, marketing, and promotional expenditures. Based on these encouraging figures, it seemed likely that a food network, executed well, could generate a solid revenue stream.

The planning group assumed the new channel's audience would be upper-middle-class women—stay-at-home moms who could watch daytime television as well as working women interested in evening entertainment. Although this would be a smaller potential audience than that of many other cable networks, the group believed the affluent, decidedly female demographics would appeal to potential advertisers.

Many problems were raised and solved during the planning process. The most pressing one was how to generate funds to launch the network. Start-up costs were estimated at $40 million for the first four years. After that, the planners believed, the network would become profitable. Since Johnson & Wales had broached the idea, they were offered the first opportunity to buy into the expanded food network concept for a portion of the $40 million. After deliberation, Johnson & Wales declined the offer: it was simply too much for the university to invest at a time when the school was rapidly expanding to new locations throughout the United States. Rather than seek other investors—and split the profits—Myhren convinced the Providence Journal board to cover the entire start-up investment.

Another serious difficulty was how to get cable operators to carry the proposed channel. At the time, many cable networks, such as ESPN, charged operators for the right to air their programs. This system worked well with the more popular networks—every operator wanted to host some channels, particularly in areas where operators competed. However, cable operators had limited bandwidth, and they could thus offer only a limited number of channels to their subscribers. With hundreds of channels available, operators could choose those they were interested in hosting, which meant that new channels often languished because they had limited access to subscribers. Moreover, a small potential audience meant that advertisers were less interested in buying time on a particular network. To surmount this obstacle, Myhren devised a plan by which operators would receive the Food Network programs at no cost for several years and would be given a small equity in the new endeavor. Consequently, adding TVFN to their offerings would cost operators little, and, if the network made a profit, the operators stood to gain financially. It was in the operators' best interest to offer the new channel to as many of their subscribers as possible. With a large subscriber base, it would be easier for TVFN to acquire major advertisers, which was precisely what Myhren intended—to finance TVFN solely through advertising revenue.

Myhren headed the group seeking to interest cable operators in the new network. In short order, several cable operators, including Cincinnati-based Scripps Howard, Boston-based Continental Cablevision, Pennsylvania-headquartered Adelphia, and others bought into the concept and became part owners of the nascent network. Myhren again approached Johnson & Wales, this time with a scaled-down proposal—for $2 million—but again the university heads declined, believing the school should focus on its students rather than move into the TV business. Meanwhile, Reese Schonfeld approached the Tribune Company, of Chicago, and made a deal to give them a larger share of TVFN in exchange for using their broadcast "must carry" rights to gain additional cable carriage. Cable operators who agreed to carriage were given positions on the TVFN board, although, as the largest investor, the Providence Journal Company maintained control of the board.

Meanwhile, in 1992, Congress passed the Cable Television Consumer Protection and Competition Act, with a series of requirements for new cable operators and programmers. To avoid these new regulations, cable networks had to be operating full-time before September 23, 1993. So that TVFN could steer clear of these regulations, TVFN acquired the rights to cooking shows previously aired on broadcast and public television stations and began running them. Creaky old cooking shows such as James Beard's *I Love to Cook*, *The Dione Lucas Cooking Show*, and Graham Kerr's *The Galloping Gourmet* were regularly rebroadcast on TVFN. Viewers were also treated to a two-hour preview devised by Joe Langhan and produced by Barry Rosenthal that featured upcoming shows slated for November 1993. The network also broadcast a couple of cooking demonstrations, along with an invitation to write to TVFN for the recipes. As soon as the channel began broadcasting, Langhan started getting requests for recipes. Soon after TVFN went live on November 23, 1993, requests for recipes grew into the thousands. While the cost of responding to these requests soared, it also provided a new way of disseminating recipes and information about TVFN's programs and provided TVFN with information on its viewers. Langhan argued successfully for the development of a Web site, unusual at the time and one of TVFN's more successful innovations. Once the TVFN Web site was live, it quickly became one of the most important elements in the success of the new network, helping further a brand that could support sales of ancillary products and services.

TVFN needed to develop a number of new programs to fill broadcast time, but at the time the decision was made to launch the network, it had no broadcast studio. Rather than construct studios in Providence, Schonfeld believed that New York was the place to be. TVFN used existing studios until Schonfeld's wife, Pat O'Gorman, took on the task of seeing to it that a new "studio, control room, editing rooms, and office space" were completed, in eighty-three days, in a New York skyscraper.[4] Since there was no ready pool of food celebrities looking for work, new talent had to be located. Schonfeld stepped in and made some crucial decisions. Having been a newsman on CNN, he wanted a news show on food. Based on previous contact he'd had with Donna Hanover, a TV journalist, he wanted her to anchor the program. At the time, her husband, Rudy Giuliani, was running for mayor of New York, and Schonfeld thought this might also create interest in the new network. Hanover herself knew nothing about food—in fact, in the early days none of those in TVFN leadership positions did—but she was an experienced television news professional and could read a script as well as any of them. An actor and food and wine writer named David Rosengarten was chosen to be Hanover's on-air partner. Rosengarten's agent had sent Schonfeld a tape of a pilot for which Rosengarten had auditioned. After a brief interview, Schonfeld promptly hired the actor to serve as the program's cohost. Rosengarten also proposed an idea for a program called *Taste*, which he would host, and Schonfeld agreed to give it a try.

Another live program on the new cable channel was *Food Talk*, hosted by Robin Leach, a celebrity-focused writer who had starred in a popular television show, *Lifestyles of the Rich and Famous*. *Food Talk* gave TVFN a late-night talk show, and Schonfeld thought that having celebrities on the show would attract a wider audience. Leach later hosted a weekend series called *Gourmet Getaways* showcasing vacation resorts around the world and their chefs.

Other programs on TVFN included *Getting Healthy*, anchored by sports broadcaster Gayle Gardner and Dr. Stephanie Beling; a baking program; one featuring restaurant reviews; and another showing how to feed a family on $99 a week, hosted by cookbook author Michele Urvater. These programs were bundled together and repeated four times every twenty-four hours, along with reruns of cooking shows previously broadcast on public television or by other cable networks.[5]

Even with these programs on its schedule, TVFN needed to locate more talent, so Langhan created the show *Chef du Jour*, featuring a different chef every week. This show uncovered the audience appeal of a number of talented chefs, including Sara Moulton, Bobby Flay, Mario Batali, and Tyler Florence—all of whom went on to have their own programs.

In addition to the shows taped in New York, other TVFN programs were recorded in Nashville, Tennessee, by Reid/Land Productions, a firm with which Schonfeld had previously done work. Schonfeld wanted a program entitled *How to Boil Water*, meant to be a simple introduction to cooking. He asked Allen Reid, a founder of Reid/Land Productions, to locate a host for this as well as other programs. Reid recommended two possibilities: Jasper White, a restaurateur in Boston, or Emeril Lagasse, former executive chef at Commander's Palace, in New Orleans; several years earlier, he had opened his own New Orleans restaurant, Emeril's, which *Esquire* had named Best New Restaurant of 1990. In 1993, Lagasse had published his first book, *Emeril's New New Orleans Cooking*. Lagasse's name had come up early in the planning for TVFN, when Ken Levy mentioned him as a Johnson & Wales graduate; cable distribution consultant Nory LeBrun recommended him also. Reid brought in a tape of Lagasse, who had appeared on a couple of broadcast television shows. Schonfeld watched the tape with his assistant, Robin Connelly. After the screening, Schonfeld asked Connelly what she thought. Her response was that Lagasse was a "hunk." That decided it—Emeril would host the *How to Boil Water* program. Lagasse flew into Nashville regularly to tape six or seven programs a day. He was paid the handsome sum of $300 per episode. The programs were scripted, Lagasse was stiff, and the show was yanked after a year. TVFN executives gave him another program, *Emeril and Friends*. It was also scripted, and also failed.

But TVFN still desperately needed programming, and Lagasse was available. He was given another opportunity, but this time, rather than tying him to a script, network executives gave him more freedom. *The Essence of Emeril*, which debuted in 1995, was filmed in New York; Lagasse flew in on Sunday mornings, taped five shows, and stayed over on Mondays and Tuesdays to tape seven or eight more shows each day before heading back to New Orleans. It was in one late-night taping session that Emeril yelled out "Bam!" to keep the film crew awake. That expletive soon became Emeril's signature. *The Essence of Emeril* quickly became the network's most popular show, and, in 1996, *Time* magazine named it one of the ten best TV shows of that year.[6] The show was nominated for two ACE awards, the cable equivalent of broadcasting's Emmy. Meanwhile, the program's ratings climbed ever higher. Network executives gave Lagasse another program, *Emeril Live*, which debuted in January 1997. This time Lagasse cooked in front of a live audience; this made a huge difference, and his popularity soared. Lagasse rose from television personality to superstar.

To fill the TVFN broadcasting day, executives at the network secured the rights to air reruns of a number of cooking shows, including those of the ever-popular Julia Child, who agreed, in April 1994, to be interviewed on TVFN, and she regularly appeared thereafter on various programs.[7] In addition, Schonfeld acquired the rights to the blockbuster Japanese cooking show, *The Iron Chef*, which introduced competitive cooking as spectator sport to American TV audiences. *Iron Chef* was such a hit that it spawned an entire new genre of cooking-competition programs.

In the early years, the heads of TVFN were convinced their main audience was women eighteen and older interested in instructional cooking shows.[8] This turned out to be the case during weekday afternoons and weekend mornings, when many women did watch these programs. For the evening shows, however, TVFN had to develop new lifestyle programs, and these soon dominated TVFN in prime time. The network's programs eventually settled into this two-tiered approach: daytime programs consisting of instructional cooking shows and nighttime programming featuring entertainment, such as cooking competitions, lighthearted surveys of food history, reality shows, and cuisine-themed travel shows.

In 1995, TVFN's name was changed to the Food Network. Although the network's audience was growing steadily, it reached only about 18 million subscribers at the time. Thirty-six million dollars had been invested, and operating profitability, though close, had not yet been achieved.

The board of TVFN's parent, Providence Journal, was well aware that an investment of two dollars per cable subscriber, in an era when such cable operators sold subscribers for seven to ten dollars in private transactions, indicated that they had a winner on their hands. But the board had bigger issues to deal with. Shareholders of this private company were in disagreement as to its future, with the heirs of some founders demanding liquidity and others wanting to reinvest in their growing enterprise. Providence Journal had begun with a newspaper 180 years earlier, but, by the 1990s, it had grown into a large, diversified media company with broadcast TV, cable TV, cable programming, magazines, newspapers, and early Internet ventures. As such, it was keenly aware of the fate of some other newspaper dynasties, where disagreement among heirs had eventually resulted in significant depreciation in the value of the corporation.

Consequently, the board felt compelled to dismantle the company. The first step was the sale of the cable operating properties to Continental Cable, of Boston. The second step was taking the remaining properties, including the Food Network, public on the New York Stock Exchange. The final step was to accept an offer from the A. H. Belo Corporation, in Dallas, for all those businesses. In order to complete this sale, Providence Journal was required to buy back shares of minority shareholders in the Food Network. One of those who sold its shares was E. W. Scripps Company.

In an unusual move, the following year Scripps acquired a 56-percent controlling interest from Belo in return for $75 million in cash and the rights to television station KENS and radio station KENS-AM, broadcast outlets in San Antonio, Texas. The package was worth an estimated $140 million. Many observers, including those from Providence Journal, were surprised that Belo had relinquished the Food Network at such a low price.

Scripps, which also owned the home and garden cable network (HGTV), focused on shifting programming away from instructional television and more toward lifestyle shows. This approach worked: by 2001, the network was reaching 75 million households, with some of the most affluent TV viewers in America. By 2007, the Food Network was being watched in 90 million homes—virtually every American home that had a cable television or satellite TV hookup.

Entertaining Effects

Julia Child wanted her viewers to cook and to cook well, but the Food Network has taken its on-air fare down a different path. As culinary historian Pauline Adema has argued, the Food Network shifted from an audience comprised of "people who like to cook to people who love to eat"[9] to one consisting of voyeurs who increasingly liked simply to watch acts of consumerism and consumption. In the process, the Food Network spawned such celebrities as Emeril Lagasse, Bobby Flay, Sara Moulton, Ming Tsai, and Rachael Ray, who have become some of America's most influential culinary luminaries. While TVFN's initial audience was primarily women, in time more men began watching the network. By 2007, almost half its viewers were male. In part this can be attributed to male food celebrities such as Lagasse, Flay, and Kaga Takeshi, who made it culturally appropriate for men to take an interest in cooking—traditionally a woman's domain.

While the Food Network found its niche in entertainment—not education—it actually taught Americans about food in a way traditional cooking shows never imagined. It brought glamour to the culinary profession and convinced thousands of Americans it was a valid and worthwhile career path. Of course, many young students attending culinary school today dream of becoming tomorrow's television chefs.

On the other hand, the Food Network's programs are watched by millions of people who have no intention of cooking dinner in their own kitchens, let alone signing up for culinary school. These viewers wish to become more knowledgeable about food so they can order properly in a restaurant or hold their own in culinary conversations with their peers. In this way, the Food Network's programs also give viewers a type of "cultural capital" that allows them to discuss the latest trends, personalities, and events in the food world.[10] With its influence now pervasive throughout America, the Food Network has gone far beyond the realm of public-TV daytime cooking shows. It has empowered its viewers "to participate in consumerism by expanding their familiarity with food traditions emblematic of elite culture."[11]

The Food Network has changed the nation's food scene through entertainment. It has also spawned hundreds of other food and cooking shows on cable and broadcast networks, and its culinary competitions have converted food into a spectator sport. The Food Network's success demonstrated that food had become a central feature in the media and American life.

Postscript

Trygve Myhren is now president of Denver-based Myhren Media, Inc., a private investment firm, and he is also deeply engaged in pro bono work. Reese Schonfeld is retired and lives in New York. Jack Clifford has retired and lives in Scottsdale, Arizona. Ken Levy is still the director of external relations for Johnson & Wales University. Joe Langhan helped set up the Wine Network and other cable channels and serves as a consultant to them. After fifteen years of successful programming, Emeril Lagasse, in 2007, left the Food Network and is currently starring in the new series *Emeril Green*, on Discovery Networks International.

Advertisement for the MacGregor's tomato, 1992 (courtesy of Marion Nestle)

29.

The Flavr Savr

O N MAY 18, 1994, the U.S. Food and Drug Administration (FDA) announced that tomatoes grown from Flavr Savr seeds, patented by Calgene, Inc., were as safe as tomatoes bred by conventional means. Newspaper reaction to this first American specimen of bioengineered produce was almost universally positive, and three days later, the new tomatoes were unveiled with great fanfare. Sales were brisk, and by June 1995, Flavr Savr tomatoes, marketed under the trade name MacGregor, were being sold in supermarkets across the country. The Flavr Savr tomato's unique feature was that scientists had inserted a gene into the plant that could "help block the rapid deterioration of vine ripened tomatoes."[1] For growers, this slow-to-rot trait meant that they would lose fewer tomatoes—and thereby less profit—through spoilage. For consumers, it meant that the tomato could be ripened on the vine rather than harvested when rock hard and green, as was the case with conventional factory-farmed tomatoes, which are treated with ethylene gas to speed "ripening" once they reach their destination. With its new biotech introduction, Calgene targeted the 25 percent of American consumers who refused to buy the rock-hard tomatoes during the off-season.[2]

Despite its great promise, all did not go well for the Flavr Savr tomato. The off-season market was complicated by hothouse tomatoes that were competitive with the Flavr Savr, and the transgenic tomatoes were significantly higher priced than ordinary tomatoes. Then there were the protests from activists, scientists, chefs, and supermarkets. Although Calgene had conducted extensive research and the FDA had approved the commercial sale of the Flavr Savr, critics raised safety concerns and condemned the bioengineered produce. Shippers and retailers found that Flavr Savr tomatoes were prone to bruising and that, even at their best, they tasted no better than other factory-farmed tomatoes. Consumer demand for them flagged once the hype had worn off, and the costs of producing and marketing the new tomato shot up. Calgene began to take on considerable debt. Less than three years after their introduction, Flavr Savr tomatoes were gone from supermarket produce bins. Yet, their introduction had opened the floodgates for other transgenic foods: within a decade, almost every American processed food contained transgenic corn or soy ingredients.

Transgenic Food

Humans have been altering the genetic makeup of plants and animals for thousands of years. Genetic mutations occur naturally in all living organisms, and when such mutations were seen as beneficial—a cow that gave more milk, a grain that survived drought, an ox that grew bigger than its sire—these advantages were reinforced through selective breeding. It took years—sometimes centuries—to develop the forerunners of today's food plants and domesticated animals. This process was sped up in the late nineteenth century with the application of the scientific method to breeding. By the 1920s, plant scientists had refined the technique of hybridization, resulting in many highly productive crops.

In the mid-twentieth century, a very different way of modifying plants and animals arose from the pioneering work of Cambridge University scientists James Watson and Francis Crick, who had deciphered the structure of the DNA molecule, discovering that it formed a double helix. In 1953, Watson and Crick submitted a one-page paper to the British journal *Nature* describing their discovery. The paper closed with the observation, "It has not escaped our notice that the specific pairing that we have postulated immediately suggests a possible copying mechanism for the genetic material."[3] Many scientists have since contributed to the basic understanding of transgenic engineering. One significant event occurred when scientists isolated a small portion of DNA from the cytoplasm of a bacterium, spliced in a gene from another bacterium, and introduced the resulting *recombinant* gene back into the original bacterium.[4] This seminal work paved the way for gene splicing in other organisms. Commercial applications for the new technology underwent exploration—first for pharmaceuticals and then for agricultural products—by start-up companies financed by venture capital. Biotech firms sprouted up, usually around universities. During the period 1971 to 1987, 350 new biotech firms sprang up; 70 new firms were formed in 1981 alone.[5]

One such company established during this time was Calgene, a small biotech start-up founded in 1980 in Davis, California. The company's work on the tomato built upon research that had been under way since 1950, when the University of California, Davis, established the Tomato Genetics Cooperative (TGC). The purpose of the TGC was to "exchange information on tomato genetic research, stimulate linkage studies and preserve and distribute germplasm." A Gene List Committee was formed to compile a list of tomato genes, and. in the decades that followed, researchers identified and categorized hundreds of those genes. Along with gene identification came a listing of sources of seeds for each gene. The TGC established a Tomato Genetics Stock Center in 1976 to facilitate access to tomato varieties with specific genes.[6] By 1977, 288 genes had been identified, and the tomato's twelve chromosomes, easily recognizable during certain stages of its reproduction, had been mapped for marker genes.[7]

A noteworthy genetic trait of the tomato is that specific functions are controlled by only one gene. This characteristic—one gene per trait—has made the tomato a relatively easy organism in which to locate exact chromosomal positions, a fact that aids bioengineering techniques. Bioengineers maintained that, with the Flavr Savr, through selective breeding and naturally occurring mutations, they had produced genetically engineered tomatoes with some qualities that breeders had sought for years. But that was just the beginning of the new genetic era.

Research into genetics encouraged further investigations into the tomato's chromosomal structure, making more sophisticated alterations possible. In the 1980s, Calgene and other biotech companies began working on splicing the tomato's DNA,[8] and, with funding from the Campbell Soup Company, Calgene succeeded in doing so in 1988.[9] Researchers were soon able to take a gene from an organism and insert it into the genetic sequence of the tomato.[10] Thomas C. Churchwell, president of Calgene Fresh, Inc., a Calgene subsidiary, stated that the rapid softening of ripe tomatoes was initiated by an enzyme called polygalacturonase, or PG. He explained that "PG breaks down the pectin in the tomato's cell walls so it will decay faster and allow the fruit's seed to spread on the ground." Calgene spliced into the tomato's genetic makeup an extra gene that would cancel out 99 percent of the effect of the PG enzyme. Churchwell continued, "Thus, the tomato remains firmer in its last week and can be left on the vine to ripen for an extra two or three days, until it begins to flush red. It can then be picked and allowed to ripen further en route without gassing to produce redness. After a week or so of extra firmness, the Calgene tomato softens and decays like other tomatoes."[11]

After extensive research, Calgene completed its work on producing a tomato with a slow-to-rot trait gene inserted, and the company was ready to put it on the market.[12] Recognizing the importance of commercializing its transgenic tomato, in August 1991 Calgene asked the FDA to review the safety of the transgenic tomato. The FDA initiated hearings on the tomato, and David A. Kessler, the FDA's commissioner, stated at one point, "I heard no dissent today on the safety evaluation of the Flavr Savr tomato, and the committee thought that the evaluation of the Flavr Savr was exceptionally thorough." The transgenic tomato sailed through the FDA's Food Advisory Committee after Calgene produced a substantial amount of scientific data to show that it was safe.[13]

Critics, meanwhile, complained about a second gene Calgene scientists had inserted "to mark the successful insertion of the one to cancel the effect of PG. This marker gene, called Kan-r, conferred resistance to the antibiotic kanamycin." The critics believed the transgenic tomato might pass the Kan-r gene to people, "negating kanamycin's effectiveness as a prescription drug to stop an infection." To counter such criticism, Calgene presented data demonstrating that the Kan-r gene was quickly denatured in the stomach and ineffective in neutralizing the antibiotic.[14]

Upon obtaining the FDA's approval, Calgene asked grocers to label the biotech tomato and distribute a brochure describing it. Despite its potential for success, the Flavr Savr was a financial failure, in part because Calgene was unable to provide a constant supply of Flavr Savr tomatoes. The problem was that the seeds had been developed in California, yet the plants were also to be grown in Florida, which has a different climate and soil composition. This resulted in poor crop yields in Florida. In 1995, Calgene made the decision to grow the tomatoes only in California and market them only west of the Rocky Mountains.[15] Even with this geographical downshift, the biotech tomato's cost was twice that of the abundant conventional tomatoes flooding supermarkets year-round. In the end, consumers perceived no real advantage in the biotech tomatoes, so they saw no reason to pay more for them. Meanwhile, the futurist Jeremy Rifkin and other critics were highly vocal in their opposition to what they viewed as the unacceptable risks to humans of transgenic engineering.[16] Many grocery stores refused to sell the tomatoes, and many restaurants and chefs threatened to boycott the "mutant tomato." As a result, Calgene racked up millions of dollars of debt each year, and, in 1996, the company withdrew the Flavr Savr tomato from the market, just two years after its introduction.

First Generation Biotech Foods

The Flavr Savr, the first transgenic whole food to be commercialized, failed, and Calgene, deeply in debt, was sold to Monsanto,[17] a chemical company known for its herbicides (including the defoliant known as Agent Orange, used by U.S. armed forces in Vietnam). Monsanto had no interest in the Flavr Savr but saw a potential in Calgene's work for biotech cotton and canola oil. Monsanto had been experimenting with biotech food since the late 1970s. Its scientists began work on genetically modifying plant cells in 1982, and, five years later, the company started field tests of transgenic crops. Rather than focusing on tomatoes, Monsanto's research was devoted to four staple crops: corn, cotton, soybeans, and canola.

Monsanto's premier product was Roundup, a nontransgenic herbicide containing glyphosate, which the company had patented in 1970. The patent was scheduled to run out in 2000, and, in 1996, Monsanto released its Roundup Ready (RR) transgenic soybeans, followed by RR corn, cotton, sorghum, canola, and alfalfa. These biotech plants were tolerant of Roundup, which meant the herbicide could be sprayed on them without harming the crop, thus increasing yields and decreasing the use of herbicides known to cause harm to the environment.

Monsanto also bioengineered corn, cotton, and other plants, with an insecticidal protein produced by the bacterium *Bacillus thuringiensis* (Bt). Bt occurs naturally in plants and in the soil. It has been used by organic farmers for fifty years to control crop-eating insects and mosquitoes. The use of transgenic Bt crops has decreased losses due to insects and lessened the application of pesticides harmful to the environment. Several potential problems have been raised, however, including the spread of Bt plants to non-Bt crops, and the possibility that the Bt gene will show up in the crops' close wild relatives, such as teosinte or *Tripsacum*, to produce a superweed that would be resistant to insects. Concern has also been expressed that the widespread presence of Bt might produce a superbug resistant to all means of eradication. To date, no such problems have been detected.[18]

One problem that did emerge, in September 2000, was the discovery of traces of Aventis Bt corn, marketed as StarLink, in taco shells manufactured by Kraft Foods and in some other food products. StarLink corn had been approved for animal but not for human consumption. In December 2000, the Environmental Protection Agency reported that an independent panel of scientists had concluded that StarLink corn had a "medium likelihood" of causing allergic reactions; several people filed lawsuits alleging they had suffered such effects after consuming items identified as potentially containing StarLink. Companies recalled 300 products possibly having traces of StarLink corn.[19] StarLink was subsequently pulled off the market in the United States.

In March 1990, the FDA approved the use of bioengineered recombinant chymosin in cheese making. The engineered chymosin is a substitute for the naturally occurring enzyme traditionally scraped from the lining of calves' stomachs. Today, about 90 percent of American hard cheese contains this transgenic enzyme, and little controversy has surrounded this application of bioengineering. But controversy greeted its next decision, three years later, when the FDA approved Monsanto's application for recombinant bovine growth hormone (rBGH), also known as recombinant bovine somatotropin (rBST), which increases lactation in dairy cows by 10 to 20 percent. This transgenic hormone, marketed under the name Posilac, is in regular use in many nonorganic dairies. The concerns relate to animal welfare, the fear the hormone will contaminate local water supplies, and potential harm to the health of those who consume milk produced by cows injected with rBGH/rBST. Others have dismissed the concerns and pointed to the environmental advantages of having fewer cows producing more milk. More than 120 studies have shown that "rBST poses no risk to human health." Whatever the debate, Monsanto estimates that one-third of all dairy cows in America are injected with Posilac.[20]

Frankenfoods

Even before the Flavr Savr's brief appearance, opposition to transgenic foods had begun to mount. In 1992, the FDA established guidelines for testing the safety of foods derived from any and all plant-breeding techniques, including transgenic ones. Having concluded that transgenic foods contained no new or special safety risks, the FDA deemed its guidelines exempted transgenic plants from case-by-case review. This raised concerns among many Americans. Sheldon Krimsky, a professor at Tufts University, wrote a *New York Times* op-ed piece, "Tomatoes May Be Dangerous to Your Health," attacking the FDA's decision not to require special safety testing for transgenic foods.[21] A Boston College English professor, Paul Lewis, responded with a letter to the editor in which the coinage "Frankenfood" first appeared, referring to all transgenic foods then under development. In 1992, a coalition of organic farmers and restaurateurs, consumer and environmental groups, and animal-welfare organizations formed the Pure Food Campaign (PFC) to stop transgenic foods. The PFC was led by San Francisco State University professor Jeremy Rifkin, who strongly opposed bioengineering, which he characterized as "a form of annihilation every bit as deadly as nuclear holocaust and even more profound."[22] In Europe, opposition to transgenic foods was even stronger, and many organizations, such as Greenpeace, an international environmental organization, oppose all biotech foods.

While there are many arguments offered against transgenic foods, the major ones are health issues, environmental concerns, the review process, labeling of transgenic foods, and corporate control of the food supply. Heath issues raised include allergenicity, as in the case of StarLink corn. Environmental concerns are many and complex, but, in large part, they relate to the possible escape of transgenic plants into wild populations. There are also concerns that transgenic plants will so dominate agriculture that plant diversity will be lost. Reliance on too few plant strains makes for a potential disaster if one of these strains is destroyed by pests or disease.

Some consumer groups are concerned about the lack of labeling of transgenic foods; many people unknowingly eat foods with transgenic ingredients. There are also concerns related to intellectual property rights. Virtually all the patents on these plants are held by large transnational corporations. Monsanto alone controls 90 percent of the patents on transgenic crops.[23] This, observers believe, gives one company too much control over the field of transgenic foods and over the American food supply as a whole.

There are those, on the other hand, who reject these concerns. "Americans have consumed more than a trillion servings of foods that contain gene-spliced ingredients," said Henry I. Miller, former head of the FDA's Office of Biotechnology from 1989 to 1993 and coauthor of *The Frankenfood Myth*. "There hasn't been a single untoward event documented, not a single ecosystem disrupted or person made ill from these foods," he claimed in 2005 during an interview with the health and nutrition author and *New York Times* columnist, Jane Brody. Miller continued: "That is not something that can be said about conventional foods, where imprecise methods of genetic modification actually have caused illnesses and deaths."[24]

Flavr Effects

Despite the Flavr Savr's financial failure, it opened the way for all the biotech foods that followed. As a result of its review of the Flavr Savr, the FDA established guidelines, in 1992, for the review process related to all transgenic foods, and, two years later, it established a consultation process to help producers meet the safety standards set forth in these guidelines. Since 1994, the FDA has judged many transgenic foods to be as safe as their conventional counterparts. In 1999,

Jim Maryanski, the biotechnology coordinator for the FDA, acknowledged the monumental role of the Flavr Savr in establishing the new industry.[25]

Since 1996, the planting of biotech crops has experienced double-digit growth every year. By 2008, transgenic plantings had swelled to 92 percent for soybeans and 80 percent for corn.[26] Similar percentages hold for crops producing cooking oil, such as cotton and canola. Since many processed foods are made using corn, soybean, or vegetable-oil products, food manufacturers routinely include transgenic ingredients in the foods they produce. In 2003, the Grocery Manufacturers of America estimated that between 70 and 75 percent of all processed foods in U.S. grocery stores may contain ingredients from transgenic plants. In the period 2002 to 2006, plantings of Bt corn and herbicide-tolerant corn skyrocketed. Although soy, corn, cotton, and canola constitute the largest proportion of transgenic crops, others, such as sweet potatoes, tomatoes, papayas, chili peppers, sweet peppers, peanuts, and sunflowers, are also currently on the market. Today, experts estimate that 80 percent of baby formulas, bread, cereal, frozen pizzas, hot dogs, tortilla chips, and sodas contain at least one transgenic ingredient.[27]

These "first generation" products will soon be joined by second-generation transgenic foods. During the past few years alone, the U.S. Department of Agriculture has approved more than 1,000 new biotech plants for use by farmers. New transgenic varieties of corn, cotton, canola, and soybeans are under development, and a number of other bioengineered foods, including apples, bananas, lettuce, potatoes, rice, strawberries, sugar beets, and wheat, are being developed. Biotech foods will likely make up an increasingly large percentage of the foods sold in supermarkets, forever altering what Americans eat.

Postscript

In August 2008, Monsanto announced the sale of Posilac to Eli Lilly and Company's subsidiary Elanco Animal Health for $300 million.[28]

Computer whiz Bill Gates has expressed considerable interest in biotech foods, especially for potential use in Africa to feed the continent's rapidly growing population.[29] In July 2008, the National Research Council, the National Academy of Science's research arm, released a report, funded by the Bill and Melinda Gates Foundation, arguing in part for the development of genetically engineered crops that could be grown in sub-Saharan Africa and South Asia.[30]

30.

Mergers, Acquisitions, and Spin-Offs

I N 1985, the tobacco giant Philip Morris acquired General Foods, the venerable American food company, in a bid to diversify and provide an income stream independent of tobacco. When Philip Morris acquired Kraft, Inc., three years later, it became the largest food company in America. Philip Morris merged General Foods with Kraft to create a single division, Kraft General Foods; its products ranged from Starbucks brand coffee, to Oreos, Oscar Mayer meats, and Swans Down Cake Flour. In the 1990s, as class action lawsuits related to smoking advanced in the courts, Philip Morris needed cash to support its legal defense and pay off settlements, and, in 2001, the company sold 16.1 percent of its wholly owned subsidiary, which was renamed Kraft Foods. By 2006, the management of Philip Morris (now renamed the Altria Group) was convinced the worst of the court cases was over and concluded it was time to begin acquiring smaller tobacco companies, particularly foreign firms. It also decided to spin off Kraft Foods, whose sales were slumping. Altria executives thus sold the remaining stock in the company's food division, and, on March 30, 2007, Kraft Foods became completely independent—and, at the same time, America's largest food company and the second largest in the world.[1]

Kraft History

Kraft Foods traces its roots back more than a century, to when James L. Kraft started selling cheese out of the back of a wagon on the streets of Chicago. Kraft, born in Ontario, Canada, in 1874, had emigrated to the United States, where he engaged in a variety of pursuits. One of his jobs was with the Buffalo Cheese Company, where he learned the business. Kraft arrived in Chicago in 1903 with sixty-five dollars in his pocket. He bought a wagon and a horse to pull it, and fifty pounds of cheese, which he peddled on the streets. Sales were slow until Kraft came up with the idea of packaging the cheese in portions in advance, rather than weighing out and wrapping pieces to each customer's specification.[2] He was joined in the business by his four brothers, and the firm grew. The brothers incorporated the company in 1909 as J. L. Kraft & Bros. They differentiated their cheeses from others on the market by prominently labeling theirs with the company name, and they also began an aggressive marketing campaign in the Chicago area. In 1914, the Kraft brothers opened their first cheese-making plant. At the time, they were selling thirty-one different cheeses and had expanded their market throughout the upper Midwest. In 1915, they began packaging their cheeses in tins. The following year, the company patented the first processed cheese made from milk solids, emulsifiers, salt, and food colorings. The advantage of processed cheese was that it could be made using by-products of regular cheese production and it had a longer shelf-life than did natural cheese.

By 1917, Kraft's earnings were $2 million. When the United States entered World War I, Kraft received a major contract to produce cheese in tins for the U.S. Army. In 1920, it purchased a Canadian firm, MacLaren's Imperial Cheese Company, Ltd., and so began selling its products in Canada. By 1923, the company's annual sales had reached $22 million. During the 1920s, Kraft began expanding abroad, opening its first office in London in 1924 and one in Germany three years later. Also during the 1920s, Kraft launched new products, such as Velveeta, which debuted in 1927.

In 1928, Kraft merged with the Phenix Cheese Company, which had been started by a group of New York dairy farmers who, around 1880, had created and begun marketing Philadelphia Cream Cheese. Both Kraft and Phenix were early producers of processed cheese, but Kraft was the first company to patent such a product. Together, the two companies were soon controlling 40 percent of the nation's cheese sales. National Dairy Products acquired Kraft and several other firms, including the Breyers Ice Cream Company, in 1930. By 1931, the company had plants in thirty-one states and several foreign countries. During the 1930s, it debuted several more products, including Miracle Whip (1930), the Kraft Macaroni and Cheese Dinner (1937), and Parkay Margarine (1940).[3]

During World War II, Kraft supplied cheese to the American armed forces and American allies abroad. In 1951, thanks to the postwar economic boom, National Dairy's gross sales surpassed the $1 billion mark. Kraft packaged the nation's first processed cheese slices in 1950, and it later introduced Cheez Whiz (1952) and Cracker Barrel Cheese (1954). One reason for the company's success was its savvy use of the national media for advertising. To promote Miracle Whip, the company sponsored, in 1933, the Kraft Music Program on NBC radio; when television emerged as a national advertising tool, the company created the Kraft Television Theatre, inaugurated in 1958.

In 1988, Kraft was acquired by Philip Morris, which had acquired the giant General Foods three years earlier. General Foods was an outgrowth of the Postum Cereal Company, founded by C. W. Post in 1895. When Post committed suicide in 1914, his daughter, Marjorie Merriweather Post, inherited the company.[4] She married the financier Edward F. Hutton in 1920, and he took over Postum Cereal. During the 1920s, Hutton went on a buying spree, acquiring fourteen other brands, including Jell-O, Swans Down Cake Flour, Minute Tapioca, Baker's Coconut, Baker's Chocolate, and Log Cabin Syrup. In 1928, Maxwell House Coffee was absorbed into Postum. The following year, Hutton acquired Clarence Birdseye's General Seafood Company and then named the new conglomerate General Foods. After the Depression and World War II, General Foods went on another buying binge, this time acquiring companies such as Perkins Products, the maker of Kool-Aid, in 1953.

In 1981, General Foods acquired Oscar Mayer & Company. The original Oscar Mayer was a German immigrant who started out working for a Detroit meat market before moving to Chicago, where he worked in the stockyards. In 1883, Mayer joined his brother, a sausage maker and ham curer, in opening a small retail butcher shop in a German neighborhood on Chicago's Near North Side. In 1904, the Mayers took the bold step of putting their own name on their products and thus began selling America's first brand-name meats. When the Meat Inspection Act was signed into law in 1906, Oscar Mayer was one of the first companies to voluntarily comply with the provisions of the new law. In 1929, the company further distinguished its products by placing a yellow paper band with the company's name on it around its hot dogs, thus becoming the first meat company to effectively employ a brand name. Oscar Mayer became famous for its Wienermobile, a hot dog–shaped vehicle that has been touring the United States since 1936.

In 1989, Philip Morris merged its two food divisions—General Foods and Kraft—to form Kraft General Foods. In 1993, Philip Morris acquired the ready-to-eat cereals division of RJR Nabisco. Philip Morris reorganized its food companies under the name Kraft Foods, Inc. In 2000, Philip Morris acquired the rest of Nabisco, which it folded into Kraft Foods. Nabisco had been formed in 1898, when the American Biscuit Company, composed of forty bakeries in the Midwest, merged with the New York Biscuit Company and the smaller United States Biscuit Company to create the National Biscuit Company, which operated under the brand name Nabisco.[5] The new company became famous for many products, including Fig Newtons, introduced in 1891; Uneeda Biscuits (1898), the first nationally advertised cracker in America; Graham Crackers (1898), which Sylvester Graham would have disowned, since they contained sugar; Triscuits (1900); Barnum's Animal Crackers (1902); Oreos (1912); Ritz Crackers (1934); and Chips Ahoy cookies (1963).

Nabisco acquired the Shredded Wheat Company in 1928 and the Cream of Wheat Company in 1962. In 1981, Nabisco merged with Standard Brands to form Nabisco Brands. Standard Brands had arisen when three nationally known brands—Fleischmann's Yeast,[6] Chase & Sanborn Coffee, and Royal Baking Powder—came together in 1929. Standard Brands became one of the largest suppliers of grocery goods to supermarkets. In 1961, Standard Brands acquired Planters Nut and Chocolate Company, which had been established in 1906 by two Italian immigrants.[7] It also acquired the Curtiss Candy Company, makers of Baby Ruth and Butterfinger candy bars.[8]

Nabisco Brands also acquired, in 1981, Life Saver Candies from the E. R. Squibb Corporation. Life Savers mints were created in 1912 and sold at bars and tobacco shops, for freshening the breath of drinkers and smokers. In 1913, the Life Savers brand was acquired by the Mint Products Company, which spun off the Life Savers Corporation in 1926. In 1956, Life Savers merged with Beech-Nut, makers of chewing gum, candy, and baby food, to form Beech-Nut Life Savers, Inc. It merged with E. R. Squibb & Sons in 1968.[9]

At about the same time that Philip Morris acquired General Foods, in 1985, R. J. Reynolds Industries acquired Nabisco. Like Philip Morris, R. J. Reynolds had already acquired some food companies in an effort to diversify its operations as the specter of antismoking sentiment and litigation loomed. In 1968, Reynolds bought the Chun King Corporation, which produced Chinese-style packaged foods, and established a subsidiary, R. J. Reynolds Foods, for other nontobacco acquisitions.[10] It had previously acquired Patio (Mexican foods), Hawaiian Punch (fruit punch), College Inn (broth and boned chicken), Brer Rabbit (molasses) and My-T Fine Desserts.[11] In 1979, Reynolds acquired Del Monte Corporation.

In 1986, the year after its merger with Nabisco, R. J. Reynolds changed its name to RJR Nabisco. Three years later, Kohlberg Kravis Roberts & Company (KKR) acquired RJR Nabisco in the largest leveraged buyout in American history.[12] To pay off its debts, KKR began selling assets, including Chun King, Hawaiian Punch, Brer Rabbit, Patio, and My-T-Fine Desserts.[13] The leadership of the Del Monte subsidiary acquired what was left—about half of the original Del Monte company—through another leveraged buyout in 1990. RJR Nabisco sold its cereal foods to Philip Morris in 1993 and finally sold the remainder of Nabisco to Philip Morris in 2000.

The merger between Nabisco and Philip Morris was approved by the Federal Trade Commission on the condition that Philip Morris divested the merged company of Jell-O, Royal brands, mints, and baking powder. In 2001, Kraft Foods began acquiring individual food brands, such as the Pasta Anytime line from Borden.

Other Mergers, Acquisitions, and Spin-Offs

The story of Kraft Foods' mergers, acquisitions, and spin-offs is not unique. Most American food corporations have gone through similar games of corporate musical chairs. Pepsi-Cola merged with Frito-Lay in 1965 to create PepsiCo. Beginning in the 1970s, PepsiCo acquired several fast-food chains, including Pizza Hut (1977), Taco Bell (1978), and Kentucky Fried Chicken (1986). It also acquired beverage companies, including Mug Root Beer (1986), Gatorade (2001), the South Beach Beverage Company (2001), and Naked Juice (2006). PepsiCo also created special relationships with California Pizza Kitchen, the Thomas J. Lipton Company, and Ocean Spray Cranberries, Inc. PepsiCo purchased the Quaker Oats Company in 2001 and Stacy's Pita Chip Company in 2006.[14]

PepsiCo saw its fast-food chains as important outlets for its soft drinks, as all its chains sold Pepsi-Cola. Other large fast-food chains, however, refused to handle PepsiCo beverages because of competition with Pepsi's fast-food chains. In 1997, PepsiCo divested itself of its restaurant subsidiaries, creating a separate corporate entity now called Yum! Brands. PepsiCo's main fast-food rival, McDonald's, has done some acquiring of its own. In 1998, it purchased a minority stake in Chipotle Mexican Grill, a chain of casual Mexican restaurants. The following year the company acquired Donato's Pizza, Inc., and in 2000, McDonald's purchased the bankrupt Boston Market chain.

In 1969, two major British firms—the candy company Cadbury and the soda company Schweppes—merged to form Cadbury Schweppes. Since then, Cadbury Schweppes has acquired many brands, including Mott's (1982), Canada Dry (1986), Hires Root Beer (1989), A&W Beverages (1993), Dr Pepper and 7-Up

(1995), Hawaiian Punch (1999), Orangina (2002), and the Snapple Beverage Group (2003). It acquired Adams Confectionery and its brands, such as Halls, Trident, Dentyne, and Hubba Bubba Bubblegum. Cadbury Schweppes is today a leading global confectionery company, the world's second-largest manufacturer of gum and the world's third-largest manufacturer of soft drinks.

John Tyson started transporting poultry from Arkansas to midwestern cities in the 1930s. The company went public in 1963 and adopted the name Tyson Foods, Inc. The company acquired its first poultry company in 1963; by 1989, it had added nineteen more. In 1977, Tyson purchased a hog company in North Carolina and shortly thereafter became the nation's largest packer of hogs. In 1983, it purchased Mexican Original, and Tyson Foods soon became the nation's largest manufacturer of tortillas. When Tyson Foods purchased Holly Farms, in 1989, it became the largest poultry producer in the United States. In 1992, the company went into seafood with the acquisition of Arctic Alaska Fisheries, Inc., and Louis Kemp Seafood. It purchased, in 1995, Cargill's U.S. broiler operation, McCarty Farms, Inc., and Culinary Foods of Chicago. Two years later, Tyson acquired Mallard's Food Products, and, in 1998, bought its largest competitor in the poultry industry, Hudson Foods. Three years later, with its purchase of IBP, Tyson Foods became America's largest producer of both beef and pork. When Kraft Foods floundered a bit in the early years of the twenty-first century, Tyson surpassed Kraft as the nation's largest food conglomerate.

Concentration of market power also occurred in other poultry and meat businesses, commodities, and food retailing. Today, the top four turkey packers control 41 percent of the market, the top four poultry packers control 58.5 percent of the broiler industry, the top four pork packers control 66 percent of the market, and the top four beef packers control some 83.5 percent of the market. The top three flour millers control 63 percent of the U.S. market, and five companies control 90 percent of the world grain trade.[15] In 1993, the top five grocery chains controlled approximately 20 percent of food sales; in 2001, this rose to 40 percent. Today the top five food retailers control 62 percent of all groceries sold in the United States,[16] and the world's top thirty food-retailing corporations account for one-third of all global grocery sales.[17]

A similar consolidation has occurred in the seed business. Thirty years ago, most commercial seed companies were small and family owned. Since then, chemical companies, such as Monsanto and DuPont, have vertically integrated with the seed and biotechnology industries. During the 1990s, Monsanto expended $8 billion in acquiring seed and biotech companies. By 2000, two companies, Monsanto and DuPont's Pioneer Hi-Bred International, had gained control of 15 percent of the world's seed market, and the percentage is much higher in specific seed sectors. Monsanto and DuPont control 73 percent of the corn seed business in the United States, for example. They also own 40 percent of all significant agri-biotech patents.[18]

Even the organic foods business has become concentrated. Conventional food corporations have continued to gobble up farms and firms producing organic and "health" foods: Cascadian Farm and Muir Glen were purchased by General Mills; Celestial Seasonings and Soy Dream, by H. J. Heinz; Odwalla by Coca-Cola; and Nature's Farm by Tyson Foods, to name just a few.

Similar consolidation has occurred in the candy industry. In 1945, an estimated 6,000 companies were manufacturing candy in the United States. Hershey acquired the H. B. Reese Candy Company, maker of Reese's Peanut Butter Cups, in 1963. In 1977, Hershey acquired Y & S Candies, makers of Twizzlers. In 1988, Hershey purchased Peter Paul brands. Hershey bought, in 1996, Leaf North America, maker of Good & Plenty, Jolly Rancher, Whoppers, Milk Duds, and PayDay. In 2000, the company acquired the Bubble Yum brand. In 1993, Russell Stover Candies, Inc., bought out Whitman Chocolates. In 1972, the Brock Candy Company purchased Schuler Chocolates, of Winona, Minnesota, and, in 1990, it acquired Shelly Brothers. In 1993, the Brock Candy Company was acquired by E. J. Brach Corporation, its biggest competitor. Today, Brach is owned by Barry Callebaut, a Swiss company, which is one of the world's leading manufacturers of chocolate products. Nestlé Food Corporation acquired Butterfinger and Baby Ruth in 1990 and today owns many other candies worldwide.

Merged Effects

Corporate consolidation is complex and at times confusing, but the importance of these transactions cannot be overstated. On the positive side, food giants may become more efficient based on economies of scale. They have more funds to invest in technology, distribution, marketing, and research. Moreover, large corporations are better able to compete successfully in the global economy.

On the negative side, large corporate structures make decisions based almost entirely on profit margins and projected growth. Large corporations often require that subsidiaries generate double-digit profits to guarantee the investment they need to acquire state-of-the-art equipment and to finance advertising. A century ago, food businesses grew because of individuals who were able to make quick decisions and were willing to take risks. In the past, too, anyone with a good idea could launch a food product on a small scale and test the market. With but a few large corporations controlling product development, however, marketing flexibility and creativity are limited. Corporate consolidation has reduced competition within significant food sectors, and some studies have suggested that, in many sectors of the food industry, concentration has produced higher prices.[19] Other studies have reported that consolidation in the seed industry has decreased research and development.[20]

Critics also worry about the political power of large food corporations. During the 2000 election year, for instance, agribusiness spent $60 million on campaign contributions and $78 million on lobbying; the food sector received $23 billion in public subsidies in 2002. Likewise, food manufacturers have constantly pressured for relaxation of rules and regulations regarding safety and labeling, the "dumbing down" of food standards, and the watering down of critical reports. They have also opposed the funding of independent research into new additives and preservatives and discouraged the hiring of inspectors to enforce federal laws.

The concentration of corporate control in agriculture, processing, and distribution have been hallmarks of the American food business for the past half century. The smaller the number of food producers, processors, and supermarket chains, the less competition that exists, which, to some observers, places too much power in the hands of too few executives. As others see it, large corporations are more efficient, and their competition is now global. In addition, they may be better able to solve the problems the food world will likely face in the near future.

Postscript

Thomas McInnerney died in 1952; James Kraft remained president of the Kraft division until his death, also in 1952. E. F. Hutton remained in charge of General Foods until 1935, when he and Marjorie Merriweather Post were divorced. He died in 1962; she died ten years later.

Epilogue

I F THESE THIRTY turning points tell us anything, it is that culinary and dietary changes are universal and constantly surprising. Oliver Evans did not expect his mill to be a major force in the development of American food processing. The individuals planning the Erie Canal did not foresee consumers in one part of America becoming dependent on farmers and millers in another region. Neither did they imagine the canal would create dislocations among eastern farmers, causing many of them to leave their homes and head for the Midwest in search of better farmland. The Delmonico brothers did not expect their restaurant would become the model for future American restaurants. Neither Evans nor the Erie Canal planners anticipated that, as a result of their creations, Sylvester Graham would launch a food-protest movement, while Graham himself certainly did not see that his culinary concerns would still be relevant 180 years later. Cyrus McCormick did not expect his reaper to help the North win the Civil War, nor did he anticipate that the mechanization of farms would contribute eventually to the development of large-scale corporate farming. When the United States acquired California and the Southwest and permitted waves of Chinese and German immigrants into the country in 1848, Anglo-Americans never imagined the exotic fare of China, Mexico, and Germany would someday be readily available in restaurants and grocery stores throughout America.

The Civil War certainly was not fought over culinary matters, but it had tremendous influences on what Americans ate: canned foods became common, African Americans carried southern food traditions throughout the nation, and legislation passed during the war created an agricultural revolution leading to further mechanization on farms, the application of science to boosting crop yields, and the eventual rise of the factory farm. The American fairs and expositions that began with Philadelphia's in 1876 were intended to disseminate new machinery, technologies, and commercial products to a wide audience, but a surprise effect was the rapid adoption of foods and beverages—such as snack foods, ethnic foods, and soft drinks—that were displayed at these fairs.

When Henry Crowell thought up the Quaker Special, he didn't anticipate the emergence of food advertising and its contribution to the gradual disappearance of generic food products sold in bulk, nor to the idea that any commercial product, properly advertised, could make a profit. The pharmacist John Pemberton would be amazed that his cocaine-spiked medicine became the basis of a multibillion-dollar global industry. Frederick and Louis Rueckheim would be shocked to know their product, Cracker Jack, had launched a multibillion-dollar snackfood industry.

Wilbur O. Atwater would be astounded to learn his work helped establish a field of nutrition research still influencing what Americans eat today. Fannie Farmer never anticipated that her self-funded *Boston Cooking-School Cook Book* would become the model for countless future cookbooks, or that her simplification of recipes would contribute to a decline in American culinary literacy. Health-food guru John Harvey Kellogg was horrified when his brother Will commercialized Toasted Corn Flakes, and neither of them could have expected they would change forever what Americans eat for breakfast. Upton Sinclair wanted a socialist revolution in America, and he was opposed to the legislation creating the Food and Drug Administration, legislation partly a consequence of the publication of his own book, *The Jungle*.

Although there had been commercial potential in frozen food prior to World War II, success in the marketplace depended on postwar sales of refrigerators and freezers, which led to the advent, in 1953, of Swanson's TV Dinner and, eventually, to the widespread use of frozen foods in homes and restaurants. Frozen foods were sold in supermarkets, which were popularized beginning in the 1930s. Supermarkets sold an enormous variety of inexpensive and convenient processed foods. Paradoxically, these changes created interest in "gourmet" food. A magazine of that name, *Gourmet*, elicited even more interest in fine food. The magazine's success encouraged the founding of other food magazines, which, collectively, contributed to Americans' becoming "food spectators," vicariously experiencing gustatory pleasures through the written word and the glossy color photo.

Continuous strides were made in American agriculture during the twentieth century, but with progress came protest. Jerome I. Rodale planned a counterrevolution when he began publishing, in 1942, a magazine entitled *Organic Gardening*. The organic food movement didn't really take off, however, until the emergence of the food counterculture, around 1970. From that counterculture came urban gardens, food co-ops, green markets, and a renewed interest in organic farming. In addition, the increasing popularity of organizations such as Slow Food USA—an outgrowth of the counterculture—has encouraged Americans to preserve their culinary heritage.

Radar technology during World War II led to an unexpected result, when, in 1944, a new type of oven was created that could cook food with unprecedented speed. The inventor of this new device, Percy Spencer, expected his invention would be adopted immediately by restaurants, but it was decades before the microwave oven was commonplace in American homes and restaurants.

The labor shortage created by World War II resulted, surprisingly, in the professionalization of the American restaurant through the creation of what became the Culinary Institute of America and other culinary schools for training workers and culinary leaders. On the other hand, the wartime labor shortage also convinced Richard and Maurice McDonald to do away with carhops and cooks at their drive-in in San Bernardino, California. The franchising of McDonald's by Ray Kroc began the era of large fast-food chains, which changed what Americans ate for lunch and dinner—and, more recently, for breakfast. The fast-food industry has, in turn, affected what farmers raise and, because of its pervasive influences, even contributed to changes in the natural environment.

Julia Child just wanted to publish a cookbook, but her subsequent television series made her America's first media food celebrity. From her position of authority, Child helped create organizations such as the American Institute of Wine and Food and the International Association of Culinary Professionals' philanthropic arm, now called the Culinary Trust, as well as foster the development of an academic field devoted to food studies. The culinary arts program at Boston University was the first such academic program in America. Alice Waters, in creating her personal vision of a French restaurant, invented and popularized California cuisine, which continues to influence American eating habits.

The Food Network's creation, in 1993, gave rise to a number of "celebrity chefs" who have become some of the country's most influential arbiters of food and cooking. Numerous other cookery programs now fill the airwaves, and culinary competition has even made cooking a spectator sport.

Yet another unanticipated effect of the changing food scene came with the introduction of the Flavr Savr tomato, the first genetically modified organism approved by the U.S. Department of Agriculture. Although the product flopped and was withdrawn a few years later, the Flavr Savr tomato paved the way for other genetically engineered foods. Today, every American who eats processed foods likely consumes genetically engineered ingredients, and more foods with bioengineered components will no doubt be marketed in the future.

At the dawn of the twenty-first century, the American foodscape remains vibrant. Immigrant populations and émigré chefs continue introducing new foods to America's table. Global trade has given Americans wider food choices than ever before and inspired a dizzying array of places to buy and enjoy that food: chic restaurants using exotic imported ingredients; fast-food chains serving vegetarian alternatives; thriving supermarkets offering tens of thousands of products; and newly revived, old-fashioned food sources such as farmers' markets, local artisan bakers, and farmstead cheese makers. As American food corporations remain at the forefront of research and applications of genetic engineering, a wider variety and more abundant supply of foods will be available in the future.

The problems facing the American food system, however, are many; the main one being that the nation's industrialized agricultural system is based largely on oil and petroleum products, such as fertilizers and synthetic pesticides. With the volatile price of oil and an estimated 30 percent of American corn being diverted to ethanol production, food prices have surged since 2002, and it is likely that more escalations are in store. As the demand for food and petroleum rise in other countries, such as China and India, hefty boosts in commodity prices are even more likely in the future.

A related concern is that America's superabundance of food is based on a global system where commodities are produced in the country with the lowest costs and shipped to (or from) the United States. The transportation and distribution systems eat up even more petroleum. In all, the agricultural system uses about 30 percent of the oil consumed in the United States.

The Foreseeable Future

It is always easier to explain past events and discuss their influence on the present than to predict future events with any degree of accuracy. Nonetheless, some near-term projections about American food are relatively easy to make. It is extremely unlikely that Americans will ever return to the culinary world of 200 years ago. It is impossible for the United States to feed its population a diverse and healthy diet exclusively through local food production. Food will always have to travel. Middle-class and well-to-do consumers will demand choices beyond the foods a particular season has to offer. Industrial food, bioengineered food, fast food, snack food, supermarkets, food television, and so on are here to stay and will surely have a strong influence on the foods Americans eat in the future. It is also likely that medium-sized farms and food corporations will expand their leverage during the next decade or so. Finally, it is likely that the government will institute more regulation and oversight in the future in order to promote public health and control abuses by large corporations.

Food prices in the United States are affected by population growth and food demand throughout the world, as well as by unprecedented world shortages of such staples as rice and wheat. In response to rising oil prices, many American farmers have switched from growing food crops, such as wheat, to growing corn for making ethanol, presumably a cheaper fuel than petroleum. But this has had an ironic, unintended consequence: corn for animal feed has become more expensive, and prices for animal-derived food products—meat, poultry, eggs, milk, and cheese—have surged. Meanwhile, higher prices for basic commodities and transportation costs have pushed up prices of processed foods as well. These changes, along with the effects of natural disasters such as floods and droughts, have also contributed to the increasing cost of food in the United States and abroad.

While petroleum and food prices have been rising, the value of the American dollar has slid against foreign currencies. Hence, the cost of imported foods, which now represent about 40 percent of all food consumed in the United States, has increased. Because of their escalating cost, it is possible that the importation of foodstuffs from abroad will decline in the near future and that American factory farms will increase production. Another possible consequence is that Americans will gain a greater appreciation for locally produced foods. Perhaps the high cost of petrochemical fertilizers will encourage the growth of organic farms, and more Americans will rediscover the pleasures of local, fresh, seasonal foods.

That scenario applies to middle- and upper-class Americans. America's poor, on the other hand, will likely face a gloomier future. Food banks are running out of money to buy food, and, without a major infusion of government funds, it is likely the amount of food available to the poor and homeless will decrease.

Still another likely effect of increasing food prices is an expansion of research into bioengineered crops. Monsanto, for instance, has announced research into genetically modified crops that will double yields during the next two decades.[1] Monsanto and other biotech corporations will likely succeed in increasing the productivity of basic crops, but the fast growth in transgenic food may well cause serious problems, as all new technologies are prone to do.

Future Scenarios

It is impossible, of course, to predict the future with any reliability beyond the next few years. But in the long run, four basic scenarios are possible. In the doomsday scenario, major crises will largely destroy the world's food systems. The most commonly discussed possible cause of this is the potential effects of global warming. It is likely that global warming will change world weather patterns, making much of America's farm belt unproductive. Large tracts of arable land may become unusable because of drought. Hurricanes, typhoons, tornadoes, floods, and tsunamis caused by climate change may create widespread agricultural dislocations and global upheavals. Possible results of the doomsday scenario are the end of industrial agriculture, perhaps a monumental loss of global population, and an exodus from large urban areas to rural communities. Food will become a matter of life and death, and its supply will be controlled by a small minority with the power to decide how to allocate available food.

A second possibility is the corporate oligarchic scenario. In this futurescape, technology and science will save the world's industrial food system and create a culinary utopia for everyone. Yes, global warming and weather-related dislocations might affect the food supply, but technology and science will solve these problems as they emerge. Energy problems will be taken care of by nuclear power. It is likely that a relatively few corporate giants—such as Monsanto, Kraft Foods, Archer Daniels Midland, and PepsiCo—will control more and more market share because they will be the only entities large enough to conduct the research and testing necessary to solve the problems that arise.

A third alternative is the green scenario, where large factory farms are broken up and medium-sized farms become the backbone of American agriculture. They shift from a complete dependence on fossil fuels to more renewable solar and other energy sources. Hormones, synthetic pesticides, and chemical fertilizers are reduced or eliminated. Likewise, small and medium-sized companies become dominant in food processing and retailing. Americans shift from buying the majority of their food from large supermarket chains to shopping at farmers' markets. Family-owned artisanal food suppliers proliferate, as do family-owned restaurants, diminishing the role of large fast-food chains.

Including aspects of these three scenarios, the most likely one is the "just muddle through" scenario. In this scenario there are problems—hunger, malnutrition, climate change, and natural disasters—even those associated with such new technologies as bioengineering. But the application of advances in industry, science, and technology will partially overcome some problems. There may well be a proliferation of medium-sized farms that can supply food to local consumers. There will also be a jump in alternative agricultural systems, the expansion of nuclear power, and the continued development of alternative-energy sources.

If there is a lesson to be taken from the thirty turning points discussed in this book, it is that we should expect the unexpected and plan for the unintended effects of any actions we take now and in the future.

Notes

Preface

1. Organic Trade Association, "U.S. Organic Sales Show Substantial Growth," May 6, 2007, Organic Trade Association, http://www.organicnewsroom.com (accessed September 20, 2008); Jack W. Plunkett, *Plunkett's Food Industry Almanac 2008* (Houston: Plunkett Research, 208).

2. "When Wal-Mart Goes Organic," *New York Times*, May 14, 2006, http://www.nytimes.com (accessed September 20, 2008).

3. *Body Bulletin* (January 2000), cited in Myrna Chandler Goldstein and Mark A. Goldstein, *Controversies in Food and Nutrition* (Westport, Conn.: Greenwood Press, 2002), 163; Suzanne Phelan and Gary D. Foster, "Environmental Challenges and Assessment," in *Handbook of Nutrition and Food*, ed. Carolyn D. Berdanier, Johanna Dwyer, and Elaine B. Feldman, 2nd ed. (Boca Raton, Fla.: Taylor & Francis, 2008), 652.

4. Brian Halweil, *Worldwatch Paper #163: Home Grown: The Case for Local Food in a Global Market* (Washington, D.C.: Worldwatch Institute, 2002), 5, 9, 18.

5. Alberto Jerardo, "The US Ag Trade Balance, More Than Just a Number," *Amber Waves* 3 (February 2004), 36–37; Economic Research Service, "Value of U.S. Trade: Agricultural, Nonagricultural, and Total—and Trade Balance, by Fiscal Year," Economic Research Service, http://www.ers.usda.gov/data/fatus/index.htm#value (accessed September 26, 2008).

6. "GE Foods in the Market," Genetically Engineered Organisms Public Issues Education Project, http://www.geo-pie.cornell.edu/crops/eating.html (accessed September 18, 2008); Linda Bren, "Genetic Engineering: The Future of Foods?" *FDA Consumer*

37 (November-December 2003), Food and Drug Administration, http://www.fda.gov /fdac/features/2003/603_food.html (accessed September 1, 2008).

Prologue

1. T. H. Breen, "An Empire of Goods: The Anglicization of Colonial America, 1690–1776," *Journal of British Studies* 25 (October 1986): 496–98.
2. Richard J. Hooker, *Food and Drink in America: A History* (Indianapolis: Bobbs-Merrill, 1981), 39.
3. Ibid., 46; Amy D. Schwartz, "New England Agriculture: Old Visions, New Directions," *Agricultural History* 69 (summer 1995): 455; James E. McWilliams, *A Revolution in Eating: How the Quest for Food Shaped America* (New York: Columbia University Press, 2005), 10, 63.
4. Hooker, *Food and Drink in America*, 24–25, 44; Max George Schumacher, *The Northern Farmer and His Markets during the Late Colonial Period* (New York: Arno Press, 1975), 152; Carole Shammas, "How Self-Sufficient Was Early America?" *Journal of Interdisciplinary History* 13 (autumn 1982): 260–61.
5. Hugh Jones, *The Present State of Virginia: From Whence Is Inferred a Short View of Maryland and North Carolina*, ed. Richard L. Morton (Chapel Hill: University of North Carolina Press, 1956), 86.
6. Albert Cook Myers, ed., *Narratives of Early Pennsylvania, West New Jersey and Delaware, 1630–1707* (New York: Scribner's, 1912), 252–53, 324–27; J. Franklin Jameson, ed., *Narratives of New Netherland, 1609–1664* (New York: Scribner's, 1909), 55, 219; Bayrd Still, *Mirror for Gotham* (New York: New York University Press, 1956), 10; McWilliams, *Revolution in Eating; How the*, 12, 186–96.
7. Hooker, *Food and Drink in America*, 55–56; Johann David Schoepf, *Travels in the Confederation* [1783–1784], trans. and ed. Alfred J. Morrison, 2 vols. (New York: Franklin, 1968), 1:113; Kenneth Roberts and Anna M. Roberts, trans. and eds., *Moreau de St. Méry's American Journey* [1793–1798] (Garden City, N.Y.: Doubleday, 1947), 280.
8. Phillips Russell, *Benjamin Franklin: The First Civilized American* (New York: Cosimo Classics, 2005), 166.
9. Julia Cherry Spruill, *Women's Life and Work in the Southern Colonies* (New York: Norton, 1972), 65; Linda K. Kerber, Jane Sherron De Hart, and Jane De Hart-Mathews, eds., *Women's America: Refocusing the Past* (New York: Oxford University Press, 1982), 27.
10. Louis B. Wright and Marion Tinling, eds., *The Secret Diary of William Byrd of Westover, 1709–1712* (Richmond, Va.: Dietz Press, 1941), 2, 6, 8, 14, 221, 394; Israel Acrelius, *A History of New Sweden*, trans. William M. Reynolds (Philadelphia: Historical Society of Pennsylvania, 1874), 158–59; John Ernest Thorrington Wright and Doris S. Corbett, *Pioneer Life in Western Pennsylvania* (Pittsburgh: University of Pittsburgh Press, 1940), 58; Hooker, *Food and Drink in America*, 39–42.
11. Ulysses Prentiss Hedrick, *A History of Agriculture in the State of New York* (New York: Hill and Wang, 1966), 74–75.
12. E. A. White, "A Study of the Plow Bottom and Its Action upon the Furrow Slice," *Journal of Agricultural Research* 12 (January 28, 1918): 173–74.

1. Oliver Evan's Automated Mill

1. John Storck and Walter Dorwin Teague, *A History of Milling Flour for Man's Bread* (Minneapolis: University of Minnesota Press, 1952), 161.

2. Henry Howe, *Memoirs of the Most Eminent American Mechanics; Also, Lives of Distinguished European Mechanics; Together with a Collection of Anecdotes, Descriptions, &C. &C., Relating to the Mechanic Arts* (New York: Blake, 1844), 73.

3. Ulysses Prentiss Hedrick, ed., *Sturtevant's Edible Plants of the World* (New York: Dover, 1972), 577–80.

4. Rolla Milton Tryon, *Household Manufactures in the United States, 1640–1860* (Chicago: University of Chicago Press, 1917), 94, 221; Richard J. Hooker, *Food and Drink in America: A History* (Indianapolis: Bobbs-Merrill, 1981), 174.

5. Jayme A. Sokolow, *Eros and Modernization: Sylvester Graham, Health Reform and the Origins of Sexuality in America* (Madison, N.J.: Fairleigh Dickinson University Press, 1983), 116.

6. Greville Bathe and Dorothy Bathe, *Oliver Evans: A Chronicle of Early American Engineering* (Philadelphia: Historical Society of Pennsylvania, 1935), 8.

7. Ibid., 9–10.

8. Siegfried Giedion, *Mechanization Takes Command: A Contribution to Anonymous History* (New York: Norton, 1969), 82.

9. Coleman Sellers Jr., "Oliver Evans and His Inventions," *Journal of the Franklin Institute* 122 (July 1886): 2–4.

10. Joseph Dart, "The Grain Elevators of Buffalo," March 13, 1865, in *Publications of the Buffalo Historical Society* (Buffalo: Bigelow, 1879), 396.

11. Bathe and Bathe, *Oliver Evans*, 25–27.

12. John W. McGrain, "Grist Mills in Baltimore County, Maryland" (typescript, Maryland Historical Society, 1980), 7, cited in Brooke Hunter, "Wheat, War, and the American Economy during the Age of Revolution," *William and Mary Quarterly* 62 (July 2005): 505–26; George Terry Sharrer, "Flour Milling and the Growth of Baltimore, 1783–1830" (Ph.D. diss., University of Maryland, 1975), 85–86.

13. Ruth Schwartz Cowan, *A Social History of American Technology* (Oxford: Oxford University Press, 1997), 72.

14. John Storck and Walter Dorwin Teague, *A History of Milling Flour for Man's Bread* (Minneapolis: University of Minnesota Press, 1952), 171; David A. Wells, ed., *Annual of Scientific Discovery: or, Year-Book of Facts in Science and Art* (Boston: Gould, Kendall, and Lincoln, 1850), 62; Sokolow, *Eros and Modernization*, 116–17; Harvey A. Leven-stein, *Revolution at the Table: The Transformation of the American Diet* (New York: Oxford University Press, 1988), 22. The main reason bread making became more expensive in cities relates to the price of wood used to heat the ovens. As forests near cities were cut down, loggers had to go greater distances for wood, increasing the price of fuel.

15. John F. G. Harrison and W. W. Nichols, "Equipment of a Modern Flour Mill," *Journal of the American Society of Mechanical Engineers* 34 (January 1912): 514.

16. Hunter, "Wheat, War, and the American Economy," 505–26.

17. James Hall, *Statistics of the West at the Close of the Year 1836* (Cincinnati: James, 1836), 265–66; Richard Bennett and John Elton, *History of Corn Milling*, 4 vols. (London: Simpkin, Marshall, 1898–1904), 3:297–304.

18. Herman Steen, *Flour Milling in America* (Minneapolis: Denison, 1963), 46; Hooker, *Food and Drink in America*, 241.

19. Bennett and Elton, *History of Corn Milling*, 194.

20. Giedion, *Mechanization Takes Command*, 85; Randolph Shipley Klein, ed., *Science and Society in Early America: Essays in Honor of Whitfield J. Bell, Jr.* (Philadelphia: American Philosophical Society, 1986), 290–91; Ralph Gray and John M. Peterson, *Economic Development of the United States*, rev. ed. (Homewood, Ill.: Irwin, 1974), 239; Martin S. Peterson and Donald Kiteley Tressler, eds., *Food Technology the World Over*, 2 vols. (Westport, Conn.: Avi, 1963–65), 1:48; Robert H. Roy, *Operations Technology: Systems and Evolution* (Baltimore: Johns Hopkins University Press, 1986), 71.

2. The Erie Canal

1. Ronald E. Shaw, *Erie Water West: A History of the Erie Canal 1792–1854* (Lexington: University of Kentucky Press, 1966), 184–85; Janey Levy, *The Erie Canal: A Primary Source History of the Canal That Changed America* (New York: Rosen Central Primary Source, 2003), 12; Peter L. Bernstein, *Wedding of the Waters: The Erie Canal and the Making of a Great Nation* (New York: Norton, 2005), 311.

2. Ulysses Prentiss Hedrick, *A History of Agriculture in the State of New York* (New York: Hill and Wang, 1966), 245.

3. Edward Everett Hale, *Memories of a Hundred Years*, rev. ed. (New York: Macmillan, 1904), 299–301.

4. Frederick Cook and George S. Conover, comps., *Journals of the Military Expedition of Major General John Sullivan Against the Six Nations of Indians in 1779* (Auburn, N.Y.: Knapp, Peck & Thomson, 1887), 110, 163, 175, 186, 188, 266, 296, 299, 301, 302, 337, 343, 362, 366, 371, 376, 415, 417, 426, 456, 530; Jayme A. Sokolow, *The Great Encounter: Native Peoples and European Settlers in the Americas, 1492–1800* (Armonk, N.Y.: M. E. Sharpe, 2003), 208.

5. Bernstein, *Wedding of the Waters*, 49, 61, 173.

6. Shaw, *Erie Water West*, 185.

7. Bernstein, *Wedding of the Waters*, 272.

8. Shaw, *Erie Water West*, 284.

9. Hedrick, *History of Agriculture in the State of New York*, 145, 247.

10. John Storck and Walter Dorwin Teague, *A History of Milling Flour for Man's Bread* (Minneapolis: University of Minnesota Press, 1952), 179.

11. Ibid., 179–180.

12. Hedrick, *History of Agriculture in the State of New York*, 248.

13. Arnold Tilden, *The Legislation of the Civil-War Period Considered as a Basis of the Agricultural Revolution in the United States* (Los Angeles: University of Southern California Press, 1937), 47.

14. Emerson David Fite, *Social and Industrial Conditions in the North During the Civil War* (New York: Smith, 1930), 1.

15. Martha H. Verbrugge, "Healthy Animals and Civic Life, Physiology of Subsistence," *Reviews in American History* 9 (September 1981): 362; Stephen Nissenbaum, *Sex, Diet, and Debility in Jacksonian America* (Westport, Conn.: Greenwood Press, 1980), ix, 137.

16. Hedrick, *History of Agriculture in the State of New York*, 247; Storck and Teague, *History of Milling Flour for Man's Bread*, 183.

17. A 1969 Department of Energy report estimates 1,300 miles for the distance grain travels from where it is grown to where it is consumed (Stephen L. Brown and Ulrich F. Pilz, *U.S. Agriculture: Potential Vulnerabilities* [Menlo Park, Calif.: Stanford Research Institute, 1969]). A 1980 report gives 1,346 miles, but the authors concluded that the distance was probably much greater (John Hendrickson, "Energy Use in the U.S. Food System: A Summary of Existing Research and Analysis," Center for Integrated Agricultural Systems, University of Wisconsin, Madison, January 1994, 8, http://www.cias. wisc.edu/farm-to-fork/energy-use-in-the-us-food-system-a-summary-of-existing-research-and-analysis [accessed September 26, 2008]). A 1997 study examining vegetables arriving in Maryland reports 1,686 miles (Matthew Hora and Judy Tick, *From Farm to Table: Making the Connection in the Mid-Atlantic Food System* [Washington, D.C.: Capital Area Food Bank, 2001]). Brian Halweil estimates somewhere between 1,500 and 2,500 miles (Brian Halweil, *Worldwatch Paper #163: Home Grown: The Case for Local Food in a Global Market* [Washington, D.C.: Worldwatch Institute, 2002], 5, 9, 18). A 2003 study reported that conventional food traveled 1,494 miles before being sold in Iowa (Rich Pirog and Andrew Benjamin, "Checking the Food Odometer: Comparing Food Miles for Local Versus Conventional Produce Sales to Iowa Institutions, Marketing and Food Systems," Leopold Center for Sustainable Agriculture, Iowa State University, Ames, July 2003, http://www.leopold.iastate.edu/pubs/staff/files/food_travel072103.pdf [accessed September 26, 2008]).

3. Delmonico's

1. Joe O'Connell, "History of Delmonico's Restaurant and Business Operations in New York," http://www.steakperfection.com/delmonico/History.html (accessed December 2, 2008).

2. H. E. Scudder, ed., *Recollections of Samuel Breck* (Philadelphia: Porter & Coates, 1877), 24–26.

3. Charles Frances Adams, ed., *Familiar Letters of John Adams and His Wife Abigail Adams during the Revolution* (New York: Hurd and Houghton, 1876), 359; Richard Osborn Cummings, *The American and His Food: A History of Food Habits in the United States* (Chicago: University of Chicago Press, 1940), 30–31; James M. Gabler, *Passions: The Wines and Travels of Thomas Jefferson* (Baltimore: Bacchus Press, 1995), 27–28.

4. James Schouler, *Thomas Jefferson* (New York: Dodd, Mead, 1893), 100.

5. Jean Anthelme Brillat-Savarin, *The Physiology of Taste; or, Meditations on Transcendental Gastronomy*, trans. M. F. K. Fisher (Washington, D.C.: Counterpoint, 1986), 271, 305.

6. *New-York Evening Post*, December 16–20, 1827, 4; Lately Thomas [pseudonym for Robert V. P. Steele?], *Delmonico's: A Century of Splendor* (Boston: Houghton Mifflin, 1967), 22.

7. Ibid., 7–11.

8. "Carte du Restaurant Français des Frères Delmonico" (New York: T. & C. Wood, 1838), reproduced on the inside cover of Thomas, *Delmonico's*.

9. Frederick Marryat, *Second Series of a Diary in America, with Remarks on Its Institutions* (Philadelphia: T. K. & P. G. Collins, 1840), 35.

10. George Augustus Sala, *America Revisited: From the Bay of New York to the Gulf of Mexico* (London: Vizetelly, 1883), 92.

11. Ibid., 90.

12. Charles Ranhofer, *The Epicurean* (New York: Ranhofer, 1894).

13. Leopold Rimmer, *A History of Old New York Life and the House of the Delmonicos* (New York, 1898), 24–25.

14. Richard J. Hooker, *Food and Drink in America: A History* (Indianapolis: Bobbs-Merrill, 1981), 237.

15. Harvey A. Levenstein, *Revolution at the Table: The Transformation of the American Diet* (New York: Oxford University Press, 1988), 192.

16. Kathleen McLaughlin, "Epicures' Retreat Opened by French," *New York Times*, May 10, 1939, 21.

17. Patric Kuh, *The Last Days of Haute Cuisine: America's Culinary Revolution* (New York: Viking, 2001), 11–12.

18. Pierre Franey with Richard Flaste and Bryan Miller, *A Chef's Tale: A Memoir of Food, France, and America* (New York: Knopf, 1994), 88–89.

19. Harvey Levenstein, "Two Hundred Years of French Food in America," *Journal of Gastronomy* 5 (spring 1989): 77; Kuh, *Last Days of Haute Cuisine*, 7, 15–16.

20. Franey, , *Chef's Tale*, 109.

21. Craig Claiborne, "In Classic Tradition; Henri Soule Had Towering Standards in Pursuit of Gastronomic Perfection," *New York Times*, January 28, 1966, 44; "Henri Soulé of Le Pavillon Dies, Had Wide Influence on French Cuisine in City and U.S.," *New York Times*, January 28, 1966, 44; Levenstein, "Two Hundred Years of French Food in America," 78.

22. Levenstein, "Two Hundred Years of French Food in America," 79.

23. Joseph Wechsberg, *Dining at the Pavillon* (Boston: Little, Brown,1962), 35.

24. Jacques Pépin, *The Apprentice: My Life in the Kitchen* (Boston: Houghton Mifflin, 2003), 145; Craig Claiborne, "Le Pavillon Shut in Gallic Pique," *New York Times*, March 3, 1960, 31.

25. "Henri Soulé of Le Pavillon Dies," 44.

26. René Verdon, *The White House Chef Cookbook* (Garden City, N.Y.: Doubleday, 1968), 17.

27. Levenstein, "Two Hundred Years of French Food in America," 80–81.

28. Levenstein, *Revolution at the Table*, 15; Carolyn Voight, "You Are What You Eat: Contemplations on Civilizing the Palette with *Gourmet*" (master's thesis, McGill University, 1996), 38.

29. Levenstein, *Revolution at the Table*, 17.

30. Thomas, *Delmonico's*, 181–82.

31. Claiborne, "In Classic Tradition," 44.

32. Ibid., 44.

33. Jane Nicholson, "News of Food: 2 Former Waiters Open French Restaurant," *New York Times*, December 28, 1954, 49.

34. Florence Fabricant, "La Caravelle, a French Legend, Is Closing After 43 Years," Dining In, Dining Out, *New York Times*, May 12, 2004.

35. Delmonico's Restaurant Web site: http://www.delmonicosny.com (accessed July 5, 2008); Judith Choate and James Canora, *Dining at Delmonico's: The Story of America's Oldest Restaurant, with More Than 80 Recipes* (New York: Stewart, Tabori & Chang, 2008), 9.

4. Sylvester Graham's Reforms

1. Sylvester Graham, *A Lecture on Epidemic Diseases Generally, and Particularly the Spasmodic Cholera: Delivered in the City of New York, March, 1832, and Repeated June, 1832, and in Albany, July 4, 1832, and in New York, June, 1833* (Boston: David Cambell, 1838).

2. Martyn Paine, *Letters on the Cholera Asphyxia, as It Has Appeared in the City of New-York: Addressed to John C. Warren, M.D., of Boston, and Originally Published in That City* (New York: Collins & Hannay, 1832).

3. *Boston Medical and Surgical Journal* 45 (1851): 316; "Life of Sylvester Graham," in Sylvester Graham, *Lectures on the Science of Human Life* (New York: Fowler & Wells, 1883), 9 ; Richard H. Shryock, "Sylvester Graham and the Popular Health Movement, 1830–1870," *Mississippi Valley Historical Review* 18 (September 1931): 172–75; Jayme A. Sokolow, *Eros and Modernization: Sylvester Graham, Health Reform and the Origins of Sexuality in America* (Madison, N.J.: Fairleigh Dickinson University Press, 1983), 55–58.

4. Sokolow, *Eros and Modernization*, 60.

5. Stephen Nissenbaum, *Sex, Diet, and Debility in Jacksonian America* (Westport, Conn.: Greenwood Press, 1980), 79.

6. Hillel Schwartz, *Never Satisfied: A Cultural History of Diets, Fantasies and Fat* (New York: Free Press, 1986), 25; Ronald L. Numbers, *Prophetess of Health: Ellen G. White and the Origins of Seventh-Day Adventist Health Reform* (Knoxville: University of Tennessee Press, 1992), 52–53; Charles Caldwell, "Thoughts of the Pathology, Prevention, and Treatment of Intemperance, as a Form of Mental Derangement," *Transylvania Journal of Medicine* 5 (September 1832): 313.

7. William Alcott, *Vegetable Diet: As Sanctioned by Medical Men, and by Experience in All Ages* (Boston: Marsh, Capen & Lyon, 1838).

8. Sokolow, *Eros and Modernization*, 101–12.

9. J. H. Appleby and J. R. Millburn, "Henry or Humphrey? The Jacksons, Eighteenth-Century Chemists," *Library* 10 (1988): 31–43.

10. Edwin G. Burrows and Mike Wallace, *Gotham: A History of New York City to 1898* (New York: Oxford University Press, 1999), 533.

11. Sylvester Graham, *A Lecture to Young Men on Chastity: Intended Also for the Serious Consideration of Parents and Guardians* (Boston: Light & Stearns, 1837); Nissenbaum, *Sex, Diet, and Debility*, 39.

12. Sylvester Graham, *A Lecture on Epidemic Diseases with an Appendix Containing Several Testimonials, Rules of the Graham Boarding House, &c.* (New York: Day, 1833); Richard Osborn Cummings, *The American and His Food: A History of Food Habits in the United States* (Chicago: University of Chicago Press, 1940), 43–46.

13. Sylvester Graham, *Treatise on Bread and Bread-Making* (Boston: Light & Stearns, 1837), 35.

14. Ibid., 33.

15. Ibid., 43.

16. Ibid., 45.

17. Ibid., 42–56, 105.

18. Ibid., 29.

19. "My Lodgings, by B.," *The New-England Magazine* 7 (July 1834): 72.

20. Wendell Phillips Garrison, "The Isms of Forty Years Ago," *Harper's New Monthly Magazine* 60 (January 1880): 190.

21. Graham, *Lectures on the Science of Human Life*, 600–13.

22. Nissenbaum, *Sex, Diet, and Debility*, 143.

23. Asenath Hatch Nicholson, *Nature's Own Book*, 2nd ed. (New York: Dorr, 1835), 14–22. For more about Nicholson, see Constance He McCarthy, "Asenath Hatch Nicholson: An Unknown American Author," (master's thesis, Southern Connecticut State University, 1975).

24. Thomas H. Le Duc, "Documents: Grahamites and Garrisonites," *New York History* 20 (April 1939): 189–91; Cummings, *American and His Food*, 48–50; Randall Herbert Balmer and John R. Fitzmier, *The Presbyterians* (Westport, Conn.: Greenwood Press, 1993), 166; Burrows and Wallace, *Gotham*, 533; Schwartz, *Never Satisfied*, 45.

25. William A. Alcott, "Abuse of Condiments," *Moral Reformer and Teacher on the Human Constitution* 1 (May 1835): 155–57.

26. William A. Alcott, *Tea and Coffee* (Boston: Light, 1839).

27. Dioclesian Lewis, *Chastity, or Our Secret Sins* (Philadelphia: Maclean, 1874), 270.

28. Richard W. Schwarz, *John Harvey Kellogg, M.D.* (Nashville, Tenn.: Southern Publishing Association, [1970]), 23.

29. Shryock, "Sylvester Graham and the Popular Health Movement, 180; William B. Walker, "The Health Reform Movement in the United States, 1830–1870" (Ph.D. diss., Johns Hopkins University, 1955), 198–202; Numbers, *Prophetess of Health*, 72–76.

30. *Health and How to Live* (Battle Creek, Mich.: Review and Herald, 1865), cited in Richard William Schwarz, "John Harvey Kellogg: American Health Reformer" (Ph.D. diss., University of Michigan, 1964), 18.

31. Nissenbaum, *Sex, Diet, and Debility*, ix, 4.

32. "Life of Sylvester Graham," 5.

33. Louisa M. Alcott, "Transcendental Wild Oats," in *Bronson Alcott's Fruitlands*, comp. Clara Endicott Sears (Boston: Houghton Mifflin, 1915), 145–174; Numbers, *Prophetess of Health*, 55; Susan Cheever, *American Bloomsbury: Louisa May Alcott, Ralph Waldo Emerson, Margaret Fuller, Nathaniel Hawthorne, and Henry David Thoreau: Their Lives, Their Loves, Their Work* (New York: Simon & Schuster, 2006), 63–67.

5. Cyrus McCormick's Reaper

1. William T. Hutchinson, *Cyrus Hall McCormick*, vol. 1, *Seed-Time, 1809–1856* (New York: Century, 1930), 71.

2. Siegfried Giedion, *Mechanization Takes Command: A Contribution to Anonymous History* (New York: Norton, 1969), 140.

3. Hutchinson, *Cyrus Hall McCormick: Seed-Time*, 336.

4. Marcus Cunliffe, "America at the Great Exhibition of 1851," *American Quarterly* 3 (summer 1951): 124.

5. D. Eldon Hall, *A Condensed History of the Origination, Rise, Progress and Completion of the "Great Exhibition of the Industry of All Nations," Held in the Crystal Palace, London, during the Summer of the Year 1851* (New York: Redfield, 1852), 77; Hutchinson, *Cyrus Hall McCormick: Seed-Time*, 466; William T. Hutchinson, *Cyrus Hall McCormick*, vol. 2, *Harvest, 1856–1884* (New York: Appleton-Century, 1935), 97.

6. Peter D. McClelland, *Sowing Modernity: America's First Agricultural Revolution* (Ithaca: Cornell University Press, 1997), 219.

7. Wayne D. Rasmussen, "The Civil War: A Catalyst of Agricultural Revolution," *Agricultural History* 39 (October 1965): 194.

8. Barton H. Wise, "Invention and Industry at the South," *Popular Science Monthly* 44 (1894): 383; James Grant Wilson and John Fiske, eds., *Appletons' Cyclopedia of American Biography*, rev. ed. (New York: Appleton, 1900), 4:95.

9. Hutchinson, *Cyrus Hall McCormick: Harvest*, 98.

10. Leo Rogin, *The Introduction of Farm Machinery in Its Relation to the Productivity of Labor in the Agriculture of the United States during the Nineteenth Century* (Berkeley: University of California Press, 1931), 91.

11. Willard W. Cochrane, *The Development of American Agriculture*, 2nd ed. (Minneapolis: University of Minnesota Press, 1993), 460.

12. Giedion, *Mechanization Takes Command*, 131.

13. E. Lee Trinkle, "Cyrus Hall McCormick: A Distinguished Virginian Who Has Contributed to World Progress" (speech, July 29, 1931), Shenandoah Valley Research and Extension Center, Virginia Agricultural Experiment Station, http://www.vaes.vt.edu /steeles/mccormick/speech.html (accessed December 2, 2008).

6. A Multiethnic Smorgasbord

1. "An Old New-Yorker Dead: William Niblo, the Theatre Manager. The Founder of Niblo's Garden Dies at the Age of 80 Years—Story of His Life—His Chop-House and His Playhouse," *New York Times*, August 22, 1878, 5; Walter Barrett [pseud. for Joseph Alfred Scoville], *The Old Merchants of New York City*, 2nd ser. (New York: Carleton, 1863), 105–6; A. C. Dayton, *Last Days of Knickerbocker Life in New York* (New York: Harlan, 1882), 9; Richard Osborn Cummings, *The American and His Food: A History of Food Habits in the United States* (Chicago: University of Chicago Press, 1940), 32; Lately Thomas [pseud. for Robert V. P. Steele?], *Delmonico's: A Century of Splendor* (Boston: Houghton Mifflin, 1967), 10.

2. For more about the Irish lack of influence on American cuisine, see Hasia R. Diner, *Hungering for America: Italian, Irish, and Jewish Foodways in the Age of Migration* (Cambridge, Mass.: Harvard University Press, 2001), 113–45.

3. Sylvia Sun Minnick, "Never Far from Home: Being Chinese in the California Gold Rush," in *Riches for All: The California Gold Rush and the World*, ed. Kenneth N. Owens (Lincoln: University of Nebraska Press, 2002), 143.

4. Ibid., 143.

5. Gunther Barth, *Bitter Strength: A History of the Chinese in the United States, 1850–1870* (Cambridge, Mass.: Harvard University Press, 1964), 82.

6. Joseph R. Conlin, *Bacon, Beans and Galantines: Food and Foodways on the Western Mining Frontier* (Reno: University of Nevada Press, 1986), 190–92.

7. William Shaw, *Golden Dreams and Waking Realities: Being the Adventures of a Gold-seeker in California and the Pacific Islands* (London: Smith, Elder, 1851), cited in J. A. G. Roberts, *China to Chinatown: Chinese Food in the West* (London: Reaktion Books, 2002), 135.

8. William Kelly, *A Stroll through the Diggings of California* (London: Simms and M'Intyre, 1852), 149–50.

9. Robert F. G. Spier, "Food Habits of Nineteenth Century California Chinese," *California Historical Quarterly* 37 (March 1958): 80.

10. Conlin, *Bacon, Beans and Galantines*, 190–92; Roberts, *China to Chinatown*, 136.

11. Roberts, *China to Chinatown*, 137.

12. Mrs. Mary Mathews, *Ten Years in Nevada* (Buffalo: Baker, Jones, 1880), 249–57.

13. Conlin, *Bacon, Beans and Galantines*, 187–92; Kenneth F. Kipple, *A Movable Feast: Ten Millennia of Food Globalization* (Cambridge: Cambridge University Press, 2007), 203.

14. Valerie Imbruce, "From the Bottom Up: The Global Expansion of Chinese Vegetable Trade in New York City Markets," in *Fast Food/Slow Food: The Cultural Economy of the Global Food System*, ed. Richard Wilk (Lanham, Md.: Altamira Press, 2006), 166.

15. Donna R. Gabaccia, *We Are What We Eat: Ethnic Food and the Making of Americans* (Cambridge, Mass.: Harvard University Press, 1998), 102–3; Roberts, *China to Chinatown*, 138, 144–52.

16. Gabaccia, *We Are What We Eat*, 102–3.

17. Roberts, *China to Chinatown*, 138–39; Hugh D. R. Baker, "Branches All Over: The Hong Kong Chinese in the United Kingdom," in *Reluctant Exiles? Migration from Hong Kong and the New Overseas Chinese*, ed. Ronald Skeldon (Armonk, N.Y.: M. E. Sharpe, 1994), 295.

18. Jessup Whitehead, *The Steward's Handbook and Guide* (Chicago: [Anderson], 1893), 280.

19. *Frank Leslie's Illustrated*, January 9, 1896, cited in Arthur Bonner, *Alas! What Brought Thee Hither? The Chinese in New York 1800–1950* (Madison, N.J.: Fairleigh Dickinson University Press, 1997), 97; Samantha Barbas, " 'I'll Take Chop Suey': Restaurants as Agents of Culinary and Cultural Change," *Journal of Popular Culture* 36 (spring 2003): 674.

20. Sunyowe Pang, "Chinese in America," *New York Times Magazine Supplement*, January 5, 1902, SM15.

21. Andy Coe, personal communication, March 13, 2008.

22. Paul Myron Linebarger, *Our Chinese Chances Through Europe's War* (Chicago: Linebarger, 1915), 159–60.

23. "Women Here and There," *New York Times Magazine Supplement*, November 17, 1901, SM13.

24. Carl Crow, "Sharks' Fins and Ancient Eggs," *Harper's Monthly Magazine*, September 1937, 425.

25. A. Elizabeth Sloan, "What, When, and Where America Eats," *Food Technology* 62 (January 2008): 27.

26. Frederick Law Olmsted, *A Journey Through Texas* (New York: Dix, Edwards, 1860), 159.

27. Stephen Powers, *Afoot and Alone: A Walk from Sea to Sea by the Southern Route* (Hartford, Conn.: Columbia Book Co., 1872), 164–65.

28. Reverend P. F. Parisot, *The Reminiscences of a Texas Missionary* (San Antonio: Johnson, 1899), 38; John G. Bourke, "The Folk-Foods of the Rio Grande Valley and Northern Mexico," *Journal of American Folk-Lore* 8 (January 1895): 62.

29. H. F. McDanield and N. A. Taylor, *The Coming Empire; or, Two Thousand Miles in Texas on Horseback* (New York: Barnes, 1878), 125–26.

30. Stephen Gould, *The Alamo City Guide* (New York: Macgowan and Slipper, 1882), 138.

31. Bourke, "Folk-Foods of the Rio Grande," 60.

32. Harris Newmark, *Sixty Years in Southern California* (1853–1913) (New York: Knickerbocker Press, 1926), 133–34.

33. Willow Borba, comp., *Loyalty Cook Book Native Daughters of the Golden West* 4th ed. (Sebastopol, Calif.: Willow Borba, 1956), 313–18.

34. S. Compton Smith, *Chile con Carne; or, The Camp and the Field* (New York: Miller & Curtis, 1857), 99.

35. *The Landmarks Club Cook Book: A California Collection of the Choicest Recipes from Everywhere* (Los Angeles: Out West, 1903), 14; Ana Bégué de Packman, *Early California Hospitality: The Cookery Customs of Spanish California, with Authentic Recipes and Menus of the Period* (Fresno, Calif.: Academy Library Guild, 1953), 114–15; Mario Montaño, "The History of Mexican Folk Foodways of South Texas: Street Vendors, Offal Foods, and Barbacoa de Cabeza" (Ph.D. diss., University of Pennsylvania, 1992), 120–22, 175; Bill Bridges, *The Great Chili Book: 101 Variations on "The Perfect Bowl of Red"* (New York: Lyons & Burford, 1994), 17.

36. Bourke, "Folk-Foods of the Rio Grande," 62.

37. Francisco J. Santamaría, *Diccionario general de americanismos*, 3 vols. (Mexico City: Robredo, 1942), 1:493.

38. Cora Brown, Rose Brown, and Bob Brown, *The South American Cook Book* (New York: Doubleday, 1939), 94.

39. Erna Fergusson, *Mexican Cookbook* (Albuquerque: University of New Mexico Press, 1934); Fabiola Cabeza de Baca Gilbert, *The Good Life: New Mexico Traditions and Food*, repr. (Santa Fe: Museum of New Mexico Press, 1982), v.

40. Maria Gargiulo and Joe Gargiulo, "Mexican Café at Maria's Pueblo" (menu, San Rafael, Calif., 1940s).

41. Carlotta Flores, *El Charro Café: The Tastes and Traditions of Tucson* (Tucson, Ariz.: Fisher Books, 1998), 2–5; Alfonso C. Pain, comp., *El Charro: Restaurant and Cocktail Lounge; Western Mexican Cook Book* (Mesa, Ariz.: El Charro, 1959).

42. Nancy Harmon Jenkins, "It's Called Mexican, But Is It Genuine?" *New York Times*, April 23, 1986, http://www.nytimes.com (accessed June 24, 2008); Gabaccia, *We Are What We Eat*, 216.

43. Glenn Hassenplug, "Texas Favorite Now a National Craze," *Corpus Christi Caller*, October 22, 1978, cited in Gabaccia, *We Are What We Eat*, 107.

44. Keith J. Guenther, "The Development of the Mexican-American Cuisine," in *Oxford Symposium 1981: National and Regional Styles of Cookery; Proceedings*, ed. Alan Davidson (London: Prospect Books, 1981), 274.

45. Diner, *Hungering for America*, 139–40.

46. Gabaccia, *We Are What We Eat*, 97–99.

47. Bruce Kraig, *Hot Dogs: A Global History* (London: Reaktion Books, 2009).

48. "Nelson Morris Dead; Financier and Pioneer Meat Packer Dies at His Home in Chicago," *New York Times*, August 28, 1907, 7; Howard Copeland Hill, "The Development of Chicago as a Center of the Meat Packing Industry," *Mississippi Valley Historical Review* 10 (December 1923): 268.

49. "German Restaurants," *New York Times*, January 19, 1873, 5.

50. Andrew F. Smith, *Hamburger: A Global History* (London: Reaktion Books, 2008), 20.

51. Richard Ellsworth Day, *Breakfast Table Autocrat: The Life Story of Henry Parsons Crowell*

(Chicago: Moody Press, 1946), 106–7; Arthur F. Marquette, *Brands, Trademarks and Good Will: The Story of the Quaker Oats Company* (New York: McGraw-Hill, 1967), 18.

52. Artemas Ward, *The Grocer's Encyclopedia* (New York: Kempster, 1911), 212.

53. Richard J. Hooker, *Food and Drink in America: A History* (Indianapolis: Bobbs-Merrill, 1981), 294, 354.

54. Richard Pillsbury, *No Foreign Food: The American Diet in Time and Place* (Boulder, Colo.: Westview Press, 1998), 177, 184; Guenther, "Mexican-American Cuisine," 275; Gabaccia, *We Are What We Eat*, 170.

55. Pillsbury, *No Foreign Food*, 177, 184; Sloan, "What, When, and Where America Eats," 22.

56. Hooker, *Food and Drink in America*, 358.

57. Gabaccia, *We Are What We Eat*, 226.

7. Giving Thanks

1. Alexander Young, *Chronicles of the Pilgrim Fathers of the Colony of Plymouth, from 1602 to 1625* (Boston: Little and Brown, 1841), 231.

2. William S. Russell, *Guide to Plymouth, and Recollections of the Pilgrims* (Boston: G. Coolidge, 1846), 95; Edwin Hall, *The Puritans and Their Principles* ([Boston], 1846), 171.

3. Letter from Shubael Breed, Norwich, Conn., to Mason Fitch Cogswell, New York, quoted in Sandra L. Oliver, *Saltwater Foodways: New Englanders and Their Food at Sea and Ashore in the Nineteenth Century* (Mystic, Conn.: Mystic Seaport Museum, 1995), 242. An earlier description of Thanksgiving dinner is cited in Helen Evertson Smith, *Colonial Days and Ways as Gathered from Family Papers* (New York: Century, 1900). It was later frequently cited. The original diary that this selection was taken from has not been located, and several statements in the published description have led many observers to question the veracity of this account. It is more likely a late nineteenth century fictional creation.

4. William Bentley, *The Diary of William Bentley, D.D.* (Salem: Essex Institute, 1905), 3:64, 202, 264.

5. Theophilus, "Thanksgiving," *American Monthly Magazine and Critical Review* 2 (December 1817): 95–96.

6. Edward E. Hale, *New England Boyhood* (New York: Cassell, 1893), 144–15.

7. Sarah Parker Goodwin, "Pleasant Memories," memoirs of Sarah Parker Rice Goodwin, 1889, Goodwin Family Papers, Strawberry Banke Museum, Portsmouth, N. H., cited in Jane C. Nylander, *Our Own Snug Fireside: Images of the New England Home, 1760–1860* (New Haven, Conn.: Yale University Press, 1994), 275.

8. U. P. Hedrick, *A History of Agriculture in the State of New York* (New York: New York State Agricultural Society, 1933), 217.

9. Corrine, "Thanksgiving," *Portland Magazine* 1 (December 1, 1834): 88.

10. Harriet Beecher Stowe, *Oldtown Folks* (Boston: Houghton, Osgood, 1878), 347.

11. Mrs. S. J. Hale, *Northwood; or, a Tale of New England* (Boston: Bowles & Dearborn, 1827), 107–11.

12. Sarah Josepha Hale, *Northwood; or, Life North and South*, 2nd ed. (New York: H. Long & Brother, 1852), iii; *Godey's Magazine* 41 (December 1850): 326; Edward T. James, ed., *Notable American Women, 1607–1950*, 3 vols. (Cambridge, Mass.: Harvard University Press, 1971), 2:110–14.

13. Henry Ware Jr., "Thanksgiving Song," In *The Works of Henry Ware, Jr.*, 4 vols. (Boston: J. Munroe, 1846), 1:237–38; Isaac McClellan, "Thanksgiving," *Living Age* 3 (December 1858): 846–47; "Lizzy Griswold's Thanksgiving," *Atlantic Monthly* 3 (March 1859): 282–89.

14. Margaret Fuller, "Thanksgiving," *New York Tribune*, December 12, 1844; Margaret Fuller, *Life Without and Life Within* (Boston: Brown, Taggard and Chase, 1859), 243, 250.

15. Hale's 1863 letter to Seward has not been located; however, Hale reports in her letter to President Lincoln in 1863 that she had written to her "friend" Seward, requesting him to confer with the president. She again made reference to the 1863 letter to Seward in a private latter to him in 1864 in which she again requested him to speak to the president. Hale then proceeded to recommend items for inclusion in the president's 1864 Thanksgiving proclamation. This implies that Seward was the one who prepared the previous Thanksgiving proclamation, and Lincoln just signed it. See Sarah J. Hale to Abraham Lincoln, September 28, 1863, and Sarah J. Hale to William H. Seward, October 9, 1864, in the Making of America database, Library of Congress Web site.

16. "Our National Thanksgiving Day," *Godey's Lady's Book* 71 (November 1865): 445.

17. Corrine, "Thanksgiving," 88.

18. "Thanksgiving," *Scribner's Magazine* 3 (December 1871): 240–41.

19. "Thanksgiving Dinner at the Five Points Ladies' Home Mission of the Episcopal Church," *Harper's Weekly* 9 (December 23, 1865): 804; *New York Times*, November 29, 1895, 2.

20. W. S. L. Jewett, "Thanksgiving: A Thanksgiving Dinner Among Their Descendants," *Harper's Weekly* 11 (November 30, 1867): 761.

21. *New York Times*, November 30, 1894, 10; *New York Times*, November 29, 1895, 2.

22. David B. Scott, *A School History of the United States, from the Discovery of America to the Year 1870* (New York: Harper & Brothers, 1874), 85.

23. Jane Austin, *Standish of Standish: A Story of the Pilgrims* (Boston: Houghton, Mifflin, 1889), 281, 283, 286.

24. "Weekly Record of New Publications," *Publisher's Weekly* 36 (December 7, 1889): 878.

25. "Pilgrim Pageant," *New York Times*, December 27, 1920, 8l; Hélène Adeline Guerber, *The Story of the Thirteen Colonies* (New York: American Book Company [1898]), 113–17; Nora A. Smith, "The First Thanksgiving Day," in *The Story Hour: A Book for the Home and the Kindergarten*, ed. Kate Douglas Wiggin and Nora A. Smith (Boston: Houghton Mifflin, 1890), 112–13; Elizabeth Pleck, "The Making of the Domestic Occasion: The History of Thanksgiving in the United States," *Journal of Social History* 32 (summer 1999): 779–80.

26. Eric Hobsbawm and Terence Ranger, eds., *The Invention of Tradition* (New York: Cambridge University Press, 1983), 279–80; Diana Karter Appelbaum, *Thanksgiving: An American Holiday, an American History* (New York: Facts on File, 1984), 218; Janet Siskind, "The Invention of Thanksgiving: A Ritual of American Nationality," *Critique of Anthropology* 12 (1992): 182–83, 186; Pleck, "Making of the Domestic Occasion, 780–81.

27. Jane Austin, *Standish of Standish*, dramatized by Annie Russell Marble (Boston: Houghton, Mifflin, 1919); "The First Thanksgiving Day," *New York Times*, November 20, 1921, 87.

28. "Two Tired Little Turkeys," lyrics by William H. Gardner, music by Louis F. Gottschalk, in *Songs for Little Folks* (Philadelphia: Presser, 1904); an excellent summary of

early literature appears in *Home Festivals: A Reference List on Hallowe'en, Thanksgiving and Christmas* (Riverside, Calif.: Riverside Public Library, 1913), 15–16; Alice M. Kellogg, ed., *How to Celebrate Thanksgiving and Christmas: Consisting of Recitations, Songs, Drills, Exercises and Complete Programs for Celebrating Autumn Day, Thanksgiving and Christmas in the Schoolroom* (Philadelphia: Penn, 1922).

29. Thomas Nast, "Uncle Sam's Thanksgiving Dinner," *Harper's Weekly* 13 (November 20, 1869): 745.

30. J. C. Leyendecker, *Pilgrim Stalking Tom Turkey*, *Saturday Evening Post*, November 23, 1907, cover.

31. Jennie Augusta Brownscombe's *The First Thanksgiving* is in the Museum of Pilgrim Treasures, in Plymouth, Mass.; Jean Louis Gerome Ferris's *First Thanksgiving* is in a private collection.

32. See, for example, the collection of first Thanksgiving stories in Robert Haven Schauffler, ed., *Thanksgiving: Its Origin, Celebration and Significance as Related in Prose and Verse* (New York: Moffat, Yard, 1907), 1–66.

33. William Alcott, "Thanksgiving," *Moral Reformer and Teacher on the Human Constitution* 1 (November 1835): 352.

34. John Harvey Kellogg, *The New Dietetics, What to Eat and How* (Battle Creek, Mich., Modern Medicine, 1921), 757.

35. Godfrey Hodgson, *A Great and Godly Adventure: The Pilgrims and the Myth of the First Thanksgiving* (New York: PublicAffairs, 2006), 119.

36. James Robertson, *American Myth, American Reality* (New York: Hill & Wang, 1980), 15.

37. James Grant Wilson and John Fiske, eds., *Appletons' Cyclopaedia of American Biography*, 6 vols. (New York: Appleton, 1889), 6:643–44.

38. *Public School Methods* (Chicago: Methods, 1918), 396; George Earlie Shankle, *American Nicknames: Their Origin and Significance* (New York: Wilson, 1955), 186; Laura Schenone, *A Thousand Years Over a Hot Stove: A History of American Women Told Through Food, Recipes, and Remembrances* (New York: Norton, 2003), 118.

8. Gail Borden's Canned Milk

1. "Startling Exposure of the Milk Trade of New York and Brooklyn," *Frank Leslie's Illustrated Newspaper* 5 (May 8, 1858): 353–54, 359.

2. Lyman Underwood, "Incidents in the Canning Industry of New England," in *A History of the Canning Industry: Souvenir of the Seventh Annual Convention of the National Canners' Association and Allied Associations*, ed. Arthur I. Judge (Baltimore: Canning Trade, 1914), 12–13; Mary B. Sim, *Commercial Canning in New Jersey: History and Early Development* (Trenton: New Jersey Agricultural Society, 1951), 14.

3. Edward F. Keuchel Jr., "The Development of the Canning Industry in New York State to 1960" (Ph.D. diss., Cornell University, 1970), 23.

4. W. V. Cruess, *Commercial Fruit and Vegetable Products: A Textbook for Student, Investigator and Manufacturer*, 2nd ed. (New York: McGraw-Hill, 1938), 34–35.

5. Julian H. Toulouse, *Fruit Jars: A Collectors' Manual* (Camden, N.J.: Nelson / Everybodys Press, 1969), 340–47; E. F. Haskell, *The Housekeeper's Encyclopedia* (New York: Appleton, 1861), 131; Andrew F. Smith, *Souper Tomatoes: The Story of America's Favorite Food* (New Brunswick, N.J.: Rutgers University Press, 2000), 53.

6. Hugh S. Orem, "Baltimore: Master of the Art of Canning," in Judge, *History of the Canning Industry*, 10.

7. Harold W. Comfort, *Gail Borden and His Heritage since 1857* (New York: Newcomen Society in North America, 1953), 10.

8. Joe B. Frantz, "Gail Borden as a Businessman," *Bulletin of the Business Historical Society* 22 (December 1948): 123–33; Joe B. Frantz, *Gail Borden, Dairyman to a Nation* (Norman: University of Oklahoma Press, 1951), 254–55; James J. Nagle, "Borden's Passes Its First Century," Business and Finance, *New York Times*, January 4, 1957, 35.

9. Richard J. Hooker, *Food and Drink in America: A History* (Indianapolis: Bobbs-Merrill, 1981), 207.

10. Richard Osborn Cummings, *The American and His Food: A History of Food Habits in the United States* (Chicago: University of Chicago Press, 1940), 53–54, 67; Frantz, *Gail Borden, Dairyman to a Nation*, 256–61; Nagle, "Borden's Passes Its First Century," 35.

11. Keuchel, "Development of the Canning Industry," 35.

12. *War of the Rebellion: Official Records of the Union and Confederate Armies*, ser. 1, vol. 5, 28–29, ser. 1, vol. 11, part 1, 169–76, ser. 1, vol. 36, part 3, 197; Thomas Wilson, *Notes on Canned Goods* (Washington, D.C.: Commissary of General Subsistence, 1870), 1–2.

13. Hooker, *Food and Drink in America*, 214.

14. W. H. H. Stevenson, "Cans and Can-Making Machinery," in Judge, *History of the Canning Industry*, 93.

15. Cruess, *Commercial Fruit and Vegetable Products*, 35–36.

16. Keuchel, "Development of the Canning Industry," 34.

17. Mark Sullivan, *Our Times in the United States 1900–1925*, 3 vols. (New York: Scribner's, 1929), 2:507.

18. Diane M. Goff and Geraldine Wine, "The Life and Art of Grace G. Drayton, Part 2," *Doll News* (summer 1988): 21; Smith, *Souper Tomatoes*, 95–96.

19. Cummings, *American and His Food*, 72–73.

20. "Campbell's Soup," *Fortune* 12 (November 1935): 68; Smith, *Souper Tomatoes*.

9. The Homogenizing War

1. "The Bombardment of Sumter; Detailed and Graphic Description of the Scene," *New York Times*, May 5, 1861, 1; Samuel Wylie Crawford, *The History of the Fall of Fort Sumter* (New York: [F. P. Harper], 1896), 434–48.

2. Many New World foods, such as cassava, sweet potatoes, corn, and peanuts were imported into Africa during the sixteenth and seventeenth centuries. For the history of the peanut's diaspora, see Andrew F. Smith, *Peanuts: The Illustrious History of the Goober Pea* (Urbana: University of Illinois Press, 2002), 3, 8.

3. David Ramsay, *The History of South Carolina*, 2 vols. (Charleston: Longworth, 1809), 2:349, 564–65; *Ballou's Pictorial Drawing-Room Companion*, February 24, 1855, 120–21.

4. For more about the development of this southern cuisine, see the historical notes and commentaries of Karen Hess in the reprint of Mary Randolph, *The Virginia House-wife* (Columbia: University of South Carolina Press, 1984).

5. Smith, *Peanuts*, 19–25; Brian W. Jones, *The Peanut Plant: Its Cultivation and Uses* (New York: Orange Judd, 1885), 58–59.

6. Abby Fisher, *What Mrs. Fisher Knows about Old Southern Cooking* (San Francisco: Women's Co-operative Printing Office, 1881).

7. Gaillard Hunt, *Life in America One Hundred Years Ago* (New York: Harper, 1914), 218–19.

8. John Chandler Gregg, *Life in the Army: In the Departments of Virginia, and the Gulf, Including Observations in New Orleans, with an Account of the Author's Life and Experience in the Ministry* (Philadelphia: Perkinpine & Higgins, 1868), 139; Thomas F. Devoe, *The Market Assistant* (New York: Hurd and Houghton, 1867), 399–400; "Foreign Trade of the United States, Annual, 1790–1929, Nuts, Domestic Exports, Imports, Reexports and Nut Balance, Quantity and Value," *Report FS 51* (Washington, D.C.: Statistical and Historical Research of the Bureau of Agricultural Economics of the USDA, July 1930), 18.

9. Henry Crittenden Morris, *The History of the First National Bank of Chicago* (Chicago: Donnelley, 1902), 181–82; "Nelson Morris Dead; Financier and Pioneer Meat Packer Dies at His Home in Chicago," *New York Times*, August 28, 1907, 7.

10. Emerson David Fite, *Social and Industrial Conditions in the North During the Civil War* (New York: Smith, 1930), 267; Jimmy M. Skaggs, *Prime Cut: Livestock Raising and Meatpacking in the United States, 1607–1983* (College Station: Texas A&M University Press, 1986), 78.

11. Arnold Tilden, *The Legislation of the Civil-War Period Considered as a Basis of the Agricultural Revolution in the United States* (Los Angeles: University of Southern California Press, 1937), 80–81.

12. T. Swann Harding, *Two Blades of Grass: A History of Scientific Developments in the U.S. Department of Agriculture* (Norman: University of Oklahoma Press, 1947), 21.

13. Tilden, *Legislation of the Civil-War Period*, 35–54.

14. Edward Danforth Eddy Jr., *Colleges for Our Land and Time: The Land-Grant Idea in American Education* (New York: Harper, 1957), 33.

15. Wayne D. Rasmussen, "The Civil War: A Catalyst of Agricultural Revolution," *Agricultural History* 39 (October 1965): 195; Tilden, *Legislation of the Civil-War Period*, 75–79.

16. Rasmussen, "Civil War," 194.

17. Ulysses S. Grant, *Personal Memoirs* (New York: Webster, 1885), 551–53.

10. The Transcontinental Railroad

1. Stephen E. Ambrose, *Nothing Like It in the World: The Men Who Built the Transcontinental Railroad 1863–1869* (New York: Simon & Schuster, 2000), 363–70.

2. Arnold Tilden, *The Legislation of the Civil-War Period Considered as a Basis of the Agricultural Revolution in the United States* (Los Angeles: University of Southern California Press, 1937), 46; T. E. Nichols Jr., "Transportation and Regional Development in Agriculture," *American Journal of Agricultural Economics* 51 (December 1969): 1457.

3. Emerson David Fite, *Social and Industrial Conditions in the North During the Civil War* (New York: Smith, 1930), 78–79; Howard Copeland Hill, "The Development of Chicago as a Center of the Meat Packing Industry," *Mississippi Valley Historical Review* 10 (December 1923): 262.

4. Tilden, *Legislation of the Civil-War Period*, 35–54.

5. Ambrose, *Nothing Like It in the World*, 198.

6. "Tomatoes from California," *American Agriculturist* 28 (August 1869): 283; *Chicago Tribune*, October 20, 1870; *Chicago Tribune*, March 4, 1871, cited in Richard Osborn Cummings, *The American and His Food: A History of Food Habits in the United States* (Chicago: University of Chicago Press, 1940), 62; Edward F. Keuchel Jr., "The Development of the Canning Industry in New York State to 1960" (Ph.D. diss., Cornell University, 1970), 40.

7. Nephtune Fogelberg and Andrew W. McKay, *The Citrus Industry and the California Fruit Growers Exchange System* (Washington, D.C.: Farm Credit Administration, 1940),13; Ralph J. Roske, *Everyman's Eden: A History of California* (New York: Macmillan, 1968), 398–99; Kevin Starr, *Inventing the Dream: California Through the Progressive Era* (New York: Oxford University Press, 1985), 133; Steven Stoll, *The Fruits of Natural Advantage: Making the Industrial Countryside in California* (Berkeley: University of California Press, 1998), 50–51.

8. Mary Yeager Kujovich, "The Refrigerator Car and the Growth of the American Dressed Beef Industry," *Business History Review* 44 (winter 1970): 460.

9. *Food Investigation Report of the Federal Trade Commission on Private Car Lines* (Washington, D.C.: Government Printing Office, 1920), 28; Louise Carroll Wade, *Chicago's Pride: The Stockyards, Packingtown, and Environs in the Nineteenth Century* (Urbana: University of Illinois Press, 2003), 104–5.

10. William Taylor, "The Influence of Refrigeration on the Fruit Industry," *Yearbook of the United States Department of Agriculture, 1900* (Washington, D.C.: Government Printing Office, 1901), 575; F. S. Earle, "Development of the Trucking Interests," *Yearbook of the United States Department of Agriculture, 1900* (Washington, D.C.: Government Printing Office, 1901), 444–46; *Food Investigation Report of the Federal Trade Commission on Private Car Lines* (Washington, D.C.: Government Printing Office, 1920), 25–26.

11. *Food Investigation Report of the Federal Trade Commission on Private Car Lines* (Washington, D.C.: Government Printing Office, 1920), 27.

12. William Taylor, "The Influence of Refrigeration on the Fruit Industry," *Yearbook of the United States Department of Agriculture, 1900* (Washington, D.C.: Government Printing Office, 1901), 574; *Food Investigation Report*, 26; William E. O'Connell Jr., "The Development of the Private Railroad Freight Car, 1830–1966," *Business History Review* 44 (summer 1970): 200.

13. O'Connell, "Development of the Private Railroad Freight Car," 201; Kujovich, "Refrigerator Car," 461.

14. Hill, "Development of Chicago," 272.

15. "Gustavus F. Swift Dead.; Head of Big Packing Company Dies from Internal Hemorrhages—Fortune Estimated at from $7,000,000 to $10,000,000," *New York Times*, March 30, 1903, 1; Hill, "Development of Chicago," 270; Wade, *Chicago's Pride*, 92.

16. Hill, "Development of Chicago," 268–89.

17. Ibid., 271; Wade, *Chicago's Pride*, 106.

18. *Food Investigation Report*, 29–30.

19. Ibid., 30.

20. Stoll, *Fruits of Natural Advantage*, 66–67; J. Ogden Armour, *The Packers, the Private Car Lines, and the People* (Philadelphia: Altemus, 1906), 25–28.

21. G. O. Virtue, "The Meat-Packing Investigation," *Quarterly Journal of Economics* 34 (August 1920): 633–34, 656–80; E. Thomas Sullivan, *The Political Economy of the Sherman Act: The First One Hundred Years* (New York: Oxford University Press, 1991), 79.

22. Charles Edward Russell, "The Greatest Trust in the World," *Everybody's Magazine* 12 (February, March 1905): 147–56, 191–200; 13 (September 1905): 380–83; Charles Edward Russell, *The Greatest Trust in the World* (New York: Ridgway-Thayer, 1905).

23. Cummings, *American and His Food*, 53, 57–59.

24. Ibid., 62.

25. Tilden, *Legislation of the Civil-War Period*, 68–70.

26. Albert Fishlow, *American Railroads and the Transformation of the Ante-Bellum Economy* (Cambridge, Mass.: Harvard University Press, 1965), 226; Nichols, "Transportation and Regional Development in Agriculture," 1457–58.

27. Harper Leech and John Charles Carroll, *Armour and His Times* (New York: Appleton-Century, 1938), 44. This quote is also attributed to others, including Gustavus Swift.

28. Nichols, "Transportation and Regional Development in Agriculture," 1461.

29. Marc Levinson, *The Box: How the Shipping Container Made the World Smaller and the World Economy Bigger* (Princeton, N.J.: Princeton University Press, 2006).

30. "Nelson Morris Dead.; Financier and Pioneer Meat Packer Dies at His Home in Chicago," *New York Times*, August 28, 1907, 7.

31. "Gustavus F. Swift Dead," 1.

32. Swift Web site: http://www.jbsswift.com (accessed July 5, 2008).

33. Douglas Brinkley, *Wheels for the World: Henry Ford, His Company, and a Century of Progress, 1903–2003* (New York: Viking, 2003), 153.

11. Fair Food

1. Frank Norton, ed., *Frank Leslie's Historical Register of the United States Centennial Exposition, 1876* (New York: Frank Leslie's Publishing House, 1877), 268.

2. Francis A. Walker, *World's Fair Philadelphia, 1876: A Critical Account* (Chicago: Barnes, 1878), 56.

3. Norton, *Frank Leslie's Historical Register*, 82; *Visitors' Guide to the Centennial Exhibition and Philadelphia* (Philadelphia: Lippincott, 1876), 16; Norton, *Frank Leslie's Historical Register*, 219; Richard J. Hooker, *Food and Drink in America: A History* (Indianapolis: Bobbs-Merrill, 1981), 232; Virginia Scott Jenkins, *The Fruit with A-Peel: The Impact of the Importation of Bananas on American Culture* (Washington, D.C.: Smithsonian Institution Press, 2000).

4. "Centennial Concession, or Extortion?" *Manufacturer and Builder* 8 (March 1876): 53.

5. J. S. Ingram, *The Centennial Exposition* (Philadelphia: Hubbard, 1876), 287–91; "Centennial Concession," 53; John J. Riley, *A History of the American Soft Drink Industry: Bottled Carbonated Beverages, 1807–1957* (Washington, D.C.: American Bottlers of Carbonated Beverages, 1958), 10–11, 60–61; J. H. Snively, "Soda-Water," *Harper's New Monthly Magazine* 45 (August 1872): 341–46; "Druggist Circular," *Confectioner's Gazette* 34 (August 10, 1913): 34, 36–37; Hooker, *Food and Drink in America*, 273–74.

6. Philip Langdon, *Orange Roofs, Golden Arches: The Architecture of American Chain Restaurants* (New York: Knopf, 1986), 9.

7. "Centennial Concession," 53; Ingram, *Centennial Exposition*, 758; "The Centennial Pop-Corn," *Frank Leslie's Illustrated Newspaper* 153 (November 18, 1876): 179, 186; *Frank Leslie's Illustrated Historical Register of the Exposition 1876* (New York: Frank Leslie's Publishing House, 1877), 56, 210, 306.

8. *A Centennial Pea Nut Merchant* (illustration of a peanut vendor, Philadelphia Centennial Exposition, 1876), Print and Picture Collection, Free Library of Philadelphia.

9. For more information about popcorn, see Andrew F. Smith, *Popped Culture: A Social History of Popcorn in America* (Columbia: University of South Carolina Press, 1999).

10. Francis A. Walker, ed., *International Exhibition, 1876: Reports and Awards; Groups 1–36* (Philadelphia: Lippincott, 1878). For more information about canning and the Campbell Soup Company, see Andrew F. Smith, *Souper Tomatoes: The Story of America's Favorite Food* (New Brunswick, N.J.: Rutgers University Press, 2000).

11. Eben Norton Horsford, *Report on Vienna Bread* (Washington, D.C.: Government Printing Office, 1875).

12. Norton, *Frank Leslie's Historical Register*, 213.

13. "German Restaurants," *New York Tribune*, January 19, 1873, 5; James Dabney McCabe, *The Illustrated History of the Centennial Exhibition, Held in Commemoration of the One Hundredth* (Philadelphia: National Publishing, 1876), 623; Donald G. Mitchell, "In and About the Fair," *Scribner's Monthly* 12 (November 1876): 889–97; *New York Tribune*, May 17, 1876, 1.

14. For more information about the history of the hamburger, see Andrew F. Smith, *Hamburger: A Global History* (London: Reaktion Books, 2008).

15. Margaret Cook, *America's Charitable Cookbooks: A Bibliography of Fund-Raising Cook Books Published in the United States (1861–1915)* (Kent, Ohio, 1971); Maria J. Moss, *A Poetical Cook-Book* (Philadelphia: Sherman, 1864).

16. Robert W. Rydell, *All the World's a Fair: Visions of Empire at American International Expositions, 1876–1916* (Chicago: University of Chicago Press, 1984), 7; Warren Belasco, *Meals to Come: A History of the Future of Food* (Berkeley: University of California Press, 2006), 167–68.

17. Sarah T. Rorer, *Recipes Used in the Illinois Corn Exhibit Model Kitchen, Women's Building, Columbian Exposition* (Chicago: Illinois Women's Exposition Board, 1893); Emma Seifrit Weigley, *Sarah Tyson Rorer: The Nation's Instructress in Dietetics and Cookery* (Philadelphia: American Philosophical Society, 1977), 93–95; Harvey A. Levenstein, *Revolution at the Table: The Transformation of the American Diet* (New York: Oxford University Press, 1988), 50–55; Belasco, *Meals to Come*, 160–61, 167–68.

18. *The "Home Queen" World's Fair Souvenir Cook Book* (Chicago: Cram Publishing, 1893), 551; Alex Jaramillo, *Cracker Jack Prizes* (New York: Abbeville Press, 1989), 8.

19. Hazel Thompson Craig, *The History of Home Economics* (New York: Practical Home Economics, 1945), 5–6; Emma Seifrit Weigley, "It Might Have Been Euthenics: The Lake Placid Conferences and the Home Economics Movement," *American Quarterly* 26 (March 1974): 82–84, 87.

20. Rydell, *All the World's a Fair*, 2; Robert W. Rydell, *World of Fairs: The Century-of-Progress Expositions* (Chicago: University of Chicago Press, 1993), 22, 31, 35.

21. Hillel Schwartz, *Never Satisfied: A Cultural History of Diets, Fantasies and Fat* (New York: Free Press, 1986), 185.

22. Donald L. Miller, *City of the Century: The Epic of Chicago and the Making of America* (New York: Simon & Schuster, 1996), 488–505; "The More You Eat," *Fortune* 35 (June 1947): 144.

12. Henry Crowell's Quaker Special

1. Richard Harrison Thornton, *The History of Quaker Oats Company* (Chicago: University of Chicago Press, 1933), 97; Richard Ellsworth Day, *Breakfast Table Autocrat: The Life Story of Henry Parsons Crowell* (Chicago: Moody Press, 1946), 79; Arthur F. Marquette, *Brands, Trademarks and Good Will: The Story of the Quaker Oats Company* (New York: McGraw-Hill, 1967), 62–64.
2. Day, *Breakfast Table Autocrat*, 112.
3. Thornton, *History of Quaker Oats*, 150–51.
4. Marquette, *Brands, Trademarks and Good Will*), 52; Pamela Walker Laird, *Advertising Progress: American Business and the Rise of Consumer Marketing* (Baltimore: Johns Hopkins University Press, 1998), 252; Thomas Hine, *The Total Package: The Evolution and Secret Meanings of Boxes, Bottles, Cans, and Tubes* (New York: Little, Brown, 1995), 62; Jerry Jankowski, *Shelf Life: Modern Package Design, 1920–1945* (San Francisco: Chronicle Books, 1992), 108, 109, 309; Harry J. Bettendorf, ed., *The Package Engineering Handbook*, 2nd ed. (Chicago: Board Products, 1954), 109.
5. Hine, *Total Package*, 79.
6. Marquette, *Brands, Trademarks and Good Will*, 50.
7. *America's Cereal Foods and How to Cook Them* (Chicago: American Cereal, 1894); Thornton, *History of Quaker Oats*, 98–101; Joe Musser, *The Cereal Tycoon: Henry Parsons Crowell, Founder of the Quaker Oats Co.; A Biography* (Chicago: Moody Press, 1997), 104.
8. Thornton, *History of Quaker Oats*, 102–10; Laird, *Advertising Progress*, 251–52.
9. "Some Food Show Exhibits.; Displays Which Prove Very Attractive to Visitors," *New York Times*, March 22, 1892, http://www.nytimes.com (accessed June 20, 2008).
10. Marquette, *Brands, Trademarks and Good Will*, 50.
11. Thornton, *History of Quaker Oats*, 97.
12. Marquette, *Brands, Trademarks and Good Will*, 46.
13. Laird, *Advertising Progress*, 252.
14. Marquette, *Brands, Trademarks and Good Will*, 6.
15. Michael Krondl, "Advertising," in *The Oxford Encyclopedia of Food and Drink in America*, ed. Andrew F. Smith, 2 vols. (New York: Oxford University Press, 2004), 1:16.

13. Wilbur O. Atwater's Calorimeter

1. Edward Atkinson, *Suggestions for the Establishment of Food Laboratories in Connection with the Agricultural Experiment Stations*, Experiment Stations Bulletin, no. 17 (Washington, D.C.: USDA, Office of Experiment Stations, 1893).
2. Harvey A. Levenstein, *Revolution at the Table: The Transformation of the American Diet* (New York: Oxford University Press, 1988), 72–73.
3. T. Swann Harding, *Two Blades of Grass: A History of Scientific Developments in the U.S. Department of Agriculture* (Norman: University of Oklahoma Press, 1947), 219.

4. Lester F. Goodchild and Harold S. Wechsler, eds., *Ashe Reader on the History of Higher Education* (Needham Heights, Mass.: Ginn Press, 1989).

5. William J. Darby, "Contributions of Atwater and USDA to Knowledge of Nutrient Requirements," *Journal of Nutrition*, suppl., 124 (September 1994): 1734S; W. O. Atwater, "Agricultural-Experiment Stations in Europe," *Report of the Commissioner of Agriculture for the Year 1875* (Washington, D.C.: Government Printing Office, 1876), 517–24.

6. Darby, "Contributions of Atwater," 1735S; Kenneth J. Carpenter, "The Life and Times of W. O. Atwater (1844–1907)," *Journal of Nutrition*, suppl., 124 (September 1994): 1708S.

7. Carpenter, "Life and Times of W. O. Atwater," 1709S–10S.

8. Laura Shapiro, *Perfection Salad: Women and Cooking at the Turn of the Century* (New York: Holt, 1987), 163.

9. W. O. Atwater, "The Chemistry of Food and Nutrition I," *Century Magazine* 34 (May 1887): 59–74; W. O. Atwater, "The Chemistry of Food and Nutrition II: How Food Nourishes the Body," *Century Magazine* 34 (June 1887): 237–52; W. O. Atwater, "The Potential Energy of Food III: The Chemistry and Economy of Food," *Century Magazine* 34 (July 1887): 397–405; W. O. Atwater, "The Chemistry of Food and Nutrition IV: The Digestibility of Food," *Century Magazine* 34 (September 1887): 733–40; W. O. Atwater, "The Chemistry of Food and Nutrition V: The Pecuniary Economy of Food," *Century Magazine* 35 (January 1888): 437–46; W. O. Atwater, "The Chemistry of Food and Nutrition VI: Food and Beverages," *Century Magazine* 36 (May 1888): 135–40; W. O. Atwater, "Food Supply of the Future," *Century Magazine* 43 (November 1891): 101–12; Naomi Aronson, "Nutrition as a Social Problem: A Case Study of an Entrepreneurial Strategy in Science," *Social Problems* 29 (June 1982): 474–87; Carpenter, "Life and Times of W. O. Atwater," 1710S.

10. Aronson, "Nutrition as a Social Problem," 475.

11. Buford L. Nichols, "Atwater and USDA Nutrition Research and Service: A Prologue of the Past Century," *Journal of Nutrition*, suppl., 124 (September 1994): 1725S–26S.

12. Judy McBride, "Wilbur O. Atwater: Father of American Nutrition Science—Includes Information on Current Research Activities," *Agricultural Research* 41 (June 1993): 11.

13. Wilbur O. Atwater, "Foods: Nutritive Value Costs," *Farmer's Bulletin* (Washington, D.C.: USDA, 1894).

14. "Protecting the American Hen.; Retaliation on the Silver Men Suggested at the Farmers' Dinner," *New York Times*, January 20, 1886, 2; Aronson, "Nutrition as a Social Problem," 476.

15. Emma Seifrit Weigley, *Sarah Tyson Rorer: The Nation's Instructress in Dietetics and Cookery* (Philadelphia: American Philosophical Society, 1977), 93–95; Levenstein, *Revolution at the Table*, 50–55.

16. Jane Addams, *Twenty Years at Hull-House, with Autobiographical Notes* (New York: Macmillan, 1910), 130.

17. Edward Atkinson, *The Cooking of Food* (Washington, D.C.: Government Printing Office, 1894), 31; Edward Atkinson, *The Science of Nutrition: Treatise upon the Science of Nutrition* (Boston: Damrell & Upham, 1896); Levenstein, *Revolution at the Table*, 54.

18. Atkinson, *Suggestions for the Establishment of Food Laboratories*.

19. Richard Osborn Cummings, *The American and His Food: A History of Food Habits in the United States* (Chicago: University of Chicago Press, 1940), 129; Harding, *Two Blades of Grass*, 219; Levenstein, *Revolution at the Table*, 72–73.

20. W. O. Atwater, "How Food Is Used in the Body: Experiments with Men in a Respiration Apparatus," *Century Magazine* 54 (June 1897): 246–52; Carpenter, "Life and Times of W. O. Atwater," 1712S.

21. W. O. Atwater and A. P. Bryant, *The Chemical Composition of American Food Materials*, Experiment Stations Bulletin, no. 28 (Washington, D.C.: USDA, Office of Experiment Stations, 1896).

22. W. O. Atwater and F. G. Benedict, *A Respiration Calorimeter with Appliances for the Direct Determination of Oxygen* (Washington, D.C.: Carnegie Institution of Washington, 1905).

23. Lulu Hunt Peters, *Diet and Health, with Key to the Calories* (Chicago: Reilly and Britton, 1918).

24. McBride, "Wilbur O. Atwater," 11; Darby, "Contributions of Atwater," 1734S; *Columbia Encyclopedia*, 6th ed. (New York: Columbia University Press, 2007), s.v. "Wilbur Olin Atwater"; Audrey H. Ensminger et al., *The Concise Encyclopedia of Foods and Nutrition* (Boca Raton, Fla.: CRC Press, 1995); "ARS Fifty Years and Growing," *Agricultural Research* 51 (November 2003): 10.

25. Rima D. Apple, *Vitamania: Vitamins in American Culture* (New Brunswick, N.J.: Rutgers University Press, 1996).

26. For more about the history of federal dietary guidance, see Marion Nestle, "Evolution of Federal Dietary Guidance Policy: From Food Adequacy to Chronic Disease Prevention," *Cadeuces* 6 (summer 1990): 43–67; Marion Nestle, *Food Politics: How the Food Industry Influences Nutrition and Health*, rev. ed. (Berkeley: University of California Press, 2007).

14. The Cracker Jack Snack

1. *The "Home Queen" World's Fair Souvenir Cook Book* (Chicago: Cram Publishing, 1893), 551; Henry G. Abbott [George H. A. Hazlitt, pseud.], *Historical Sketch of the Confectionery Trade of Chicago* (Chicago: Jobbing Confectioners Association, 1905), 51; Alex Jaramillo, *Cracker Jack Prizes* (New York: Abbeville Press, 1989), 8.

2. "The More You Eat," *Fortune* 35 (June 1947): 144; *Fifty Years* (Chicago: Cracker Jack, 1922); "How 'Cracker Jack' Was Given Its Name," (broadside, Chicago, Cracker Jack Co., ca. 1950); "Information from the Cracker Jack History Book #1—To 1954," 1982, collection of Harriet Joyce, Debary, Fla.

3. George Henry Lewes, *The Physiology of Common Life*, 2 vols. (New York: Appleton, 1860), 1:192; "Serious Effects of Eating Between Meals," *Eclectic Magazine* 58 (March 1863): 393; Worthington Hooker and Joseph Addison Sewall, *Hooker's New Physiology: Designed as a Text-book for Institutions of Learning* (New York: Sheldon, 1874), 93.

4. William Barnard Sharp, *The Foundation of Health: A Manual of Personal Hygiene for Students*, 3rd ed. (Philadelphia: Lea & Febiger, 1930), 242.

5. Thomas A. Horrock, " 'The Poor Man's Riches, The Rich Man's Bless,' Regimen, Reform and the *Journal of Health* 1829–1833," in *Proceedings, American Philosophical Society* 139, no. 2 (1995): 127; John Harvey Kellogg, *Second Book in Physiology and Hygiene* (New York: American Book Co., 1894), 59.

6. *Fifty Years*; "The More You Eat," 144; Jaramillo, *Cracker Jack Prizes*, 8.

7. *Fifty Years*; "The More You Eat," 144; Jaramillo, *Cracker Jack Prizes*, 8.

8. "*Home Queen,*", 551; Jaramillo, *Cracker Jack Prizes*, 8.

9. *Official Gazette*, United States Trademark No. 28,016, registered March 24, 1896.

10. *Grocery World* 22 (July 13, 1896): 8, 23, 25.

11. Henry G. Eckstein, diary, in the collection of Ronald Toth Jr.

12. "Take Me Out to the Ball Game," lyrics by Jack Norworth, music by Albert Von Tilzer, sung by Edward Meeker, Edison's National Phonograph Co., 1908, from *Performing Arts Encyclopedia*, Library of Congress, http://lcweb2.loc.gov/diglib/ihas/loc.natlib .ihas.200153239/default.html (accessed September 28, 2008).

13. Abbott, *Historical Sketch*, 51; George William Myers, *Myers Arithmetic: Book 1* (Chicago: Scott, Foresman, 1908), 144.

14. *Billboard* 14 (August 9, 1902): 28.

15. "Shortage of Popcorn Production," *Confectioner's Gazette* 34 (October 12, 1912): 12; *Confectioner's Gazette* 35 (February 10, 1914): 10.

16. Ravi Piña, *Cracker Jack Collectibles with Price Guide* (Atglen, Pa.: Schiffer, 1995); undated photocopied material on Cracker Jack, from Forest Wanberg Jr., former vice president for operations of Borden's Cracker Jack division.

17. "Information from the Cracker Jack History Book #1"; Jerry L. Hess, *Snack Food: A Bicentennial History* (New York: Harcourt Brace Jovanovich, 1976), 204.

18. *Billboard* 49 (April 16, 1937): 94; "The More You Eat," 144.

19. James D. Russo, *Cracker Jack Collecting for Fun and Profit* (printed for the author, 1976), 17; Hess, *Snack Food*, 204.

20. Phillip P. Gott and L. F. Van Houten, *All About Candy and Chocolate: A Comprehensive Study of the Candy and Chocolate Industries* (Chicago: National Confectioners' Association, 1958), 153–54; Joël Glenn Brenner, *The Emperors of Chocolate: Inside the Secret World of Hershey and Mars* (New York: Broadway Books, 2000), 8; Robert M. Rees, "Bite Sized Marketing: Candy Bars," in *Chocolate: Food of the Gods*, ed. Alex Szogyi (Westport, Conn.: Greenwood Press, 1997), 127; Gail Cooper, "Love, War, and Chocolate: Gender and the American Candy Industry," in *His and Hers: Gender, Consumption, and Technology*, ed. Roger Horowitz and Arwen Mohun (Charlottesville: University Press of Virginia, 1998), 75.

21. *Collier's* 78 (July 31, 1926): 21; Ray Broekel, *The Great American Candy Bar Book* (Boston: Houghton Mifflin, 1982), 22–25.

22. For more about candy bars and chocolate, see Brenner, *Emperors of Chocolate*; Broekel, *Great American Candy Bar Book*; Tim Richardson, *Sweets: A History of Candy* (New York: Bloomsbury, 2002).

23. For more about the histories of popcorn and peanuts, see Andrew F Smith, *Popped Culture: A Social History of Popcorn in America* (Columbia: University of South Carolina Press, 1999); Andrew F. Smith, *Peanuts: The Illustrious History of the Goober Pea* (Urbana: University of Illinois Press, 2002).

24. Michael A. Kirkman, "Global Markets for Processed Potato Products," in *Potato Biology and Biotechnology*, ed. Dick Vreugdenhil et al. (San Diego: Elsevier, 2007), 28.

25. *Des Moines Register*, January 2, 1945 (clipping file, State Historical Society of Iowa Library, Des Moines); "Pop Goes the Corn," *Time* 46 (November 19, 1945): 88.

26. "Candy," *Progressive Grocer* 87 (May 2008): 10; "SFA Installs New Chairman," *Snack World* (April 2008): 20.

15. Fannie Farmer's Cookbook

1. Laura Shapiro, *Perfection Salad: Women and Cooking at the Turn of the Century* (New York: Holt, 1987), 112.
2. Pierre Blot, *What to Eat, and How to Cook It* (New York: Appleton, 1863); Helen S. Conant, "Kitchen and Dining Room," *Harper's New Monthly Magazine* 54 (February 1877): 429; Albert Rhodes, "What Shall We Eat?" *Galaxy* 22 (November 1876): 666; Jan Longone, "Professor Blot and the First French Cooking School in New York, Part 1," *Gastronomica* 1 (spring 2001): 65–71; Jan Longone, "Professor Blot and the First French Cooking School in New York, Part 2," *Gastronomica* 1 (summer 2001): 53–60.
3. Juliet Corson, *Cooking School Text Book and Housekeepers' Guide* (New York: Orange Judd, 1879); F. E. Fryatt, "The New York Cooking School," *Harper's New Monthly Magazine* 60 (December 1879): 22–29; George Augustus Sala, *America Revisited*, 3rd ed., 2 vols. (London: Vizetelly, 1883), 1:177–78; "The New-York Cooking School," *New York Times*, November 18, 1885, 2.
4. Sarah Emery Hooper, "History of the Boston Cooking School Established 1879" (manuscript, 1884, Boston Athenaeum).
5. Mrs. D. A. Lincoln, *Mrs. Lincoln's Boston Cook Book* (Boston: Roberts, 1884).
6. Shapiro, *Perfection Salad*, 109.
7. Sarah Tyson Rorer, "Early Dietetics," in *Essays of History of Nutrition and Dietetics*, comp. Adelia M. Beeuwkes, E. Neige Todhunter, and Emma Seifrit Weigley (Chicago: American Dietetic Association, 1967), 215.
8. Fannie Merritt Farmer, *The Boston Cooking-School Cook Book* (Boston: Little, Brown, 1896), XXX.
9. Ibid.
10. Ibid., 28; Hazel Thompson Craig and Blanche Margaret Stover, *The History of Home Economics* (New York: Practical Home Economics, 1946), 5; Clarence Lewis et al., *The New Century Cyclopedia of Names*, XX vols. (New York: Appleton-Century-Crofts, 1954), 2:1515; Shapiro, *Perfection Salad*, chap. 5.
11. *Literary World* 28 (January 23, 1897): 28.
12. Shapiro, *Perfection Salad*, 112.
13. A. Elizabeth Sloan, "What, When, and Where America Eats," *Food Technology* 62 (January 2008): 20.

16. The Kelloggs' Corn Flakes

1. *Kellogg Toasted Corn Flakes Co. v. Quaker Oats*, F. 235 (October-November 1916): 660–66; Nancy Rubin, *American Empress: The Life and Times of Marjorie Merriweather Post* (New York: Villard Books, 1995), 47.
2. Harvey A. Levenstein, *Revolution at the Table: The Transformation of the American Diet* (New York: Oxford University Press, 1988), 15–16.
3. Thomas Low Nichols, *Forty Years of American Life 1821–1861*, 2 vols. (London: Maxwell, 1864), 1:360.
4. Richard H. Shryock, "Sylvester Graham and the Popular Health Movement, 1830–1870," *Mississippi Valley Historical Review* 18 (September 1931): 180; William B. Walker,

"The Health Reform Movement in the United States, 1830–1870" (Ph.D. diss., Johns Hopkins University, 1955), 198–202; Nettie Leitch Major, *C. W. Post: The Hour and the Man; A Biography with Genealogical Supplement* (Washington, D.C.: Judd & Detweiller, 1963), 28.

5. Gerald Carson, *Cornflake Crusade* (New York: Rinehart, 1957), 67; *Dansville Advertiser*, April 12, 1883, cited in Gerald Carson, "Bloomers and Bread Crumbs," *New York History* 38 (July 1957): 303, 308; "Granula," *Laws of Life* 30 (February 1887): 64.

6. Ellen G. White to "Bro. and Sister Lockwood," September 14, 1864, cited in Ronald L. Numbers, *Prophetess of Health: Ellen G. White and the Origins of Seventh-Day Adventist Health Reform* (Knoxville: University of Tennessee Press, 1992), 202–5.

7. White claimed that her vision occurred on June 5, 1863, well before she visited Jackson's Our Home. Historian Ronald L. Numbers offers a convincing case that Seventh-Day Adventists had been visiting Our Home since the early 1860s, and that many members were knowledgeable about Jackson's views. Numbers also points out that White admitted to having read an article written by Jackson, published in January 15, 1863, that spelled out his views on health reform, which were similar to those later expressed by White. White's first statement about her vision did not appear in print until 1865 (Numbers, *Prophetess of Health*, 77–101).

8. Ibid., 93–104.

9. M. G. Kellogg, *Notes Concerning the Kellogg's* (Battle Creek, Mich., 1927), 3; Richard William Schwarz, "John Harvey Kellogg: American Health Reformer" (Ph.D. diss., University of Michigan, 1964), 17–18, 21; Richard W. Schwarz, *John Harvey Kellogg, M.D.* (Nashville, Tenn.: Southern Publishing Association, 1970), 31–36, 61.

10. Schwarz, *John Harvey Kellogg*, 28–29, 66–68; Numbers, *Prophetess of Health*, 123–28; Hillel Schwartz, *Never Satisfied: A Cultural History of Diets, Fantasies and Fat* (New York: Free Press, 1986), 183; Scott Bruce and Bill Crawford, *Cerealizing America: The Unsweetened Story of American Breakfast Cereal* (Boston: Faber and Faber, 1995), 13.

11. Carson, *Cornflake Crusade*, 93–94; Schwarz, *John Harvey Kellogg*, 117.

12. See, for an example, the "Granola Crust" recipe in E. E. K., "The Cooking School," in J. H. Kellogg, *Practical Manual of Health and Temperance* (Battle Creek, Mich.: Good Health, 1885), 46; Mrs. E. E. Kellogg, *Science in the Kitchen* (Battle Creek, Mich.: Health, 1892), 91, 293, 337; E. E. Kellogg, *Every-Day Dishes and Every-Day Work* (Battle Creek, Mich.: Modern Medicine, 1897), 139–41.

13. Schwarz, *John Harvey Kellogg*, 117.

14. James A. Holechek, *Henry Perky: The Shredded Wheat King* (New York: iUniverse, 2007), 181–82.

15. Carson, *Cornflake Crusade*, 120–22.

16. Holechek, *Henry Perky*, 194–95.

17. Fannie Merritt Farmer, *The Boston Cooking-School Cook Book* (Boston: Little, Brown, 1896), 513; Gesine Lemcke, *Chafing-Dish Recipes* (New York: Appleton, 1896), 74.

18. H. D. Perky and Harriet A. Higbee, *The Vital Question and Our Navy 1898* (Worcester, Mass.: Perky, 1897).

19. "General Booth's Eureka: 'I Have Found the Ideal Food.': The Romance of Shredded Wheat," in "Wake Up John Bull," supplement no. 18, *Review of Reviews* 26 (December 15, 1902): 649–54.

20. Major, *C. W. Post*, 29; Rubin, *American Empress*, 6.

21. C. W. Post, *I Am Well! The Modern Practice: Natural Suggestion, or Scientia Vitae* (Battle Creek, Mich.: La Vita Inn, 1894).

22. Major, *C. W. Post*, 32.

23. Holechek, *Henry Perky*, 218.

24. C. W. Post, *The Road to Wellville* (Battle Creek, Mich.: Postum, n.d.).

25. "C. W. Post, Faker," *Collier's* 46 (December 24, 1910): 13–15; "Disputes That Came Up When Collier's Refused to Advertise Grape Nuts: A Lying Advertisement," *Collier's* 46 (December 31, 1910): 21.

26. Robert J. Collier, *The $50,000 Verdict: An Account of the Action of Robert J. Collier vs. The Postum Cereal Co., Ltd. for Libel; In which the Plaintiff Recovered $50,000 Damages; Also Certain Truths about the Nature of Grape-Nuts, Postum, and C. W. Post* (New York: Collier, 1911), 40.

27. Rubin, *American Empress*, 47.

28. J. H. Kellogg, *The Battle Creek Sanitarium System: History, Organization, Methods* (Battle Creek, Mich.: Kellogg, 1908), 207.

29. Schwarz, "John Harvey Kellogg," 281–82; Schwarz, *John Harvey Kellogg*, 120.

30. *New York World*, September 7, 1902, cited in Horace B. Powell, *The Original Has This Signature: W. K. Kellogg* (Englewood Cliffs, N.J.: Prentice-Hall, 1956), 99–101.

31. Schwarz, "John Harvey Kellogg," 422–23.

32. Mrs. E. E. Kellogg, comp., *Healthful Cookery: A Collection of Choice Recipes for Preparing Foods, with Special Reference to Health* (Battle Creek, Mich.: Modern Medicine, 1904), 203.

33. Schwarz, *John Harvey Kellogg*, 210–13.

34. Major, *C. W. Post*, 92.

35. *Kellogg Toasted Corn Flakes Co. v. Quaker Oats*, 660. For more information about Charles D. Bolin, see Walter B. Stevens, *Centennial History of Missouri (The Center State) One Hundred Years in the Union, 1820–1921* (St. Louis: Clarke, 1921), 346–47.

36. *Kellogg Toasted Corn Flakes Co. v. Quaker Oats*, 660; "Kellogg Toasted Corn Flakes," *McClure's* 28 (November 1906): 166; "Kellogg Toasted Corn Flakes," *Boston Cooking-School Magazine* 11 (November 1906): ix; "Kellogg Toasted Corn Flakes," *Christian Family* 2 (November 1907): 522; Harry Tipper et al., *Advertising: Its Principles and Practice* (New York: Ronald Press, 1915), 290–91; *Trade-Mark Reporter* (New York: Trade-Mark Association, 1913), 3:404–5; Carson, *Cornflake Crusade*, 209–10.

37. *Kellogg Toasted Corn Flakes Co. v. Quaker Oats*, 660; Schwarz, *John Harvey Kellogg*, 212–13.

38. Levenstein, *Revolution at the Table*, 33–43.

39. Bruce and Crawford, *Cerealizing America*, xv; Katherine Battle Horgan, Molly Choate, and Kelly D. Brownell, "Television Food Advertising: Targeting Children in a Toxic Environment," in *Handbook of Children and the Media*, ed. Dorothy G. Singer and Jerome L. Singer (Thousand Oaks, Calif.: Sage, 2001), 447–61; Sandra L. Calvert and Barbara J. Wilson, eds., *The Handbook of Children, Media, and Development* (Malden, Mass.: Blackwell, 2008).

40. M. F. K. Fisher, *Among Friends* (Washington, D.C.: Shoemaker & Hoard, 2004), 280.

41. Numbers, *Prophetess of Health*, 191–98.

42. Schwartz, *Never Satisfied*, 184.

17. Upton Sinclair's Jungle

1. Upton Sinclair, *The Brass Check: A Study of American Journalism* (Pasadena, Calif.: self-published, 1920), 32–49.

2. Ibid., 27.

3. Upton Sinclair, *Autobiography* (New York: Harcourt, Brace & World, 1962), 108–9.

4. Ann Barton, *Mother Bloor: The Spirit of 76* (New York: Workers Library, 1937); A.M. Simons, *Packingtown* (Chicago: Kerr, 1899); Ernest Poole, "The Meat Strike," *Independent* (July 1904): 179–84; Ernest Poole, "From Lithuania to the Chicago Stockyards: An Autobiography," *Independent* 57 (August 4, 1904): 241–48. The series written by Adolph Smith was: "The Stockyards and Packing Town: Insanitary Condition of the World's Largest Meat Market," *Lancet* 165 (January 7, 1905): 49–52; "Chicago: The Dark and Insanitary Premises Used for the Slaughtering of Cattle and Hogs; The Government Inspection," *Lancet* 165 (January 14, 1905): 120–23; "Chicago: Tuberculosis Among the Stockyard Workers; Sanitation in Packingtown; The Police and the Dumping of Refuse; Vital Statistics," *Lancet* 165 (January 21, 1905): 183–85; "Chicago: Unhealthy Work in the Stockyards; Shameless Indifference to the Insanitary Condition of the Buildings and the Cattle Pens; Pollution of the Subsoil; The Need for Legislative Interference," *Lancet* 165 (January 28, 1905): 258–60.

5. Sinclair, *Brass Check*, 32–49.

6. Ibid., 44.

7. Upton Sinclair, "The Condemned-Meat Industry: A Reply to Mr. J. Ogden Armour," *Everybody's Magazine* 14 (May 1906): 612–13; Sinclair, *Brass Check*, 32–38.

8. Upton Sinclair, "What Life Means to Me," *Cosmopolitan* 45 (October 1906): 591–95.

9. Upton Sinclair, *The Jungle* (New York: Doubleday, Page, 1906), 161–62.

10. Charles Edward Russell, "The Greatest Trust in the World," *Everybody's Magazine* 12 (February 1905): 147–56; *Everybody's Magazine* 12 (March 1905): 191–200; *Everybody's Magazine* 13 (September 1905): 380–83; Charles Edward Russell, *The Greatest Trust in the World* (New York: Ridgway-Thayer, 1905); Donald Bragaw, "Soldier for the Common Good: The Life and Career of Charles Edward Russell" (Ph.D. diss., Syracuse University, 1970), 153.

11. Richard Osborn Cummings, *The American and His Food: A History of Food Habits in the United States* (Chicago: University of Chicago Press, 1940), 96–97.

12. Mark Sullivan, *Our Times in the United States 1900–1925*, 3 vols. (New York: Scribner's, 1929), 2:518; C[ornelius] C. Regier, *The Era of the Muckrakers* (Chapel Hill: University of North Carolina Press, 1932), 180; James Harvey Young, "The Science and Morals of Metabolism: Catsup and Benzoate," *Journal of the History of Medicine and Allied Sciences* 33 (1968): 88.

13. Stephen Wilson, *Food and Drug Regulation* (Washington, D.C.: American Council on Public Affairs, 1942), 12; Young, "Science and Morals of Metabolism," 87; James Harvey Young, *Pure Food: Securing the Federal Food and Drugs Act of 1906* (Princeton, N.J.: Princeton University Press, 1989), 180.

14. Charles F. Loudon, "Preservatives and Artificial Coloring in Food Products: A Manufacturer's Views," *What to Eat* 17 (September 1904): 131.

15. Young, *Pure Food*, 179–80; Robert C. Alberts, *The Good Provider: H. J. Heinz and His 57 Varieties* (Boston: Houghton Mifflin, 1973), 176–77.

16. H. B. Meyer, ed. and comp., *Journal of Proceedings of the Seventh Annual Convention of the National Association of State Dairy and Food Departments*, (St. Paul, Minn., 1903), 6.

17. *Testimony of E. O. Grosvenor, Curtice Brothers v. Harry E. Barnard et al., in the United States Circuit Court of Appeals*, vol. 5, 3987, National Archives: Great Lakes Region, Chicago.

18. *Baltimore Sun*, November 27, 1904, 16; *Philadelphia Record*, February 15, 1905.

19. "The Year of the Food Law," *Nation*, 1905, cited in Philip J. Hilts, *Protecting America's Health: The FDA, Business, and One Hundred Years of Regulation* (New York: Knopf, 2003), 46.

20. "Meat Inspection Bill Passes the Senate; Added Without Debate to Agricultural Bill as a Rider. Its Adoption Unexpected Direct Consequence of the Disclosures Made in Upton Sinclair's Novel, 'The Jungle.' Meat Inspection Bill Passes the Senate," *New York Times*, May 26, 1906, 1.

21. Ibid.

22. Hilts, *Protecting America's Health*, 53–54.

18. Frozen Seafood and TV Dinners

1. Wilfred Thomason Grenfell, *Labrador, the Country and the People*, new ed. (New York: Macmillan, 1913), 450.

2. For more on the history of the ice industry, see Richard O. Cummings, "The American Ice Industry and the Development of Refrigeration, 1790–1860" (Ph.D. diss., Harvard University, 1935).

3. James Troubridge Critchell, *A History of the Frozen Meat Trade, an Account of the Development and Present Day Methods of Preparation, Transport, and Marketing of Frozen and Chilled Meats* (London: Constable, 1912), 164, 190–91, 246; Oscar Edward Anderson, *Refrigeration in America: A History of a New Technology and Its Impact* (Princeton, N.J.: published for the University of Cincinnati by Princeton University Press, 1953), 57–61; Edwin W. Williams, *Frozen Food: Biography of an Industry* (Boston: Cahners Book Division, 1963), 2.

4. Donald K. Tressler and Clifford F. Evers, *The Freezing Preservation of Foods* (New York: Avi, 1943), 63–67; Robert G. Phipps, *The Swanson Story: When the Chicken Flew the Coop* (Omaha, Neb.: Carl and Caroline Swanson Foundation, 1977), 68; Elaine Schwartz, "Birdseye," in *Encyclopedia of New Jersey*, ed. Maxine N. Lurie and Marc Mappen (New Brunswick, N.J.: Rutgers University Press, 2004), 77.

5. Clarence Birdseye, "Packaging Perishables for Quick Freezing," *Canning Age* 11 (1930): 329; Harvey Levenstein, *Paradox of Plenty: A Social History of Eating in Modern America* (New York: Oxford University Press, 1993), 106–7.

6. C. Lester Walker, "What's in the Deep Freeze?" *Harper's Magazine* 198 (June 1949): 41; John Stuart, "Frozen Food Industry Is Traced to Labrador Fur Trapper in 1915; Clarence Birdseye, Founder of Quick-Freeze Company, Pioneering in New Field," *New York Times*, June 20, 1954, F1; "Clarence Birdseye Is Dead at 69; Inventor of Frozen-Food Process," *New York Times*, October 9, 1956, http://www.nytimes.com (accessed June 20, 2008); "Just Heat and Serve," *Time*, December 7, 1959, http://www.time.com (accessed August 4, 2008).

7. Phipps, *Swanson Story*, 69.

8. Williams, *Frozen Food*, 42.

9. Jane Holt, "News of Food: To Save the Post-war Housewife Time and Work," *New York Times*, April 11, 1945, 20; James Lee, *Operation Lifeline: History and Development of the Naval Air Transport Service* (Chicago: Ziff-Davis, 1947), 151; Adel P. Den Hartog, "Technological Innovations and Eating Out as a Mass Phenomenon in Europe," in *Eating Out in Europe: Picnics, Gourmet Dining, and Snacks since the Late Eighteenth Century*, ed. Marc Jacobs and Peter Scholliers (Oxford: Berg, 2003), 272.

10. "News of Food; French Fried Potatoes in Frozen Form Need Only Be Heated in Oven 20 Minutes," *New York Times*, February 6, 1946, 22; Phipps, *Swanson Story*, 73–74; Carroll Pursell, *Technology in Postwar America: A History* (New York: Columbia University Press, 2007), 100.

11. Williams, *Frozen Food*, 66; Karal Ann Marling, *As Seen on TV: The Visual Culture of Everyday Life in the 1950s* (Cambridge, Mass.: Harvard University Press, 1994), 232; *Quick Frozen Foods* (January 1955): 63, cited in Laura Shapiro, *Something from the Oven: Reinventing Dinner in 1950s America* (New York: Penguin, 2004), 18–20; "Everyday Mysteries," Library of Congress, http://www.loc.gov/rr/scitech/mysteries/tvdinner.html, accessed June 22, 2008.

12. Tressler and Evers, *Freezing Preservation of Foods*, 311; Walker, "What's in the Deep Freeze?" 46–47; Williams, *Frozen Food*, 10–11, 58–60, 85–86; Levenstein, *Paradox of Plenty*, 107; Sidney Mintz, "Frozen in Time: The Other Orangemen," *Wall Street Journal*, June 23, 2000, 13.

13. "Big Butter-and-Egg Man," *Fortune Magazine* 28 (October 1943): 123.

14. Phipps, *Swanson Story*, 69.

15. "Big Butter-and-Egg Man," 122; Phipps, *Swanson Story*, 45–46.

16. Phipps, *Swanson Story*, 75–77.

17. Gerry Thomas, "TV Dinners: A Firsthand Account," in *The Oxford Encyclopedia of Food and Drink in America*, ed. Andrew F. Smith (New York: Oxford University Press, 2004), 524–25. Jerry Thomas died a few months after the publication of his entry. Columnist Roy Rivenburg proclaimed in the *Los Angeles Times* that the story that Thomas told was not true (Roy Rivenburg, "A Landmark Idea, Yes, but Whose?" *Los Angeles Times*, November 23, 2003; and Roy Rivenburg, "False Tales of Turkey on a Tray," *Los Angeles Times*, July 31, 2005, http://www.LATimes.com [accessed June 22, 2008]).

18. Phipps, *Swanson Story*, 77–80; Gerry Thomas, "TV Dinners: A Firsthand Account," personal communication to the author; Gerry Thomas, interview by author, August 20, 2004.

19. Norge W. Jerome, "Frozen (TV) Dinners: The Staple Emergency Meals of a Changing Modern Society," in *Food in Perspective: Proceedings of the Third International Conference on Ethnological Food Research*, ed. Alexander Fenton and Trefor M. Owen (Edinburgh: Donald, 1981), 145–46; Thomas, "TV Dinners," personal communication; Thomas, interview by author, August 20, 2004.

20. Phipps, *Swanson Story*, 78; Marling, *As Seen on TV*, 232.

21. Lori F. Brost, "Television Cooking Shows: Defining the Genre" (Ph.D. diss., Indiana University, 2000), 50–51.

22. Marling, *As Seen on TV*, 232, 233–34.

23. Phipps, *Swanson Story*, 79–80.

24. Warren Belasco, *Meals to Come: A History of the Future of Food* (Berkeley: University of California Press, 2006), 197.

25. Levenstein, *Paradox of Plenty*, 105–6; Thomas L. Harris, *Value-Added Public Relations: The Secret Weapon of Integrated Marketing* (Lincolnwood, Ill.: NTC Business Books, 1998), 114–15.

26. Marling, *As Seen on TV*, 188–89.

27. Paul Roberts, *The End of Food* (Boston: Houghton Mifflin, 2008), xvii–xviii.

28. Andrew Hamilton, "Heat and Eat Meals," *Nation's Business* 43 (July 1955): 56; "Just Heat and Serve"; "Campbell's Mr. Soup, William B. Murphy," *Time*, September 26, 1960, http://www.time.com (accessed August 4, 2008).

29. "Clarke Swanson," *Omaha World*, April 16, 1961; "Gilbert Swanson," *Omaha World*, March 9, 1968.

19. Michael Cullen's Super Market

1. "M. J. Cullen Is Dead; Chain Store Owner," *New York Times*, April 26, 1936, N10; M. M. Zimmerman, *The Super Market: A Revolution in Distribution* (New York: McGraw-Hill, 1955), 37–38; Lloyd Singer, "Michael J. Cullen: An American Innovator," *Newsday Magazine* 1 (May 6, 1990): 21; James M. Mayo, *The American Grocery Store: The Business Evolution of an Architectural Space* (Westport, Conn.: Greenwood Press, 1993), 130–45; Richard W. Longstreth, *The Drive-In, the Supermarket, and the Transformation of Commercial Space in Los Angeles, 1914–1941* (Cambridge, Mass.: MIT Press, 1999), 37.

2. "Holiday Goods.; The Great American Tea Company," *New York Times*, December 24, 1872, http://www.nytimes.com (accessed August 21, 2008); William I. Walsh, *The Rise and Decline of the Great Atlantic and Pacific Tea Company* (Secaucus, N.J.: Stuart, 1986), 20–32.

3. Walsh, *Rise and Decline of the Great Atlantic and Pacific Tea Company*, 34.

4. Joe Blackstock, "One-Stop Shopping Got Started in Downtown Pomona," *Inland Valley Daily Bulletin*, December 23, 2005, http://www.dailybulletin.com (accessed August 21, 2008); Raj Patel, *Stuffed and Starved: The Hidden Battle for the World Food System* (Brooklyn: Melville House, 2008), 218.

5. Patel, *Stuffed and Starved*, 218–22.

6. Lucius P. Flint, "The Los Angeles Super," *Chain Store Age* (Grocery Managers' Edition) 26 (June 1950): J34–J35; Frank J. Charvat, *Supermarketing* (New York: Macmillan, 1961), 19; Longstreth, *Drive-In, the Supermarket, and the Transformation of Commercial Space in Los Angeles*, 82–89, 110–11.

7. "M. J. Cullen Is Dead," N10; Mayo, *American Grocery Store*, 130–45.

8. "New Market Plan Stirs Food Trade; 'Big Bear' and Other 'Price' Units Will Spread Through East, Mr. Dawson Says. Industry Fights Trend Chains, Independents and Jobbers Hostile to Establishments: Seek Check Through New Laws," Financial News, *New York Times*, February 19, 1933, N15; Emanuel B. Halper, *Shopping Center and Store Leases* (New York: Law Journal Press, 2001), 40–57.

9. "New Market Plan Stirs Food Trade," N15.

10. Warren Belasco, *Meals to Come: A History of the Future of Food* (Berkeley: University of California Press, 2006), 194.

11. Mayo, *American Grocery Store*, 80–136.

12. Harvey Levenstein, *Paradox of Plenty: A Social History of Eating in Modern America* (New York: Oxford University Press, 1993), 113.

13. Mayo, *American Grocery Store*, 150.

14. Ibid., 114.

15. "Supermarket Facts," Food Marketing Institute, http://www.fmi.org/facts_figs /?fuseaction=superfact (accessed December 2, 2008).

16. Mary Hendrickson, William D. Heffernan, Philip H. Howard, and Judith B. Heffernan, "Consolidation in Food Retailing and Dairy," *British Food Journal* 103, no. 10 (2001): 717; TDLinx (Nielsen), cited in *Progressive Grocer* 87 (May 2008): 20–125.

17. Levenstein, *Paradox of Plenty*, 114–15.

18. Ruth Winter, *Poisons in Your Food* (New York: Crown, 1969), 2, 185–86; Richard J. Hooker, *Food and Drink in America: A History* (Indianapolis: Bobbs-Merrill, 1981), 349–50.

19. Lyall Watson, *The Omnivorous Ape* (New York: Coward, McCann & Geoghegan, 1971), 54–55, 214–15.

20. David Merrefield, "Supermarkets Reach a Milestone: The 75th Anniversary," *Supermarket News*, August 29, 2005, http://www.supermarketnews.com (accessed September 13, 2008).

20. Earle MacAusland's *Gourmet*

1. Margaret Leibenstein, "Earle MacAusland," in *Culinary Biographies*, ed. Alice Arndt (Houston: Yes Press, 2006), 249.

2. Philip H. Dougherty, "Advertising: Waxing Fat Off the Calories," Business and Finance, *New York Times*, May 3, 1968, 77; Leibenstein, "Earle MacAusland," 249.

3. Anne Mendelson, "60 Years of Gourmet," *Gourmet* 61 (September 2001): 71.

4. Samuel Chamberlain, "Burgundy at a Snail's Pace," *Gourmet* 1 (January 1941): 6; Samuel Chamberlain, *Etched in Sunlight* (Boston: Boston Public Library, 1958), 10; Craig Claiborne, "He Even Has Recipes to Induce Gout," Family/Style, *New York Times*, August 17, 1967, 40.

5. Clementine Paddleford, "Food Flashes," *Gourmet* 1 (January 1941): 28.

6. Earle R. MacAusland, "Editorial," *Gourmet* 1 (January 1941): 4.

7. Eric Pace, "Gladys G. Straus, 84, A Nutrition Expert," Metropolitan, *New York Times*, March 15, 1980, 24; Leibenstein, "Earle MacAusland," 250.

8. Phineas Beck [pseud. for Samuel Chamberlain], *Clémentine in the Kitchen* (New York: Hastings House, 1943); Laura Shapiro, *Something from the Oven: Reinventing Dinner in 1950s America* (New York: Penguin, 2004), 203–7; Chamberlain, *Etched in Sunlight*, 10–11, 152, 158, 161–62, 175; Samuel Chamberlain, *Bouquet de France, an Epicurean Tour of the French Provinces: Recipes Translated from the French and Adapted by Narcissa Chamberlain* (New York: Gourmet, 1952); Anne Mendelson, *Stand Facing the Stove: The Story of the Women Who Gave America "The Joy of Cooking"; The Lives of Irma S. Rombauer and Marion Rombauer Becker* (New York: Holt, 1996), 254.

9. It was rumored that the section in *Gourmet* titled "Menus Classiques," with Diat's byline, was actually written by Helen E. Ridley, which could well be true. After Diat's death in 1957, Ridley published *The Ritz-Carlton Cook Book and Guide to Home Entertaining* under her own name.

10. "Contributors," *Gourmet* 61 (September 2001): 30, 32; F. Scott Fitzgerald, "Tender Is the Turkey," in "Sound Bites," *Gourmet* 61 (September 2001): 117.

11. Dougherty, "Advertising," 77.

12. Mendelson, "60 Years of Gourmet," 71.

13. Pace, "Gladys G. Straus," 24; Leibenstein, "Earle MacAusland," 250.

14. Charlotte Turgeon, "A Lot of Good Things to Eat," *New York Times Book Review*, February 25, 1951, 223.

15. Other cookbooks include a second volume of *The Gourmet Cookbook*, *The Gourmet Menu Cookbook*, *Gourmet's Basic French Cookbook* (published posthumously under Louis Diat's name), and *Gourmet's Old Vienna Cookbook*, by longtime contributor Lillian Langseth-Christensen.

16. Leibenstein, "Earle MacAusland," 51.

17. N. R. Kleinfield, "A Growing Appetite For Food Magazines; A Refined Monthly Emphasis Is Changed," Family/Style, *New York Times*, July 1, 1980, B10.

18. N. R. Kleinfield, "Knapp Publishes the Good Life; Knapp's Magazines Show Rapid Growth With the Appeal of the Good Life," Business and Finance, *New York Times*, February 9, 1979, D16.

19. Kleinfield, "Growing Appetite for Food Magazines," B10; Michael Batterberry, interview by author, March 5, 2008.

20. Kleinfield, "Growing Appetite For Food Magazines," B10.

21. Other important culinary magazines include *Cooking Light*, *Taste of Home*, *Saveur*, *Eating Well*, *Vegetarian Times*, *Everyday Food*, *Good Food*, *Cuisine at Home*, and *Fine Cooking*.

22. Carolyn Voight, "You Are What You Eat: Contemplations on Civilizing the Palette with *Gourmet*" (master's thesis, McGill University, 1996), 5–6, 44.

21. Jerome I. Rodale's *Organic Gardening*

1. Amy Bentley, *Eating for Victory: Food Rationing and the Politics of Domesticity* (Urbana: University of Illinois Press, 1998), 117.

2. Robert Leslie Jones, *History of Agriculture in Ohio to 1860* (Kent, Ohio: Kent State University Press, 1983), 65–66; Samuel Fromartz, *Organic, Inc.: Natural Foods and How They Grew* (New York: Harcourt, 2007), 7–8.

3. Samuel Fromartz, *Organic, Inc.: Natural Foods and How They Grew* (New York: Harcourt, Inc., 2007), 7.

4. G. J. Leign, *The World's Greatest Fix: A History of Nitrogen and Agriculture* (New York: Oxford University Press, 2004), 121–63; Michael Pollan, *The Omnivore's Dilemma: A Natural History of Four Meals* (New York: Penguin, 2006), 43–44.

5. Harvey Levenstein, *Paradox of Plenty: A Social History of Eating in Modern America* (New York: Oxford University Press, 1993), 109.

6. "J. I. Rodale Dead; Organic Farmer; Espoused the Avoidance of Chemical Fertilizers," *New York Times*, June 8, 1971, 42; J. I. Rodale, *Autobiography* (Emmaus, Pa.: Rodale Press, 1965); Carlton Jackson, *J. I. Rodale: Apostle of Nonconformity* (New York: Pyramid Books, 1974), 29.

7. Warren J. Belasco, *Appetite for Change: How the Counterculture Took on the Food Industry*

1966–1988 (New York: Pantheon, 1989), 71–72; J. I. Rodale, *Pay Dirt: Farming and Gardening with Composts* (New York: Devin-Adair, 1945).

8. "J. I. Rodale Dead," 42; Belasco, *Appetite for Change*, 71–72; Jackson, *J. I. Rodale*, 33.

9. Rodale, *Pay Dirt*, 179; William F. Longgood, *The Poisons in Your Food* (New York: Simon & Schuster, 1960); Rachel Carson, *Silent Spring* (Boston: Houghton Mifflin, 1962); Jackson, *J. I. Rodale*, 33–34.

10. Levenstein, *Paradox of Plenty*, 162.

11. Belasco, *Appetite for Change*, 161.

12. Frances Moore Lappé, *Diet for a Small Planet* (New York: Ballantine Books, 1971); Belasco, *Appetite for Change*, 45–47, 56–57, 60.

13. Frances Moore Lappé and Anna Lappé, *Hope's Edge: The Next Diet for a Small Planet* (New York: Putnam, Tarcher, 2003).

14. Levenstein, *Paradox of Plenty*, 165.

15. Melanie Warner, "Wal-Mart Eyes Organic Foods, and Brand Names Get in Line," *New York Times*, May 12, 2006, 1.

16. "When It Pays to Buy Organic," *Consumer Reports* (February 2006), http://www.consumer.org (accessed June 20, 2008); Organic Trade Association, "U.S. Organic Sales Show Substantial Growth," May 6, 2007, http://www.organicnewsroom.com (accessed September 20, 2008).

17. "The Soil and Health by Sir Albert Howard," *Commonweal* 45 (March 21, 1947): 24; Julie Guthman, *Agrarian Dreams: The Paradox of Organic Farming in California* (Berkeley: University of California Press, 2004), 4; Mary Choate, *Organic Lies: Misconceptions of the United States Organic Act in America and the World* (Arvada, Colo.: Coastalfields Press, 2007), 11–12; V. A. Parthasarathy, K. Kandiannan, and V. Srinivasan, *Organic Spices* (New Delhi: New India, 2008), 26.

18. Jackson, *J. I. Rodale*, 224–26.

19. Rodale Institute, http://www.rodaleinstitute.org/history (accessed June 11, 2008).

22. Percy Spencer's Radar

1. *Missile Messenger*, cited in Otto J. Scott, *The Creative Ordeal: The Story of Raytheon*. (New York: Atheneum, 1974), 180; John Osepchuk, "A History of Microwave Applications," *IEEE Transactions on Microwave Theory and Technique* 32 (September 1984): 1204; John A. Alic et al., *Beyond Spinoff: Military and Commercial Technologies in a Changing World* (Boston: Harvard Business School Press, 1992), 58–59; Elmer J. Gorn, Chief Patent Attorney, Raytheon Company, "Micro Wave Cooking: The Story of a Man and His Invention" (unpublished paper, Raytheon Company, Waltham, Mass., ca. 1970), 3; Percy Spencer, U.S. Patent 2,480,629, issued October 8, 1945; William M. Hall and Fritz A. Gross, U.S. Patent 2,500,676, registered to Raytheon Manufacturing Corporation, applied for January 14, 1947, issued March 14, 1950.

2. Robert Buderi, *The Invention That Changed the World: How a Small Group of Radar Pioneers Won the Second World War and Launched a Technological Revolution* (New York: Simon & Schuster, 1997), 85–90.

3. Ibid., 82–83, 89; Charles R. Buffler, *Microwave Cooking and Processing: Engineering Fundamentals for the Food Scientist* (New York: Avi Books, 1993), 14.

4. Osepchuk, "History of Microwave Applications," 1203.
5. Ibid., 1204; Charles W. Behrens, "The Development of the Microwave Oven," *Appliance Manufacturer* 24 (November 1976): 72; Norman Krim, Raytheon historian, interview by author, August 14, 1997.
6. Behrens, "Development of the Microwave Oven," 72; Osepchuk, "History of Microwave Applications," 1205, 1207.
7. Donald Kiteley Tressler and Clifford F. Evers, *The Freezing Preservation of Foods*, 3rd ed. (Westport, Conn.: Avi, 1957), 482.
8. C. Lon Enloe et al., *Physical Science: What the Technology Professional Needs to Know* (New York: Wiley, 2001), 26.
9. Behrens, "Development of the Microwave Oven," 72; Steven P. Schnaars, *Managing Imitation Strategies: How Later Entrants Seize Markets from Pioneers* (New York: Free Press, 1994), 113.
10. Osepchuk, "History of Microwave Applications," 1208.
11. Ibid., 1211.
12. Behrens, "Development of the Microwave Oven," 72; Sandra L. Newsome, William R. Spillers, and Susan Finger, eds., *Design Theory '88: Proceedings of the 1988 NSF Grantee Workshop on Design Theory and Methodology* (New York: Springer-Verlag, 1989), 3; Buderi, *Invention That Changed the World*, 256; Robert D. Hershey Jr., "George Foerstner, 91, Amana Founder and Advocate of the Microwave Oven," *New York Times*, January 24, 2000, http:www.nytimes.com (accessed June 22, 2008).
13. Tadashi Sasaki and Yoshihiro Kase, "Growth of the Microwave Oven Industry in Japan," *Journal of Microwave Power* 6 (December 1971): 283.
14. Osepchuk, "History of Microwave Applications," 1211; Susan Strasser, *Never Done: A History of American Housework* (New York: Pantheon, 1982), 277; Wayne R. Tinga, "Microwave Ovens: History and Future," *Transactions of the International Microwave Power Institute* 6 (1976): 3.
15. Andrew F. Smith, *Popped Culture: A Social History of Popcorn in America* (Columbia: University of South Carolina Press, 1999), 144–45.
16. *The Popcorn Market* (New York: Packaged Facts, 1989), 63.
17. Mona Doyle, quoted in Dena Kleiman, "Fast Food? It Just Isn't Fast Enough Anymore," *New York Times*, December 6, 1989, 1.
18. Alic, *Beyond Spinoff*, 59.

23. Frances Roth and Katharine Angell's CIA

1. Elise Biesel, "The First Cook in the Land," *Good Housekeeping* 58 (March 1914): 421.
2. Lawrence Timothy Ryan, "The Culinary Institute of America: A History" (Ed.D. diss., University of Pennsylvania, 2003), 67.
3. Ibid., 36, 71–72.
4. Ibid., 46, 77, 85; LeRoi A. Folsom, ed., *The Professional Chef. Prepared by the Culinary Institute of America, Inc. and the Editors of Institutions Magazine* (Chicago: Institutions Magazine, 1968).
5. Ryan, "Culinary Institute of America, 95, 104, 139.
6. Jacques Pépin, *The Apprentice: My Life in the Kitchen* (Boston: Houghton Mifflin, 2003), 241–42.

7. Pépin, *Apprentice*, 242.
8. Craig Claiborne, "Food News: From Court to Kitchen," *New York Times*, January 25, 1960, 20.

24. McDonald's Drive-In

1. Henry Wansey, *Henry Wansey and His American Journal, 1794*, ed. David John Jeremy (Philadelphia: American Philosophical Society, 1970), 57.
2. Adam Hodgson, *Remarks During a Journey Through North America in the Years 1819, 1820, and 1821* (New York: Whiting, 1823), 106.
3. Basil Hall, *Travels in North America, in the Years 1827 and 1828*, 3 vols. (London: Simpkin and Marshall, 1829), 1:31–32.
4. Aleksander B. Lakier, *A Russian Looks at America: The Journey of Aleksander B. Lakier in 1857* (Chicago: University of Chicago Press, 1979), 61–62; see also citations in Hillel Schwartz, *Never Satisfied: A Cultural History of Diets, Fantasies and Fat* (New York: Free Press, 1986), 42.
5. "The United States," *Blackwood's Edinburgh Magazine* 50 (December 1841): 822.
6. Andrew F. Smith, *Hamburger: A Global History* (London: Reaktion Books, 2008), 16–20.
7. David Gerard Hogan, *Selling 'em by the Sack: White Castle and the Creation of American Food* (New York: New York University Press, 1997), 25–29.
8. Smith, *Hamburger*, 29–37.
9. Ibid., 39–40.
10. John F. Love, *McDonald's: Behind the Arches*, rev. ed. (New York: Bantam Books, 1995), 160; Ray Kroc with Robert Anderson, *Grinding It Out: The Making of McDonald's* (Chicago: Regnery, 1977), 128.
11. Phillip Fitzell, "The Man Who Sold the First McDonald's Hamburger," *Journal of American Culture* 1 (summer 1978): 393.
12. Fitzell, "Man Who Sold the First McDonald's Hamburger," 392.
13. Alan Hess, "The Origins of McDonald's Golden Arches," *Journal of the Society of Architectural Historians* 45 (March 1986): 60–67.
14. Philip Langdon, *Orange Roofs, Golden Arches: The Architecture of American Chain Restaurants* (New York: Knopf, 1986), 92; James W. McLamore, *The Burger King: Jim McLamore and the Building of an Empire* (New York: McGraw-Hill, 1997), 15–18.
15. Eric Schlosser, *Fast Food Nation: The Dark Side of the All-American Meal* (Boston: Houghton Mifflin, 2001), 21.
16. Hogan, *Selling 'em by the Sack*, 153.
17. Love, *McDonald's*, 25.
18. McLamore, *Burger King*, 18.
19. Kroc, *Grinding It Out*, 6–13.
20. John A. Jakle and Keith A. Sculle, *Fast Food: Roadside Restaurants in the Automobile Age* (Baltimore: Johns Hopkins University Press, 1999), 69–73.
21. Kroc, *Grinding It Out*, 113–15.
22. For more on Hamburger University, see Sarah Sanderson King and Michael J. King, "Hamburger University," *Journal of American Culture* 1 (summer 1978): 412–23.
23. "The Burger That Conquered the Country," *Time*, September 17, 1973, 84–92.

24. Smith, *Hamburger*, 64–75.

25. James L. Watson, ed., *Golden Arches East: McDonald's in East Asia* (Stanford, Calif.: Stanford University Press, 1997), 24.

26. Love, *McDonald's*, 454–56.

27. David Kaimowitz, Benoit Mertens, Sven Wunder, and Pablo Pacheco, "Hamburger Connection: Cattle Ranching and Deforestation in Brazil's Amazon," Center for International Forestry Research, http://www.cifor.cgiar.org/publications/pdf_files /media/Amazon.pdf (accessed September 1, 2008); Danielle Nierenberg, "Rethinking the Global Meat Industry," in *State of the World: A Worldwatch Institute Report on Progress Toward a Sustainable Society*, ed. Danielle Nierenberg (New York: Norton, 2006), 37; Mark Edelman, "From Costa Rican Pasture to North American Hamburger," in *Food and Evolution, Toward a Theory of Human Food Habits*, ed. Marvin Harris and Eric B. Ross (Philadelphia: Temple University Press, 1987), 545–48.

28. Marc Kaufman, "New Allies on The Amazon: McDonald's, Greenpeace Unite To Prevent Rainforest Clearing," *Washington Post*, April 24, 2007, D1.

29. Schlosser, *Fast Food Nation*, 9.

30. Ibid., 244.

31. George Ritzer, *The McDonaldization of Society*, rev. ed. (Thousand Oaks, Calif.: Pine Forge Press, 1996), 13–15.

32. http://www.mcdonalds.com/corp/about.html (accessed September 1, 2008).

33. "The Burger That Conquered the Country," 5; Kroc, *Grinding It Out*, 116.

34. Kroc, *Grinding It Out*, inside cover flap; Ellen Graham, "McDonald's Pickle: He Began Fast Food but Gets No Credit," *Wall Street Journal*, August 15, 1991, A1.

25. Julia Child, the French Chef

1. Noël Riley Fitch, *Appetite for Life: The Biography of Julia Child* (New York: Doubleday, 1997), 276–77; Bill Buford, "Notes of a Gastronome: TV Dinners; The Rise of Food Television," *New Yorker* 82 (October 2, 2006): 45; Julia Child with Alex Prud'Homme, *My Life in France* (New York: Knopf, 2006), 236–37; Regina Schrambling with William Grimes, "Julia Child, the French Chef for a Jell-O Nation, Dies at 91," *New York Times*, August 14, 2004, 1.

2. Fitch, *Appetite for Life*, 68, 78.

3. Child, *My Life in France*, 12.

4. "Everyone's in the Kitchen," *Time*, November 25, 1966, http://www.time.com (accessed August 4, 2008); Fitch, *Appetite for Life*, 130; Laura Shapiro, *Something from the Oven: Reinventing Dinner in 1950s America* (New York: Penguin, 2004), 218; Laura Shapiro, *Julia Child: A Penguin Life* (New York: Penguin, 2007), 19, 23, 27.

5. Fitch, *Appetite for Life*, 148–49, 167.

6. Ibid., 175, 182; David Kamp, *The United States of Arugula: How We Became a Gourmet Nation* (New York: Broadway Books, 2006), 195.

7. Fitch, *Appetite for Life*, 187–88, 192; Shapiro, *Julia Child*, 40–45.

8. Louisette Bertholle, Simone Beck, and Helmut Ripperger, *What's Cooking in France* (New York: Washburn 1952). This work was subsequently published in London and self-published in Paris (Louisette Bertholle, Simone Beck, and Helmut Ripperger, *What's Cuisine in France* [Paris: Fischbacher, 1953]; Louisette Bertholle, *What's Cook-*

ing in France [London: MacGibbon & Kee, 1955]); Craig Claiborne, "Cookbook Review: Glorious Recipes," *New York Times*, October 18, 1961, 47; Fitch, *Appetite for Life*, 187–91; Shapiro, *Something from the Oven*, 220–21; Jane Nickerson, "News of Food," *New York Times*, May 5, 1952, 20.

9. Child, *My Life in France*, 117, 132.

10. Bernard DeVoto, "The Easy Chair," *Harper's* 203 (November 1951): 95–98; Fitch, *Appetite for Life*, 197–98; Child, *My Life in France*, 138–39, 177, 208–10.

11. Fitch, *Appetite for Life*, 259; Shapiro, *Julia Child*, 89.

12. Judith Jones, *The Tenth Muse: My Life in Food* (New York: Knopf, 2007), 61.

13. Child, *My Life in France*, 220, 222–23, 226, 230.

14. These include Louis Diat's *French Cooking for Americans*, Dione Lucas's *The Cordon Bleu Cook Book*, James Beard's *Paris Cuisine*, Ali-Bab and Bart Keith Winer's *The Art of French Cooking*, Elizabeth David's *French Country Cooking*, Robert J. Courtine's *Real French Cooking*, and Fernande Garvin's *The Art of French Cooking*. In 1961 alone, several significant French culinary works were published, including *Gourmet's Basic French Cookbook*, *Vogue's French Cookery Book*, Jean Conil's *Haute Cuisine*, Curnonsky's *Traditional Recipes of the Provinces of France*, and André Simon's *Menus for Gourmets*. That year also saw the publication of an American edition of *Larousse gastronomique*, a comprehensive encyclopedia of French cuisine, which was edited by Julia Child's friend from Smith College, Charlotte Snyder Turgeon.

15. Bertholle, Beck, and Ripperger, *What's Cooking in France*, back cover.

16. Kamp, *United States of Arugula*, 85.

17. Jones, *Tenth Muse*, 69; Craig Claiborne, "Delight in Keeping Up With Cuisine; Couple's Cooking Zeal Mounted, During a Paris Sojourn Fresh Herbs Grow in Penthouse Garden in Manhattan," Food Fashions Family Furnishings, *New York Times*, August 3, 1961, 10; Craig Claiborne, "Cookbook Review: Glorious Recipes; Art of French Cooking Does Not Concede to U.S. Tastes Text Is Simply Written for Persons Who Enjoy Cuisine," *New York Times*, October 18, 1961, 47.

18. Child, *My Life in France*, 231; Kamp, *United States of Arugula*, 86.

19. Child, *My Life in France*, 230, 235.

20. Fitch, *Appetite for Life*, 277.

21. Shapiro, *Julia Child*, 101.

22. Ryan Scott Eanes, "From Stovetop to Screen: A Cultural History of Food Television" (master's thesis, New School, 2008), 17.

23. "Brief Biographies of Television's Best Cooks," in William Irving Kaufman, *Cooking with the Experts* (New York: Random House, 1955); Lori F. Brost, "Television Cooking Shows: Defining the Genre" (Ph.D. diss., Indiana University, 2000), 77–80; Kamp, *United States of Arugula*, 10; John E. Finn, "Julia," *Gastronomica* 7 (fall 2007): 96; Eanes, "From Stovetop to Screen," 10–15.

24. Brost, "Television Cooking Shows," 93.

25. Fitch, *Appetite for Life*, 286; Julia Child, interview by Harvey Levenstein, quoted in Harvey Levenstein, *Paradox of Plenty: A Social History of Eating in Modern America* (New York: Oxford University Press, 1993), 143.

26. Shapiro, *Julia Child*, 104.

27. Julia Child, "The Potato Show," *The French Chef*, vol. 1, first selection, DVD (Boston: WGBH Boston Video, 2005); Shapiro, *Julia Child*, 118–20.

28. "Everyone's in the Kitchen," 74.

29. Shapiro, *Julia Child*, 92.

30. Fitch, *Appetite for Life*, 276–79, 311–13, 332; Shapiro, *Something from the Oven*, 222–26; Claiborne, "Cookbook Review," 47; Nadine Brozan, "Cookbooks: The Books Publishers Love Best," *New York Times*, December 2, 1974, 40; Shapiro, *Julia Child*, 92.

31. Val Adams, "Radio and TV Scored as 11 Get Peabody Awards," Business Financial, *New York Times*, April 27, 1965, 75; "Julia Child, the Master Chef, *Life*, October 21, 1966, 45–46; "Everyone's in the Kitchen," 74; Fitch, *Appetite for Life*, 309–10.

32. Fitch, *Appetite for Life*, 313; Schrambling, "Julia Child," 1.

33. Fitch, *Appetite for Life*, 275.

34. Patric Kuh, *The Last Days of Haute Cuisine: America's Culinary Revolution* (New York: Viking, 2001), 178.

35. Betty Fussell, *My Kitchen Wars* (New York: North Point Press, 2000), 154.

36. Jacques Pépin, *The Apprentice: My Life in the Kitchen* (Boston: Houghton Mifflin, 2003), 182.

37. Ibid., 253–54, 265.

38. Julia Child's other television series were *Julia Child and Company, Julia Child and More Company, Dinner at Julia's, Cooking with Master Chefs, Baking with Julia*, and *Julia and Jacques: Cooking at Home*. Her other books include: *The French Chef Cookbook; Mastering the Art of French Cooking, Volume Two* (with Simone Beck); *From Julia Child's Kitchen; Julia Child and Company; Julia Child and More Company; The Way to Cook; Julia Child's Menu Cookbook; Cooking with Master Chefs; In Julia's Kitchen with Master Chefs*; and *Baking with Julia*.

26. Jean Nidetch's Diet

1. Jean Nidetch, *The Story of Weight Watchers* (New York: New American Library, 1979), 2–3, 6, 77–89, 92–4, 111–14.

2. Hillel Schwartz, *Never Satisfied: A Cultural History of Diets, Fantasies and Fat* (New York: Free Press, 1986), 21–24, 73.

3. Sylvester Graham, *Lectures on the Science of Human Life* (New York: Fowler & Wells, 1883), 579.

4. Laura Fraser, *Losing It: America's Obsession with Weight and the Industry That Feeds on It* (New York: Dutton, 1997), 16–49.

5. Richard W. Schwarz, *John Harvey Kellogg, M.D.* (Nashville, Tenn.: Southern Publishing Association, 1970), 45; Schwartz, *Never Satisfied*, 186–87.

6. Upton Sinclair, *The Fasting Cure* (New York: Kennerley, 1911), 5, 86.

7. Irving Fisher, "A New Method for Indicating Food Values," *American Journal of Physiology* 15 (1906): 417–32.

8. Robert H. Rose, *Eat Your Way to Health, a Scientific System of Weight Control*, 2nd ed. (New York: Funk & Wagnalls, 1924); Lulu Hunt Peters, *Diet and Health, with Key to the Calories* (Chicago: Reilly and Britton, 1918); *Who Was Who in America*, rev. ed., 3 vols. (Chicago: Marquis, 1967), 1:964; Schwartz, *Never Satisfied*, 175; Elizabeth Sharon Hayenga, "Dieting through the Decades: A Comparative Study of Weight Reduction in America as Depicted in Popular Literature and Books from 1940 to the Late 1980s" (Ph.D. diss., University of Minnesota, 1988), 88; Fraser, *Losing It*, 56.

9. "American Fruit in Demand; Belgian Women Take Especially to the Grapefruit Diet," *New York Times*, February 7, 1932, E4 153.

10. Jack LaLanne, *Eat the LaLanne Way to Promote Health, Preserve Youth, Prolong Life* (Oakland, Calif.: Fontes, 1954); Fraser, *Losing It*, 58–59.

11. Michel Hersen, Richard M. Eisler, and Peter M. Miller, *Progress in Behavior Modification* (New York: Academic Press, 1982), 12:136; Hayenga, "Dieting through the Decades," 180–82; Fraser, *Losing It*, 150–51; Take Off Pounds Sensibly Web site: http://www.tops. org (accessed June 30, 2008).

12. Bill B., *Compulsive Overeater: The Basic Text for Compulsive Overeaters* (Minneapolis: CompCare, 1981); Rozanne S., *Beyond Our Wildest Dreams: A History of Overeaters Anonymous as Seen by a Cofounder* (Rio Rancho, N.M.: Overeaters Anonymous, 1996), 8–11; Overeaters Anonymous Web site: http://www.oa.org (accessed June 30, 2008).

13. Schwartz, *Never Satisfied*, 246.

14. Robert Hutchison, *Food and the Principles of Dietetics* (New York: Wood, 1903), 487; W. Gilman Thompson, *Practical Dietetics with Special Reference to Diet in Disease*, 3rd ed. (New York: Appleton, 1906), 687; "Saccharin Advertised as a Sugar Substitute," *Printers Ink* 109 (October 2, 1919): 40; Rich Cohen, *Sweet and Low: A Family Story* (New York: Farrar, Straus and Giroux, 2006), 103.

15. H. W. Lewis, *Technological Risk* (New York: Norton, 1990), 150.

16. Cohen, *Sweet and Low*, 114–15; Hayenga, "Dieting through the Decades," 150–52, 274.

17. Hayenga, "Dieting through the Decades," 187–89.

18. Sibel Roller and Sylvia A. Jones, eds., *Handbook of Fat Replacers* (Boca Raton, Fla.: CRC Press, 1996), 15; Marion Nestle, *Food Politics: How the Food Industry Influences Nutrition and Health*, rev. ed. (Berkeley: University of California Press, 2007), 338–39, 345–47.

19. Laura Fraser, *Losing It*, 100–104.

20. Hayenga, "Dieting through the Decades," 93, 293.

21. John P. Morgan, Doreen V. Kagan, and Jane S. Brody, eds., *Phenylpropanolamine: Risks, Benefits, and Controversies* (New York: Praeger, 1985); U.S. Food and Drug Administration Web site: http://www.fda.gov/cder/drug/infopage/ppa/advisory.htm (accessed July 1, 2008).

22. Howard Brody, *Hooked: Ethics, the Medical Profession, and the Pharmaceutical Industry* (Lanham, Md.: Rowman & Littlefield, 2007), 269–70; U.S. Food and Drug Administration Web site: http://www.fda.gov/cder/news/feninfo.htm (accessed July 1, 2008).

23. Hayenga, "Dieting through the Decades," 302–3, 317, 332.

24. Gary Taubes, "What If It's All Been a Big Fat Lie?" *New York Times Magazine*, July 7, 2002, http://www.nytimes.com (accessed July 1, 2008).

25. Hayenga, "Dieting through the Decades," 60.

26. *Clinical Guidelines on the Identification, Evaluation, and Treatment of Overweight and Obesity in Adults: The Evidence Report* (Bethesda, Md.: NHLBI Obesity Education Initiative, National Heart, Lung, and Blood Institute, in cooperation with the National Institute of Diabetes and Digestive and Kidney Diseases, National Institutes of Health, 1998), http://www.nhlbi.nih.gov/guidelines/obesity/ob_gdlns.htm (accessed December 2, 2008); C. L. Ogden, M. D. Carroll, M. A. McDowell, and K. M. Flegal, *Obesity among Adults in the United States—No Change since 2003-2004*, NCHS data brief no. 1 (Hyattsville, Md.: National Center for Health Statistics, 2007), 1–8.

27. Alan Zarembo, "Child Obesity Rate in U.S. Hits a Plateau, Researchers Say; the Percentage of Children Who Are Obese Has Been Roughly Stable since 1999, but No One Knows Why. The Level Is 'Still Too High,' the Study's Author Says," *Los Angeles Times*, May 28, 2008, http://articles.latimes.com/2008/may/28/science/sci-obesity28 (accessed July 4, 2008).

28. A. E. Field, S. B. Austin, M. W. Gillman, B. Rosner, H. R. Rockett, and G. A. Colditz, "Snack Food Intake Does Not Predict Weight Change among Children and Adolescents," *International Journal of Obesity* 28, no. 10 (2004): 1210–16.

27. Alice Waters's Chez Panisse

1. Jeremiah Tower, *California Dish: What I Saw (and Cooked) at the American Culinary Revolution* (New York: Free Press, 2003), 111.

2. Patric Kuh, *The Last Days of Haute Cuisine: America's Culinary Revolution* (New York: Viking, 2001), x, 147; Tower, *California Dish*, 130.

3. Kuh, *Last Days of Haute Cuisine*, x.

4. Joan Reardon, *M. F. K. Fisher, Julia Child, and Alice Waters: Celebrating the Pleasures of the Table* (New York: Harmony Books, 1994), 207.

5. Reardon, *M. F. K. Fisher, Julia Child, and Alice Waters*, 210; Thomas McNamee, *Alice Waters and Chez Panisse: The Romantic, Impractical, Often Eccentric, Ultimately Brilliant Making of a Food Revolution* (New York: Penguin, 2007), 29.

6. Reardon, *M. F. K. Fisher, Julia Child, and Alice Waters*, 213.

7. Ibid., 215.

8. David Kamp, *The United States of Arugula: How We Became a Gourmet Nation* (New York: Broadway Books, 2006), 123.

9. McNamee, *Alice Waters and Chez Panisse*, 45.

10. Reardon, *M. F. K. Fisher, Julia Child, and Alice Waters*, 222.

11. Alice B. Toklas, *The Alice B. Toklas Cookbook* (New York: Harper, 1954); Tower, *California Dish*, 90; Kamp, *United States of Arugula*, 156.

12. Tower, *California Dish*, 93.

13. Robert Clark, *James Beard: A Biography* (New York: HarperCollins, 1993), 281.

14. Caroline Bates, "Spécialités de la Maison: California," *Gourmet* 35 (October 1975): 11–12; Harvey Levenstein, "Two Hundred Years of French Food in America," *Journal of Gastronomy* 5 (spring 1989): 85; Joan Reardon, *Poet of the Appetites: The Lives and Loves of M. F. K. Fisher* (New York: North Point Press, 2004), 235–37; Leslie Brenner, *American Appetite: The Coming of Age of a Cuisine* (New York: Avon Books, 1999), 125, 144.

15. Charles Ranhofer, *The Epicurean* (New York: Ranhofer, 1894), 256; Tower, *California Dish*, 27, 103, 110.

16. Reardon, *M. F. K. Fisher, Julia Child, and Alice Waters*, 218.

17. Patric Kuh, *Last Days of Haute Cuisine*, 168.

18. Alice Waters in collaboration with Linda P. Guenzel, *The Chez Panisse Menu Cookbook* (New York: Random House, 1982); Alice Waters with Patricia Curtan, Kelsie Kerr, and Fritz Streiff, *The Art of Simple Food: Notes, Lessons, and Recipes from a Delicious Revolution* (New York: Clarkson Potter, 2007).

19. Reardon, *M. F. K. Fisher, Julia Child, and Alice Waters*, 235.

20. Ibid., 288.

21. James Beard, *Savvy* magazine, quoted in Roman Czajkowsky, "The 'Mother' of California Cuisine: Alice Waters," *Nation's Restaurant News*, February 13, 1984, http://www.findarticles.com (accessed June 22, 2008); Caroline Bates, "Pure Waters," *Gourmet* 61 (September 2001): 44.

22. R. W. Apple Jr., quoted in McNamee, *Alice Waters and Chez Panisse*, xi.

23. Ibid., 6.

24. Reardon, *M. F. K. Fisher, Julia Child, and Alice Waters*, 285, 287; McNamee, *Alice Waters and Chez Panisse*, 7.

25. Laura Shapiro, *Julia Child: A Penguin Life* (New York: Penguin, 2007), 165.

28. TVFN

1. Nadine Brozan, "Chronicle," *New York Times*, December 29, 1993, http://www.nytimes.com (accessed June 20, 2008); David Rosengarten, interview by author, April 15, 2008.

2. Pauline Adema, "Vicarious Consumption: Food, Television and the Ambiguity of Modernity," *Journal of American Culture and Comparative Studies* 23 (fall 2000): 115.

3. Other key players in the early stages of the development of TVFN were Andrew Thatcher, Jack Clifford's assistant, Bruce Clark, the president of Colony Communications, Paul Silva, the vice president of Colony Communications, and Jeff Wayne, the vice president of marketing and programming of Colony Communications.

4. Reese Schonfeld, *Me and Ted against the World: The Unauthorized Story of the Founding of CNN* (New York: HarperCollins, 2001), 334.

5. Walter Goodman, "Review/Television; What? Eat Pretzels with All This on the Screen?" *New York Times*, January 26, 1994, C8.

6. Marcia Layton Turner, *Emeril! Inside the Amazing Success of Today's Most Popular Chef* (Hoboken, N.J.: Wiley, 2004), 72–77.

7. Noël Riley Fitch, *Appetite for Life: The Biography of Julia Child* (New York: Doubleday, 1997), 482.

8. Morrie Gelman, "Tastes Good Like a Network Should," *Emmy* (December 1993): 44.

9. Adema, "Vicarious Consumption," 115.

10. The notion of cultural capital was coined by Pierre Bourdieu and Jean-Claude Passeron in "Cultural Reproduction and Social Reproduction," in *Knowledge, Education, and Cultural Change: Papers in the Sociology of Education*, ed. Richard Brown (London: Tavistock, 1973), 75.

11. Adema, "Vicarious Consumption," 117–18.

29. The Flavr Savr

1. David Goll, "Calgene Claims Breakthrough That Will Lead to 'Supertomato'," *Sacramento Union*, August 16, 1988, cited in Belinda Martineau, *First Fruit: The Creation of the Flavr Savr Tomato and the Birth of Biotech Food* (New York: McGraw-Hill, 2001), 1.

2. Sheldon Krimsky and Roger P. Wrubel, *Agricultural Biotechnology and the Environment: Science, Policy, and Social Issues* (Urbana: University of Illinois Press, 1996), 100.

3. James Watson and Francis Crick, "Molecular Structure of Nucleic Acids," *Nature* 171 (April 25, 1953): 737–38.

4. Stanley Cohen, Annie C. Y. Chang, Herbert W. Boyert, and Robert B. Helling, "Construction of Biologically Functional Bacterial Plasmids in Vitro," *Proceedings of the National Academy of Sciences* 70 (November 1973): 3240–44.

5. William F. Hamilton, Joaquim Vilà, and Mark D. Dibner, "Patterns of Strategic Choice in Emerging Firms: Positioning for Innovation in Biotechnology," *California Management Review* 32 (spring 1990): 76; Office of Technology Assessment, cited in Krimsky and Wrubel, *Agricultural Biotechnology and the Environment*, 3.

6. R. W. Robinson, "A History of the Tomato Genetics Cooperative," *Report of the Tomato Genetics Cooperative No. 32* (May 1982): 1–2.

7. Charles Rick, "Research Notes," *Report of the Tomato Genetics Cooperative No. 5* (January 1955): 8–13; Charles Rick, "Linkage Summary," *Report of the Tomato Genetics Cooperative No. 27* (February 1977): 2–5; Robinson, "History of the Tomato Genetics Cooperative," 1–2.

8. Charles Rick, "Genetic Resources in *Lycopersicon*," in *Tomato Biotechnology*, ed. Donald J. Nevins and Richard A. Jones (New York: Liss, 1987), 19; Benedict Carey, "Tasty Tomatoes: Now There's a Concept," *Health* 7 (July-August 1993): 26; Donald Woutat, "Toward a Tastier Tomato," *Los Angeles Times*, July 7, 1993; John Seabrook, "Tremors in the Hot House," *New Yorker* 69 (July 19, 1993): 32–41.

9. Martineau, *First Fruit*, 1, 11.

10. It was also possible to take an antifreeze gene from a fish and insert it into a tomato's genetic makeup; this was first accomplished by Pam Dunsmuir and her fellow researchers at DNA Plant Technology Corporation, in Oakland, California. There were numerous complaints about this experimental "mutant fish-tomato," and it was never commercialized or even field-tested (Nina V. Fedoroff and Nancy Marie Brown, *Mendel in the Kitchen: A Scientist's View of Genetically Modified Foods* [Washington, D.C.: Henry Press, 2004], 91–92).

11. Philip Hilts, "Genetically Altered Tomato Moves Toward U.S. Approval," *New York Times*, April 9, 1994, 7.

12. For the research on the Flavr Savr, see Keith Redenbaugh et al., *Safety Assessment of Genetically Engineered Fruits and Vegetables: A Case Study of the Flavr Savr Tomato* (Boca Raton, Fla.: CRC Press, 1992).

13. Hilts, "Genetically Altered Tomato," 7.

14. *Request for Advisory Opinion: Flavr Savr Tomato; Status as Food* (Davis, Calif.: Calgene, 1991); G. Kalloo, ed., *Genetic Improvement of Tomato* (New York: Springer-Verlag, 1991); Redenbaugh, *Safety Assessment of Genetically Engineered Fruits and Vegetables*; Hilts, "Genetically Altered Tomato ," 143.

15. Martineau, *First Fruit*, 216–17.

16. Ibid., 191; Marion Nestle, *Safe Food: Bacteria, Biotechnology, and Bioterrorism* (Berkeley: University of California Press, 2003), 211–13.

17. Martineau, *First Fruit*, 219–21.

18. For more on *Bacillus thuringiensis*, see Travis R. Glare and Maureen O'Callaghan, *Bacillus thuringiensis: Biology, Ecology and Safety* (New York: Wiley, 2000); Jeremy Rifkin, *The Biotech Century: Harnessing the Gene and Remaking the World* (New York: Putnam, Tarcher, 1998), 82–90; Krimsky and Wrubel, *Agricultural Biotechnology and the Environment*, 56–58.

19. Neil E. Harl, Roger G. Ginder, Charles R. Hurburgh, and Steve Moline, "The StarLink Situation," http://www.mindfully.org/GE/StarLink-Situation-15mar01.htm (accessed August 25, 2008).

20. Nestle, *Safe Food*, 197–207; Monsanto Web site: http://www.monsantodairy.com/about/general_info/index.html (accessed August 25, 2008); Henry I. Miller, "Don't Cry Over rBST Milk," *New York Times*, June 29, 2007, http://www.nytimes.com (accessed August 26, 2008).

21. Sheldon Krimsky, "Tomatoes May Be Dangerous to Your Health," *New York Times*, June 1, 1992, A17.

22. Nestle, *Safe Food*, 213; Rifkin, *Biotech Century*; Ted Howard and Jeremy Rifkin, *Who Should Play God? The Artificial Creation of Life and What It Means for the Future of the Human Race* (New York: Delacorte Press, 1977), 9–10; Pure Food Campaign Web site: http://www.foet.org/past/PureFoodCampaign.html (accessed August 25, 2008).

23. Hendrickson et al., "Consolidation in Food Retailing and Dairy," 715–28; MacDonald et al., *Consolidation in U.S. Meatpacking*, 8–11; Schlosser, *Fast Food Nation*, 137–38; Hendrickson and Heffernan, "Concentration in Agricultural Markets.".

24. Henry I. Miller, *The Frankenfood Myth: How Protest and Politics Threaten the Biotech Revolution* (Westport, Conn.: Praeger, 2004); Jane Brody, "Personal Health; Facing Biotech Foods Without the Fear Factor," *New York Times*, January 11, 2005, http://www.nytimes.com (accessed July 7, 2008).

25. Martineau, *First Fruit*, 224–25.

26. "Adoption of Genetically Engineered Crops in the U.S.," *Economic Research Service*, July 2, 2008, http://www.ers.usda.gov/Data/BiotechCrops/ (accessed August 26, 2008).

27. Nestle, *Safe Food*, 150; Linda Bren, "Genetic Engineering: The Future of Foods?" *FDA Consumer* 37 (November-December 2003), http://www.fda.gov/fdac/features/2003/603_food.html (accessed September 1, 2008).

28. "Eli Lilly to Buy Monsanto's Dairy Cow Hormone for $300 Million," *New York Times*, August 20, 2008, http://www.nytimes.com (accessed August 25, 2008).

29. Bill Gates, "Will Frankenfood Feed the World?" *Time*, June 19, 2000, http://www.time.com (accessed September 11, 2008).

30. Board on Agriculture and Natural Resources, National Research Council, *Emerging Technologies to Benefit Farmers in Sub-Saharan Africa and South Asia* (Washington, D.C.: National Academies Press, 2008).

30. Mergers, Acquisitions, and Spin-Offs

1. "Company News; Kraft Deal Settled, Philip Morris Says," *New York Times*, December 6, 1988, http://www.nytimes.com (accessed July 1, 2008); Andrew Martin, "Wall Street Finds a Lot to Like About Tobacco," *New York Times*, January 31, 2007, A1. In 2005 Kraft Foods slipped behind Tyson Foods and was downgraded to the second largest food corporation in America.

2. Glenn A. Bishop and Paul Thomas Gilbert, comps., *Chicago's Accomplishments and Leaders* (Chicago: Bishop, 1932), 290; Laura Enright, *Chicago's Most Wanted: The Top 10 Book of Murderous Mobsters, Midway Monsters, and Windy City Oddities* (Washington, D.C.: Potomac Books, 2005), 114.

3. The product line Parkay was subsequently sold to ConAgra.

4. Nancy Rubin, *American Empress: The Life and Times of Marjorie Merriweather Post* (New York: Villard Books, 1995), 89–101.

5. The National Biscuit Company did not officially change its name to Nabisco until 1971.

6. Fleischmann's was subsequently sold to ConAgra.

7. Harper W. Boyd Jr., Richard M. Clewett, and Ralph Westfall, *Cases in Marketing Strategy* (Homewood, Ill.: Irwin, 1958), 206.

8. The Baby Ruth and Butterfinger candy bars were sold to Nestlé in 1990.

9. Kraft Foods sold LifeSaver Candies to Wrigley in 2004.

10. Reynolds sold Chun King frozen foods to ConAgra in 1986. Reynolds sold the Chun King trademark and its shelf-stable foods to Singapore investors in 1989.

11. *Annual Report* (Winston-Salem, N.C.: R.J. Reynolds Tobacco Co., 1969), 11; Vartanig G. Vartan, "Tobacco Stocks Gain; Diversity Aiding Cigarette Makers," Business and Finance, *New York Times*, November 1, 1970, 141.

12. Bryan Burrough and John Helyar, *Barbarians at the Gate: The Fall of RJR Nabisco* (New York: Harper & Row, 1990), 190–259.

13. Reynolds transferred Hawaiian Punch to Del Monte in 1981; Proctor & Gamble acquired it in 1990, and Proctor & Gamble sold it to Cadbury Schweppes Americas Beverages in 1999. Brer Rabbit molasses, developed by Penick & Ford, was sold to B&G Food.

14. "PepsiCo Inc.," *Notable Corporate Chronologies*, online ed. (Gale, 2007).

15. Mary Hendrickson, William D. Heffernan, Philip H. Howard, and Judith B. Heffernan, "Consolidation in Food Retailing and Dairy," *British Food Journal* 103, no. 10 (2001): 715–28; J.M. MacDonald, M.E. Ollinger, K.E. Nelson, and C.R. Handy, *Consolidation in U.S. Meatpacking*, Agricultural Economic Report no. 785 (Washington, D.C.: Food and Rural Economics Division, Economic Research Service, U.S. Department of Agriculture, 2000); Eric Schlosser, *Fast Food Nation: The Dark Side of the All-American Meal* (Boston: Houghton Mifflin, 2001), 137–38; Mary Hendrickson and William Heffernan, "Concentration in Agricultural Markets" (report to the National Farmers Union, 2007), http://www.nfu.org/news (accessed July 2, 2008).

16. Hendrickson et al., "Consolidation in Food Retailing and Dairy," 716; TDLinx (Nielsen), cited in *Progressive Grocer* 87 (May 2008): 20–125.

17. TDLinx, 20–125.

18. Helena Paul and Ricarda Steinbrecher with Devlin Kuyek and Lucy Michaels, *Hungry Corporations: Transnational Biotech Companies Colonise the Food Chain* (London: Zed Books / New York: Palgrave, 2003), 82, 85–86.

19. Sanjib Bhuyan and Rigoberto A. Lopez, "Oligopoly in the Food and Tobacco Industries," *American Journal of Agricultural Economics* 7 (August 1997): 1041; Rigoberto A. Lopez, Azzeddine M. Azzam, and Carmen Liron-Espana, "Market Power and/or Efficiency: A Structural Approach," *Review of Industrial Organization* 20 (March 2002): 121; Raj Patel, *Stuffed and Starved: The Hidden Battle for the World Food System* (Brooklyn: Melville House, 2008), 104.

20. Jorge Fernandez-Cornejo and David Schimmelpfennig, "Have Seed Industry Changes Affected Research Effort?" *Amber Waves* 2 (February 2004): 18–19; Patel, *Stuffed and Starved*, 105.

Epilogue

1. Andrew Pollack, "Monsanto Seeks Big Increase in Crop Yields," *New York Times*, June 5, 2008, http://www.nytimes.com (accessed June 20, 2008).

Bibliography

General

Belasco, Warren. *Meals to Come: A History of the Future of Food*. Berkeley: University of California Press, 2006.

Civitello, Linda. *Cuisine and Culture: A History of Food and People*. 2nd ed. New York: Wiley, 2008.

Cummings, Richard Osborn. *The American and His Food: A History of Food Habits in the United States*. Chicago: University of Chicago Press, 1940.

Flandrin, Jean-Louis, and Massimo Montanari, general eds., Albert Sonnenfeld, ed., English edition. *Food: A Culinary History from Antiquity to the Present*. New York: Columbia University Press, 1999.

Haber, Barbara. *From Hardtack to Home Fries: An Uncommon History of American Cooks and Meals*. New York: Free Press, 2002.

Hooker, Richard J. *Food and Drink in America: A History*. Indianapolis: Bobbs-Merrill, 1981.

Levenstein, Harvey A. *Revolution at the Table: The Transformation of the American Diet*. New York: Oxford University Press, 1988.

——. *Paradox of Plenty: A Social History of Eating in Modern America*. New York: Oxford University Press, 1993.

Chapter 1: Oliver Evans's Automated Mill

Bathe, Greville, and Dorothy Bathe. *Oliver Evans: A Chronicle of Early American Engineering*. Philadelphia: Historical Society of Pennsylvania, 1935.

Bibliography

Bennett, Richard, and John Elton. *History of Corn Milling.* 4 vols. London: Simpkin, Marshall, 1898–1904.

Cowan, Ruth Schwartz. *A Social History of American Technology.* Oxford: Oxford University Press, 1997.

Dupaigne, Bernard. *The History of Bread.* New York: Abrams, 1999.

Ferguson, Eugene S. *Oliver Evans: Inventive Genius of the Industrial Revolution.* Greenville, Del.: Hagley Museum, 1980.

Giedion, Siegfried. *Mechanization Takes Command: A Contribution to Anonymous History.* New York: Norton, 1969.

Hamper, Karol Redfern. *A Romance with Baking: A Millennium Dedication to the American Flour Milling Industry.* N.p.: K. R. Hamper, 2000.

Hess, John, and Karen Hess. *The Taste of America.* Urbana: University of Illinois Press, 2000.

Hess, Karen. "A Century of Change in the American Loaf; or, Where Are the Breads of Yesteryear?" Paper delivered at the Smithsonian Institution, Washington, D.C., April 29–30, 1994.

Jacob, H. E. *Six Thousand Years of Bread: Its Holy and Unholy History.* Garden City, N.Y.: Doubleday, Doran, 1944.

Kuhlman, Charles B. *The Development of the Flour-Milling Industry in the United States.* Clifton, N.J.: Kelley, 1973.

Panschar, William G. *Baking in America.* Evanston, Ill.: Northwestern University Press, 1956.

Pyler, E. J. *Baking Science and Technology.* 3rd ed. Merriam, Kan.: Sosland, 1988.

Sellers, Coleman, Jr. "Oliver Evans and His Inventions." *Journal of the Franklin Institute* 122 (July 1886): 1–16.

Storck, John, and Walter Dorwin Teague. *A History of Milling Flour for Man's Bread.* Minneapolis: University of Minnesota Press, 1952.

Chapter 2: The Erie Canal

Bernstein, Peter L. *Wedding of the Waters: The Erie Canal and the Making of a Great Nation.* New York: Norton, 2005.

Levy, Janey. *The Erie Canal: A Primary Source History of the Canal That Changed America.* New York: Rosen Central Primary Source, 2003.

Nissenbaum, Stephen. *Sex, Diet, and Debility in Jacksonian America.* Westport, Conn.: Greenwood Press, 1980.

Shaw, Ronald E. *Erie Water West: A History of the Erie Canal 1792–1854.* Lexington: University of Kentucky Press, 1966.

Sheriff, Carol. *The Artificial River: The Erie Canal and the Paradox of Progress, 1817–1862.* New York: Hill & Wang, 1996.

Storck, John, and Walter Dorwin Teague. *A History of Milling Flour for Man's Bread.* Minneapolis: University of Minnesota Press, 1952.

Chapter 3: Delmonico's

Batterberry, Michael, and Ariane Batterberry. *On the Town in New York: The Landmark History of Eating and Entertainments from the American Revolution to the Food Revolution.* New York: Routledge, 1999.

Brown, Henry Collins. *Delmonico's: A Story of Old New York*. New York: Valentine's Manual, 1928.

Choate, Judith, and James Canora. *Dining at Delmonico's: The Story of America's Oldest Restaurant, with More Than 80 Recipes*. New York: Stewart, Tabori & Chang, 2008.

Mariani, John. *America Eats Out: An Illustrated History of Restaurants, Taverns, Coffee Shops, Speakeasies, and Other Establishments That Have Fed Us for 350 Years*. New York: Morrow, 1991.

Pillsbury, Richard. *From Boarding House to Bistro: The American Restaurant Then and Now*. Boston: Unwin Hyman, 1990.

Ranhofer, Charles. *The Epicurean*. New York: Ranhofer, 1894.

Thomas, Lately [pseud. for Robert V. P. Steele?]. *Delmonico's: A Century of Splendor*. Boston: Houghton Mifflin, 1967.

Trubek, Amy B. *Haute Cuisine: How the French Invented the Culinary Profession*. Philadelphia: University of Pennsylvania Press, 2000.

Chapter 4: Sylvester Graham's Reforms

Bruce, Scott, and Bill Crawford. *Cerealizing America: The Unsweetened Story of American Breakfast Cereal*. Boston: Faber and Faber, 1995.

Graham, Sylvester. *Treatise on Bread and Bread-Making*. Boston: Light & Stearns, 1837.

——. *Lectures on the Science of Human Life*. New York: Fowler & Wells, 1883.

Nissenbaum, Stephen. *Sex, Diet, and Debility in Jacksonian America*. Westport, Conn.: Greenwood Press, 1980.

Shryock, Richard H. "Sylvester Graham and the Popular Health Movement, 1830–1870." *Mississippi Valley Historical Review* 18 (September 1931): 172–83.

Sokolow, Jayme A. *Eros and Modernization: Sylvester Graham, Health Reform and the Origins of Sexuality in America*. Madison, N.J.: Fairleigh Dickinson University Press, 1983.

Chapter 5: Cyrus McCormick's Reaper

Aldrich, Lisa J. *Cyrus McCormick and the Mechanical Reaper*. Greensboro, N.C.: Morgan Reynolds, 2002.

Cochrane, Willard W. *The Development of American Agriculture*. 2nd ed. Minneapolis: University of Minnesota Press, 1993.

Fitzgerald, Deborah. *Every Farm a Factory: The Industrial Ideal in American Agriculture*. New Haven, Conn.: Yale University Press, 2003.

Giedion, Siegfried. *Mechanization Takes Command: A Contribution to Anonymous History*. New York: Norton, 1969.

Hutchinson, William T. *Cyrus Hall McCormick*. Vol. 1, *Seed-Time, 1809–1856*. New York: Century, 1930.

——. *Cyrus Hall McCormick*. Vol. 2, *Harvest, 1856–1884*. New York: Appleton-Century, 1935.

Lyons, Norbert. *The McCormick Reaper Legend: The True Story of a Great Invention*. New York: Exposition Press, 1955.

McClelland, Peter D. *Sowing Modernity: America's First Agricultural Revolution*. Ithaca: Cornell University Press, 1997.

Rogin, Leo. *The Introduction of Farm Machinery in Its Relation to the Productivity of Labor in the Agriculture of the United States During the Nineteenth Century.* Berkeley: University of California Press, 1931.

Trinkle, E. Lee. "Cyrus Hall McCormick: A Distinguished Virginian Who Has Contributed to World Progress." Speech, July 29, 1931, http://www.vaes.vt.edu/steeles/mccormick/speech.html]

Chapter 6: A Multiethnic Smorgasbord

Barbas, Samantha. "'I'll Take Chop Suey': Restaurants as Agents of Culinary and Cultural Change." *Journal of Popular Culture* 36 (spring 2003): 669–86.

Belasco, Warren J. "Ethnic Fast Foods: The Corporate Melting Pot." *Food and Foodways* 2, no. 1 (1987): 1–30.

Bonner, Arthur. *Alas! What Brought Thee Hither? The Chinese in New York 1800–1950.* Madison, N.J.: Fairleigh Dickinson University Press, 1997.

Brown, Linda Keller, and Kay Mussell, eds. *Ethnic and Regional Foodways in the United States: The Performance of Group Identity.* Knoxville: University of Tennessee Press, 1984.

Diner, Hasia R. *Hungering for America: Italian, Irish, and Jewish Foodways in the Age of Migration.* Cambridge, Mass.: Harvard University Press, 2001.

Gabaccia, Donna R. *We Are What We Eat: Ethnic Food and the Making of Americans.* Cambridge, Mass.: Harvard University Press, 1998.

Smith, Andrew F. "Tacos, Enchiladas and Refried Beans: The Invention of Mexican-American Cookery." In *Cultural and Historical Aspects of Foods,* edited by Mary Wallace Kelsey and ZoeAnn Holmes, 183–203. Corvallis: Oregon State University Press, 1999.

Zanger, Mark H. *The American Ethnic Cookbook for Students.* Phoenix, Ariz.: Oryx Press, 2001.

Chapter 7: Giving Thanks

Abrams, Ann Uhry. *The Pilgrims and Pocahontas: Rival Myths of American Origin.* Boulder, Colo.: Westview Press, 1999.

Appelbaum, Diana Karter. *Thanksgiving: An American Holiday, an American History.* New York: Facts on File, 1984.

Baker, James W., with Elizabeth Brabb. *Thanksgiving Cookery.* New York: Brick Tower Press, 1994.

Curtin, Kathleen, Sandra L. Oliver, and Plimoth Plantation. *Giving Thanks: Thanksgiving Recipes and History, from Pilgrims to Pumpkin Pie.* New York: Clarkson Potter, 2005.

Davis, Kenneth C. *America's Hidden History: Untold Tales of the First Pilgrims, Fighting Women, and Forgotten Founders Who Shaped a Nation.* New York: Smithsonian Books, 2008.

Hodgson, Godfrey. *A Great and Godly Adventure: The Pilgrims and the Myth of the First Thanksgiving.* New York: PublicAffairs, 2006.

Love, W. DeLoss, Jr. *The Fast and Thanksgiving Days of New England.* Boston: Houghton, Mifflin, 1895.

Pelton, Robert W. *Historical Thanksgiving Cookery: Favorite Recipes from the Revolutionary War through the Time of the Civil War.* Haverford, Penn.: Infinity, 2003.

Schauffler, Robert Haven, ed. *Thanksgiving: Its Origin, Celebration and Significance as Related in Prose and Verse*. New York: Moffat, Yard, 1907.

Scherer, Margaret. *Thanksgiving and Harvest Festival*. New York: Metropolitan Museum of Art, 1942.

Smith, Andrew F. "The First Thanksgiving." *Gastronomica* 3 (fall 2003): 79–85.

——. *The Turkey: An American Story*. Champagne: University of Illinois Press, 2006.

——. "Thanksgiving." In *Entertaining from Ancient Rome to the Super Bowl*, edited by Melitta Weiss Adamson and Francine Segan, 2:511–18. Westport, Conn.: Greenwood Press, 2008.

——. "Talking Turkey: Thanksgiving in Canada and the U.S." In *What's for Dinner: The Daily Meal Through History*. Montreal: McGill-Queens University Press, forthcoming.

Chapter 8: Gail Borden's Canned Milk

Collins, James H. *The Story of Canned Foods*. New York: Dutton 1924.

Comfort, Harold W. *Gail Borden and His Heritage since 1857*. New York: Newcomen Society in North America, 1953.

Fite, Emerson David. *Social an Industrial Conditions in the North During the Civil War*. New York: Smith, 1930.

Frantz, Joe B. "Gail Borden as a Businessman." *Bulletin of the Business Historical Society* 22 (December 1948): 123–33.

——. *Gail Borden, Dairyman to a Nation*. Norman: University of Oklahoma Press 1951.

——. "Borden at the Century Mark: Case Study of a Centennial Observance." *Business History Review* 33 (winter 1959): 469–94.

Judge, Arthur I., ed. *A History of the Canning Industry: Souvenir of the Seventh Annual Convention of the National Canners' Association and Allied Associations*. Baltimore: Canning Trade, 1914.

Keuchel, Edward F., Jr. "The Development of the Canning Industry in New York State to 1960." Ph.D. diss., Cornell University, 1970.

May, Earl Chapin. *The Canning Clan: A Pageant of Pioneering Americans*. New York: Macmillan, 1937.

Chapter 9: The Homogenizing War

The Confederate Receipt Book. Introduction by E. Merton Coulter. Richmond, Va.: West & Johnson, 1863. Reprint, Athens: University of Georgia Press, 1989.

Harding, T. Swann. *Two Blades of Grass: A History of Scientific Developments in the U.S. Department of Agriculture*. Norman: University of Oklahoma Press, 1947.

Lonn, Ella. *Salt as a Factor in the Confederacy*. Southern Historical Publications, no. 4. Tuscaloosa: University of Alabama Press, 1965.

Porcher, Francis Peyre. *Resources of the Southern Fields and Forests, Medical, Economical and Agricultural*. Charleston, S.C.: Evans & Cogswell, 1863.

Rogin, Leo. *The Introduction of Farm Machinery in Its Relation to the Productivity of Labor in the Agriculture of the United States During the Nineteenth Century*. Berkeley: University of California Press, 1931.

Spaulding, Lily May, and John Spaulding, eds. *Civil War Recipes: Receipts from the Pages of Godey's Lady's Book*. Lexington: University of Kentucky Press, 1999.

Tilden, Arnold. *The Legislation of the Civil-War Period Considered as a Basis of the Agricultural Revolution in the United States*. Los Angeles: University of Southern California Press, 1937.

Vevier, Charles. "American Continentalism: An Idea of Expansion, 1845–1910." *American Historical Review* 65 (January 1960): 323–35.

Chapter 10: The Transcontinental Railroad

Ambrose, Stephen E. *Nothing Like It in the World: The Men Who Built the Transcontinental Railroad 1863–1869*. New York: Simon & Schuster, 2000.

Armour, J. Ogden. *The Packers, the Private Car Lines, and the People*. Philadelphia: Altemus, 1906.

Bain, David Haward. *Empire Express: Building the First Transcontinental Railroad*. New York: Viking, 1999.

Cummings, Richard Osborn. *The American and His Food: A History of Food Habits in the United States*. Chicago: University of Chicago Press, 1940.

Food Investigation Report of the Federal Trade Commission on Private Car Lines. Washington, D.C.: Government Printing Office, 1920.

Galloway, John Debo. *The First Transcontinental Railroad: Central Pacific, Union Pacific*. New York: Simmons-Boardman, [1950].

Goodspeed, Thomas Wakefield. "Gustavus Franklin Swift, 1838–1903." In *University of Chicago Biographical Sketches*, 1:171–97. Chicago: University of Chicago Press, 1922.

Hill, Howard Copeland. "The Development of Chicago as a Center of the Meat Packing Industry." *Mississippi Valley Historical Review* 10 (December 1923): 253–73.

Horowitz, Roger. *Putting Meat on the American Table: Taste, Technology, Transformation*. Baltimore: Johns Hopkins University Press, 2006.

Kujovich, Mary Yeager. "The Refrigerator Car and the Growth of the American Dressed Beef Industry." *Business History Review* 44 (winter 1970): 460–82.

Leech, Harper, and John Charles Carroll. *Armour and His Times*. New York: Appleton-Century, 1938.

Nichols, T. E., Jr. "Transportation and Regional Development in Agriculture." *American Journal of Agricultural Economics* 51 (December 1969): 1455–63.

O'Connell, William E., Jr. "The Development of the Private Railroad Freight Car, 1830–1966." *Business History Review* 44 (summer 1970): 190–209.

Skaggs, Jimmy M. *Prime Cut: Livestock Raising and Meatpacking in the United States, 1607–1983*. College Station: Texas A&M University Press, 1986.

Swift, Helen. *My Father and My Mother*. Chicago: [Lakeside Press, Donnelley & Sons], 1937.

Swift, Louis. *The Yankee of the Yards*. Chicago: Shaw, 1927.

Wade, Louise Carroll. *Chicago's Pride: The Stockyards, Packingtown, and Environs in the Nineteenth Century*. Urbana: University of Illinois Press, 2003.

Yeager, Mary. *Competition and Regulation: The Development of Oligopoly in the Meat Packing Industry*. Greenwich, Conn.: Jai Press, 1981.

Chapter 11: Fair Food

Belasco, Warren. *Meals to Come: A History of the Future of Food.* Berkeley: University of California Press, 2006.

Bolotin, Norm, and Christine Laing. *The World's Columbian Exposition: The Chicago World's Fair of 1893.* Washington, D.C.: Preservation Press, 1992.

Rydell, Robert W. *All the World's a Fair: Visions of Empire at American International Expositions, 1876–1916.* Chicago: University of Chicago Press, 1984.

——. *World of Fairs: The Century-of-Progress Expositions.* Chicago: University of Chicago Press, 1993.

Women's Centennial Executive Committee. *National Cookery Book Compiled from Original Receipts for the Women's Centennial Committees of the International Exhibition.* Philadelphia: Women's Centennial Executive Committee, 1876. Reprint, Bedford, Mass.: Applewood Books, 2005. Introduction by Andrew F. Smith.

Chapter 12: Henry Crowell's Quaker Special

Day, Richard Ellsworth. *Breakfast Table Autocrat: The Life Story of Henry Parsons Crowell.* Chicago: Moody Press, 1946.

Hine, Thomas. *The Total Package: The Evolution and Secret Meanings of Boxes, Bottles, Cans, and Tubes.* New York: Little, Brown, 1995.

Laird, Pamela Walker. *Advertising Progress: American Business and the Rise of Consumer Marketing.* Baltimore: Johns Hopkins University Press, 1998.

Lears, Jackson. *Fables of Abundance: A Cultural History of Advertising in America* (New York: Basic Books, 1994.

Marquette, Arthur F. *Brands, Trademarks and Good Will: The Story of the Quaker Oats Company.* New York: McGraw-Hill, 1967.

Michman, Ronald D., and Edward M. Mazze. *The Food Industry Wars: Marketing Triumphs and Blunders.* Westport, Conn.: Quorum, 1998.

Musser, Joe. *The Cereal Tycoon: Henry Parsons Crowell, Founder of the Quaker Oats Co.; A Biography.* Chicago: Moody Press, 1997.

Thornton, Richard Harrison. *The History of Quaker Oats Company.* Chicago: University of Chicago Press, 1933.

Chapter 13: Wilbur O. Atwater's Calorimeter

Atkinson, Edward. *Suggestions for the Establishment of Food Laboratories in Connection with the Agricultural Experiment Stations of the United States.* Experiment Stations Bulletin, no. 17. Washington, D.C.: USDA, Office of Experiment Stations, 1893.

Atwater, W. O., and A. P. Bryant. *The Chemical Composition of American Food Materials.* Experiment Stations Bulletin, no. 28. Washington, D.C.: Government. Printing Office, 1896.

Carpenter, Kenneth J. "The Life and Times of W. O. Atwater (1844–1907)." *Journal of Nutrition*, suppl., 124 (September 1994): 1707S–14S.

Conover, Milton. *The Office of Experiment Stations: Its History, Activities and Organization.* Baltimore: Johns Hopkins University Press, 1924.

Darby, William J. "Contributions of Atwater and USDA to Knowledge of Nutrient Requirements." *Journal of Nutrition*, suppl., 124 (September 1994): 1733S–37S.

Gratzer, Walter. *Terrors of the Table: The Curious History of Nutrition*. New York: Oxford University Press, 2005.

Harding, T. Swann. *Two Blades of Grass: A History of Scientific Developments in the U.S. Department of Agriculture*. Norman: University of Oklahoma Press, 1947.

Levenstein, Harvey A. *Revolution at the Table: The Transformation of the American Diet*. New York: Oxford University Press, 1988.

McBride, Judy. "Wilbur O. Atwater: Father of American Nutrition Science—Includes Information on Current Research Activities." *Agricultural Research* 41 (June 1993): 5–11.

Shapiro, Laura. *Perfection Salad: Women and Cooking at the Turn of the Century*. New York: Holt, 1987.

True, Alfred C. *A History of Agricultural Experimentation and Research in the United States, 1607–1925*. USDA Miscellaneous Publication, no. 251. Washington, D.C.: USDA, 1937.

Chapter 14: The Cracker Jack Snack

Brenner, Joël Glenn. *The Emperors of Chocolate: Inside the Secret World of Hershey and Mars*. New York: Broadway Books, 2000.

Broekel, Ray. *The Great American Candy Bar Book*. Boston: Houghton Mifflin, 1982.

——. *The Chocolate Chronicles*. Lombard, Ill.: Wallace-Homestead Book Co., 1985.

Pottker, Janice. *Crisis in Candyland: Melting the Chocolate Shell of the Mars Family Empire*. Bethesda, Md.: National Press Books, 1995.

Smith, Andrew F. *Popped Culture: A Social History of Popcorn in America*. Columbia: University of South Carolina Press, 1999.

——. *Peanuts: The Illustrious History of the Goober Pea*. Urbana: University of Illinois Press, 2002.

——. *The Encyclopedia of Junk Food and Fast Food*. Westport, Conn.: Greenwood Press, 2006.

Snack Food Association. *Fifty Years: A Foundation for the Future*. Alexandria, Va.: Snack Food Association, 1987.

Snack Foods: A Global Strategic Business Report. San Jose, Calif.: Global Industry Analysts, 2008.

Szogyi, Alex, ed. *Chocolate: Food of the Gods*. Westport, Conn.: Greenwood Press, 1997.

Chapter 15: Fannie Farmer's Cookbook

Cunningham, Marion. *The Fannie Farmer Cookbook*. 13th ed. New York: Knopf, 1996.

Endrijonas, Erika Anne. "No Experience Required: American Middle-Class Families and Their Cookbooks, 1945–1960." Ph.D. diss., University of Southern California, 1996.

Farmer, Fannie Merritt. *The Boston Cooking-School Cook Book*. Boston: Little, Brown, 1896.

Harding, T. Swann. *Two Blades of Grass: A History of Scientific Developments in the U.S. Department of Agriculture*. Norman: University of Oklahoma Press, 1947.

Hooper, Sarah Emery. "History of the Boston Cooking School Established 1879." Manuscript, 1884, Boston Athenaeum, 18 pp.

Lincoln, Mrs. D. A. *Mrs. Lincoln's Boston Cook Book*. Boston: Roberts, 1884.

Longone, Jan. "Professor Blot and the First French Cooking School in New York, Part 1." *Gastronomica* 1 (spring 2001): 65–71.

Richards, Ellen. *The Chemistry of Cooking and Cleaning: A Manual for Housekeepers*. Boston: Estes & Lauriat, 1882.

Shapiro, Laura. *Perfection Salad: Women and Cooking at the Turn of the Century*. New York: Holt, 1987.

Chapter 16: The Kelloggs' Corn Flakes

Carson, Gerald. *Cornflake Crusade*. New York: Rinehart, 1957.

Deutsch, Ronald M. *The Nuts among the Berries*. New York: Ballantine Books, 1961.

Holechek, James A. *Henry Perky: The Shredded Wheat King*. New York: iUniverse, 2007.

Kellogg, M. G. *Notes Concerning the Kellogg's*. Battle Creek, Mich., 1927.

Kellogg, Mrs. E. E. *Science in the Kitchen*. Battle Creek, Mich.: Health Publishing, 1892.

Major, Nettie Leitch. *C. W. Post: The Hour and the Man; A Biography with Genealogical Supplement*. Washington, D.C.: Judd & Detweiller, 1963.

Powell, Horace B. *The Original Has This Signature: W. K. Kellogg*. Englewood Cliffs, N.J.: Prentice-Hall, 1956.

Rubin, Nancy. *American Empress: The Life and Times of Marjorie Merriweather Post*. New York: Villard Books, 1995.

Schwarz, Richard William. "John Harvey Kellogg: American Health Reformer." Ph.D. diss., University of Michigan, 1964.

Schwarz, Richard W. *John Harvey Kellogg, M.D.* Nashville, Tenn.: Southern Publishing Association [1970].

Smith, Andrew F. *Peanuts: The Illustrious History of the Goober Pea*. Urbana: University of Illinois Press, 2002.

Chapter 17: Upton Sinclair's Jungle

Anderson, Oscar E., Jr. *The Health of a Nation: Harvey W. Wiley and the Fight for Pure Food*. Chicago: University of Chicago Press, 1958.

Bausum, Ann. *Muckrakers: How Ida Tarbell, Upton Sinclair, and Lincoln Steffens Helped Expose Scandal, Inspire Reform, and Invent Investigative Journalism*. Washington, D.C.: National Geographic, 2007.

Bragaw, Donald. "Soldier for the Common Good: The Life and Career of Charles Edward Russell." Ph.D. diss., Syracuse University, 1970.

Coppin, Clayton, and Jack High. *The Politics of Purity: Harvey Washington Wiley and the Origins of Federal Food Policy*. Ann Arbor: University of Michigan Press, 1999.

Filler, Louis. *The Muckrakers*. Stanford, Calif.: Stanford University Press, 1993.

Goodwin, Lorine Swainston. *The Pure Food, Drink, and Drug Crusaders, 1879–1914*. Jefferson, N.C.: McFarland, 1999.

Hawthorne, Fran. *Inside the FDA: The Business and Politics Behind the Drugs We Take and the Food We Eat*. Hoboken, N.J.: Wiley, 2005.

Hilts, Philip J. *Protecting America's Health: The FDA, Business, and One Hundred Years of Regulation*. New York: Knopf, 2003.

Nestle, Marion. *Food Politics: How the Food Industry Influences Nutrition and Health*. Rev. ed. Berkeley: University of California Press, 2007.

Okun, Mitchell. *Fair Play in the Marketplace: The First Battle for Pure Food and Drugs*. De Kalb: Northern Illinois University Press, 1986.

Sinclair, Upton. *The Jungle*. New York: Doubleday, Page, 1906.

Weinberg, Arthur, and Lila Weinberg, eds. *The Muckrakers*. Urbana: University of Illinois Press, 2001.

Young, James Harvey. *Pure Food: Securing the Federal Food and Drugs Act of 1906*. Princeton, N.J.: Princeton University Press, 1989.

Chapter 18: Frozen Seafood and TV Dinners

Anderson, Oscar Edward. *Refrigeration in America: A History of a New Technology and Its Impact*. Princeton, N.J.: published for the University of Cincinnati by Princeton University Press, 1953.

Evans, Judith A., ed. *Frozen Food Science and Technology*. Oxford: Blackwell, 2008.

Hui, Y. H., ed. *Handbook of Frozen Foods*. New York: Dekker, 2004.

Jerome, Norge W. "Frozen (TV) Dinners: The Staple Emergency Meals of a Changing Modern Society." In *Food in Perspective: Proceedings of the Third International Conference on Ethnological Food Research*, edited by Alexander Fenton and Trefor M. Owen, 145–56. Edinburgh: Donald, 1981.

Marling, Karal Ann. *As Seen on TV: The Visual Culture of Everyday Life in the 1950s*. Cambridge, Mass.: Harvard University Press, 1994.

Phipps, Robert G. *The Swanson Story: When the Chicken Flew the Coop*. Omaha, Neb.: Carl and Caroline Swanson Foundation, 1977.

Shapiro, Laura. *Something from the Oven: Reinventing Dinner in 1950s America*. New York: Penguin, 2004.

Smith, Andrew F. *The Turkey: An American Story*. Urbana: University of Illinois Press, 2006.

Sun, Da-Wen, ed. *Handbook of Frozen Food Packaging and Processing*. Boca Raton, Fla.: Taylor & Francis, 2006.

Williams, Edwin W. *Frozen Food: Biography of an Industry*. Boston: Cahners Book Division, 1963.

Chapter 19: Michael Cullen's Super Market

Charvat, Frank J. *Supermarketing*. New York: Macmillan, 1961.

Deville, Nancy. *Death by Supermarket: The Fattening, Dumbing Down, and Poisoning of America*. Fort Lee, N.J.: Barricade Books, 2007.

Dumas, Lynne S. *Elephants in My Backyard: Alex Aidekman's Own Story of Founding the Pathmark Supermarket Powerhouse*. New York: Vantage Press, 1988.

Humphrey, Kim. *Shelf Life: Supermarkets and the Changing Culture of Consumption*. Cambridge: Cambridge University Press, 1998.

Kahn, Barbara E., and Leigh McAlister. *Grocery Revolution: The New Focus on the Consumer*. Reading, Mass.: Addison Wesley Longman, 1997.

Lewis, Len. *The Trader Joe's Adventure: Turning a Unique Approach to Business into a Retail and Cultural Phenomenon*. Chicago: Dearborn Trade, 2005.

Longstreth, Richard W. *The Drive-In, the Supermarket, and the Transformation of Commercial Space in Los Angeles, 1914–1941.* Cambridge, Mass.: MIT Press, 1999.

Marnell, William H. *Once Upon a Store: A Biography of the World's First Supermarket.* New York: Herder and Herder, 1971.

Mayo, James M. *The American Grocery Store: The Business Evolution of an Architectural Space.* Westport, Conn.: Greenwood Press, 1993.

Nestle, Marion. *What to Eat: An Aisle-by-Aisle Guide to Savvy Food Choices and Good Eating.* New York: North Point Press, 2006.

Seth, Andrew, and Geoffrey Randall. *The Grocers: The Rise and Rise of the Supermarket Chains.* 2nd ed. Dover, N.H.: Kogan Page, 2001.

——. *Supermarket Wars: Global Strategies for Food Retailers.* New York: Palgrave Macmillan, 2005.

Walsh, William I. *The Rise and Decline of the Great Atlantic and Pacific Tea Company.* Secaucus, N.J.: Stuart, 1986.

Zimmerman, M. M. *The Super Market: A Revolution in Distribution.* New York: McGraw-Hill, 1955.

Chapter 20: Earle MacAusland's *Gourmet*

Chamberlain, Samuel. *Etched in Sunlight.* Boston: Boston Public Library, 1958.

Leibenstein, Margaret. "Earle MacAusland." In *Culinary Biographies,* edited by Alice Arndt. Houston: Yes Press, 2006.

Mendelson, Anne. *Stand Facing the Stove: The Story of the Women Who Gave America "The Joy of Cooking"; The Lives of Irma S. Rombauer and Marion Rombauer Becker.* New York: Holt, 1996.

——. "60 Years of Gourmet." *Gourmet* 61 (September 2001): 71, 110–11, 133, 153, 203, 219.

Shapiro, Laura. *Something from the Oven: Reinventing Dinner in 1950s America.* New York: Penguin, 2004.

Voight, Carolyn. "You Are What You Eat: Contemplations on Civilizing the Palette with *Gourmet.*" Master's thesis, McGill University, 1996.

Chapter 21: Jerome I. Rodale's *Organic Gardening*

Barton, Gregory. "Sir Albert Howard and the Forestry Roots of the Organic Farming Movement." *Agricultural History* 75 (spring 2001): 168–87.

Belasco, Warren J. *Appetite for Change: How the Counterculture Took on the Food Industry 1966–1988.* New York: Pantheon, 1989.

Fromartz, Samuel. *Organic, Inc.: Natural Foods and How They Grew.* New York: Harcourt, 2007.

Jackson, Carlton. *J. I. Rodale: Apostle of Nonconformity.* New York: Pyramid Books, 1974.

Lappé, Anna, and Bryant Terry. *Grub: Ideas for an Urban Home Garden.* New York: Penguin, Tarcher, 2006.

Lappé, Frances Moore. *Diet for a Small Planet.* New York: Ballantine Books, 1971.

Lappé, Frances Moore, and Anna Lappé. *Hope's Edge: The Next Diet for a Small Planet.* New York: Putnam, Tarcher, 2003.

Bibliography

Leign, G. J. *The World's Greatest Fix: A History of Nitrogen and Agriculture*. New York: Oxford University Press, 2004.

Myers, Adrian. *Organic Futures: The Case for Organic Farming*. Totnes, U.K.: Green Books, 2005.

Nestle, Marion. *Food Politics: How the Food Industry Influences Nutrition and Health*. Berkeley: Rev. ed. University of California Press, 2007.

Pawlick, Thomas F. *The End of Food: How the Food Industry Is Destroying Our Food Supply; And What You Can Do about It*. Fort Lee, N.J.: Barricade Books, 2006.

Planck, Nina. *Real Food: What to Eat and Why*. New York: Bloomsbury, 2006.

Pollan, Michael. *The Omnivore's Dilemma: A Natural History of Four Meals*. New York: Penguin, 2006.

——. *In Defense of Food: An Eater's Manifesto*. New York: Penguin, 2008.

Roberts, Paul. *The End of Food*. Boston: Houghton Mifflin, 2008.

Wells, Betty, Shelly Gradwell, and Rhonda Yoder. "Growing Food, Growing Community: Community Supported Agriculture in Rural Iowa." In *Food in the USA: A Reader*, edited by Carole M. Counihan, 401–8. New York: Routledge, 2002.

Chapter 22: Percy Spencer's Radar

Armbruster, Gertrude, et al. *Microwave Research Bibliography, 1970 to 1983*. [Clifton, Va.]: International Microwave Power Institute, [1988?].

Brown, David E., Lester C. Thurow, and James Burke. *Inventing Modern America: From the Microwave to the Mouse*. Cambridge, Mass.: MIT Press, 2002.

Buderi, Robert. *The Invention That Changed the World: How a Small Group of Radar Pioneers Won the Second World War and Launched a Technological Revolution*. New York: Simon & Schuster, 1997.

Buffler, Charles R. *Microwave Cooking and Processing: Engineering Fundamentals for the Food Scientist*. New York: Avi Books, 1993.

Carlisle, Rodney P. *Scientific American Inventions and Discoveries: All the Milestones in Ingenuity; From the Discovery of Fire to the Invention of the Microwave Oven*. Hoboken, N.J.: Wiley, 2004.

Osepchuk, John. "A History of Microwave Applications." *IEEE Transactions on Microwave Theory and Technique* 32 (September 1984): 1200–24.

Smith, Andrew F. *Popped Culture: A Social History of Popcorn in America*. Columbia: University of South Carolina Press, 1999.

Strasser, Susan. *Never Done: A History of American Housework*. New York: Pantheon, 1982.

Chapter 23: Frances Roth and Katharine Angell's CIA

Culinary Schools. 10th ed. Princeton, N.J.: Peterson's, 2007.

Klein, Camille. *The Professional Cook: His Training, Duties, and Rewards*. New York: Helios Books, 1965.

Mandabach, Keith H. "American Professional Culinary Education Prior to World War II: The History of the Founding of the Washburne Trade School Chef's Training Program." Ed.D. diss., University of Houston, 1998.

Ryan, Lawrence Timothy. "The Culinary Institute of America: A History." Ed.D. diss., University of Pennsylvania, 2003.

Scotto, Charles. "What to Do about Apprentices for Our American Kitchens? Reviewing the Various Methods Followed to Assure Trained and Efficient Future Workers." *Hotel Bulletin and Nation's Chefs* 46 (June 1931): 543–44.

Trubek, Amy. *Haute Cuisine: How the French Invented the Culinary Profession*. Philadelphia: University of Pennsylvania Press, 2000.

Chapter 24: McDonald's Drive-In

Boas, Max, and Steve Chain. *Big Mac: The Unauthorized Story of McDonald's*. New York: New American Library, 1977.

Décsy, Gyula. *Hamburger for America and the World: A Handbook of the Transworld Hamburger Culture*. Transworld Identity Series, vol. 3. Bloomington, Ind.: Europa, European Research Association, 1984.

Edelman, Mark. "From Costa Rican Pasture to North American Hamburger." In *Food and Evolution, Toward a Theory of Human Food Habits*, edited by Marvin Harris and Eric B. Ross, 541–61. Philadelphia: Temple University Press, 1987.

Edge, John T. *Hamburgers and Fries: An American Story*. New York: Putnam, 2005.

Fishwick, Marshall, ed. "The World of Ronald McDonald." Special issue, *Journal of American Culture* 1 (summer 1978): 332–474.

Graulich, David. *The Hamburger Companion: A Connoisseur's Guide to the Food We Love*. New York: Lebhar-Friedman Books, 1999.

Hogan, David Gerard. *Selling 'em by the Sack: White Castle and the Creation of American Food*. New York: New York University Press, 1997.

Huddleston, Eugene L. "A Burger Bibliography." *Journal of American Culture* 1 (summer 1978): 466–71.

Kincheloe, Joe L. *The Sign of the Burger: McDonald's and the Culture of Power*. Philadelphia: Temple University Press, 2002.

Kroc, Ray, with Robert Anderson. *Grinding It Out: The Making of McDonald's*. Chicago: Regnery, 1977.

Love, John F. *McDonald's: Behind the Arches*. Rev. ed. New York: Bantam Books, 1995.

McDonald, Ronald L. *The Complete Hamburger: The History of America's Favorite Sandwich*. Secaucus, N.J.: Carol, 1997.

Nierenberg, Danielle. *Happier Meals: Rethinking the Global Meat Industry*. Washington, D.C.: Worldwatch Institute, 2005.

Ozersky, Josh. *Hamburgers: A Cultural History*. New Haven, Conn.: Yale University Press, 2008.

Ritzer, George. *The McDonaldization of Society*. Rev. ed. Thousand Oaks, Calif.: Pine Forge Press, 1996.

Schlosser, Eric. *Fast Food Nation: The Dark Side of the All-American Meal*. Boston: Houghton Mifflin, 2001.

Smith, Andrew F. *Hamburger: A Global History*. London: Reaktion Books, 2008.

Tennyson, Jeffrey. *Hamburger Heaven: The Illustrated History of the Hamburger*. New York: Hyperion, 1993.

Thomas, David R. *Dave's Way*. New York: Putnam, 1991.

Chapter 25: Julia Child, the French Chef

Barr, Nancy Verde. *Backstage with Julia: My Years with Julia Child.* Hoboken, N.J.: Wiley, 2007.

Child, Julia, with Alex Prud'Homme. *My Life in France.* New York: Knopf, 2006.

Finn, John E. "Julia." *Gastronomica* 7 (fall 2007): 95–97.

Fitch, Noël Riley. *Appetite for Life: The Biography of Julia Child.* New York: Doubleday, 1997.

——. "Notre Dame de la Cuisine and the Prince des Gastronomes." *Gastronomica* 5 (summer 2005): 73–78.

Hersh, Stephanie. "A Full Measure of Humor." *Gastronomica* 5 (summer 2005): 15–16.

Jones, Judith. "Ever-Curious Cook." *Gastronomica* 5 (summer 2005): 26–28.

——. *The Tenth Muse: My Life in Food.* New York: Knopf, 2007.

Jordi, Nathalie. "Samuel Chamberlain's *Clémentine in the Kitchen.*" *Gastronomica* 7 (fall 2007): 42–52.

Julier, Alice. "Julia at Smith." *Gastronomica* 5 (summer 2005): 44–49.

McWilliams, Julia. "A Woman of Affairs." *Gastronomica* 5 (summer 2005): 39.

Moulton, Sara. "Julia's Greatest Lesson: Get On with It!" *Gastronomica* 5 (summer 2005): 19.

Pépin, Jacques. "My Friend Julia." *Gastronomica* 5 (summer 2005): 9–14.

Reardon, Joan. *M. F. K. Fisher, Julia Child, and Alice Waters: Celebrating the Pleasures of the Table.* New York: Harmony Books, 1994.

——. "*Mastering the Art of French Cooking*: A Near Classic or a Near Miss." *Gastronomica* 5 (summer 2005): 62–72.

Shapiro, Laura. *Something from the Oven: Reinventing Dinner in 1950s America.* New York: Penguin, 2004.

——. "Sacred Cows and Dreamberries: In Search of the Flavor of France." *Gastronomica* 5 (summer 2005): 54–61.

——. *Julia Child: A Penguin Life.* New York: Penguin, 2007.

Chapter 26: Jean Nidetch's Diet

Beller, Anne Scott. *Fat and Thin: A Natural History of Obesity.* New York: Farrar, Straus and Giroux, 1977.

Bray, George A. *The Battle of the Bulge: A History of Obesity.* Pittsburgh, Pa.: Dorrance, 2006.

Brownell, Kelly D., and Katherine Battle Horgen. *Food Fight: The Inside Story of the Food Industry, America's Obesity Crisis, and What We Can Do about It.* Chicago: Contemporary Books, 2004.

Campos, Paul. *The Obesity Myth: Why America's Obsession with Weight Is Hazardous to Your Health.* New York: Gotham Books, 2004.

Chase, Chris. *The Great American Waistline: Putting It on and Taking It Off.* New York: Coward, McCann & Geoghegan, 1981.

Cohen, Rich. *Sweet and Low: A Family Story.* New York: Farrar, Straus and Giroux, 2006.

Critser, Greg. *Fat Land: How Americans Became the Fattest People in the World.* Boston: Houghton Mifflin, 2003.

Fraser, Laura. *Losing It: America's Obsession with Weight and the Industry That Feeds on It.* New York: Dutton, 1997.

Hayenga, Elizabeth Sharon. "Dieting through the Decades: A Comparative Study of Weight Reduction in America as Depicted in Popular Literature and Books from 1940 to the Late 1980s." Ph.D. diss., University of Minnesota, 1988.

Nidetch, Jean. *The Story of Weight Watchers.* New York: New American Library, 1979.

Oliver, J. Eric. *Fat Politics: The Real Story Behind America's Obesity Epidemic.* New York: Oxford University Press, 2005.

Schwartz, Hillel. *Never Satisfied: A Cultural History of Diets, Fantasies and Fat.* New York: Free Press, 1986.

Stearns, Peter N. *Fat History: Bodies and Beauty in the Modern West.* New York: New York University Press, 1997.

Wyden, Peter. *The Overweight Society: An Authoritative, Entertaining Investigation into the Facts and Follies of Girth Control.* New York: Morrow, 1965.

Chapter 27: Alice Waters's Chez Panisse

Bates, Caroline. "Spécialités de la Maison: California." *Gourmet* 35 (October 1975): 11–12.

Kuh, Patric. *The Last Days of Haute Cuisine: America's Culinary Revolution.* New York: Viking, 2001.

McNamee, Thomas. *Alice Waters and Chez Panisse: The Romantic, Impractical, Often Eccentric, Ultimately Brilliant Making of a Food Revolution.* New York: Penguin, 2007.

Reardon, Joan. *M. F. K. Fisher, Julia Child, and Alice Waters: Celebrating the Pleasures of the Table.* New York: Harmony Books, 1994.

Ross, Drew Eliot. "Topography of Taste: Globalization, Cultural Politics, and the Making of California Cuisine." Ph.D. diss., University of Wisconsin, Madison, 1999.

Shapiro, Laura. *Julia Child: A Penguin Life.* New York: Penguin, 2007.

Tower, Jeremiah. *California Dish: What I Saw (and Cooked) at the American Culinary Revolution.* New York: Free Press, 2003.

Waters, Alice, in collaboration with Alan Tangren and Fritz Streiff. *Chez Panisse Fruit.* New York: HarperCollins, 2002.

Waters, Alice, in collaboration with Linda P. Guenzel. *The Chez Panisse Menu Cookbook.* New York: Random House, 1982.

Waters, Alice, with Patricia Curtan, Kelsie Kerr, and Fritz Streiff. *The Art of Simple Food: Notes, Lessons, and Recipes from a Delicious Revolution.* New York: Clarkson Potter, 2007.

Chapter 28: TVFN

Adema, Pauline. "Vicarious Consumption: Food, Television and the Ambiguity of Modernity." *Journal of American Culture and Comparative Studies* 23 (fall 2000): 113-23.

Brost, Lori F. "Television Cooking Shows: Defining the Genre." Ph.D. diss., Indiana University, 2000.

Buford, Bill. "Notes of a Gastronome: TV Dinners; The Rise of Food Television." *New Yorker* 82 (October 2, 2006): 42–47.

Chan, Andrew. "'La grande bouffe': Cooking Shows as Pornography." *Gastronomica* 3 (fall 2003): 47–53.

De Solier, Isabelle. "TV Dinners: Culinary Television, Education and Distinction." *Continuum: Journal of Media and Cultural Studies* 19 (December 2005): 465–81.

Bibliography

Eanes, Ryan Scott. "From Stovetop to Screen: A Cultural History of Food Television." Master's thesis, New School, 2008.

Ketchum, Cheri. "Lost in the Public Imagination: The Dismissal of Political Consumerism in News and Entertainment Food Media." Ph.D. diss., University of California, San Diego, 2004.

——. "The Essence of Cooking Shows: How the Food Network Constructs Consumer Fantasies." *Journal of Communication Inquiry* 29 (July 2005): 217–34.

Lurie, Karen. *TV Chefs: The Dish on the Stars of Your Favorite Cooking Shows.* Los Angeles: Renaissance Books, 1999.

Polan, Dana. *The French Chef.* Durham, N.C.: Duke University Press, forthcoming.

Ray, Krishnendu. "Domesticating Cuisine: Food and Aesthetics on American Television." *Gastronomica* 7 (winter 2007): 50–63.

Schonfeld, Reese. *Me and Ted against the World: The Unauthorized Story of the Founding of CNN.* New York: HarperCollins, 2001.

Turner, Marcia Layton. *Emeril! Inside the Amazing Success of Today's Most Popular Chef.* Hoboken, N.J.: Wiley, 2004.

Chapter 29: The Flavr Savr

Avise, John. *The Hope, Hype and Reality of Genetic Engineering: Remarkable Stories from Agriculture, Industry, Medicine, and the Environment.* New York: Oxford University Press, 2004.

Brookes, Graham, and Peter Barfoot. *GM Crops: The First Ten Years; Global Socio-Economic and Environmental Impacts.* Brief 36. Dorchester, U.K.: International Service for the Acquisition of Agro-Biotech Applications, 2006.

Charles, Daniel. *Lords of the Harvest: Biotech, Big Money and the Future of Food.* Cambridge, Mass.: Perseus, 2001.

Kloppenberg, Jack Ralph. *First the Seed: The Political Economy of Plant Biotechnology 1492–2000.* Cambridge: Cambridge University Press, 1990.

Krimsky, Sheldon, and Roger P. Wrubel. *Agricultural Biotechnology and the Environment: Science, Policy, and Social Issues.* Urbana: University of Illinois Press, 1996.

Martineau, Belinda. *First Fruit: The Creation of the Flavr Savr Tomato and the Birth of Biotech Food.* New York: McGraw-Hill, 2001.

Mather, Robin. *A Garden of Unearthly Delights: Bioengineering and the Future of Food.* New York: Dutton, 1995.

Miller, Henry I. *The Frankenfood Myth: How Protest and Politics Threaten the Biotech Revolution.* Westport, Conn.: Praeger, 2004.

Nestle, Marion. *Safe Food: Bacteria, Biotechnology, and Bioterrorism.* Berkeley: University of California Press, 2003.

Nottingham, Stephen. *Genescapes: The Ecology of Genetic Engineering.* London: Zed Books, 2002.

Paul, Helena, and Ricarda Steinbrecher with Devlin Kuyek and Lucy Michaels. *Hungry Corporations: Transnational Biotech Companies Colonise the Food Chain.* London: Zed Books / New York: Palgrave, 2003.

Pringle, Peter. *Food, Inc.: Mendel to Monsanto; The Promises and Perils of Biotech Harvest.* New York: Simon & Schuster, 2003.

Rifkin, Jeremy. *The Biotech Century: Harnessing the Gene and Remaking the World*. New York: Putnam, Tarcher, 1998.

Schrepfer, Susan R., and Phillip Scranton, eds. *Industrializing Organisms: Introducing Evolutionary History*. New York: Routledge, 2004.

Chapter 30: Mergers, Acquisitions, and Spin-Offs

Allen, Gary, and Ken Albala, eds. *The Business of Food: Encyclopedia of the Food and Drink Industries*. Westport, Conn.: Greenwood Press, 2007.

Braznell, William. *California's Finest: The History of the Del Monte Corporation and the Del Monte Brand*. San Francisco: Del Monte, 1982.

Burrough, Bryan, and John Helyar. *Barbarians at the Gate: The Fall of RJR Nabisco*. New York: Harper & Row, 1990.

Cahn, William. *Out of the Cracker Barrel: From Animal Crackers to Zu Zu's*. New York: Simon & Schuster, 1969.

Food Business Mergers and Acquisitions. Fair Lawn, N.J.: Food Institute, 2007.

Fusario, Dave. "Food Processing Top 100, 2006." *Food Processing* 67 (August 2006): 34–48.

Patel, Raj. *Stuffed and Starved: The Hidden Battle for the World Food System*. Brooklyn: Melville House, 2008.

Pollan, Michael. *The Omnivore's Dilemma: A Natural History of Four Meals*. New York: Penguin, 2006.

Rama, Ruth, ed. *Multinational Agribusinesses*. Binghamton, N.Y.: Food Products Press, 2005.

Roberts, Paul. *The End of Food*. Boston: Houghton Mifflin, 2008.

Schlosser, Eric. *Fast Food Nation: The Dark Side of the All-American Meal*. Boston: Houghton Mifflin, 2001.

Tansey, Geoff, and Tamsin Rajotte, eds. *The Future Control of Food: An Essential Guide to International Negotiations and Rules on Intellectual Property, Biodiversity and Food Security*. London: Earthscan / Ottawa, Ont.: International Development Research Centre, 2008.

Index